Global Economic Prospects

A World Bank Group
Flagship Report

JANUARY 2021

Global
Economic
Prospects

 **WORLD BANK GROUP**

ISBN (paper): 978-1-4648-1612-3
ISBN (electronic): 978-1-4648-1613-0
DOI: 10.1596/978-1-4648-1612-3

Cover design: Bill Pragluski (Critical Stages).

The cutoff date for the data used in this report was December 18, 2020.

Summary of Contents

Table of Contents

Acknowledgments

This World Bank Group Flagship Report is a product of the Prospects Group in the Equitable Growth, Finance and Institutions (EFI) Vice Presidency. The project was managed by M. Ayhan Kose and Franziska Ohnsorge.

Global and regional surveillance work was coordinated by Carlos Arteta. The report was prepared by a team that included John Baffes, Justin-Damien Guénette, Jongrim Ha, Osamu Inami, Alain Kabundi, Sergiy Kasyanenko, Sinem Kilic Celik, Gene Kindberg-Hanlon, Patrick Kirby, Hideaki Matsuoka, Peter Nagle, Yoki Okawa, Cedric Okou, Franz Ulrich Ruch, Rudi Steinbach, Naotaka Sugawara, Ekaterine Vashakmadze, Dana Vorisek, Collette Mari Wheeler, Takefumi Yamazaki, and Lei Sandy Ye.

Research assistance was provided by Damien M. V. Boucher, Hrisyana Doytchinova, Fuda Jiang, Maria Hazel Macadangdang, Julia Roseman Norfleet, Ipek Ceylan Oymak, Vasiliki Papagianni, Shijie Shi, Kaltrina Temaj, Jingran Wang, Jinxin Wu, Heqing Zhao, and Juncheng Zhou. Modeling and data work were provided by Rajesh Kumar Danda, Vasiliki Papagianni, and Shijie Shi.

Online products were produced by Graeme Littler. Mark Felsenthal and Alejandra Viveros managed communications and media outreach with extensive support from the World Bank's media team. Torie Smith and Yanan Zhao produced social media and data visualization with extensive support from the World Bank's digital media teams. Graeme Littler provided editorial support, with contributions from Adriana Maximiliano.

The print publication was produced by Maria Hazel Macadangdang and Adriana Maximiliano, in collaboration with Luiz H. Almeida, Andrew Charles Berghauser, Cindy A. Fisher, Michael Harrup, and Jewel McFadden.

Regional projections and write-ups were produced in coordination with country teams, country directors, and the offices of the regional chief economists.

Many reviewers provided extensive advice and comments. The analysis also benefited from comments and suggestions by staff members from World Bank Group country teams and other World Bank Group Vice Presidencies as well as Executive Directors in their discussion of the report on December 15, 2020. However, both forecasts and analysis are those of the World Bank Group staff and should not be attributed to Executive Directors or their national authorities.

Foreword

Following the devastating health and economic crisis caused by COVID-19, the global economy appears to be emerging from one of its deepest recessions and beginning a subdued recovery. Beyond the short term economic outlook, this edition of *Global Economic Prospects* makes clear, policymakers face formidable challenges—in public health, debt management, budget policies, central banking and structural reforms—as they try to ensure that this still-fragile global recovery gains traction and sets a foundation for robust growth and development in the longer run.

Governments, households, and firms all need to embrace a changed economic landscape. While protecting the most vulnerable, successful policies will be needed that allow capital, labor, skills, and innovation to shift to new purposes in order to build a greener, stronger post-COVID economic environment. Some countries already moving toward this type of dynamism and resilience, will need to redouble their efforts. For others, change is especially critical now, when fiscal positions are severely stretched by the pandemic and other drivers of long-term growth have weakened.

Investment, in particular, collapsed in 2020 in many emerging market and developing economies, following a decade of persistent weakness. Investment growth is expected to resume in 2021, but, despite an uplift from advances in digital technology, not add enough to reverse the large 2020 decline. The experience of past crises raises a further concern—without urgent course correction, investment could remain feeble for years to come.

To counter the investment headwind, there needs to be a major push to improve business environments, increase labor and product market flexibility, and strengthen transparency and governance. These can re-kindle investment and help allocate it more effectively, but unsustainable debt burdens are a major obstacle. Already at record levels before the pandemic, both domestic and external debt burdens have become much

heavier due to the devastating contraction in incomes across emerging market and developing economies.

To address the external debt burden, a comprehensive set of policy interventions is needed: broader participation by all private and official bilateral creditors in existing debt service relief efforts; deep debt reduction for countries in debt distress to increase the attractiveness for investment; better debt transparency practices that overcome secrecy and restrictions in debt contracts; legislative reforms to expedite the restructuring of private sector debt; and enhanced sequencing of these processes, which may involve countries running arrears with creditors as they work with international financial institutions to achieve debt sustainability.

Complicating the debt sustainability problem is the possibility that contingent liabilities from soaring private debt may be added to already high public debt. During the pandemic, many governments have supported lending to firms to address liquidity constraints, including loan guarantees, payment moratoria, and regulatory forbearance. These interventions highlight the challenge of balancing efforts to increase the availability of credit while maintaining proper regulatory standards to mitigate financial risks. As the health and economic crisis abates, these policies need to be reassessed periodically to ensure asset quality transparency and avoid undermining bank capitalization.

Policymakers also need to enhance supervisory assessments of loan quality and improve resolution and recovery regimes to address the potential challenges associated with elevated corporate debt levels. With non-performing loans likely to rise, more rapid bankruptcy and domestic debt resolution processes will be important in allowing assets to be relieved of litigation and repurposed for new uses. Adding new investment to productive existing assets will be vital for sustainable development.

In both the external and internal debt resolution processes, transparency is critical to bolster accountability, make future investment and debt more productive, and support the economic recoveries that are crucial for poverty reduction. Left unaddressed, the problem of unsustainable debt, and restructurings that do too little, will delay vital recoveries, especially in the poorest countries.

Mounting climate and environmental challenges add to the urgency of policy action, including on debt reduction and an improved investment framework. As countries formulate policies for recovery, they have a chance to embark on a greener, smarter, and more equitable development path. Investing in green infrastructure projects, phasing out fossil fuel subsidies, and offering incentives for environmentally sustainable technologies can buttress long-term growth, lower carbon output, create jobs, and help adapt to the effects of climate change.

Making the right investments now is vital both to support the recovery when it is urgently needed and foster resilience. Our response to the pandemic crisis today will shape our common future for years to come. We should seize the opportunity to lay the foundations for a durable, equitable, and sustainable global economy.

David Malpass
President
World Bank Group

Executive Summary

Although the global economy is emerging from the collapse triggered by the pandemic, the recovery is projected to be subdued. Global economic output is expected to expand 4 percent in 2021 but still remain more than 5 percent below its pre-pandemic trend. Moreover, there is a material risk that setbacks in containing the pandemic or other adverse events derail the recovery. Growth in emerging market and developing economies (EMDEs) is envisioned to firm to 5 percent in 2021, but EMDE output is also expected to remain well below its pre-pandemic projection. The pandemic has exacerbated the risks associated with a decade-long wave of global debt accumulation. Debt levels have reached historic highs, making the global economy particularly vulnerable to financial market stress. The pandemic is likely to steepen the long-expected slowdown in potential growth over the next decade, undermining prospects for poverty reduction. The heightened level of uncertainty around the global outlook highlights policy makers' role in raising the likelihood of better growth outcomes while warding off worse ones. Limiting the spread of the virus, providing relief for vulnerable populations, and overcoming vaccine-related challenges are key immediate priorities. With weak fiscal positions severely constraining government support measures in many countries, an emphasis on ambitious reforms is needed to rekindle robust, sustainable and equitable growth. Global cooperation is critical in addressing many of these challenges. In particular, the global community needs to act rapidly and forcefully to make sure the ongoing debt wave does not end with a string of debt crises in EMDEs, as was the case with earlier waves of debt accumulation.

Global Outlook. Following a collapse last year caused by the COVID-19 pandemic, global economic output is expected to expand 4 percent in 2021 but still remain more than 5 percent below pre-pandemic projections. Global growth is projected to moderate to 3.8 percent in 2022, weighed down by the pandemic's lasting damage to potential growth. In particular, the impact of the pandemic on investment and human capital is expected to erode growth prospects in emerging market and developing economies (EMDEs) and set back key development goals. The global recovery, which has been dampened in the near term by a resurgence of COVID-19 cases, is expected to strengthen over the forecast horizon as confidence, consumption, and trade gradually improve, supported by ongoing vaccination.

Although aggregate EMDE growth is envisioned to firm to an average of 4.6 percent in 2021-22, the improvement largely reflects China's expected rebound. Absent China, the recovery across EMDEs is anticipated to be more muted, averaging 3.5 percent in 2021-22, as the pandemic's lingering effects continue to weigh on consumption and investment. Despite the recovery, aggregate EMDE output in 2022 is expected to remain about 6 percent below its pre-pandemic projection.

Downside risks to this baseline predominate, including the possibility of a further increase in the spread of the virus, delays in vaccine procurement and distribution, more severe and longer-lasting effects on potential output from the pandemic, and financial stress triggered by high debt levels and weak growth.

Limiting the spread of the virus, providing relief for vulnerable populations, and overcoming vaccine-related challenges are key immediate policy priorities. As the crisis abates, policy makers need to balance the risks from large and growing debt loads with those from slowing the economy through premature fiscal tightening. To confront the adverse legacies of the pandemic, it will be critical to foster resilience by safeguarding health and education, prioritizing investments in digital technologies and green infrastructure, improving governance, and enhancing debt transparency. Global cooperation will be key in addressing many of these challenges.

Regional Prospects. The pandemic has exacted substantial costs on all EMDE regions. Although all regions are expected to grow this year, the pace of the recovery varies considerably, with greater weakness in countries that have larger outbreaks or greater exposure to global spillovers through tourism and industrial commodity exports. The East Asia and Pacific region is envisioned to show notable strength in 2021 due to a solid rebound in China, whereas activity is projected to be weakest in the Middle East and North Africa and Sub-Saharan Africa regions. Many countries are expected to lose a decade or more of per capita income gains. Risks to the outlook are tilted to the downside. In addition to region-specific risks, all regions are vulnerable to renewed outbreaks and logistical impediments to the distribution of effective vaccines, financial stress amid elevated debt levels, and the possibility that the impact of the pandemic on growth and incomes may be worse than expected over the longer term. In a downside scenario of a more severe and prolonged pandemic, growth would be lowest among the six EMDE regions in Latin America and the Caribbean, the Middle East and North Africa, and Sub-Saharan Africa, reflecting these regions' reliance on exports of oil and industrial commodities, the prices of which would be reduced by weak global demand.

This edition of *Global Economic Prospects* also includes analytical chapters on the implications of the pandemic for long-term growth prospects, as well as on benefits and risks of recent unconventional monetary policy measures in EMDEs.

Global Economy: Heading into a Decade of Disappointments? The COVID-19 pandemic has caused major disruptions in the global economy. Economic activity has been hit by reduced personal interaction, owing both to official restrictions and private decisions; uncertainty about the post-pandemic economic landscape and policies has discouraged investment; disruptions to education have slowed human capital accumulation; and concerns about the viability of global value chains and the course of the pandemic have weighed on international trade

and tourism. As with previous economic crises, the pandemic is expected to leave long-lasting adverse effects on global economic activity and per capita incomes. It is likely to steepen the slowdown in the growth of global potential output—the level of output the global economy can sustain at full employment and capacity utilization—that had earlier been projected for the decade just begun. If history is any guide, unless there are substantial and effective reforms, the global economy is heading for a decade of disappointing growth outcomes. Especially given weak fiscal positions and elevated debt, institutional reforms to spur growth are particularly important. A comprehensive policy effort is needed to rekindle robust, sustainable, and equitable growth. A package of reforms to increase investment in human and physical capital and raise female labor force participation could help avert the expected impact of the pandemic on potential growth in EMDEs over the next decade. In the past, the growth dividends from reform efforts were recognized and anticipated by investors in upgrades to their long-term growth expectations.

Asset Purchases in Emerging Markets: Unconventional Policies, Unconventional Times. Central banks in some EMDEs have employed asset purchase programs, in many cases for the first time, in response to pandemic-induced financial market pressures. These programs, along with spillovers from accommodative monetary policies in advanced economies, appear to have helped stabilize EMDE financial markets. However, the governing framework, scale, and duration of these programs have been less transparent than in advanced economies, and the effects on inflation and output in EMDEs remain uncertain. In EMDEs where asset purchases continue to expand and are perceived to finance unsustainable fiscal deficits, these programs risk eroding hard-won central bank operational independence and de-anchoring inflation expectations. Ensuring that asset purchase programs are conducted with credible commitments to central bank mandates and with transparency regarding their objectives and scale can support their effectiveness.

Abbreviations

AE	advanced economy
BIS	Bank for International Settlements
CA	Central Asia
CDS	credit default swap
CE	Central Europe
CEPR	Center for Economic and Policy Research
DeMPA	Debt Management Performance Assessments
EAP	East Asia and Pacific
ECA	Europe and Central Asia
ECB	European Central Bank
EE	Eastern Europe
EMBI	Emerging Market Bond Index
EMDE	emerging market and developing economy
EM-DAT	Emergency Events Database
EU	European Union
FAO	Food and Agriculture Organization of the United Nations
FDI	foreign direct investment
G7	Group of Seven: Canada, France, Germany, Italy, Japan, the United Kingdom, and the United States.
G20	Group of Twenty: Argentina, Australia, Brazil, Canada, China, France, Germany, India, Indonesia, Italy, Japan, Republic of Korea, Mexico, Russia, Saudi Arabia, South Africa, Turkey, United Kingdom, United States, and the European Union.
GCC	Gulf Cooperation Council
GDP	gross domestic product
GEP	Global Economic Prospects
GFC	global financial crisis
GNFS	goods and nonfactor services
HIPC	heavily indebted poor countries
ICRG	International Crisis Risk Group
IDA	International Development Association
IDB	Inter-American Development Bank
IEA	International Energy Agency
ILO	International Labour Organization
IMF	International Monetary Fund
IP	industrial production
LAC	Latin America and the Caribbean
LIC	low-income country
LSAP	large-scale asset purchase
MNA/MENA	Middle East and North Africa
MERS	Middle East Respiratory Syndrome
MIC	middle-income country
NBER	National Bureau of Economic Research

OECD	Organisation for Economic Co-operation and Development
OPEC	Organization of the Petroleum Exporting Countries
OPEC+	OPEC and Azerbaijan, Bahrain, Brunei, Kazakhstan, Malaysia, Mexico, Oman, Russia, Sudan, and South Sudan
PMI	Purchasing Managers' Index
PPP	purchasing power parity
SAR	South Asia Region
SARS	Severe Acute Respiratory Syndrome
SCC	South Caucasus
SDG	Sustainable Development Goal
SIR	Susceptible-Infected-Removed model
SSA	Sub-Saharan Africa
TFP	total factor productivity
UN	United Nations
UNCTAD	United Nations Conference on Trade and Development
UNESCO	United Nations Educational, Scientific and Cultural Organization
UNICEF	United Nations Children's Fund
VAR	vector autoregression
VIX	Chicago Board Options Exchange Volatility Index
WAEMU	West African Economic and Monetary Union
WBK	Western Balkans
WFP	World Food Program
WHO	World Health Organization
WTO	World Trade Organization

CHAPTER 1

GLOBAL OUTLOOK

Following a collapse last year caused by the COVID-19 pandemic, global economic output is expected to expand 4 percent in 2021 but still remain more than 5 percent below pre-pandemic projections. Global growth is projected to moderate to 3.8 percent in 2022, weighed down by the pandemic's lasting damage to potential growth. In particular, the impact of the pandemic on investment and human capital is expected to erode growth prospects in emerging market and developing economies (EMDEs) and set back key development goals. The global recovery, which has been dampened in the near term by a resurgence of COVID-19 cases, is expected to strengthen over the forecast horizon as confidence, consumption, and trade gradually improve, supported by ongoing vaccination. Downside risks to this baseline predominate, including the possibility of a further increase in the spread of the virus, delays in vaccine procurement and distribution, more severe and longer-lasting effects on potential output from the pandemic, and financial stress triggered by high debt levels and weak growth. Limiting the spread of the virus, providing relief for vulnerable populations, and overcoming vaccine-related challenges are key immediate policy priorities. As the crisis abates, policy makers need to balance the risks from large and growing debt loads with those from slowing the economy through premature fiscal tightening. To confront the adverse legacies of the pandemic, it will be critical to foster resilience by safeguarding health and education, prioritizing investments in digital technologies and green infrastructure, improving governance, and enhancing debt transparency. Global cooperation will be key in addressing many of these challenges.

Summary

COVID-19 caused a global recession whose depth was surpassed only by the two World Wars and the Great Depression over the past century and a half. Although global economic activity is growing again, it is not likely to return to business as usual for the foreseeable future. The pandemic has caused a severe loss of life, is tipping millions into extreme poverty, and is expected to inflict lasting scars that push activity and income well below their pre-pandemic trend for a prolonged period.

The incipient recovery was initially supported by a partial easing of stringent lockdowns. Various restrictive measures have been reintroduced, however, as COVID-19 has continued to spread around the world. Some areas have experienced a sharp resurgence of infections, and daily new cases remain high (figure 1.1.A). That said, there has been substantial progress in the development of effective vaccines, and inoculation has begun in some countries. A more general rollout in advanced economies and major emerging market

and developing economies (EMDEs) is expected to proceed early this year. Most other EMDEs, however, face greater constraints in vaccine procurement and distribution. Until vaccines are widely distributed, effective containment strategies to limit the spread of COVID-19 remain critical.

Following the initial rebound in mid-2020, the global economic recovery has slowed (figure 1.1.B). Whereas activity and trade in the goods sector have improved, the services sector remains anemic, with international tourism, in particular, still depressed. The fall in global investment has been pronounced, particularly for EMDEs excluding China (figure 1.1.C). Even though financial conditions remain very loose, reflecting exceptional monetary policy accommodation, underlying financial fragilities are mounting. Most commodity prices rebounded from their mid-2020 lows as strict lockdowns were gradually lifted and demand firmed, especially from China; however, the recovery in oil prices was more modest amid concerns over the pandemic's lasting impact on oil demand.

In all, the global economy is estimated to have contracted 4.3 percent in 2020—a 0.9 percentage point smaller collapse than was expected in June forecasts (figure 1.1.D). In advanced economies, the initial contraction was less severe than anticipated, but the ensuing recovery has been dampened by a substantial resurgence of COVID-19 cases. Meanwhile, output in China is estimated

_____

Note: This chapter was prepared by Carlos Arteta, Justin-Damien Guénette, Patrick Kirby, and Collette Mari Wheeler, with contributions from Rudi Steinbach, John Baffes, Osamu Inami, Sergiy Kasyanenko, Gene Kindberg-Hanlon, Peter Nagle, Cedric Okou, Franz Ulrich Ruch, and Ekaterine Vashakmadze. Research assistance was provided by Damien M. V. Boucher, Hrisyana Doytchinova, Fuda Jiang, Maria Hazel Macadangdang, Julia Roseman Norfleet, Ipek Ceylan Oymak, Vasiliki Papagianni, Shijie Shi, Kaltrina Temaj, Jinxin Wu, and Juncheng Zhou.

TABLE 1.1 Real GDP[1]
(Percent change from previous year)

Percentage point differences from June 2020 projections

	2018	2019	2020e	2021f	2022f	2020e	2021f
World	**3.0**	**2.3**	**-4.3**	**4.0**	**3.8**	**0.9**	**-0.2**
Advanced economies	**2.2**	**1.6**	**-5.4**	**3.3**	**3.5**	**1.6**	**-0.6**
United States	3.0	2.2	-3.6	3.5	3.3	2.5	-0.5
Euro area	1.9	1.3	-7.4	3.6	4.0	1.7	-0.9
Japan	0.6	0.3	-5.3	2.5	2.3	0.8	0.0
Emerging market and developing economies	**4.3**	**3.6**	**-2.6**	**5.0**	**4.2**	**-0.1**	**0.4**
EMDEs excluding China	3.2	2.3	-5.0	3.4	3.6	-0.7	0.1
Commodity-exporting EMDEs	2.0	1.6	-4.8	3.0	3.2	0.1	0.0
Other EMDEs	5.7	4.8	-1.3	6.1	4.8	-0.2	0.6
Other EMDEs excluding China	4.8	3.2	-5.3	3.9	4.1	-1.7	0.1
East Asia and Pacific	6.3	5.8	0.9	7.4	5.2	0.4	0.8
China	6.6	6.1	2.0	7.9	5.2	1.0	1.0
Indonesia	5.2	5.0	-2.2	4.4	4.8	-2.2	-0.4
Thailand	4.1	2.4	-6.5	4.0	4.7	-1.5	-0.1
Europe and Central Asia	3.4	2.3	-2.9	3.3	3.9	1.8	-0.3
Russian Federation	2.5	1.3	-4.0	2.6	3.0	2.0	-0.1
Turkey	3.0	0.9	0.5	4.5	5.0	4.3	-0.5
Poland	5.4	4.5	-3.4	3.5	4.3	0.8	0.7
Latin America and the Caribbean	1.9	1.0	-6.9	3.7	2.8	0.3	0.9
Brazil	1.8	1.4	-4.5	3.0	2.5	3.5	0.8
Mexico	2.2	-0.1	-9.0	3.7	2.6	-1.5	0.7
Argentina	-2.6	-2.1	-10.6	4.9	1.9	-3.3	2.8
Middle East and North Africa	0.5	0.1	-5.0	2.1	3.1	-0.8	-0.2
Saudi Arabia	2.4	0.3	-5.4	2.0	2.2	-1.6	-0.5
Iran, Islamic Rep. [3]	-6.0	-6.8	-3.7	1.5	1.7	1.6	-0.6
Egypt, Arab Rep. [2]	5.3	5.6	3.6	2.7	5.8	0.6	0.6
South Asia	6.5	4.4	-6.7	3.3	3.8	-4.0	0.5
India [3]	6.1	4.2	-9.6	5.4	5.2	-6.4	2.3
Pakistan [2]	5.5	1.9	-1.5	0.5	2.0	1.1	0.7
Bangladesh [2]	7.9	8.2	2.0	1.6	3.4	0.4	0.6
Sub-Saharan Africa	2.6	2.4	-3.7	2.7	3.3	-0.9	-0.4
Nigeria	1.9	2.2	-4.1	1.1	1.8	-0.9	-0.6
South Africa	0.8	0.2	-7.8	3.3	1.7	-0.7	0.4
Angola	-2.0	-0.9	-4.0	0.9	3.5	0.0	-2.2
Memorandum items:							
Real GDP[1]							
High-income countries	2.2	1.6	-5.4	3.2	3.5	1.4	-0.6
Developing countries	4.4	3.7	-2.3	5.2	4.3	0.1	0.5
Low-income countries	4.4	4.0	-0.9	3.3	5.2	-0.8	-0.6
BRICS	5.4	4.7	-1.1	6.1	4.5	0.6	0.8
World (2010 PPP weights) [4]	3.6	2.8	-3.7	4.3	3.9	0.4	0.0
World trade volume [5]	**4.3**	**1.1**	**-9.5**	**5.0**	**5.1**	**3.9**	**-0.3**
Commodity prices [6]							
Oil price	29.4	-10.2	-33.7	8.1	13.6	14.2	-10.7
Non-energy commodity price index	1.7	-4.2	2.2	2.4	1.3	8.1	-0.6

Source: World Bank.
1. Headline aggregate growth rates are calculated using GDP weights at 2010 prices and market exchange rates.
2. GDP growth rates are on a fiscal year basis. Aggregates that include these countries are calculated using data compiled on a calendar year basis. Pakistan's growth rates are based on GDP at factor cost. The column labeled 2019 refers to FY2018/19.
3. Columns indicate fiscal year. For example, 2018 refers to FY2018/19.
4. World growth rates are calculated using purchasing power parity (PPP) weights, which attribute a greater share of global GDP to emerging market and developing economies (EMDEs) than market exchange rates.
5. World trade volume of goods and nonfactor services.
6. Oil price is the simple average of Brent, Dubai, and West Texas Intermediate prices. The non-energy index is the weighted average of 39 commodity prices (7 metals, 5 fertilizers, 27 agricultural commodities). For additional details, please see https://www.worldbank.org/commodities.
Note: e = estimate; f = forecast. World Bank forecasts are frequently updated based on new information. Consequently, projections presented here may differ from those contained in other World Bank documents, even if basic assessments of countries' prospects do not differ at any given date. Country classifications and lists of EMDEs are presented in table 1.2. BRICS include: Brazil, the Russian Federation, India, China, and South Africa. Due to lack of reliable data of adequate quality, the World Bank is currently not publishing economic output, income, or growth data for Turkmenistan and República Bolivariana de Venezuela. Turkmenistan and República Bolivariana de Venezuela are excluded from cross-country macroeconomic aggregates.

and ultimately mitigate its compounding effects on the ongoing structural decline in long-term growth (chapter 3).

The prospect of a protracted period of low inflation and interest rates has important implications for both monetary and fiscal policy. In advanced economies, where the room for additional monetary policy support is limited, central bank frameworks are being reassessed, while fiscal policy is playing a more prominent role in macroeconomic stabilization. Over the longer run, the pandemic has highlighted the urgent need for reforms in advanced economies that harness the productivity benefits of sectoral reallocation and bolster the adoption of automation and digital technologies, along with the strengthening of social safety nets to facilitate this process.

In EMDEs, monetary policy is likely to remain generally accommodative in the near term, helped by subdued inflationary pressures and expectations of prolonged expansionary monetary policy stances in advanced economies. Several EMDE central banks have continued to employ asset purchase programs. These purchases appear to have been effective at stabilizing financial markets during the height of financial stress last March-April. Nevertheless, asset purchase programs need to be accompanied by clearly articulated policy mandates and objectives to avoid the risk that they would erode institutional independence and de-anchor inflation expectations (chapter 4). In addition, EMDEs increasingly face the challenge of preserving financial stability while maintaining accommodative macroprudential policy stances—such as lowered capital and liquidity requirements—to help facilitate credit availability and support the recovery.

Despite high debt levels, many EMDEs have implemented unprecedented fiscal support in response to COVID-19 to protect lives and livelihoods, confront the collapse in activity, and bolster the eventual recovery. Nevertheless, relative to advanced economies, the amount of support in EMDEs has been far more limited—particularly in countries facing narrower fiscal space, such as LICs. In most advanced economies and EMDEs,

FIGURE 1.2 Global risks and policy challenges

The pandemic is tipping millions back into poverty and reversing earlier per capita income gains. Downside risks to the growth outlook predominate, and the uncertain evolution of the pandemic, influenced in part by vaccine-related developments, suggests that various growth scenarios are possible. Even after the crisis subsides, the long-term damage caused by the pandemic is expected to weaken potential growth. Many countries have provided exceptional levels of fiscal support, which are expected to be withdrawn amid sharply higher debt levels. In the longer run, a concerted push toward productivity-enhancing structural reforms will be required to offset the pandemic's scarring effects.

A. Reversals of EMDE per capita income gains in 2020, by number of years

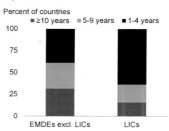

B. Possible scenarios of global growth

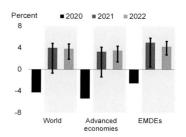

C. Estimated impact of the pandemic on global potential growth

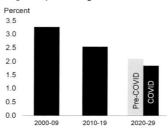

D. Global fiscal impulses

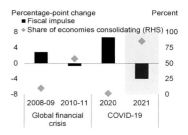

E. Government debt

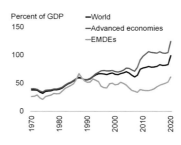

F. Cumulative response of long-term growth forecasts after institutional-reform advances and setbacks

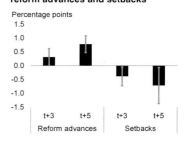

Sources: Consensus Economics; International Crisis Risk Group (database); International Monetary Fund; Kilic Celik, Kose, and Ohnsorge (2020); World Bank.
Note: EMDEs = emerging market and developing economies; LICs = low-income countries.
A.-C. Aggregates calculated using U.S. dollar GDP per capita at 2010 prices and market exchange rates.
A. Figure shows percentage of EMDEs by number of years of lost per capita income gains.
B.D. Shaded areas indicate forecasts.
B. Black vertical lines are the lower and upper bounds of growth in the scenarios described in box 1.4.
C. Potential growth based on production function estimates. Shaded area indicates pre-COVID baseline. Sample includes 30 advanced economies and 50 EMDEs.
D. Fiscal impulse defined as change in the cyclically-adjusted primary balance (CAPB) from previous year. Decline in the CAPB indicates fiscal consolidation; increase in the CAPB indicates fiscal expansion. Sample includes 61 economies.
E. Aggregates calculated using current GDP in U.S. dollars as weights. Data for 2020 are estimates.
F. Coefficients of a local projection estimation of 10-year-ahead growth forecasts on reform advances and setbacks in 57 countries during 1990-2020. For more details, see chapter 3.

much of the fiscal support provided last year is expected to be withdrawn, weighing on growth (figure 1.2.D). Whereas deficits are generally expected to shrink over the forecast, they will nonetheless contribute to rising debt, potentially planting the seeds for future problems— particularly if borrowing is not used efficiently (figure 1.2.E).

Against this backdrop, EMDE policy makers will need to tackle the challenge of avoiding premature fiscal tightening in the short term, but unwinding fiscal support measures and ensuring fiscal sustainability over the medium term. This will be especially difficult for some countries, given the substantial deterioration of fiscal positions that has occurred in the past year. Accordingly, there is a pressing need for EMDEs to improve domestic revenue mobilization and prioritize expenditures that yield large growth dividends. Additionally, the erosion of public balance sheets may call for the global community to provide assistance—in some cases including immediate debt relief—for hard-hit fiscally constrained EMDEs to support their most vulnerable populations through the crisis.

EMDE policy makers will also need to make sustained efforts to attenuate the pandemic's long-term damage to underlying growth and incomes. Addressing the recent increase in food insecurity and safeguarding access to education are essential to promoting the development of human capital. Simultaneously, far-reaching investment in digital and green infrastructure can facilitate sectoral reallocation while enhancing environmental resilience. Improved governance and reduced corruption can lay the foundations for higher long -run growth (figure 1.2.F). Increased debt transparency will be key to mitigate the risk of sovereign debt and financial crises, one of the most pressing threats to growth prospects.

Global cooperation will be essential for supporting vulnerable populations and achieving a sustainable and inclusive global recovery. In light of substantial fiscal constraints and high debt levels, globally coordinated debt relief, predicated on debt transparency, could help many economies— particularly LICs—and provide much-needed

fiscal resources to support social protection programs. More broadly, deeper global collaboration will be needed to develop equitable and sustainable solutions to the world's most pressing long-term challenges, including tackling climate change and eliminating extreme poverty.

Global context

COVID-19 has continued to spread around the world, resulting in the re-imposition of lockdown measures and a slowdown in the pace of the recovery. Although global trade in goods has largely rebounded, trade in services remains feeble. Global financial conditions are being supported by monetary policy accommodation, but financial systems in many countries are showing signs of underlying strain. Whereas most commodity prices, particularly those of metals, rebounded in the second half of the year as demand firmed, the recovery in oil prices has been more modest.

Pandemic developments

COVID-19 continued to spread in the second half of 2020, with steady increases in confirmed cases in some countries and renewed outbreaks in others (figures 1.3.A and 1.3.B). In recent months, advanced economies—particularly the United States and several euro area countries—have accounted for an increasing share of cases; in EMDEs, outbreaks in the South Asia, Latin America and the Caribbean, and Europe and Central Asia regions have continued to grow. Deaths from COVID-19 in Sub-Saharan Africa have remained low despite fears that limited healthcare capacity made it vulnerable, reflecting its young population (WHO 2020). High positive test rates in some countries and evidence from antibody tests suggest the virus is far more prevalent than indicated by confirmed cases (figure 1.3.C).

Growing outbreaks have forced many governments to maintain or reintroduce some lockdown measures (figure 1.3.D). Nonetheless, pandemic-control measures have become better targeted and less economically disruptive. For example, extensive mask usage appears to be a minimally disruptive way of slowing the spread of the virus, and some countries that adopted widespread test-and-trace policies have suffered fewer health and economic consequences (Konda et al. 2020; Schünemann et al. 2020).

Several vaccine candidates are in development, and some have already been used in countries such as the Russian Federation and China. With the completion of some Phase 3 trials, vaccination has begun in a number of advanced economies. A more general rollout of several effective vaccines is envisioned to proceed in early 2021 in advanced economies and major EMDEs, starting with vulnerable populations. It is expected that the vaccine rollout will be considerably slower in other EMDEs and LICs as a result of difficulties with procurement and distribution.

Global trade

Global trade collapsed last year as border closures and supply disruptions interrupted the international provision of goods and services. Goods trade fell more rapidly and recovered more swiftly than during the global financial crisis, while services trade remains depressed (figure 1.4.A). Relative strength in manufacturing, alongside persistent weakness in services, reflects the unusual nature of the recession, which has shifted consumption patterns toward goods and away from services requiring face-to-face interactions (figure 1.4.B). The recovery in global merchandise trade has also benefited from the resilience of global value chains to supply disruptions (Hyun, Kim, and Shin 2020).

Continued impediments to international travel and tourism are contributing to persistent weakness in services. International travel has recovered from its April trough but has stabilized far below pre-pandemic levels (figure 1.4.C). In the decade following the global financial crisis, rising trade intensity of global activity was almost entirely driven by trade in services (figure 1.4.D). The same is unlikely to be the case in the current recovery, as services will struggle to rebound until countries loosen international travel restrictions.

Although there have been some steps toward trade liberalization, such as the African Continental Free Trade Area agreement and the Regional

FIGURE 1.3 Pandemic developments

COVID-19 continued to spread in the second half of 2020, with renewed outbreaks in some countries. Advanced economies have accounted for an increasing share of cases, with particularly large concentrations in Europe and the United States. High positive test rates in some regions suggest the virus is far more prevalent than indicated by confirmed cases. The growing number of COVID-19 cases has forced many governments to maintain or reintroduce lockdown measures.

A. Evolution of the pandemic in advanced economies

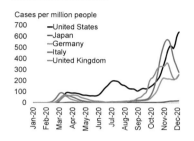

B. Evolution of the pandemic in EMDEs

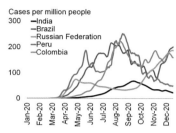

C. Positive COVID-19 test rate by region

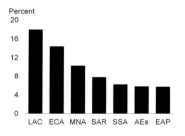

D. Stringency of pandemic-control measures

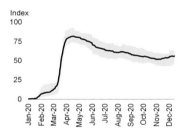

Sources: Hale et al. (2020); Our World in Data (database); World Bank.
Note: AEs = advanced economies; EMDEs = emerging market and developing economies; EAP = East Asia and Pacific, ECA = Europe and Central Asia, LAC = Latin America and the Caribbean, MNA = Middle East and North Africa, SAR = South Asia, SSA = Sub-Saharan Africa.
A.B. Figures show seven-day moving average of the daily new COVID-19 cases per million people. Last observation is December 15, 2020.
C. Figure shows the three-month average of the share of total COVID-19 tests that were positive for each region. Last observation is December 15, 2020.
D. Figure shows the simple average stringency index for EMDEs. Shaded area indicates the regional range. The stringency index refers to the average sub-indexes of nine mitigation measures: School closings, workplace closings, cancellation of public events, cancellation of public transport, restriction on gatherings, stay-home requirements and restrictions to international and domestic travel and public information campaigns. The stringency index range is between 0 and 100, with 100 being the most stringent. Last observation is December 13, 2020.

Comprehensive Economic Partnership, higher tariffs on U.S.-China trade remain in effect, and there has been little recent progress toward "deep" trade agreements that foster broader economic integration (Mattoo, Rocha, and Ruta 2020; World Bank 2020a). Trade policy uncertainty has fallen from its highs in 2019 but is still above historic norms, in part due to the potential of renewed trade tensions between major economies. The recently announced Brexit deal between the United Kingdom and the European Union is

FIGURE 1.4 Global trade

Goods trade fell more rapidly and recovered more swiftly than during the global financial crisis. It benefited from the substitution of demand from services toward manufactures, as well as the resilience of global value chains. In contrast, services trade remains depressed, in part owing to travel restrictions constraining tourism. A slow recovery in services trade—a key engine of trade growth following the global financial crisis—is expected to reduce the trade intensity of activity.

A. Trade in goods and services

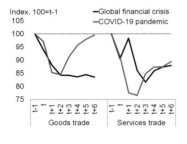

B. Cumulative deviation of global manufacturing and services PMI since January 2020

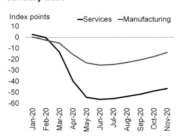

C. International tourist arrivals

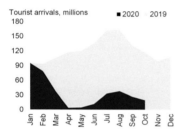

D. Growth in exports of goods and services, 2010-19

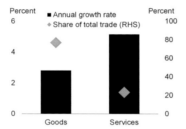

Sources: CPB Netherlands Bureau for Economic Policy Analysis; Haver Analytics; World Bank; World Tourism Organization; World Trade Organization.
A. Goods trade is in real terms from the CPB Netherlands Bureau for Economic Policy Analysis, whereas services trade is in values from the WTO. For global financial crisis, t = November 2008; for COVID-19, t = March 2020.
B. Manufacturing and services are measured by the Purchasing Managers' Index (PMI). PMI readings above 50 indicate expansion in economic activity; readings below 50 indicate contraction. Figure shows the cumulative deviation from 50 since January 2020. Last observation is November 2020.
C. Figure shows international tourist arrivals between 2019 and 2020.
D. Figure shows the average annual growth rate for goods and services exports between the year 2010 and 2019.

likely to contribute to a further decline in trade uncertainty.

Global trade is projected to contract by 9.5 percent in 2020—comparable to the decline during the 2009 global recession but affecting a markedly larger share of economies—before growing by an average of 5.1 percent in 2021-22. The moderate pickup in global trade reflects persistently subdued global investment and the gradual and incomplete recovery of global travel, and is expected to result in a further decline in the trade intensity of activity.

Financial markets

Aggressive policy actions by central banks kept the global financial system from falling into crisis last year. Financial conditions are generally loose, as suggested by low borrowing costs, abundant credit issuance, and a recovery in equity market valuations amid positive news about vaccine developments (figure 1.5.A; Altavilla et al. 2020). This masks rising underlying vulnerabilities, however, including rising debt levels and weakening bank balance sheets.

Debt burdens have increased as corporates have faced a period of sharply reduced sales and sovereigns have financed large stimulus packages (box 1.1). This follows a decade in which global debt had already risen to a record high of 230 percent of GDP by 2019. High debt levels leave borrowers vulnerable to a sudden change in investor risk appetite. This is especially true for riskier borrowers and EMDEs dependent on capital inflows to finance large fiscal and external current account deficits (figure 1.5.B). Capital inflows to many EMDEs remain soft, with significant weakness in both foreign direct investment (FDI) and portfolio flows (figure 1.5.C; World Bank 2020b). This, alongside a collapse of export revenues, has led to substantial currency depreciations and rising borrowing costs in some countries, particularly commodity exporters (figure 1.5.D; Hofmann, Shim, and Shin 2020; Hördahl and Shim 2020).

Banks' capital buffers are under pressure due to falling profitability and asset quality deterioration. Defaults have already surged in the hardest-hit sectors and countries, and rising credit downgrades point to further strains in the future (Banerjee, Cornelli, and Zakrajšek 2020). These developments reduce the resilience of financial systems, particularly in countries with weaker banking systems or without the policy space to provide sufficient support to stressed financial institutions.

Commodity markets

Most commodity prices rebounded in the second half of last year; however, the pickup in oil prices lagged the broader recovery in commodity prices due to the prolonged impact of the pandemic on global oil demand (figure 1.6.A; World Bank 2020c). Crude oil prices averaged $41/bbl in 2020, a 34 percent fall from 2019. Oil demand fell 9 percent last year—the steepest one-year decline on record—as a result of pandemic-control measures and the associated plunge in global demand, which was partly offset by historically large production cuts among OPEC+ (Organization of the Petroleum Exporting Countries, as well as Russia and other non-OPEC oil exporters; figure 1.6.B). Oil prices are forecast to remain close to current levels and average $44/bbl in 2021 before rising to $50/bbl in 2022. The main risk to this forecast relates to the evolution of the pandemic, with oil demand particularly susceptible to lockdown measures and reduced mobility; however, positive vaccine news has reduced this risk somewhat.

Base metal prices were, on net, broadly flat in 2020, as sharp falls in the first half of the year were followed by a strong recovery in the second half due to rising demand from China (figure 1.6.C). Prices are expected to increase 5 percent in 2021 alongside the expected rebound in global demand. Agricultural prices rose 4 percent in 2020, largely driven by supply shortfalls and stronger-than-expected demand in edible oils and meals. Some regions experienced localized food price spikes, and a decline in household incomes—particularly among the poorest populations—has increased the risk of food insecurity (figure 1.6.D). Agricultural prices are forecast to see a further modest increase in 2021.

Major economies: Recent developments and outlook

In advanced economies, a sharp resurgence of COVID-19 cut short an incipient economic rebound in the second half of 2020. The expected recovery in 2021 and beyond will depend heavily on the evolution of the pandemic, which will in turn be influenced by the possibility of widespread effective vaccination. In China, the economic rebound has been rapid but uneven, with consumer services trailing industrial production.

FIGURE 1.5 Global finance

After tightening early last year, global financial conditions have eased considerably. Nevertheless, many underlying vulnerabilities have risen. Credit spreads and debt inflows remain sensitive to investor sentiment. Although capital flows to most emerging market and developing economies (EMDEs) have stabilized, they remain soft, and foreign direct investment inflows have declined substantially. In some EMDEs, large capital outflows and a collapse of export revenues have led to substantial currency depreciations.

A. Global financial conditions

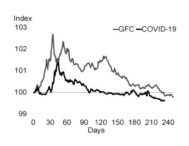

B. EMDE debt flows and credit spreads

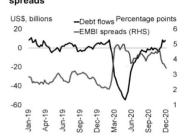

C. Capital flows to EMDEs

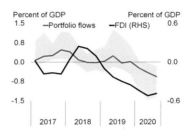

D. EMDE exchange rate depreciations

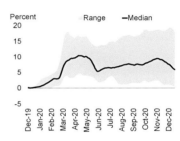

Sources: Bloomberg; Goldman Sachs; Haver Analytics; International Institute of Finance; International Monetary Fund; J.P. Morgan; Moody's; World Bank.
A. Index rescaled to equal 100 at the start of the corresponding event (t=0): September 9, 2008, for the global financial crisis (GFC) and January 21, 2020, for COVID-19. An increase (decrease) in the index indicates a tightening (loosening) of financial conditions, while a value above (below) 100 indicates that financial conditions are tighter (looser) than their average since 2000. Based on Goldman Sachs Financial Conditions Index (FCI) for 12 advanced economies, the euro area, and 12 emerging market and developing economies (EMDEs). Aggregates calculated using U.S. dollar GDP weights at 2010 prices and market exchange rates. The FCI is a weighted sum of short-term bond yields, long-term corporate yields, exchange rates, and stock market valuations. Last observation is December 11, 2020.
B. Portfolio debt inflows are shown as cumulative 12-week flows to nine EMDEs with weekly data available, excluding China. Emerging Market Bond Index (EMBI) spreads show the difference between credit spreads for high-yield (HY) and investment grade (IG) borrowers classified based on Moody's sovereign credit ratings. The EMBI Index tracks the performance of U.S. dollar-denominated sovereign bonds issued by EMDEs. Last observation is December 11, 2020.
C. FDI = foreign direct investment. Portfolio flows and FDI are as a percent of GDP and are calculated using nominal U.S. dollar GDP; GDP data for 2019 are used for 2020. Gross FDI inflows are shown as four-quarter cumulative sums and are shown as a deviation from the 2016-2019 average (2 percent of GDP). Portfolio flows are calculated as the median for a sample of 19 EMDEs, with shaded area indicating the 25-75 percentile range. Sample for FDI inflows includes 28 EMDEs, with data available through 2020Q3.
D. Change in nominal exchange rates since start of 2020. Shaded area indicates 25-75 percentile range. Sample includes 23 EMDEs with free floating or floating exchange rate regimes: 8 commodity importers and 15 commodity exporters. Last observation is December 15, 2020.

In advanced economies, precautionary social distancing and stringent lockdowns in response to surging COVID-19 cases triggered an unprecedented collapse in the demand and supply of services in mid-2020 (figures 1.7.A and 1.7.B;

BOX 1.1 How has the pandemic made the fourth wave of debt more dangerous?

The COVID-19 global recession and economic policy response have triggered a surge in debt levels in emerging market and developing economies (EMDEs). Even before the pandemic, however, a rapid buildup in these economies—dubbed the "fourth wave" of debt accumulation—had raised concerns about debt sustainability and the possibility of financial crisis. The pandemic has made the fourth wave even more dangerous by exacerbating debt-related risks. The global community needs to act rapidly and forcefully to make sure the fourth wave does not end with a string of debt crises in EMDEs, as earlier waves did.

Introduction

The COVID-19 pandemic has triggered a massive increase in global debt levels, including in emerging market and developing economies (EMDEs). Among EMDEs, government debt is expected to increase by 9 percentage points of GDP in 2020—its largest increase since the late 1980s when EMDEs saw a series of debt crises. The jump in government debt has been broad-based, with a large increase in all regions and all major EMDEs.[a] Private sector debt is also expected to rise sharply as firms deal with the fallout of the global recession.

Even before the pandemic, however, debt in EMDEs had risen to record levels (Kose, Nagle et al. 2020). Starting in 2010, a new wave of global debt accumulation was underway, with the largest, fastest, and most broad-based increase in global debt in five decades, led by EMDEs. Total debt in EMDEs reached 176 percent of GDP in 2019, driven by private debt which rose to 123 percent of GDP. The rapid increase in debt was a major cause of concern, as similar previous waves of debt have ended with widespread financial crises, such as the Latin American debt crisis in the 1980s, and the East Asia financial crisis in the late 1990s.

The pandemic has further exacerbated the debt-related risks in EMDEs. Against this backdrop, this box addresses the following questions:

- What was the status of the fourth wave before the pandemic?

- Why is the fourth wave even more dangerous now?

- What are the risks of inaction?

- What new policy challenges has the pandemic created?

The box updates earlier work on the risks associated with the debt buildup over the past decade (Kose, Nagle et al. 2020). It expands this work by examining in greater detail the challenges of debt resolution in the current context, drawing on lessons from past restructurings.

Prior to the pandemic: The fourth wave of debt accumulation

Prior to the COVID-19 pandemic, starting in 2010, a fourth wave of global debt accumulation was underway, with the largest, fastest, and most broad-based increase in global debt in five decades. Global debt had risen to a record high 230 percent of GDP in 2019 and government debt to a record 83 percent of GDP. In EMDEs, total debt had reached 176 percent of GDP, led by private debt which rose to 123 percent of GDP. This increase was mainly, but not solely, driven by China: in about 80 percent of EMDEs, debt was higher in 2019 than in 2010 and, in a half of them, 20 percentage points of GDP higher.

This wave was preceded by three previous debt waves since the 1970s, all of which ended with widespread financial crises. The first global wave of debt spanned the 1970s and 1980s, with borrowing by governments in Latin America and in low-income countries, particularly in sub-Saharan Africa. This wave saw a series of financial crises in the early 1980s. The second wave ran from 1990 until the early 2000s as banks and corporations in East Asia and the Pacific and governments in Europe and Central Asia borrowed heavily, and ended with a series of crises in these regions in 1997-2001. The third wave was a runup in private sector borrowing in Europe and Central Asia (as well as in advanced economies), which ended when the global financial crisis disrupted bank financing in 2007-09 and tipped many economies into sharp recessions.

The fourth wave of debt shared several features with the previous three waves: a low interest rate environment and the emergence of new financial instruments or financial market actors. Of particular concern was that the fourth wave had seen a protracted period of weak investment and slowing growth despite surging debt (chapter 3, box 3.2). In other respects, the fourth wave differed from its

---

Note: This box was prepared by Ayhan Kose, Peter Nagle, Franziska Ohnsorge, and Naotaka Sugawara.

[a] South Asia has seen the steepest increases, with India's government debt expected to rise by 17 percentage points of GDP amid a severe output contraction of more than 9 percent.

BOX 1.1 How has the pandemic made the fourth wave of debt more dangerous? (*continued*)

predecessors: policy frameworks were stronger in some EMDEs and debt in advanced economies was broadly flat.

Yet, even before the pandemic, there was no room for complacency. Previous crises had frequently been triggered by exogenous shocks that resulted in a sharp increase in investor risk aversion and sudden stops of capital flows. Global growth slowdowns were often catalysts for crises.

Implications of the pandemic for debt-related risks

The pandemic has made the fourth wave of debt even more dangerous by increasing its risky features. The sheer magnitude and speed of the debt buildup heightens the risk that not all of it will be used for productive purposes. For now, unprecedented monetary policy accommodation has calmed financial markets, reduced borrowing costs, and supported credit extension. However, amid the economic disruption caused by the pandemic, historically low global interest rates may conceal solvency problems that will surface in the next episode of financial stress or capital outflows. In addition, recent policy moves may erode some of the improvements that have occurred in EMEs in monetary, financial and fiscal policy frameworks, central bank credibility, and fiscal sustainability (Kose and Ohnsorge 2019, chapters 3 and 4).

Size and speed of increase in debt. As a result of sharp output collapses combined with unprecedented policy stimulus, debt-to-GDP ratios are set to rapidly reach new highs. Global government debt is expected to reach 99 percent of GDP for the first time on record in 2020 (figure B1.1.1). Among EMDEs, total debt had already risen by about 7 percentage points of GDP each year prior to the crisis; in 2020, government debt alone is expected to rise by 9 percentage points of GDP, while corporate indebtedness is also likely to sharply increase. [b]

Low global interest rates. At the onset of the pandemic, financial markets came under considerable strain, with sharply rising sovereign bond spreads for highly indebted EMDEs, a historic flight to safety, and record capital outflows from EMDEs (World Bank 2020d). Financial conditions have since eased due to unprecedented central

bank easing in major advanced economies. All major advanced economy central banks launched or expanded asset purchase programs, and several EMDE central banks have joined them (chapter 4). Real policy rates are negative in advanced economies, as in the first wave of debt.

Policy frameworks. While necessary to soften the impact of the pandemic-induced recession, some recent policy moves may erode policy frameworks.

- *Central bank credibility.* Monetary, financial, and fiscal policy frameworks in EMDEs improved significantly in the 2000s, helping these countries weather the global recession of 2009 and bouts of volatility over the subsequent decade (Kose and Ohnsorge 2019). In 2020, several EMDE central banks expanded their remit by starting asset purchase programs to stabilize financial markets (Arslan, Drehmann, and Hofmann 2020; IMF 2020a). While appropriate in the midst of a deep recession, the prolonged use of these tools could dampen investor confidence and risk de-anchoring inflation expectations if central bank credibility is undermined by extended funding of large fiscal deficits (chapter 4).

- *Credibility of fiscal rules.* In the face of unprecedented fiscal stimulus requirements, fiscal rules risk being eroded. Many fiscal rules have escape clauses intended to be invoked in time of major economic stress, and a large number of countries have already activated these clauses as a result of the pandemic (Budina et al. 2012; IMF 2020b). It is important, however, that the use of this flexibility is temporary and transparent. While exact timelines for a return to normal will vary, clear communication will be critical: if countries fail to reverse their path to these escape clauses as the recovery gains traction, investors may begin to question the long-term sustainability of government finances.

Changes in financial markets. With the onset of COVID-19, several new developments have spurred financial market activity in the midst of a collapse in output: the reach of central banks into new financial market segments has broadened; governments have heavily encouraged credit extension; and regulators and supervisors have eased restrictions.

- *Central banks.* Quantitative easing by EMDE central banks has eased borrowing conditions in financial market segments that would otherwise only be indirectly affected by monetary policy rate cuts. This has ensured continued access to finance in the midst

---

[b] In contrast to EMDEs, total advanced economy debt was little changed during the fourth wave as private sector deleveraging was offset by a modest increase in public sector debt. However, this is expected to shift dramatically in 2020, with a sharp increase in both public and private sector debt. Government debt alone is expected to rise by 20 percentage points of GDP to 124 percent of GDP in advanced economies (IMF 2020c).

BOX 1.1 How has the pandemic made the fourth wave of debt more dangerous? (*continued*)

FIGURE B1.1.1 Debt and policy measures during the pandemic

The pandemic has made the fourth wave of debt even more dangerous by strengthening its risky features. The sheer magnitude and speed of the debt buildup runs the risk that not all of it will be used for productive purposes. For now, unprecedented monetary policy accommodation has calmed financial markets, reduced borrowing costs, and supported credit extension. However, amid the economic disruption caused by the pandemic, historically low global interest rates may conceal solvency problems that will surface in the next episode of financial stress. In addition, some recent policy moves may erode central bank credibility and fiscal sustainability.

A. Global debt

B. Debt in EMDEs

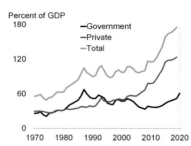

C. Changes in debt

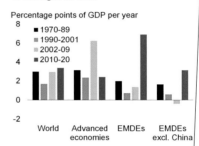

D. Policy rates

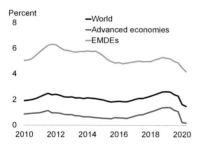

E. Asset purchases in EMDEs

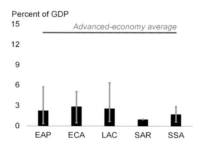

F. Fiscal measures in response to the COVID-19 pandemic

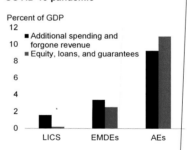

Sources: Bank for International Settlements; Haver Analytics; International Monetary Fund; Kose, Nagle et al. (2020); Kose, Sugawara, and Terrones (2020); OECD; World Bank.

Note: AEs = advanced economies, EMDEs = emerging market and developing economies, EAP = East Asia and Pacific, ECA = Europe and Central Asia, LAC = Latin America and the Caribbean, SAR = South Asia, SSA = Sub-Saharan Africa.

A.B. Aggregates are calculated using current GDP in U.S. dollars as a weight, based on data for up to 182 countries, including up to 145 EMDEs. Shaded area refers to forecasts for 2021-22; data for 2020 are estimates.

C. Rate of changes calculated as changes in total debt-to-GDP ratios over the denoted periods, divided by the number of years in each of them. Total debt is defined as a sum of government and private debt. Aggregates are calculated using current GDP in U.S. dollars as a weight. Total debt in 2020 is obtained under the assumption that it changes at the same pace as government debt in respective country groups.

D. Quarterly nominal policy rates. Aggregates are calculated using real GDP in U.S. dollars as a weight. Sample includes 123 countries, consisting of 36 advanced economies and 87 EMDEs. Last observation is 2020Q2.

E. Announced or completed purchases (where no announcement exists) relative to 2019 nominal GDP as of November 2020. Bar shows average in each region. Orange whiskers show regional range. Red line shows average of advanced economy programs launched in 2020.

F. Data are as of June 12, 2020. Country groups are weighted by GDP in purchasing power parity-adjusted current U.S. dollars. Revenue and spending measures exclude deferred taxes and advance payments.

of the recession but this may crowd out private sector investors if sustained over a prolonged period in illiquid EMDE financial markets (chapter 4).

- *Governments.* Government support packages have encouraged continued credit extension to corporates.

About 40 percent of the fiscal support from governments in EMDEs constitutes liquidity support measures such as loans, equity injections, and guarantees (IMF 2020c). Some governments have also encouraged banks to make use of available capital and liquidity buffers to support lending (Feyen et al.

BOX 1.1 How has the pandemic made the fourth wave of debt more dangerous? (*continued*)

2020; IMF 2020b, 2020d). While these are necessary to avoid widespread bankruptcies, they may support nonviable "zombie" firms. These contingent liabilities could eventually migrate onto government balance sheets, either in a financial crisis or, indirectly, in a period of sustained low growth (Mbaye, Moreno-Badia, and Chae 2018).

- *Bank supervision and regulation.* The global banking industry has asked regulators to relax or delay post-crisis rules on capital, liquidity, and accounting standards as a result of the pandemic, with some countries agreeing to delays or postponement of new regulations (IMF 2020c). Regulatory forbearance has increased. Unless comprehensive reporting of asset quality is assured, these measures risk eroding the transparency regulators and investors need to assess financial institutions' balance sheets.

Use of debt. Rising debt is less of a concern if it is used to finance growth-enhancing investments, particularly if they boost exports (World Bank 2017). During the first three waves of debt, borrowing was often used to finance productive investments. However, there are also many examples where debt was employed for less productive uses, including favoring domestic industries, or financing construction and property booms that did not raise productivity. A surge in debt without an increase in growth-enhancing investment projects is one of the factors that led to debt crises (Kose, Nagle et al. 2020, chapter 3, box 3.2). The COVID-19 pandemic has necessitated large-scale borrowing to finance many critical fiscal support measures. However, the scale and speed at which these measures were introduced creates considerable potential for diversion and misuse of funds.

Consequences of inaction

The previous waves of debt ended with widespread financial crises. When debt resolution was protracted, growth was often slow to recover or even resulted in a lost decade of growth.

Financial crises. Since 1970, about half of all countries that experienced a rapid buildup of debt also experienced a financial crisis. Where debt accumulation episodes were accompanied by crises, output and investment were significantly lower even several years after the end of the episode than in countries without crises (figure B1.1.2). There is a risk that the fourth wave, like its predecessors, also ends with a major financial crisis, with some countries already experiencing debt distress. Of particular concern is

that the current buildup is spread across both private and public sector debt, as well as across advanced economies, EMDEs, and LICs. Several countries eligible for International Development Association (IDA) lending are already in debt distress or are close to it.

Protracted resolution. During the first wave of debt, widespread sovereign debt defaults in Latin America and LICs in the early 1980s took many years to be resolved, with debt continuing to rise after the initial default. Debt relief only occurred in Latin America with the Brady Plan in 1989, while in LICs, meaningful debt relief did not occur until the Heavily Indebted Poor Countries (HIPC) initiative and Multilateral Debt Relief Initiative (MDRI) in 1996 and 2005, respectively. In contrast, during the second and third waves of debt, which mainly involved the private sector, debt resolution occurred more rapidly, but at a substantial cost to governments that frequently assisted through bank recapitalization and other support schemes.

Lost decade of growth. Prolonged periods of debt restructuring were associated with a lost decade of growth in Latin America and, in LICs, negative per capita income growth over several years. The COVID-19 pandemic is likely to deepen and prolong a slowdown in output, productivity, and investment growth that has been underway for a decade (chapter 3).[c] Weak growth will further increase debt burdens and erode borrowers' ability to service debt. For some countries in debt distress, the economic outlook may only improve once debt relief via debt write-offs occurs, rather than rescheduling (Reinhart and Trebesch 2016). Preemptive debt restructurings have generally been associated with better macroeconomic outcomes rather than restructurings that occur after a default has occurred (Asonuma et al. 2020).

New policy challenges

Several countries, particularly low-income countries, are already in, or at risk of, debt distress (IMF 2020e). In addition, the characteristics of the debt buildup of the fourth wave also raise new challenges and again highlight the major difficulties in achieving lasting debt relief.

Debt service costs. Many countries, particularly LICs, face large debt-servicing costs, with several already in debt distress. Debt service standstills can provide a temporary solution by providing breathing room to continue critical spending while allowing time for a comprehensive

---

[c] See Dieppe (2020); Kilic Celik, Kose, and Ohnsorge (2020); and Kose and Ohnsorge (2019).

BOX 1.1 How has the pandemic made the fourth wave of debt more dangerous? (*continued*)

FIGURE B1.1.2 **Cost of inaction, new challenges**

Past episodes of rapid debt accumulation were often associated with financial crises. When debt resolution was protracted, as it was in the 1980s and 1990s in Latin America and low-income countries, growth was often slow to recover or even resulted in a lost decade of growth. At present, several countries are already in debt distress or are close to it. The rapid increase in nonconcessional debt and lack of debt transparency also raise new challenges for achieving lasting debt relief.

A. **Rapid debt accumulation episodes associated with financial crises**

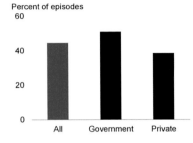

B. **Outcomes of rapid government debt accumulation episodes**

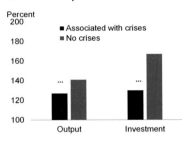

C. **Government debt in LICs and LAC**

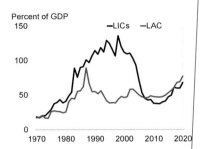

D. **Risk of external debt distress in selected countries**

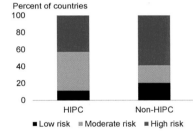

E. **Nonconcessional debt in EMDEs**

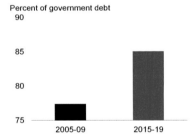

F. **Countries meeting selected DeMPA minimum requirements**

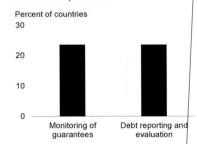

Sources: Haver Analytics; International Monetary Fund; Kose, Nagle et al. (2020); Kose, Sugawara, and Terrones (2020); World Bank.
Note: EMDEs = emerging market and developing economies; HIPC = Heavily Indebted Poor Countries; LAC = Latin America and the Caribbean; LICs = low-income countries.
A. "Episodes associated with crises" are episodes of rapid debt accumulation which experienced financial crises (banking, currency, and debt crises, as in Laeven and Valencia, 2020) during or within two years after the end of episodes. For definition of episodes and sample, see Kose, Nagle et al. (2020).
B. Median for episodes with data available for at least 8 years from the beginning of the episode. Year "t" refers to the beginning of rapid government debt accumulation episodes. Episodes associated with crises are episodes of rapid debt accumulation that experienced financial crises (banking, currency, and debt crises, as in Laeven and Valencia, 2020) during or within two years after the end of episodes. "***" denotes that medians between episodes associated with crises and those with no crises are different with statistical difference at the 1 percent level, based on Wilcoxon rank-sum tests. Cumulative percent increase from t, based on real growth rates for output and investment. Government debt accumulation episodes defined as in Kose, Nagle et al. (2020).
C. Three-year moving averages. Shaded area indicates forecast for 2020.
D. Defined as in IMF (2020). Based on a sample of 69 economies with available data, as of September 30, 2020.
E. Nonconcessional external debt as a share of general government debt. Averages over the denoted periods on the horizontal axis. Median of up to 120 EMDEs, with a smaller sample size for earlier years.
F. Figure shows share of 17 LICs meeting minimum standards as defined by Debt Management Performance Assessments (DeMPA) in December 2018.

assessment of debt sustainability that can lead to more lasting changes (Buchheit and Gulati, forthcoming). By avoiding short-term cash shortages, they can prevent a liquidity crisis becoming a solvency crisis. The External Debt Service Suspension Initiative (DSSI) is one example. As of November, 44 of the world's poorest countries have applied for the DSSI and benefited from an estimated $5.3 billion in debt service relief from official bilateral creditors,

complementing emergency financing provided by the World Bank and the International Monetary Fund. However, it is critical that these policies are only temporary measures to make space until permanent solutions can be secured. Debt standstills defer payments of interest and principal, but do not reduce debt levels. During the Latin American debt crisis, repeated debt reschedulings prolonged debt crises without resolving

BOX 1.1 How has the pandemic made the fourth wave of debt more dangerous? (*continued*)

them, and resulted in additional debt buildup and long-term debt overhangs. In addition, there can be hurdles to implementing debt standstills. For example, only 44 of the 73 countries eligible for the DSSI have requested assistance, held back by concerns that applying for the DSSI would affect their sovereign credit rating and restrict their access to new borrowing.

Fragmented creditor base. In the event of a debt crisis, its resolution will likely be more complex than earlier crises since there are many creditors with diverse motivations (international financial institutions, Paris Club bilateral lenders, non-Paris Club bilateral lenders including public owned policy institutions like the China Development Bank, and private sector lenders). The importance of bilateral non-Paris Club lenders has increased significantly, and China is now the largest official creditor to developing countries (Horn, Reinhart, and Trebesch 2020).

Lack of debt and investment transparency. The growing diversity of creditors and complexity of debt instruments has been associated with greater uncertainty about the level and composition of debt, as not all creditors are bound by a single set of reporting standards and loan terms are often confidential. In 2019, of the 17 LICs with available data, minimum requirements in debt recording were met by only eight, and monitoring guarantee requirements were met by only four. Due to shortcomings in accuracy, timeliness, coverage, and completeness of debt records, only four of these 17 countries met the minimum requirements for debt reporting and evaluation (Essl et al. 2019; World Bank 2019). Of 59 countries eligible for IDA borrowing, only one-third reported private sector external debt statistics (World Bank and IMF 2018). This raises the risk that public sector debt is higher in some EMDEs than reported. In addition, a lack of clarity about commitments encumbers debt restructuring negotiations, scrutiny of borrowing decisions, and efforts to ensure that borrowed funds are well spent. Debt sustainability can be undermined by policies that impose strict nondisclosure clauses on government borrowers, require major liens and collateralization, and place guaranteed debt repayments in state-owned enterprises.

Governance shortcomings. Many EMDEs, particularly LICs, still fall short in the strength of institutions that create distance between borrowing decisions and political pressures, as reflected in the low share of LICs that meet minimum requirements for debt administration, legal frameworks, and audit practices (World Bank 2019). This increases the risk that borrowing is excessive and not used for productive purposes.

Global debt resolution practices. In several dimensions, the playing field is currently tilted in favor of creditors and discourages prompt and comprehensive debt resolution. For example, financial centers that adjudicate disputes related to debt restructuring—especially New York, where two-thirds of outstanding sovereign bonds are governed—have provisions that favor hold-out bond holders. These include prejudgment penalties, large exemptions for buying bonds at steep discounts before default with the intent of suing subsequently, and modest taxes on excess capital gains (Stiglitz and Rashid 2020). While 91 percent of sovereign bond issuance since 2014 has included collective action clauses that facilitate restructuring, a large legacy stock without such clauses remains: about 50 percent of outstanding international debt does not include collective action clauses (IMF 2020e).

Policy implications

The COVID-19 pandemic has caused a surge in debt levels and exacerbated existing debt-related risks and vulnerabilities, leading to debt distress in some countries. Debt is likely to rise further as governments and financial systems finance the recovery by facilitating the move of capital, labor, skills, and innovation to a post-pandemic economic environment. Policy makers will also need to act to prevent short-term cash flow shortages from derailing the recovery in business activity and to provide space to assess debt sustainability, as well as to consider the best approaches to resolving debt if it becomes unsustainable.

In the short term, efforts to broaden the scope of debt covered by debt service standstills, notably by including the private sector, will provide additional breathing space for countries at risk of debt distress (World Bank 2020e, f; Bolton et al. 2020; Okonjo-Iweala et al. 2020).[d] However, such solutions will only be stop-gaps while a lasting solution is found. In the past, excessive debt has been resolved in one or more of six ways: three orthodox policy choices including growth, fiscal austerity, and privatization, and three heterodox approaches including unexpected inflation, often in combination with financial repression, debt relief, and taxing wealth (Reinhart, Reinhart, and Rogoff 2015; Reinhart and Sbrancia 2015). Each of these approaches is associated with challenging trade-offs such that choices need to be carefully tailored to country circumstances.

---

[d] The implementation of such an expansion would be a formidable challenge because it would involve coordination of numerous different stakeholders, including private creditors, official and multilateral creditors, and debtor countries (Gelpern, Hagan, and Mazarei 2020).

BOX 1.1 How has the pandemic made the fourth wave of debt more dangerous? (*continued*)

Where debt restructurings prove necessary, both creditors and debtors should aim for ambitious restructurings.[e] There is historical precedent for centrally orchestrated debt restructurings, including the London Debt Agreement of 1953; the Brady Plan in 1989-1994; and the HIPC initiative in 1996 (Guinnane 2015; Kaiser 2013; Kose, Nagle et al. 2020; Reinhart and Trebesch 2016). The Group of Twenty Common Framework that was reached in November 2020 is a step beyond the DSSI (G20 2020). The objective of the framework is to facilitate timely and orderly debt treatment for DSSI-eligible countries, and encourage broad creditor participation, including the private sector.

International financial institutions can also use lending conditionality to incentivize sovereign debtors and their creditors to aim for more ambitious restructurings (IMF 2020e). The IMF's "lending into arrears" (LIA) program, which had its origins in the Brady Plan in 1989, is one such lever (Truman 2020).[f] The LIA is conditional on a member "pursuing appropriate policies and making a "good faith effort" to reach a collaborative agreement with its private creditors," which incentivizes the debtor to

reach an agreement (IMF 2013). At the same time, the program neutralizes the possibility that private sector creditors could use the IMF's "no arrears" rule as negotiating leverage over debtors (Buchheit and Lastra 2007). In addition, financial centers that adjudicate disputes related to debt restructuring could level the playing field, which is currently tilted in favor of creditors (Stiglitz and Rashid 2020).

Longer term, measures are needed to strengthen the transparency of borrowing processes, borrowing amounts and terms, and spending of borrowed funds. Improved debt transparency is associated with lower borrowing costs and improves debt management practices (Kubota and Zeufack 2020). Several countries have made progress in this regard, including increased access to data on SOE debt and collateralized loans (World Bank 2020g). However, further progress is needed, especially in the context of transparency of debt contracts. Creditors can help by refraining from confidentiality clauses, allowing borrowers to publish detailed information, and themselves disseminating data on their lending. Beyond debt transparency, reforms to make debt management more effective can be complemented by other reforms that develop the institutional capacity and good governance to identify and monitor risks as well as conduct strategic planning. For the private sector, robust corporate governance can help ensure that private debt is well-spent in support of productivity-driven growth. Measures to improve and strengthen insolvency frameworks will also be critical amid rising rates of bankruptcies.

[e] Shallow agreements that avoid face value reductions can usher in, or extend, a protracted series of modest restructurings that last for many years until a more permanent resolution is found (Kose et al. 2020).

[f] "Lending into arrears" describes the situation where the IMF extends financial assistance to a member country that is in arrears to private creditors. Ordinarily, the IMF does not lend to countries in arrears.

Fernandez-Villaverde and Jones 2020). Robust retail sales powered a rebound in the third quarter of last year, but the recovery stalled following a resurgence of COVID-19 infections (figure 1.7.C).

Rapidly diminished momentum points to a slow and challenging recovery ahead, as was the case following the global financial crisis (figure 1.7.D). Subdued demand and heightened economic uncertainty, combined with disruptions to schooling and employment, are weighing heavily on labor productivity.

Following a 5.4 percent contraction in aggregate advanced economy GDP last year—with output declines in virtually all economies—activity is

forecast to expand 3.3 percent this year, in tandem with improved management of the pandemic and ongoing vaccination. Growth is then expected to edge further up to 3.5 percent in 2022, supported by widespread inoculation. Despite this recovery, the level of output by the end of the forecast horizon will remain 3.2 percent below pre-pandemic projections. This outlook is predicated on continued monetary and fiscal support.

United States

The fall in U.S. activity in the first half of 2020 was nearly three times as large as the peak decline during the global financial crisis, underscoring the depth of the recession (figure 1.8.A). For 2020 as a whole, U.S. output is estimated to have fallen by

3.6 percent. Although the pandemic's economic impact was not as severe as envisioned in previous projections, last year's contraction was more than one percentage point larger than that of 2009. Substantial fiscal support to household incomes—far exceeding similar measures delivered during the global financial crisis—contributed to a robust initial rebound in the third quarter of 2020, which was subsequently cut short by a broad resurgence of the pandemic (figures 1.8.B and 1.8.C).

Growth is forecast to recover to 3.5 percent in 2021—0.5 percentage point lower than previously projected, held down in the early part of the year by subdued demand amid renewed restrictions and a broad-based resurgence of COVID-19. Activity is expected to strengthen in the second half of this year and firm further next year, as improved COVID-19 management—aided by ongoing vaccination—allows for an easing of pandemic-control measures. Despite a 3.3 percent expansion in 2022, output is projected to remain 2.1 percent below pre-pandemic trends in that year, weighed down by labor market hysteresis and the scarring of potential output (figure 1.8.D). The potential for additional fiscal support and improved pandemic management during the forecast horizon could result in stronger-than-expected growth outcomes.

Euro area

Following the historic pandemic-induced collapse, an emerging rebound in economic activity in the third quarter of last year was cut short by a sharp resurgence of COVID-19, which prompted many member countries to reimpose stringent lockdown measures (figures 1.9.A and 1.9.B). Several services sectors vital to the area's economy—tourism in particular—remain depressed and are unlikely to recover until effective management of the pandemic improves confidence in the safety of face-to-face interactions (figure 1.9.C). Despite a worsening pandemic, manufacturing has continued to recover, supported by strengthening foreign demand.

Against the backdrop of a historic recession, the policy response has been far-reaching and sustained. National fiscal support packages were bolstered by grants from the European Union to

FIGURE 1.6 Commodity markets

Most commodity prices rebounded over the second half of 2020. Oil prices partially recovered as production fell sharply, particularly among OPEC+; however, this rebound was more modest than the broader recovery in commodity prices as oil demand disappointed. The rise in metal prices was mainly driven by strong demand from China. Some regions experienced localized food price spikes, which exceeded the rise at the global level.

A. Commodity price indexes

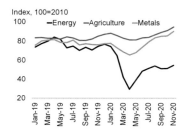

B. OPEC+ crude oil production

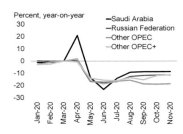

C. Metal prices

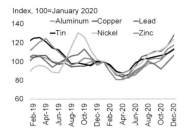

D. Regional and world food prices

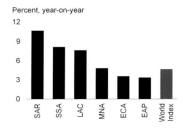

Sources: Bloomberg; International Energy Agency (database); Organization of Petroleum Exporting Countries (OPEC); World Bank.
Note: OPEC+ = OPEC plus 10 additional oil exporters; EAP = East Asia and Pacific, ECA = Europe and Central Asia, LAC = Latin America and the Caribbean, MNA = Middle East and North Africa, SAR = South Asia, SSA = Sub-Saharan Africa.
A. Last observation is November 2020.
B. "Other OPEC" includes all current OPEC countries except Saudi Arabia, and Iran, Libya, and República Bolivariana de Venezuela, which are exempt from production cuts. "Other OPEC+" includes Azerbaijan, Bahrain, Brunei, Kazakhstan, Malaysia, Oman, South Sudan, and Sudan. Last observation is November 2020.
C. Data for December represent averages of daily prices. Last observation is December 15, 2020.
D. Regional aggregates follow World Bank classifications and are based on averages of over 155 countries. Price change has been calculated as the year-on-year percent change for each month, averaged over January to November 2020. "World Index" represents the corresponding change of the World Bank's Food Commodity Price Index.

the hardest-hit member countries, which are expected to support activity starting in 2021 (figure 1.9.D).

In all, following a sharp contraction of 7.4 percent in 2020, growth is forecast to rebound to 3.6 percent in 2021, underpinned by improved COVID-19 management, an initial vaccine roll-out, and rising external demand, particularly from China. Growth is projected to strengthen further to 4 percent in 2022 as widespread vaccination

FIGURE 1.7 Advanced economies

The collapse in economic activity in the second quarter of 2020 was largely driven by sharp declines in the demand and supply of services. A lull in the COVID-19 outbreak in the second half of last year allowed for a solid rebound, powered largely by retail sales, but the more recent rise in COVID-19 cases has slowed the recovery. The level of output is expected to remain below its pre-crisis peak for a prolonged period, as was the case following the global financial crisis.

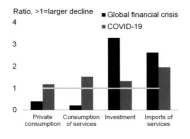

A. Ratio of decline in select GDP sub-components relative to decline in GDP

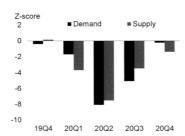

B. Demand and supply sentiments extracted from earning calls

C. Retail sales relative to pre-pandemic trend in advanced economies

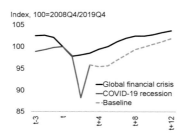

D. Advanced-economy GDP

Sources: Haver Analytics; Loughran and McDonald (2011); OECD (database); Oxford Economics; Securities and Exchange Commission; Seeking Alpha; Taskin (forthcoming); World Bank.
A. "Investment" corresponds to gross fixed capital formation. Bars represent ratios of cumulative change in sub-component relative to GDP change. For each episode, period is identified using pre-crisis peak and crisis trough of GDP. Value of 1 equals same degree of change. Data are simple average of nominal local-currency cumulative change across Group of Seven (G7) member countries which include Canada, France, Germany, Italy, Japan, the United Kingdom, and the United States.
B. The sentiment scores are calculated using earnings call transcripts of publicly listed firms in the United States. The listed companies are headquartered in 53 countries, including advanced economies (38) and EMDEs (15). Demand sentiment score for each call is calculated as (number of positive tone words - number of negative tone words)/(total number of words) around demand-related words (demand, export, exports). Each call's supply sentiment score is calculated using the same formula around supply-related words (supply, supplier, suppliers, import, imports). The call-level sentiment scores are aggregated using market capitalization values of companies as weights. The sentiment score formulas follow Hassan et al. (2019) and Taskin (forthcoming). The lists of negative and positive tone words are borrowed from Loughran and McDonald (2011). Z-scores represent the difference between raw values and their long-term average, divided by their long-term standard deviation. Mean and standard deviation are calculated over the period 2010Q1-2019Q4. Last observation is December 17, 2020.
C. Figure shows the percent difference between the level of realized real retail sales and their pre-pandemic trend. Pre-pandemic trend excludes pandemic developments by assuming that sales grow at their 2019 average rate starting in February 2020. Last observation is October 2020.
D. Figure shows the index of aggregated quarterly GDP history and projection for advanced economies. The blue line shows GDP history from 2007Q1 to 2010Q4, the red line shows GDP history from 2019Q4 to 2020Q3, and the dashed line shows baseline GDP projection from 2020Q4 to 2022Q4. The index is set to 100=2008Q4 for the blue line and 100=2019Q4 for the other lines. Sample includes 25 advanced economies.

contributes to firming consumption and investment—still above potential growth, but leaving output 3.8 percent below pre-pandemic trends.

Japan

Early effective management of COVID-19, coupled with unprecedented fiscal support, powered a rebound in activity in the third quarter of 2020. This nascent recovery quickly lost momentum as a resurgence of COVID-19 dampened consumption, even though the manufacturing sector continued to firm.

After contracting by an estimated 5.3 percent in 2020, activity is expected to expand by 2.5 percent in 2021 as additional fiscal stimulus is implemented and, with new COVID-19 cases brough down to low levels, pandemic-control measures are gradually phased out. Growth is projected to tick down to 2.3 percent in 2022, leaving output 2.4 percent below its pre-pandemic trend.

China

Growth decelerated to an estimated 2 percent in 2020—the slowest pace since 1976 but above previous projections, helped by effective control of the pandemic and public investment-led stimulus. The recovery has been solid but uneven, with consumer services trailing industrial production (figure 1.10.A). For most of last year, import growth lagged a rebound in exports, contributing to a widening current account surplus (figure 1.10.B).

Accommodative fiscal and monetary policies led to a sharp increase in the government deficit and total debt (figures 1.10.C and 1.10.D; World Bank 2020h). Fiscal policy support, which initially focused on providing relief and boosting public investment, is starting to moderate.

Growth is forecast to pick up to 7.9 percent in 2021, above previous projections due to the release of pent-up demand, and moderate to 5.2 percent in 2022 as deleveraging efforts resume. Even as GDP returns to its pre-pandemic level in 2021, it is still expected to be about 2 percent below its pre-pandemic projections by 2022, with the crisis accentuating preexisting vulnerabilities and imbalances (World Bank 2020i).

Emerging market and developing economies

Activity in EMDEs fell 2.6 percent in 2020 as a result of the COVID-19 pandemic. Although aggregate EMDE growth is projected to pick up to 5 percent in 2021 and moderate to 4.2 percent in 2022, output will remain well below pre-pandemic projections throughout the forecast horizon. The pandemic is expected to inflict long-term damage on EMDE growth prospects by depressing investment and human capital. Progress on critical development goals has been set back by several years, as the pandemic has disproportionately affected vulnerable groups and is driving poverty rates sharply higher.

Recent developments

The health and economic crisis triggered by COVID-19 caused EMDE output to shrink an estimated 2.6 percent in 2020—the worst rate since at least 1960, the earliest year with available aggregate GDP data. Excluding the recovery in China, the contraction in EMDE output last year is estimated to have been 5 percent, reflecting recessions in over 80 percent of EMDEs—a higher share than during the global financial crisis, when activity shrank in about a third of EMDEs. The economies that suffered the worst declines were those with a heavy reliance on services and tourism (Cabo Verde, Maldives, Montenegro, the Caribbean, the Seychelles), those with large domestic outbreaks (Argentina, India, Mexico, Peru), and those that faced sharp declines in industrial-commodity exports due to the fall in external demand (Ecuador, Oman; figure 1.11.A).

Services activity contracted last year as consumers shifted away from activities requiring face-to-face interactions amid severe and prolonged weakness in international travel (figure 1.11.B). In the average EMDE, services accounted for more than half of the value-added GDP prior to the pandemic. The relatively higher share in countries dependent on tourism helps to explain why they have experienced relatively deeper contractions (figure 1.11.C).

FIGURE 1.8 **United States**

The output collapse in the first half of 2020 dwarfs declines during the global financial crisis and other previous recessions. Large-scale emergency support to household incomes—well above that of the global financial crisis—helped power a rebound in a broad range of indicators starting in mid-2020, which was subsequently halted by a resurgence of COVID-19. Going forward, the recovery is likely to face headwinds from labor market scarring, with long-term unemployment rising at a faster rate than during the global financial crisis.

A. GDP decline in historical comparison

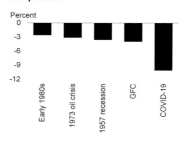

B. Personal consumption expenditures and disposable income

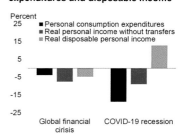

C. Selected indicators of economic activity

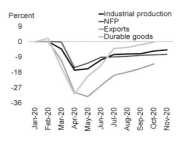

D. Long-term unemployment

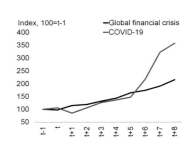

Sources: Federal Reserve Bank of St. Louis (database); U.S. Bureau of Economic Analysis (database); World Bank.
Note: GFC = global financial crisis; NFP = total nonfarm private payroll employment; Durable goods = manufacturer's new orders of durable goods.
A. Figure shows the percentage difference for U.S. real GDP between the peak before the crisis and the lowest point during the crisis. The "Early 1980s" is 1981Q4 to 1982Q1, "1973 Oil crisis" is 1974Q1 to 1975Q1, "1957 recession" is 1957Q4 to 1958Q1, "GFC" is 2008Q1 to 2009Q2, and "COVID-19" is 2020Q1 to 2020Q2.
B. Figure shows the percentage difference between peak values and lowest point during recessions. Date for pre-recession peak of GFC is June 2008 and trough is March 2009, date for pre-recession peak of COVID-19 recession is February 2020 and trough is April 2020.
C. Figure shows values for the United States as percentage changes since January 2020. Last observation is November 2020 for industrial production and NFP and October 2020 for durable goods and exports.
D. Figure shows the number of people unemployed for 27 weeks and over during the global financial crisis period and COVID-19 in the United States. "t" represents November, 2008 for the global financial crisis period, and March, 2020 for the COVID-19 period.

Substantial macroeconomic support helped soften the decline in activity. The fall in investment was partly curbed by policy rate cuts and macro-prudential support measures, which provided liquidity and promoted lending, as well as by sizable fiscal packages, which increased capital on health and information technology. The fall in

FIGURE 1.9 Euro area

The output collapse in the first half of 2020 far exceeded that of previous crises. The recovery that followed lost some momentum as COVID-19 cases surged in the second half of 2020. Tourism—a vital economic sector for several member economies—experienced a particularly acute decline and remains deeply depressed. The European Union's recovery fund is expected to provide significant support to hard-hit members facing fiscal constraints.

A. Euro area GDP decline in historical comparison

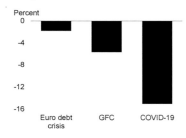

B. Selected indicators of economic activity in the euro area

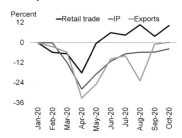

C. Decline in tourism in euro area member countries with large tourism sectors

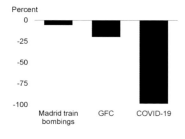

D. European Union recovery fund allocation for select members

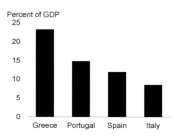

Sources: European Central Bank (database); European Commission; European Statistical Recovery Dashboard (database); Federal Reserve Bank of St. Louis (database); World Bank; World Travel & Tourism Council (database).
Note: GFC = global financial crisis; IP = industrial production.
A. Figure shows the percentage difference for euro area quarterly real GDP between the pre-crisis peak and the lowest point during the crisis. The GFC is from 2008Q2 to 2009Q2, Euro debt crisis is from 2011Q3 to 2013Q1, and the COVID-19 recession is 2020Q1 to 2020Q2.
B. Figure shows percentage changes since January 2020. Last observation is October 2020.
C. Figure shows peak declines for the year-on-year percentage change of nights spent at tourist accommodation establishments by non-residents. The regional aggregate is calculated as the average of the euro area members where tourism's contribution to GDP is above the euro area median value in 2019. "Madrid train bombings" refers to the terrorist attack that occurred in Madrid, Spain, on March 11, 2004.
D. Figure shows, as a percent of 2019 GDP, the total preliminary estimated Next Generation EU grants plus loans using European Commission's allocation key.

private consumption was less severe in EMDEs that used available fiscal policy space to expand social safety nets and support employment. The resilience of remittances in some countries also helped to cushion the blow to households (figure 1.11.D; Quayyum and Kpodar 2020; World Bank 2020j). Despite these mitigating factors, mounting job losses resulted in labor incomes falling between 10 to 15 percent across EMDE regions (figure 1.11.E; ILO 2020).

In *commodity exporters*, the dual shock of pandemic-related economic disruptions and plunging commodity prices generated substantial headwinds to activity in 2020. The rebound in industrial production across commodity exporters has been tepid, with production remaining below pre-pandemic levels (figure 1.11.F). The weakness reflects a decline in extractive investment and, for oil exporters, OPEC+ oil production cuts and still-subdued oil prices (World Bank 2020c).

In several *low-income countries*, rising caseloads forced governments to keep some containment measures in effect during the second half of 2020 (Ethiopia, Mozambique, Rwanda, Uganda; box 1.2). In all, output in LICs is estimated to have shrunk 0.9 percent in 2020—the group's first contraction in a generation. Among fragile and conflict-affected LICs—already struggling with limited fiscal space and state capacity—the collapse in activity was far steeper, with output falling by an estimated 3.9 percent (Afghanistan, Central African Republic). Output among other LICs also weakened appreciably, as tourism revenues tumbled, consumption fell, and investment came to a halt (Madagascar, Rwanda).

Outlook

Growth outlook

COVID-19 has dealt a substantial blow to the outlook in all EMDE regions (box 1.3; chapter 2). The pandemic is estimated to have erased at least 10 years of per capita income gains in more than a quarter of EMDEs in 2020 (figure 1.12.A). EMDE output is projected to expand 5 percent in 2021, predicated on firming external demand and improved pandemic management, aided by vaccine rollouts in major EMDEs (figure 1.12.B). Excluding China, however, growth for EMDEs this year will be more subdued, at only 3.4 percent, reflecting lingering disruptions from outbreaks in many EMDEs. Despite the projected aggregate recovery in 2021, forecasts in roughly two-thirds of EMDEs were downgraded—especially in Europe and Central Asia (ECA), where a number of economies are experiencing a sharp resurgence of the virus.

EMDE growth is envisioned to moderate in 2022, to 4.2 percent, near its potential pace. Despite the recovery, aggregate EMDE activity next year is expected to remain 6 percent below pre-pandemic forecasts. The shortfall is broad based, with more than 90 percent of EMDEs projected to register lower output levels in 2022 than previously anticipated.

Headwinds to activity remain particularly pronounced for economies with large services sectors, including those that rely on tourism, as social-distancing measures and sustained weakness in international travel weigh on hospitality and transportation (OECD 2020a). Economies with large services sector are envisioned to recover more slowly than other EMDEs, expanding an average of 3.2 percent over 2021-22. Similarly, growth in industrial-commodity exporters is expected to be anemic, averaging 2.8 percent over 2021-22, as many have tightened fiscal stances due to the collapse in revenues.

The pandemic is expected to exacerbate the slowdown in productivity and potential output through its scarring effects on investment, labor supply, and human capital (Dieppe 2020; World Bank 2020k). Investment, which had decelerated in the past decade, is expected to weaken further as elevated uncertainty and impaired corporate profitability dent confidence (figure 1.12.C). After contracting in nearly all EMDEs in 2020, investment is forecast to shrink again this year in more than a quarter of economies—primarily in Sub-Saharan Africa (SSA), where investment gaps were already large prior to the pandemic. The drop in FDI inflows to EMDEs will further hinder capital accumulation (UNCTAD 2020).

COVID-19 is also likely to set back human capital development (World Bank 2020l). Longer unemployment spells may discourage workers from remaining in the labor force, which could appreciably erode skills given steep job losses. In previous economic crises, vulnerable groups faced higher rates of school dropout and reduced skills development, which increased income disparities (Shmis et al. 2020). School closures are expected to reduce the learning-adjusted years of education across EMDE regions by roughly a third to a full year (figure 1.12.D; Azevedo et al. 2020). This,

FIGURE 1.10 China

The recovery in China has been solid but uneven, with consumer services trailing industrial production. Import growth has lagged the ongoing rebound in exports, contributing to a widening current account surplus. Sizable policy support has pushed total debt to new highs.

A. Activity indicators

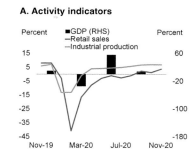

B. Balance of payments

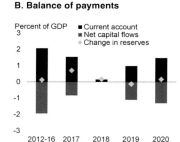

C. Fiscal support measures, augmented fiscal deficit, and government debt

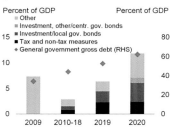

D. Total non-financial-sector credit and GDP growth

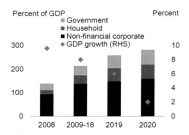

Sources: Bank for International Settlements; Haver Analytics; Institute of International Finance; International Monetary Fund; National Bureau of Statistics of China; World Bank.
A. Figure shows quarter-on-quarter annualized change of real GDP in 2015 prices, and year-on-year change of total real industrial value added (2005=100) and non-seasonally adjusted nominal retail sales. Last observation is 2020Q3 for GDP, and November 2020 for industrial production and retail sales.
B. Net capital flows and change in reserves are estimates. Net capital inflows include net capital and financial account balance, errors and omissions. 2020 is based on January-September official balance of payments statistics. Last observation is 2020Q3.
C. Centr. gov. bonds = Central government special bonds. Figure shows estimated fiscal support by categories, including investment, tax and non-tax measures, and other spending, which includes transfers to households. Augmented fiscal deficit includes net borrowing for the consolidated balance of four separate budgetary accounts: i) public finance budget balance, ii) government finance budget (including investment financed by local government bonds and land sales), iii) social security fund balance, and iv) SOE management fund balance. Government debt includes contingent debt associated with liabilities of local government finance vehicles. "Other" includes transfers to households. General government gross debt in 2019 and 2020 are estimates.
D. Total credit to non-financial sector includes household, non-financial corporate, and public sector debt. Total debt and GDP growth for 2020 are forecasts. Last observation is 2020Q1 for debt and 2020Q2 for GDP growth. Data for 2020 are estimates.

combined with deskilling due to prolonged unemployment, will likely lower future earnings and dent human capital (Fasih, Patrinos, and Shafiq 2020; Fuchs-Schündeln et al. 2020). Overall, COVID-19 could reduce EMDE potential growth by a further 0.6 percentage point, to 3.4 percent, over the next decade absent reforms to boost underlying drivers of long-term growth (boxes 3.1 and 3.2).

FIGURE 1.11 Recent developments in emerging market and developing economies

Emerging market and developing economies have been hard hit by COVID-19, especially those with the highest number of cases and those reliant on services, tourism, or industrial commodity exports. Retail sales have stabilized at low levels amid large job and income losses, although the latter has been partially offset by resilient remittance inflows in some economies. The pickup in industrial activity has been tepid in commodity exporters due to weak extractive investment.

A. Average contraction in output in 2020, by EMDE group

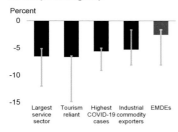

B. EMDE commercial-services exports and tourist arrivals, excluding China

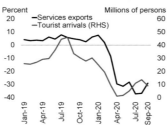

C. Share of services in 2019, by EMDE group

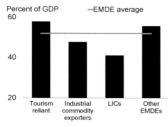

D. Retail sales volumes and remittance inflows in 2020

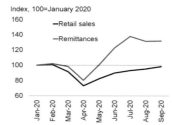

E. Job losses in EMDEs as a share of employment

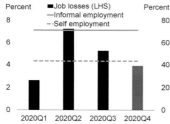

F. EMDE industrial production in 2020

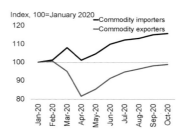

Sources: Haver Analytics; International Labour Organization; Johns Hopkins University; Quayyum and Kpodar (2020); World Bank; World Tourism Organization; World Trade Organization.

Note: EMDEs = emerging market and developing economies; LICs = low-income countries. "Industrial commodity exporters" indicates EMDEs that export either energy or metals. "Largest service sector" includes EMDEs in the top quartile of services as a share of the economy. "Tourism reliant" includes EMDEs in the top quartile of inbound tourism expenditure as a share of GDP. "Highest COVID-19 cases" includes countries in the top quartile of COVID-19 cases per capita.

A. Data for 2020 are estimates. Aggregates calculated using 2020 U.S. dollar GDP at 2010 prices and market exchange rates. Yellow lines indicate the interquartile range. Sample includes 113 EMDEs.

B. Figure shows the year-on-year growth of commercial-services exports measured in millions of U.S. dollars. Sample includes 18 EMDEs for services exports and 27 EMDEs for tourist arrivals. Last observation is September 2020.

C. Figure shows services measured as value added as a share of GDP. Orange horizontal line indicates the simple average in EMDEs, which is about 52 percent. Sample includes 115 EMDEs.

D. Data are seasonally adjusted, based on data and methodology from Haver Analytics and Quayyum and Kpodar (2020). Last observation is September 2020 for retail sales and remittances. Sample includes 22 EMDEs.

E. Figure shows the equivalent number of full-time jobs (48 hours/week as measured by the International Labor Organization) lost in 2020 as a percentage of the total employment for EMDEs in 2019. Data for 2020Q4 are International Labour Organization forecasts. "Informal employment" is defined as in the January 2019 *Global Economic Prospects* report.

F. Last observation is October 2020.

Among LICs, growth is forecast to resume at a moderate pace, reaching 3.3 percent in 2021—less than two-thirds of the average pre-pandemic pace—and subsequently firming to 5.2 percent in 2022 (box 1.2). This pickup in LIC activity assumes that external demand from key trading partners, particularly China, recovers as expected and that containment measures are gradually relaxed as effective vaccines are rolled out domestically by early 2022. Long-standing logistical challenges in LICs are expected to delay the vaccine distribution and weigh on the recovery. Moreover, ballooning government debt burdens across LICs—which rose by an estimated 7 percentage points to 69 percent of GDP in 2020—are envisaged to severely constrain fiscal policy (The Gambia, Mozambique, Zimbabwe; Essl et al. 2019; World Bank 2020k). Globally coordinated debt relief, predicated on debt transparency, could assist several LICs in providing the fiscal support and social protection needed to bolster the recovery (box 1.1).

Poverty and per capita income growth

The poorest and most vulnerable countries and populations have been hard hit by the pandemic, putting several of the Sustainable Development Goals (SDGs) even further out of reach. The pandemic has reversed the downward trend in global poverty for the first time in a generation and is projected to push more than 100 million people into extreme poverty, even though there is heightened uncertainty about the ultimate outcome (figure 1.13.A; Lackner et al. 2021; World Bank 2020m). More than one-half of this increase is expected to occur in South Asia—where substantial gains in poverty reduction had previously been made—and about one-third in Sub-Saharan Africa—where four in ten people already live in extreme poverty.

Inequality is also likely to worsen, partly reflecting the fact that the pandemic is expected to have a disproportionately negative effect on the incomes of vulnerable groups (Furceri et al. 2020; ILO 2020). These include women, migrant workers, those employed in lower-skilled occupations or informal sectors, and those with limited assets and thus constrained access to credit (Azcona et al. 2020; Islam et al. 2020). Rising inequality magnifies the impact of the global recession on poverty, with even modest increases in inequality indicators associated with tens of millions more people falling below the international poverty line (Lakner et al. 2020). The longer-term impacts of disruptions to schooling, which have been more prolonged in EMDEs and LICs, are also likely to particularly affect those populations with limited access to infrastructure and technology, such as the internet or personal computers, and leave more lasting scars (figures 1.13.B and 1.13.C; chapter 3; Azevedo et al. 2020; Copley et al. 2020).

Although EMDE per capita incomes are expected to begin to recover in 2021-22 as activity gradually picks up, they are expected to remain well below pre-pandemic projections (figure 1.13.D). In over one-half of EMDEs, five or more years of per capita incomes gains have been lost, while in more than one-quarter of economies—many of which are clustered in Latin America and the Caribbean (LAC), the Middle East and North Africa (MENA), and SSA—all progress made over the 2010s has been erased. In all, per capita GDP levels are projected to be lower in 2022 than in 2019 for about two-thirds of EMDEs.

Global outlook and risks

Although global activity is projected to recover as the pandemic is gradually brought under control, it is not expected to return to its pre-crisis trend. The baseline forecast is subject to several risks. The spread of the pandemic could accelerate, particularly if the vaccination process is delayed, and economic weakness and impaired banking systems may lead to financial crises. In the medium term, the crisis may lower global potential output as a result of lasting damage to health, education, and balance sheets. Declining global cooperation may lead to greater uncertainty and less effective policy actions.

Global outlook

Global activity is estimated to have contracted 4.3 percent in 2020 as a result of COVID-19, making it the fourth most severe global recession of the past 150 years, exceeded only by the first World War, the Great Depression, and the Second

FIGURE 1.12 **Prospects for growth in emerging market and developing economies**

COVID-19 has reversed at least a decade of per capita income gains in about a quarter of emerging market and developing economies (EMDEs). Although activity in EMDEs is projected to firm over the forecast horizon, output levels will remain well below their pre-pandemic projections. In low-income countries, where activity contracted for the first time in a generation last year, growth is expected to resume at a moderate pace. The pandemic is expected to dent longer-term prospects partly through its impact on investment and schooling.

A. Reversals of EMDE per capita income gains in 2020, by number of years

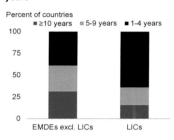

B. GDP in EMDEs

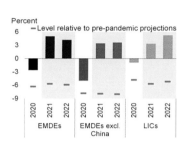

C. Investment gaps with pre-pandemic levels

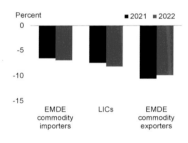

D. Impact of COVID-19 on learning-adjusted years of schooling

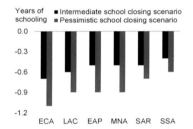

Sources: Azevedo et al. (2020); World Bank.
Note: EMDEs = emerging market and developing economies; LICs = low-income countries; EAP = East Asia and Pacific, ECA = Europe and Central Asia, LAC = Latin America and the Caribbean, MNA = Middle East and North Africa, SAR = South Asia, SSA = Sub-Saharan Africa. Data for 2020 are estimates.
A. Aggregates calculated using U.S. dollar GDP per capita at 2010 prices and market exchange rates. Figure shows the percentage of EMDEs by number of years of lost per capita income gains, measured as the difference between 2020 and the latest year of per capita income that is below 2020 value over the 2000-19 period.
B. Data for 2020 are estimates. Shaded areas indicate forecasts. Aggregates calculated using U.S. dollar GDP at 2010 prices and market exchange rates. Dashes correspond to the percent difference between the latest projected levels of GDP and those in the January 2020 *Global Economic Prospects* report.
C. Aggregates calculated using U.S. dollar GDP at 2010 prices and market exchange rates. Bars correspond to the percent difference between the latest projected levels of investment and those in the January 2020 *Global Economic Prospects* report.
D. Figure shows the simulated impact of COVID-19 school closures on schooling from the pre-pandemic baseline, as in Azevedo et al. (2020). The intermediate and pessimistic scenarios assume schools are closed for 5 and 7 months, respectively.

World War. Given the unprecedented nature of the pandemic, prospects for the global economy are uncertain, and several growth outcomes are possible. In the baseline forecast, global growth is expected at 4 percent in 2021, and is projected to

FIGURE 1.13 Poverty and per capita income in emerging market and developing economies

Global extreme poverty is set to rise markedly as a result of the pandemic, with sharp increases in South Asia and Sub-Saharan Africa. Relative to advanced economies, disruptions to schooling have, on average, been more prolonged in emerging market and developing economies (EMDEs), including in low-income countries. Such disruptions are likely to disproportionately affect more vulnerable groups owing to lack of access to distance learning. Although EMDE per capita incomes are projected to firm in 2021-22, their levels will remain well-below pre-pandemic trends.

A. Increase in global extreme poverty headcounts by 2021

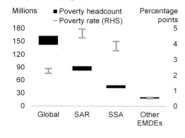

B. Duration of school closures

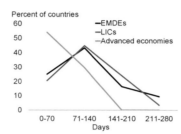

C. Access to technology of EMDE schoolchildren

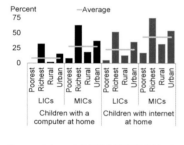

D. EMDE per capita GDP relative to pre-pandemic projections

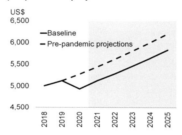

Sources: Lakner et al. (2021); UNESCO (database); UNICEF; World Bank; World Bank (2020m).
Note: EMDEs = emerging market and developing economies; LICs = low-income countries; MICs = middle-income countries; SAR = South Asia; SSA = Sub-Saharan Africa.
A. Figure shows the additional number of people pushed into poverty by 2021 as a result of the COVID-19 pandemic. Lower ends of the bars and whiskers reflect the baseline scenario; upper ends reflect the downside scenario. The increase in extreme poverty headcounts by 2021 due to the pandemic is calculated by comparing poverty using pre- and post-pandemic growth forecasts available as of October 2020; the former are used as a counterfactual series for poverty in a world without COVID-19 (Lakner et al. 2020).
B. Data correspond to the number of days country school systems in each grouping were categorized as "closed due to COVID-19". Countries where school systems are classified as "partially open" are excluded. "EMDEs" excludes LICs. Last observation is December 16, 2020.
C. Bars denote averages. "Poorest" reflects the poorest income quintile, and "Richest" the richest income quintile. Sample includes 15 MICs and 5 LICs that participated in the latest UNICEF Multiple Indicator Cluster Survey (MICS6 in 2017-19).
D. Data are in constant 2010 U.S. dollars. Shaded area indicates forecasts. Trend is assumed to grow at the regression-estimated trend rate of 2010-19. Baseline output is latest baseline forecast over 2020-22 and, for 2023 onwards, computed using long-term consensus forecasts published in October 2020.

moderate further in 2022, to 3.8 percent. Even by 2022, global GDP is forecast to be 4.4 percent below pre-pandemic projections, with the gap in EMDEs nearly twice as large as in advanced economies, highlighting the massive economic costs inflicted by COVID-19 (figure 1.14.A). Risks to this outlook are tilted to the downside,

with the probability of markedly worse-than-expected outcomes being nearly five times higher than the historical average (figure 1.14.B).

The collapse in global activity in 2020 is estimated to have been slightly less severe than previously expected, mainly due to shallower contractions in major advanced economies and a more solid recovery in China. Economic disruptions in many other EMDEs were worse than expected, however, resulting in a predominance of downgrades, including for large economies such as Argentina, India, Mexico, and Thailand (figure 1.14.C). Forecasts for activity in 2021 have also been revised down in the majority of both advanced economies and EMDEs, resulting in a downgrade to global growth.

The forecast for global growth depends on the weighting methodology being used. Advanced economies account for 60 percent of global activity according to the market exchange rate weights used in the baseline projections. In contrast, these economies only account for 40 percent of global activity when using purchasing power parity (PPP) weights—a methodology that places greater weight on faster-growing EMDEs. Since advanced economies generally suffered deeper recessions and are forecast to have slower recoveries than EMDEs—especially China, which is rebounding particularly strongly—the profile for global activity is weaker when using market exchange rate weights compared to PPP weights. As a result, global GDP is estimated to have contracted 3.7 percent in 2020 and is forecast to expand 4.3 percent in 2021 using PPP weights—slightly higher than the projections using market exchange rates (table 1.1).

The baseline outlook assumes that pandemic-control measures are able to reduce the daily number of infections in the first half of 2021. Moreover, the deployment of effective vaccines, which has begun in some countries, is envisioned to gather pace in early 2021 in advanced economies and major EMDEs, with widespread vaccination achieved by late 2021. The process for other EMDEs and for LICs is expected to take place with a lag of two to four quarters, respectively, partly reflecting distribution impediments. Vaccine deployment is assumed to bolster a recovery in consumer and business confidence and buttress financial market sentiment. As a result, consumption is expected to continue to strengthen and investment to recover. Macroeconomic policy is assumed to remain accommodative during the forecast horizon, with continued support from monetary policy and deficits remaining wide despite some fiscal tightening.

Risks to the outlook

The recovery expected in the baseline forecast could be derailed by the materialization of a number of risks. The spread of the virus could accelerate if pandemic-control measures fail or if there are delays in the deployment of vaccines. This would interrupt the already-slow recovery and deepen the damage to the global economy. It would also exacerbate existing strains—prolonged economic weakness could trigger a wave of bankruptcies; banking balance sheets could be further impaired; governments might be unable to continue providing support; and, in some circumstances, temporary bouts of unemployment and business shutdowns could become permanent.

Given the crucial importance of the progression of the pandemic in shaping the global outlook, a set of scenarios described in box 1.4 explores the economic impact of alternative assumptions about the spread of the virus and progress in administering vaccinations (figure 1.14.D). In the upside scenario, effective COVID-19 management, aided by the rapid deployment of highly effective vaccines, could allow for markedly faster easing of the pandemic, triggering a sharp rise in consumer confidence and unleashing pent-up demand. Industrial commodity exporters and countries with greater exposure to trade and tourism would be expected to benefit most from a faster resolution of the pandemic.

In the downside scenario, new cases of COVID-19 would remain persistently higher than in the baseline in many parts of the world and the vaccine rollout process would be slowed by logistical impediments and reluctance toward immunization. In these circumstances, global growth would be much more subdued, only recovering to 1.6 percent in 2021 and 2.5 percent

FIGURE 1.14 Outlook and risks

Although global activity is projected to recover as the pandemic is gradually brought under control, it is not expected to return to its pre-crisis trend over the forecast horizon. The baseline outlook is subject to considerable uncertainty, and the balance of risks is to the downside. In contrast to those in advanced economies, growth estimates for 2020 have been revised down in the majority of emerging market and developing economies. Growth forecasts hinge on assumptions about the spread of the virus and progress in vaccination, which drive different scenarios of growth.

A. Gaps with pre-pandemic projections

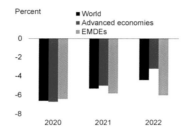

B. Probability of global growth being 1 percentage point below current baseline

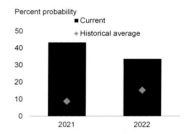

C. Share of countries with forecast revisions

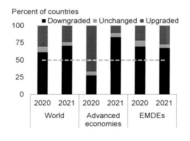

D. Possible scenarios of global growth

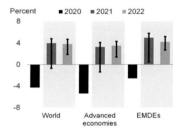

Sources: Bloomberg; Consensus Economics; World Bank.
Note: EMDEs = emerging market and developing economies.
A. Figure shows the gaps between the current projections and the forecasts reported in the January 2020 edition of the *Global Economic Prospects* report.
B. Probabilities for the forecast distribution of global growth are generated using time-varying estimates of the standard deviation and skewness extracted from the forecast distribution of three underlying risk factors (oil price futures, S&P 500 equity price futures, and term spread forecasts). The weight of each of the risks factors is derived from the model described in Ohnsorge, Stocker, and Some (2016). Values for 2021 are computed from the forecast distribution of 12-month-ahead oil price futures, S&P 500 equity price futures, and term spread forecasts. Values for 2022 are based on 24-month-ahead forecast distributions. Last observation for S&P 500 and oil price futures is December 16, 2020, while term spread forecasts are from November 2020.
C. Figure shows the share of EMDEs and advanced economies with forecast upgrades, downgrades, and no forecast changes since the June 2020 *Global Economic Prospects* report.
D. Black vertical lines indicate ranges based on the lower and upper bounds of growth in the scenarios described in box 1.4. Aggregate growth calculated using U.S. dollar GDP weights at 2010 prices and market exchange rates. Shaded areas indicate forecasts.

in 2022. Advanced economies would expand a meager 0.6 percent in 2021, while EMDEs would grow by 3.1 percent—and only 1.6 percent excluding China.

In an even more severe downside scenario, renewed financial stress would contribute to

BOX 1.2 Recent developments and outlook for low-income countries

The COVID-19 pandemic has dealt a devastating blow to low-income countries (LICs). Economic activity fell by 0.9 percent last year—the steepest decline in three decades—with an even deeper contraction among the fragile and conflict-affected LICs. As a result, gains in living standards have been eroded, tipping tens of millions of people into extreme poverty cumulatively in 2020-21. The legacy of the pandemic is expected to be long-lasting. Growth among LICs is projected to average 4.3 percent in 2021-22, well below pre-pandemic rates, with recoveries dampened in part by higher debt burdens and financial fragilities. Risks to the outlook for LICs are tilted firmly to the downside, and include a slower vaccine rollout, reduced development spending amid severely constrained fiscal space, increased inequality, and growing insecurity.

Recent developments

The COVID-19 pandemic has dealt a heavy blow to low-income countries (LICs). In 2020, disruptions to activity due to social distancing and lockdowns implemented to mitigate the pandemic's spread were worsened by sharply lower external demand, falling industrial commodity prices—particularly oil—and a collapse in tourism activity. Although the virus so far appears to have spread more slowly through LICs than previously expected—likely due in part to more limited testing capacity understating the true size of the pandemic and a younger population than in most other economies—the number of new cases remained elevated during the second half of last year (Ethiopia, Mozambique, Uganda; figure B1.2.1.A and B1.2.1.B). Output among LICs is estimated to have fallen by 0.9 percent in 2020—the steepest contraction in three decades (figure B1.2.1.C). As a result, a decade or more of per capita income gains has been reversed in about 15 percent of LICs (figure B1.2.1.D).

Fragile and conflict-affected LICs have been particularly hard hit by the pandemic, with activity contracting by an estimated 3.9 percent. The resultant fall in per capita GDP is expected to set average living standards back by a decade or more in 25 percent of fragile and conflict-affected LICs. Four of the five most severe COVID-19 outbreaks among LICs, in cases per million, have been in fragile and conflict-affected LICs (Afghanistan, Central African Republic, Guinea-Bissau, The Gambia). The adverse effects of the pandemic have been exacerbated by the underlying vulnerabilities of these economies. Weak state capacity and limited fiscal space have constrained the scope for authorities to respond decisively to the pandemic. In Sudan, output fell an estimated 8.4 percent in 2020 as the pandemic's impact on activity was compounded by civil unrest, sharp declines in real income from a tripling of

inflation, and falling agricultural production amid a locust infestation and severe flooding (FAO 2020a). In Afghanistan, the disruptions to domestic trade and commerce contributed to a 5.5 percent drop in output (World Bank 2020j).

Activity also weakened markedly among other LICs, with growth slowing to an estimated 2.2 percent last year. Growth in Ethiopia—the largest LIC economy—decelerated sharply to 6.1 percent in the 2020 fiscal year, which ended in early July. With the pandemic in Ethiopia gathering significant pace in the second half of last year, activity at the start of the 2021 fiscal year has been tepid. In other countries, the pandemic and lockdown measures substantially reduced tourism revenues, weighed on consumption and investment, and disrupted exports (Guinea, Rwanda).

Current account deficits widened in three-quarters of LICs last year, as reduced external demand and lower industrial commodity prices, particularly oil, weighed on export revenues in several countries (Chad, Democratic Republic of Congo, South Sudan; figure B1.2.1.E). Remittance inflows have fallen amid widespread job losses in host countries, weighing further on current account balances in several economies (Rwanda, Tajikistan). Despite global financial conditions easing appreciably in 2020, financing of current account deficits has remained challenging for many LICs that have limited access to international financial markets and are reliant on official development assistance.

The pandemic led to a sharp increase in government indebtedness last year, as revenues collapsed along with economic activity while government spending rose to address the health crisis and mitigate the pandemic's adverse economic impacts (figure B1.2.1.F). Contractions in activity also contributed to higher debt-to-GDP ratios. In the average LIC, government debt jumped 7 percentage points to 69 percent of GDP. In fragile and conflict-affected LICs, where fiscal positions were already weaker, government debt rose to 73 percent.

Note: This section was prepared by Cedric Okou and Rudi Steinbach. Research assistance was provided by Maria Hazel Macadangdang.

BOX 1.2 Recent developments and outlook for low-income countries *(continued)*

FIGURE B1.2.1 Recent developments

The number of new COVID cases remained elevated during the second half of 2020; nonetheless, limited testing capacity in many LICs likely understates the true magnitude of domestic outbreaks. Pandemic-related disruptions in 2020 led to the first contraction in LIC output in a generation, with the outlook subject to substantial downside risks. As a result, a decade or more of per capita GDP gains has been erased in about 15 percent of LICs and 25 percent of fragile and conflict-affected LICs. Steep falls in revenues and costly fiscal support measures have contributed to sharply higher government debt.

A. COVID-19 infections in LICs

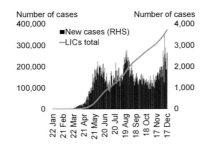

B. COVID-19 testing and cases

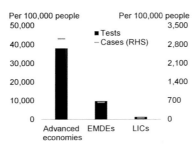

C. GDP growth

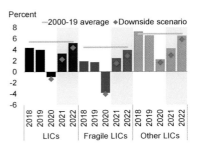

D. Years of per capita GDP gains reversed in 2020

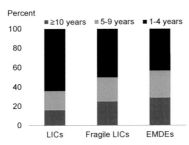

E. Current account balances

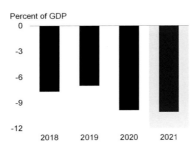

F. Government debt

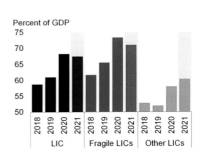

Sources: Hasell et al (2020); International Monetary Fund; John Hopkins University; World Bank.
Note: Shaded area indicates forecasts. EMDEs = emerging market and developing economies; LICs = low-income countries; Fragile LICs = fragile and conflict-affected LICs.
A. Sample includes 28 countries. Last observation is December 17, 2020.
B. Last observation is December 17, 2020.
C. Aggregate growth rates calculated using GDP weights at 2010 prices and market exchange rates. Diamonds correspond to the downside scenario.
D. Aggregates calculated using U.S. dollar GDP per capita at 2010 prices and market exchange rates. Figure shows the share of countries by number of years of lost per capita income gains, measured as the difference between 2020 and the latest year of per capita income that is below 2020 value over the 2000-19 period. Sample includes 25 LIC economies, 16 fragile and conflict-affected LICs, and 146 EMDEs.
E. F. Unweighted averages.

Outlook

Growth in LICs is projected to return to 3.3 percent in 2021—well below earlier forecasts and the pre-pandemic average pace—before firming to 5.2 percent in 2022. The pickup in activity partly reflects an expected recovery in external demand. Despite the resumption of growth, the level of activity by 2022 is forecast to remain 5.2 percent below its pre-pandemic trend. As a result, per capita

incomes are projected to be lower in 2022 than the levels recorded in 2019 in 56 percent of LICs (figure B1.2.2.A).

The growth forecast in LICs is based on the assumption that one or more approved vaccines will be widely distributed starting in the second half of 2021 in advanced economies and major EMDEs. In LICs, however, it is expected to only be available four quarters after the roll out starts in advanced economies. This group faces more

BOX 1.2 Recent developments and outlook for low-income countries *(continued)*

FIGURE B1.2.2 **Outlook and risks**

Despite the projected pickup in LIC growth in 2021-22, activity is projected to remain well below its pre-pandemic trend, especially among fragile and conflict-affected LICs. After falling sharply last year, per capita incomes are projected to edge up in 2021-22—but the rebound is envisioned to be smaller in fragile and conflict-affected LICs. The steep deterioration in living standards is set to push many millions of people into extreme poverty. Rising debt servicing costs, along with severely constrained fiscal space, may raise debt sustainability concerns. Growing insecurity and frequent natural disasters pose additional risks.

A. Level of LIC activity relative to pre-pandemic trend

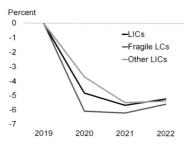

B. Growth per capita

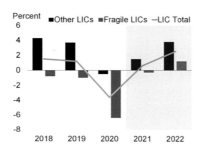

C. Poverty headcounts in LICs

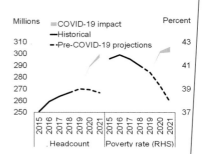

D. Debt service costs in LICs, by risk of debt stress

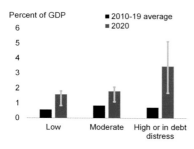

E. Violence against civilians

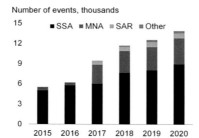

F. Frequency of natural disasters

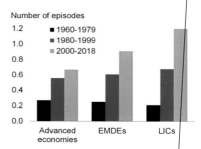

Sources: Armed Conflict Location & Event Data Project (ACLED), https://www.acleddata.com; EM-DAT (database); International Monetary Fund; Lakner et al. (2021); World Bank; World Bank (2020m).

Note: Shaded area indicates forecasts. AEs = advanced economies; LICs = low-income countries; Fragile LICs = fragile and conflict-affected LICs.

A. Pre-pandemic trend corresponds to January 2020 forecasts in the *Global Economic Prospects* report.

B. Aggregate growth rates calculated using GDP weights at 2010 prices and market exchange rates. Aggregate per capita growth rates calculated using the total GDP for each subgroup divided by its total population.

C. Lower (upper) edge of the shaded area reflects the baseline (downside) projection for the impact of the pandemic on poverty headcounts and rates in LICs.

D. Aggregates represent the estimated amount of interest and principal due on total sovereign debt in 2020 and 2021 as a share of 2019 nominal GDP.

E. Number of acts of violence against civilians. Last observation is December 12, 2020.

F. Average number of natural disaster episodes per country per year, by income group (Dieppe 2020).

binding logistical hurdles than other EMDEs in the effective nationwide distribution of vaccines. These include lacking infrastructure such as transport networks and reliable cold chains to distribute temperature-sensitive vaccines, weak health systems, and limited state capacities (Guignard et al. 2019; Kartoglu and Milstien 2014; World Bank 2020g). Moreover, severe fiscal space constraints mean that many LICs will likely also have limited scope to

procure sufficient quantities of vaccines, absent coordinated international support.

The recovery among fragile and conflict-affected LICs is projected to be sluggish, with growth resuming at 2.4 percent in 2021, before firming to 4 percent in 2022. Despite the pickup in growth, activity in these economies in 2022 would remain 5.6 percent below its pre-pandemic

BOX 1.2 Recent developments and outlook for low-income countries *(continued)*

TABLE 1.2.1 Low-income country forecasts [a]
(Real GDP growth at market prices in percent, unless indicated otherwise)

Percentage point differences from June 2020 projections

	2018	2019	2020e	2021f	2022f	2020e	2021f
Low Income Country, GDP [b]	**4.4**	**4.0**	**-0.9**	**3.3**	**5.2**	**-0.8**	**-0.6**
Afghanistan	1.2	3.9	-5.5	2.5	3.3	0.0	1.5
Burkina Faso	6.8	5.7	-2.0	2.4	4.7	-4.0	-3.4
Burundi	1.6	1.8	0.3	2.0	2.5	-0.7	-0.3
Central African Republic	3.7	3.1	0.0	3.2	4.1	-0.8	-0.3
Chad	2.4	3.2	-0.8	2.4	3.3	-0.6	-2.3
Congo, Dem. Rep.	5.8	4.4	-1.7	2.1	3.0	0.5	-1.4
Eritrea	13.0	3.7	-0.6	3.5	5.5	0.1	-2.2
Ethiopia [c]	8.4	9.0	6.1	0.0	8.7	2.9	-3.6
Gambia, The	6.5	6.0	-1.8	3.1	5.3	-4.3	-3.4
Guinea	6.2	5.6	5.2	5.5	5.2	3.1	-2.4
Guinea-Bissau	3.8	4.6	-2.4	3.0	4.0	-0.8	-0.1
Haiti [c]	1.7	-1.7	-3.8	1.4	1.5	-0.3	0.4
Liberia	1.2	-2.3	-2.9	3.2	3.9	-0.3	-0.8
Madagascar	4.6	4.8	-4.2	2.0	5.8	-3.0	-2.0
Malawi	3.2	4.4	1.3	3.3	4.9	-0.7	-0.2
Mali	4.7	5.0	-2.0	2.5	5.2	-2.9	-1.5
Mozambique	3.4	2.2	-0.8	2.8	4.4	-2.1	-0.8
Niger	7.0	5.8	1.0	5.1	11.8	0.0	-3.0
Rwanda	8.6	9.4	-0.2	5.7	6.8	-2.2	-1.2
Sierra Leone	3.4	5.5	-2.3	4.1	4.6	0.0	0.1
South Sudan [c]	-3.5	-0.3	9.3	-3.4	0.0	13.6	20.2
Sudan	-2.3	-2.5	-8.4	2.5	3.1	-4.4	2.0
Tajikistan	7.3	7.5	2.2	3.5	5.5	4.2	-0.2
Togo [d]	4.9	5.3	0.0	3.0	4.5	-1.0	-1.0
Uganda [c]	6.2	6.8	2.9	2.8	5.9	-0.4	-0.9

Source: World Bank.
Note: e = estimate; f = forecast. World Bank forecasts are frequently updated based on new information and changing (global) circumstances. Consequently, projections presented here may differ from those contained in other Bank documents, even if basic assessments of countries' prospects do not significantly differ at any given moment in time.
a. The Democratic People's Republic of Korea, Somalia, the Syrian Arab Republic, and the Republic of Yemen are not forecast due to data limitations.
b. Aggregate growth rates are calculated using GDP weights at 2010 prices and market exchange rates.
c. GDP growth based on fiscal year data. For South Sudan, the year 2019 refers to FY2018/19.
d. For Togo, growth figures in 2018 and 2019 are based on pre-2020 rebasing GDP estimates.

trend. In Sudan, the implementation of deep structural reforms amid external support is expected to gradually set the foundation for greater macroeconomic stability and a return to growth. The pace of recovery in Afghanistan is expected to be constrained amid continued insecurity and political uncertainty. In a few fragile LICs, the recovery will be dampened as persistently elevated inflation continues to erode real incomes (Haiti, South Sudan).

Among other LICs, the rebound is projected to be more pronounced, with growth rising to an average of 5.3 percent in 2021-22. In Ethiopia, growth is expected to

BOX 1.2 Recent developments and outlook for low-income countries *(continued)*

strengthen as the COVID-19 outbreak is brought under control and as exports, foreign direct investment, and remittance inflows gradually recover. Improving exports are also expected to support the recovery in Rwanda, along with efforts to improve public service delivery and efficiency through performance-based salary incentives, increased training and capacity building of public servants, and streamlining of operational procedures. The growth pickup in Guinea is expected to be underpinned by continued mining-related infrastructure investment and the implementation of structural reforms to strengthen governance and bolster the business climate.

The pandemic has severely set back living standards. Per capita income levels in LICs fell by 3.6 percent last year and are expected to edge up by an average of only 1.6 percent in 2021-22 (figure B1.2.2.B). Among fragile and conflict-affected LICs—where the incidence of extreme poverty is highest—per capita incomes declined 6.4 percent last year and are projected to fall by a further 0.3 percent this year, before firming only marginally in 2022. As a result of the deterioration in living standards, extreme poverty headcounts among LICs are projected to increase by tens of millions of people cumulatively in 2020 and 2021, while the share of the population living in extreme poverty could rise by as much as 4 percentage points—reversing five years of progress in poverty reduction (figure B1.2.2.C; World Bank 2020m).

Risks

Risks to the outlook are tilted firmly to the downside. Although the growth rebound is expected to be stronger than previously projected in China, forecast downgrades in other major economies and key LIC trading partners—notably the euro area and the United States—could further dampen the rebound. Renewed headwinds to global growth would weigh on the recovery in many LICs through subdued export demand and reduced investment.

The pandemic may persist for longer than expected, perhaps because of setbacks in the production, and rollout of vaccines, weighing further on the global economy. Delays to the distribution of vaccines could be compounded in LICs by the logistical challenges these countries are likely to face in vaccine distribution. Many LICs also have large informal sectors, which raises the likelihood that outbreaks of infections persist because informal workers often operate in close proximity to each other in crowded spaces.

Over the long term, the pandemic could have outsized and lasting scarring effects on activity in LICs due to the effects on labor productivity of higher unemployment, loss of income, lost schooling, and degraded health outcomes—especially as disruptions to immunization programs and maternal health services disproportionately affect women and children, likely exacerbating inequality.

With government debt rising sharply, some LICs face a stark tradeoff: continued government primary deficits, rising debt service costs, and weak growth may raise concerns about sovereign debt sustainability, while at the same time, governments need to support vulnerable groups, and facilitate the recovery (figure B1.2.2.D). To ease this debt burden while countries continue to grapple with substantial COVID-related spending needs, 21 LICs have accessed the temporary debt relief offered by the G20 Debt Service Suspension Initiative (box 1.1).

Growing insecurity and political unrest pose a key risk in a number of LICs (figure B1.2.2.E). Terrorist activity is increasingly becoming a major security threat in many countries in the Sahel (Burkina Faso, Mali, Niger). Protracted political instability in many countries could further impede growth prospects in LICs by amplifying the socio-economic vulnerabilities already worsened by the pandemic.

The pandemic has disrupted the food supply and damaged household incomes—which are critical to food security—in many LICs (FAO 2020b). These disruptions have exacerbated LICs' outsized exposure to unfavorable climate events that damage agricultural crops and often trigger food shortages and price spikes (figure B1.2.2.F; Dieppe 2020; Jafino, Hallegatte, and Walsh 2020).

Although downside risks predominate the outlook, positive outcomes can materialize if policy makers employ the necessary reforms to improve growth outcomes. The pandemic could create a window of opportunity to accelerate the shift of resources from agriculture to higher value-added manufacturing and services in many LICs. The resultant sectoral reallocation could facilitate LICs' participation in global value chains, boost labor productivity, and strengthen growth, if accompanied by policies that foster competition and attract domestic and foreign investments. A widespread use of digital technologies could also spur sectoral productivity gains, with positive spillovers among LICs.

widespread corporate and sovereign defaults. If this scenario were to materialize, global growth could even be negative in 2021, with countries with lingering financial fragilities and large funding needs suffering particularly extreme dislocations.

Even if the pandemic is brought under control as envisioned in the baseline forecast, the damage from last year's global recession could prove deeper than expected. Consumers and businesses may become more cautious, resulting in even weaker spending and investment. Very low interest rates may allow otherwise unviable firms to survive, crowding out the more dynamic firms that drive productivity growth. The elevated debt levels of corporates and sovereigns may weigh on activity through deleveraging pressures.

The risk of financial turmoil has been magnified by the rise in debt levels as a result of the pandemic. Shifts in investor sentiment could make it difficult for sovereigns or corporates to finance existing debt loads, while banking system buffers have already been eroded by widespread corporate bankruptcies. An extended period of very low interest rates and a spike in charge-offs on impaired loans would erode bank profitability, undermine capital buffers, and set the stage for bank failures. A wave of defaults could lead to financial crises, especially if overstretched sovereigns lack the resources to provide public support to stressed financial institutions.

Other risks also loom over the outlook. There has been a steady erosion in international cooperation and coordination, as exemplified by tensions related to COVID-19 restrictions and vaccine distribution, as well as lingering trade disputes between the United States and China. Restrictions imposed to slow the spread of COVID-19 could persist even after the health crisis ends, leading to lower productivity as the global system of trade becomes more fragmented. On a regional level, civil unrest, drought, conflict, or persistently low commodity prices could derail activity in certain groups of countries.

In contrast, stronger-than-expected growth outcomes could take place. Beyond the possibility

of better pandemic management and rapid vaccine deployment, the shared global experience of combatting COVID-19 could contribute to an increase in the extent and effectiveness of multilateralism. Alternatively, the accelerated adoption and globalization of digital services or other practices and technologies introduced during the pandemic could help bolster future productivity growth.

Continued spread of the pandemic with delayed or incomplete vaccine deployment

Even with social distancing, universal masking, and other pandemic-control measures, additional waves of contagion will remain a risk until widespread effective vaccination is achieved. All countries, including those that have suffered the largest outbreaks of COVID-19, remain well below the threshold required to achieve enhanced community resistance (figure 1.15.A). Flare-ups could arise from the appearance of new, more virulent strains of COVID-19; premature efforts to relax containment measures, such as fully reopening schools or businesses when the rate of contagion is still high; or by a lack of adherence to health guidelines (figure 1.15.B).

As detailed in box 1.4, the baseline forecast assumes that the ongoing vaccination rollout gathers pace in early 2021 in advanced economies and major EMDEs, starting with vulnerable groups and becoming widespread near the end of the year. The process in other countries would proceed with a delay of two to four quarters. The pandemic is ultimately expected to be brought under control in large parts of the world during the second half of 2022.

There is, however, a possibility of delayed or insufficient vaccination, as the distribution timeline could be postponed in a variety of ways. Vaccine development or production could encounter technical problems. Heightened reluctance by parts of the population to seek vaccination could delay the rollout or leave some communities vulnerable to further outbreaks. Many EMDEs may experience more difficulties with procurement and distribution or receive a less effective vaccine than currently assumed, especially

FIGURE 1.15 Risk of continued pandemic with delayed vaccine deployment

Even in countries that have experienced significant outbreaks, the vast majority of the population remains susceptible to COVID-19. As such, epidemiological models highlight a risk of significantly higher caseloads in the near term.

A. Estimated cases of COVID-19 compared to threshold for achieving community resistance

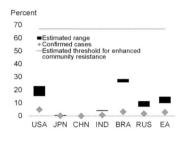

B. Range of model forecasts for COVID-19 cases in advanced economies

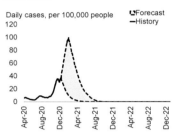

Sources: European Centre for Disease Prevention and Control (ECDC); Institute for Health Metrics and Evaluation; Johns Hopkins University; MRC Centre for Global Infectious Disease Analysis, Imperial College London; Our World in Data (database); United Nations Population Division; World Bank; Zhou and Ji (2020).
Note: BRA = Brazil, CHN = China, EA = euro area, IND = India, JPN = Japan, RUS = Russian Federation, USA = United States of America.
A. The estimated range is based on model outcomes from the Imperial College of London and the Institute for Health Metrics and Evaluation. The orange line shows the estimated threshold for enhanced community resistance to COVID-19. Last observation is December 15, 2020 for confirmed cases, December 4, 2020 for Imperial College London's estimation, and December 7, 2020 for Institute for Health Metrics and Evaluation's estimation.
B. Figure shows the 17.5 percent and 82.5 percent prediction interval obtained from simulating a stochastic Susceptible-Infected-Removed (SIR) model as in Zhou and Ji (2020). Model is augmented with the baseline assumption for vaccination described in box 1.4. Advanced economy aggregate proxied by the sum of confirmed case predictions for the Group of Seven (G7) divided by population. G7 economies include Canada, France, Germany, Italy, Japan, the United Kingdom, and the United States.

in the face of supply bottlenecks and vaccine hoarding. In the downside scenario in box 1.4, general vaccine deployment is markedly slower, with widespread global coverage only achieved outside of the forecast horizon.

A protracted upsurge in cases across many countries would interrupt the recovery in consumer and business confidence. News of a significant delay in vaccine deployment could be one trigger for a sudden worsening of financial conditions, including a sharp drop in equity valuations and a flight to safety that would add to the financial pressures on riskier borrowers. Private consumption would be depressed for several quarters and investment would soften as growth prospects are downgraded. Activity in sectors sensitive to public interactions would be hardest hit, with any recovery in domestic and foreign tourism held off until the second half of 2022. Some countries may be unable to provide further

policy support, more businesses would fall into bankruptcy, and more workers would be at risk of long-term unemployment. In these circumstances, the global recovery in 2021 would be stunted, and lingering fears of the pandemic combined with accumulated supply-side scarring would weigh heavily on growth in 2022.

Financial crises

The risks of financial crises are increasing owing to surging debt, weak activity, eroded capital buffers in the banking system, and elevated risk asset valuations (figure 1.16.A; box 1.1). These developments follow a decade which featured the largest, fastest, and most broad-based increase in debt on record (Kose et al. 2020a). Fiscal support and private sector borrowing to weather the shock from COVID-19 have pushed debt even higher (figure 1.16.B). Although low interest rates mitigate risks for some countries, elevated debt levels nonetheless increase the vulnerability to a shift in market conditions and make costly financial crises more likely—about half of all episodes of government and private debt accumulation in the last 50 years were associated with financial crises (figure 1.16.C).

Many borrowers would struggle to finance fiscal and current account deficits if investor sentiment were to deteriorate suddenly. Underdeveloped capital markets in many EMDEs pose risks to banking, corporate, and government funding in the event of a renewed tightening in global financial conditions (IOSCO 2020). Higher funding costs could lead to forced austerity or disruptive defaults that result in lost access to international debt markets. In the past, investor appetite for EMDE debt has proved sensitive to perceptions of risk, domestic inflation pressures, and the return on safe assets. An increase in any of these could trigger a reversal of the private capital inflows needed to finance elevated levels of debt. Capital outflows would also result in currency depreciation pressures and a surge in external borrowing costs for both sovereigns and corporates.

Central bank easing has been successful in averting a liquidity crisis, but may not be able to address a

BOX 1.3 Regional perspectives: Recent developments and outlook

The pandemic has exacted substantial costs on all emerging market and developing economy (EMDE) regions. Although all regions are expected to grow this year, the pace of the recovery varies considerably, with greater weakness in countries that have larger outbreaks or greater exposure to global spillovers through tourism and industrial commodity exports. The East Asia and Pacific region is envisioned to show notable strength in 2021 due to a solid rebound in China, whereas activity is projected to be weakest in the Middle East and North Africa and Sub-Saharan Africa regions. Many countries are expected to lose a decade or more of per capita income gains. Risks to the outlook are tilted to the downside. In addition to region-specific risks, all regions are vulnerable to renewed outbreaks and logistical impediments to the distribution of effective vaccines, financial stress amid elevated debt levels, and the possibility that the impact of the pandemic on growth and incomes may be worse than expected over the longer term. In a downside scenario of a more severe and prolonged pandemic, the lowest growth rates among the six EMDE regions would be in Latin America and the Caribbean, the Middle East and North Africa, and Sub-Saharan Africa, reflecting these regions' reliance on exports of oil and industrial commodities, the prices of which would be reduced by weak global demand.

East Asia and Pacific. Regional growth slowed to an estimated 0.9 percent in 2021—the lowest rate since 1967—and is projected to expand 7.4 percent in 2021. Even by 2022, the level of activity is forecast to be more than 3 percent below pre-pandemic projections. Whereas China is expected to recover strongly, the rest of the region is only expected to return to a level around 7.5 percent below pre-pandemic projections in 2022, with significant cross-country differences. Key downside risks to the outlook include heightened financial stress amplified by elevated debt levels, and persistent policy uncertainty and subdued investment amid lingering trade tensions.

Europe and Central Asia. Activity in the region is estimated to have fallen by 2.9 percent in 2020. Due to a resurgence of COVID-19, the pace of recovery in 2021 is projected to be slower than originally anticipated, at 3.3 percent. Growth is projected to accelerate to 3.9 percent in 2022 as the effects of the pandemic gradually wane and the recovery in trade and investment gathers momentum. The pandemic is expected to erase at least five years of per capita income gains in about a fifth of the region's economies. Economies with strong trade or financial linkages to the euro area and those heavily dependent on services and tourism have been hardest hit. The outlook remains highly uncertain, however, and growth could be weaker than expected if external financing conditions tighten, or if geopolitical tensions escalate.

Latin America and the Caribbean. Pandemic-control measures, risk aversion by households and firms, and spillovers from a shrinking global economy resulted in the region's economy contracting by an estimated 6.9 percent

in 2020, more than any of the other EMDE regions. The forecast for 2021 is for a modest recovery, reaching 3.7 percent growth as restrictions are relaxed, vaccines are rolled out, oil and metals prices rise, and external conditions improve. Six of the 10 EMDEs with the highest COVID-19 deaths per capita in the world are in LAC, including five of the region's six largest economies. Risks to the outlook remain tilted to the downside, and include external financing stress amid elevated debt, a resurgence of social unrest, and disruptions related to climate change and natural disasters.

Middle East and North Africa. Output in the region is estimated to have contracted 5 percent in 2020, as countries struggled with significant disruptions from COVID-19 and a sharp fall in oil demand. This contraction adds to already slowing growth in the region and compounds pre-pandemic per capita income losses. Growth is expected to improve to a modest 2.1 percent in 2021, as the pandemic is brought under control and lockdown restrictions are eased, global oil demand rises, and policy support continues. The pandemic is expected to leave lasting economic scars on the region, which will likely dampen potential growth going forward. Disruptions related to geopolitical tensions and political instability, renewed downward pressure on oil prices, and additional balance of payments stress are key downside risks to the outlook.

South Asia. Regional economic activity is estimated to have contracted by 6.7 percent in 2020, led by a deep recession in India, where the economy was already weakened before the pandemic by stress in non-bank financial corporations. The region is projected to grow by 3.3 percent in 2021 and 3.8 percent in 2022. By 2022, the level of activity is forecast to be about 16 percent below pre-pandemic projections, the largest gap of all EMDE regions. Risks remain tilted to the downside, and include

Note: This box was prepared by Patrick Kirby with contributions from Cedric Okou, Franz Ulrich Ruch, Rudi Steinbach, Ekaterine Vashakmadze, Dana Vorisek, and Collette Wheeler. Research assistance was provided by Maria Hazel Macadangdang.

BOX 1.3 Regional perspectives: Recent developments and outlook *(continued)*

FIGURE B1.3.1 Regional growth

The pandemic has had a devastating impact on all emerging market and developing economy (EMDE) regions, which could worsen further if a downside scenario materializes. The downturn has been particularly severe in Latin America and South Asia, which have suffered from large outbreaks, and regions more vulnerable to global spillovers through, for example, tourism and industrial commodity exports. In about a quarter of EMDEs, COVID-19 has reversed a decade or more of per capita income gains. COVID-19 is expected to leave lasting economic scars that will likely keep the level of activity from returning to its pre-pandemic trend.

A. Regional growth

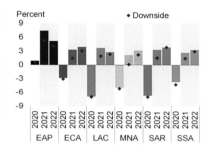

B. Reversals of EMDE per capita income gains in 2020, by number of years

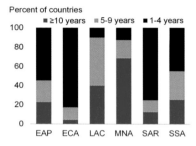

C. Gaps with pre-pandemic projections by 2022

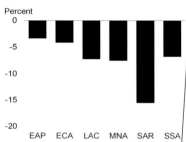

Source: World Bank.
Note: EAP = East Asia and Pacific, ECA = Europe and Central Asia, LAC = Latin America and the Caribbean, SAR = South Asia, SSA = Sub-Saharan Africa.
A. Bars denote latest forecast; diamonds denote regional growth downside scenarios. Aggregate growth rates calculated using GDP weights at 2010 prices and market exchange rates. Since largest economies account for about 50 percent of GDP in some regions, weighted averages predominantly reflect the developments in the largest economies in each region.
B. Aggregates calculated using U.S. dollar GDP per capita at 2010 prices and market exchange rates. Figure shows the percentage of EMDEs by number of years of lost per capita income gains, measured as the difference between 2020 and the latest year of per capita income that is below 2020 value over the 2000-19 period.
C. Figure shows the gaps between the current projections and the forecasts in the January 2020 edition of the *Global Economic Prospects* report.

financial distress related to an abrupt tightening of financing conditions or widespread corporate bankruptcies, extreme weather and climate change, weaker-than-expected recoveries in key partner economies, and a worsening of policy- and security-related uncertainty.

Sub-Saharan Africa. Activity in the region is estimated to have shrunk by 3.7 percent last year, setting living standards in many countries back by a decade. Growth is forecast to resume at a moderate pace of 2.9 percent in 2021—essentially zero in per capita terms and well below

previous projections. COVID-19 is likely to weigh on growth in SSA for an extended period, as the rollout of vaccines in the region is expected to lag that of major economies and many other EMDEs. Millions of people in the region could be pushed into extreme poverty in 2020 and 2021. Risks to the regional outlook are tilted to the downside, and include weaker-than-expected recoveries in key trading partners, logistical hurdles that further impede vaccine distribution, and scarring to productivity that weakens potential growth and income over the longer term.

growing wave of business insolvencies. Survey data suggest that a high proportion of businesses have limited cash on hand and have either fallen into arrears or will soon do so (Apedo-Amah et al. 2020). As regulatory forbearance wanes, continued weakness of household incomes and corporate earnings risks triggering a wave of bankruptcies, which could have a heavy and long-lasting impact on unemployment (Banerjee, Kharroubi, and

Lewrick 2020). This would erode capital buffers and slow the flow of credit, increasing the probability of financial crises. EMDEs that entered the pandemic with thinly capitalized banks and with limited policy space to provide capital support to the banking sector are particularly vulnerable, especially when there is a high degree of interconnectedness between the government and the banking system that could amplify financial stress. The growing role of nonbank financial companies adds further uncertainty about financial sector dynamics, as these companies are more opaque than conventional banks and may react in unpredictable ways during periods of stress (ESRB 2019).

Recessions that feature financial crises are significantly deeper and longer than recessions that do not (figure 1.16.D). Against this backdrop, widespread financial crises, combined with a prolonged pandemic and delayed vaccination, could result in a double-dip global recession, with a further contraction in activity this year, as illustrated by the severe downside scenario presented in box 1.4.

Greater long-term damage from the pandemic

Both recessions and epidemics can have lasting negative effects on the growth of affected countries through a variety of channels (figure 1.17.A; Arthi and Parman 2020; Dieppe 2020). These events can bankrupt otherwise viable firms, keep workers from jobs, damage financial systems, and increase debt burdens. Epidemics also lead to lost schooling and worse health outcomes. COVID-19 is expected to cause a significant drop in potential output growth relative to pre-pandemic trends (figure 1.17.B; chapter 3). The fact that the ongoing pandemic and ensuing global recession have been more widespread, more severe, and more long-lasting than any of the previous episodes over the past eight decades raises the possibility of even more significant economic damage (Chudik et al. 2020). The very severity of the shock may cause behavioral changes—a persistent increase in people's assessment of the probability of an extreme negative shock would reduce the return on investment and result in a smaller stock of capital (Kozlowski, Veldkamp, and Venkateswaran 2020).

The risk of greater long-term damage becomes more likely if the pandemic lasts longer than expected and cannot be brought fully under control, if infections cause severe chronic health effects, or if waning policy support impedes a meaningful recovery. Costly reconfigurations of production could cause some economies to reach

FIGURE 1.16 Risk of financial crises

Risks in the financial system are increasing. Market optimism and policy support have fueled a growing gap between equity market valuations and the halting progress of the recovery. Global debt rose sharply in 2020, adding to the significant increase seen in the past decade. Nearly half of debt accumulation episodes in the last 50 years were associated with financial crises. Recessions that feature financial crises are significantly deeper and longer than recessions that do not.

A. Price-to-earnings ratios of select stock indexes

B. Government debt

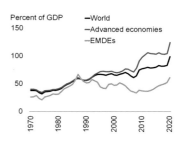

C. Debt accumulation episodes associated with crises

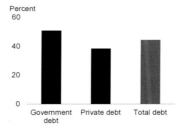

D. Output during government debt accumulation episodes

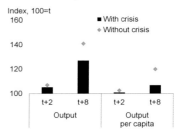

Sources: Bloomberg; International Monetary Fund; Kose, Lakatos et al. (2020); Laeven and Valencia (2020); World Bank.
A. Figure shows Bloomberg estimates of price-to-earnings ratios for major stock markets from North America, Europe, and Asia. Last observation is December 16, 2020.
B. Aggregates are calculated using current GDP in U.S. dollars as weights. Data for 2020 are estimates.
C. Figure shows the share of rapid debt accumulation episodes that are associated with financial crises, as defined by Laeven and Valencia (2020). An episode of rapid debt accumulation is defined as a period during which the debt-to-GDP ratio rises from trough to peak by more than one (country-specific) ten-year rolling standard deviation. The trough-peak years are identified with the algorithm in Harding and Pagan (2002). Sample includes 267 episodes of government debt and 280 episodes of private debt in 100 EMDEs over 1970-2019.
D. Medians for pooled government and private episodes with data available for at least eight years from the beginning of the episode. Year "t" refers to the beginning of rapid private or government debt accumulation episodes. All variables are scaled to 100 at t=0. Episodes associated with crises are those associated with financial crises (that is banking, currency, and debt crises, as in Laeven and Valencia 2020) during or within two years after the end of episodes. The medians between episodes associated "With crisis" and "Without crisis" are statistically different at 1 percent levels based on Wilcoxon rank-sum tests. Based on cumulative real growth rates for output and output per capita from the start of the government debt accumulation episode.

supply constraints earlier than expected, which could contribute to an earlier-than-expected resurgence in inflation. If monetary stimulus is withdrawn as a result, high debt levels would raise the risk of financial crises.

The debt accumulated during the pandemic will represent a heavy burden for some borrowers for a

FIGURE 1.17 Risk of greater long-term damage from the pandemic

Both recessions and pandemics inflict lasting economic damage on affected countries. The current recession comes on the heels of a long period of slowing potential growth and is likely to accelerate this trend. Potential output could slow further if private investment does not fully recover, or if disruptions to schooling persist.

A. Cumulative response of potential output after recessions and investment after epidemics

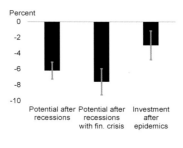

B. Estimated impact of the pandemic on global potential growth

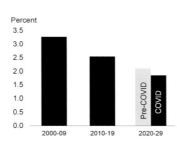

C. Real investment growth

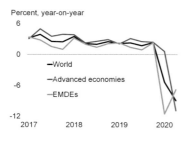

D. Estimated impact of schooling on income, by region and gender

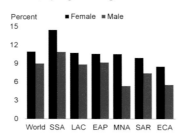

Sources: EM-DAT (database); Haver Analytics; Kilic Celik, Kose, and Ohnsorge (2020); Organisation for Economic Co-operation and Development; World Bank.
Note: EMDEs = emerging market and developing economies; EAP = East Asia and Pacific, ECA = Europe and Central Asia, LAC = Latin America and the Caribbean, MNA = Middle East and North Africa, SAR = South Asia, SSA = Sub-Saharan Africa.
A. fin. = financial. Vertical lines show 90 percent confidence intervals. The "Potential after recessions" and "Potential after recessions with fin. crisis" bars show impulse responses for 75 EMDEs from local projections model five years after the event. Dependent variable is defined as cumulative slowdown in potential output after a recession event. Bars show coefficient estimates. Data and methodology are detailed in box 3.1 and annex 3.4 of the June 2020 edition of *Global Economic Prospects* report. The "Investment after epidemics" bar shows the estimated impacts two years after the four most severe biological epidemics on output. The four epidemics considered are SARS (2002-03), MERS (2012), Ebola (2014-15), Zika (2015-16). Swine flu (2009), which coincided with the 2008-09 global financial crisis, is excluded to limit possible confounding effects. An episode dummy for a specific type of event is 1 if the event occurs at least once (>=1) in a country-year pair and 0 otherwise. The sample includes 116 economies: 30 advanced economies and 86 EMDEs.
B. Aggregates of production function-based potential growth estimates calculated using real U.S. dollar GDP at 2010 prices and market exchange rates. Shaded area indicates pre-COVID baseline. Sample includes 30 advanced economies and 50 EMDEs.
C. Figure shows year-on-year growth in quarterly real investment (gross fixed capital formation). Sample includes 78 countries, consisting of 36 advanced economies and 42 EMDEs. Aggregate growth is calculated with real investment at 2010 prices and market exchange rates as weights.
D. Figure shows the median percentage increase in wages associated with each additional year of schooling, by country group and gender according to the 2018 edition of the *World Development Report*.

protracted period. By choice or out of necessity, some sovereigns may improve budget deficits through austerity measures and cuts to public investment. Private investment plummeted during the crisis, and the recovery may be particularly

tepid if the corporate sector becomes crowded with highly indebted "zombie" firms that are not able to invest or innovate (figure 1.17.C; Banerjee and Hofmann 2020). The increase in households' precautionary savings may persist in the face of higher debt and weaker incomes, and banks' need to repair balance sheets may limit credit availability. These developments would be consistent with a rise in global savings and fall in investment as economic agents attempt to deleverage in tandem, leading to persistently weak growth and little actual progress at lowering debt—the so-called "paradox of thrift" (Fornaro and Romei 2019).

The pandemic has also had a negative impact on the accumulation of human capital. On a global level, an additional year of schooling is associated with a 10 percent increase in wages, suggesting that productivity will likely suffer from the fact that more than 90 percent of all students had their education disrupted to some extent last year, with about 40 percent losing the majority of the school year (figure 1.17.D; World Bank 2018a, UNESCO 2020). Many on-the-job training opportunities have been lost alongside the equivalent of almost 500 million full-time jobs destroyed by the pandemic (ILO 2020). Income losses are likely to result in higher malnutrition in some regions, which may further stunt the development and future productivity of those affected (FAO et al. 2020). The overall impacts are likely to be more severe for poorer EMDEs as a result of their less developed health systems and lower capacity for remote work and virtual education.

Waning global integration

The increasing integration of the global economy played an important role in the sharp decline in extreme global poverty in recent decades, and it was made possible in part because of the general use of a set of predictable rules for economic relations. This has been waning in recent years, contributing to higher tariff barriers, greater policy uncertainty, and market volatility.

A continuing move toward more contentious relations in international affairs could result in

BOX 1.4 Global growth scenarios

The highly uncertain evolution of the pandemic, influenced in part by government actions, social behavior, and vaccine-related developments, will play a critical role in shaping the global recovery's strength and durability. This box describes possible global growth outcomes under different pandemic assumptions. In the baseline scenario, social distancing and a gradual vaccination process allow policy makers to make significant inroads containing the pandemic. In a downside scenario, insufficient pandemic control efforts accompanied by delayed vaccination leads to persistently higher infection levels and a materially worse growth outcome. In a severe downside scenario, these disappointing epidemiological developments combine with a sharp increase in risk aversion to trigger financial crises in many countries. In contrast, in an upside scenario, effective management of the pandemic combine with rapid vaccine deployment to set the stage for stronger growth outcomes.

Introduction

With the COVID-19 pandemic still spreading across the world, and caseloads reaching record levels in many economies, the global outlook will remain heavily dependent on the pandemic's evolution. Turning the tide of the pandemic in the near term will be challenging, requiring voluntary social distancing on the part of households and the imposition of a variety of pandemic management measures by governments. The widespread deployment of effective vaccines will play a key role in halting the pandemic's progression, and is also expected to strengthen economic activity by raising confidence and improving financial market conditions. This box presents four scenarios to illustrate the implications of alternative pandemic outcomes on the global economy in 2021-22 (figure B1.4.1). These scenarios differ in their assumptions on the evolution of COVID-19 caseloads, vaccine deployment, voluntary social distancing by households, the stringency of pandemic-control policies imposed by governments, and financial market stress.

The *baseline scenario* assumes that voluntary and mandatory pandemic control measures are diligently maintained over the next several quarters until after widespread vaccination becomes available. From its recent increases in several major economies, the daily number of infections is assumed to decline in the first half of 2021 in most countries. In advanced economies and major EMDEs, vaccination campaigns proceed in early in 2021 and reach widespread coverage in the second half of 2021; this vaccination process would be delayed by two to four quarters in other EMDEs and LICs partly due to logistical impediments. Activity is expected to improve as the pandemic abates, vaccines are rolled out, and financial conditions remain benign, supported by exceptionally accommodative monetary policy.

The *downside scenario* assumes a persistently higher level of new cases in many regions throughout the forecast horizon. In advanced economies and major EMDEs, the vaccination proceeds at a much slower pace than under the baseline—with an additional delay of two to four quarters in other EMDEs and LICs—and is limited by a reluctance of a sizeable share of the population to be immunized. Activity would remain depressed as authorities struggle to contain the pandemic, while financial conditions would deteriorate markedly.

The *severe downside scenario* extends the downside scenario by exploring the possibility that authorities cannot contain widespread financial stress caused by a sharp rise in risk aversion after disappointing pandemic developments and widespread bankruptcies. Amid heightened financial vulnerabilities, financial crises would erupt in several countries.

In contrast, the *upside scenario* assumes more effective management of the pandemic, coupled with the rapid deployment of highly effective vaccines. This would trigger a faster easing of social distancing and a stronger recovery in activity.

Methodology. The global growth scenarios are developed using a combination of models and assumptions.[a] A Susceptible-Infected-Recovered (SIR) model is used to evaluate the impact of alternative vaccine assumptions on the evolution of the pandemic. Correlations based on cross-country regressions are used to project forward the stringency of pandemic-control policies conditional on caseloads. Regression estimates are then used to map the impact of voluntary social distancing—proxied by projected caseloads—and involuntary social distancing on private consumption. These consumption shocks, which

---

Note: This box was prepared by Justin-Damien Guénette under the supervision of Carlos Arteta, with contributions from Alain Kabundi, Hideaki Matsuoka, and Takefumi Yamazaki.

[a] The baseline and downside scenarios are an aggregation of individual country scenarios, while the upside and severe downside scenarios are model-based. The baseline and downside scenarios cover 182 countries, including 146 EMDEs. The model-based upside and severe downside scenarios are modelled as deviations from the baseline and the downside scenario, respectively.

BOX 1.4 Global growth scenarios *(continued)*

represent a mixture of voluntary and involuntary social distancing, are integrated into a macroeconometric model.[b] Scenarios are further enhanced with assumptions of financial stress, which are modeled as spikes in financial market volatility (annex 1.1).

Baseline scenario

Pandemic assumptions. In the baseline scenario, following a sharp resurgence that began toward the end of last year, many economies are able to reduce the daily number of infections in the first half of 2021. The reduction in caseloads is made possible by a combination of stringent lockdown measures as well as less costly pandemic-control policies such as social distancing guidelines and universal masking. In advanced economies and major EMDEs (including China, India, and Russia), inoculation with highly effective vaccines proceeds in the first quarter of 2021—first to vulnerable groups and subsequently to the general population—and becomes widespread in the second half of 2021 (figure B1.4.2).[c] Social distancing eases gradually through the remainder of the forecast horizon. The vaccination process is expected to be delayed by two quarters in most other EMDEs and by four quarters in LICs, owing to logistical impediments to vaccine production and distribution.

Macroeconomic channels. Activity is assumed to recover gradually as caseloads decline and social distancing efforts are relaxed, enticing households to increase their consumption of contact-intensive services. Firms grow cautiously optimistic in the face of a recovery in aggregate demand and a decline in pandemic policy uncertainty, and take advantage of historically low interest rates to modestly increase the pace of investment and boost hiring. Sustained fiscal support assists displaced workers and cash-strapped firms in major economies and many EMDEs,

while EMDEs facing fiscal space constraints manage to avoid harsh austerity. The vaccine rollout, coupled with accommodative monetary policy, underpins the continuation of benign financial conditions.

Growth outcome. The baseline scenario projects a moderate expansion in global activity of 4.0 percent in 2021, following a 4.3 percent collapse in 2020 (Table 1.1). Global growth is then envisioned to slow to 3.8 percent in 2022. Despite the projected recovery in 2021 and 2022, output is expected to remain well below pre-pandemic trends at the end of the projection horizon. Growth in EMDEs is expected to bounce back to 5 percent in 2021 from a 2.6 percent contraction in 2020, before slowing to 4.2 percent in 2022. The modest rebound in EMDE growth would not be enough to restore debt sustainability in some EMDEs, with the gap between the debt-stabilizing and the actual primary balance for EMDEs remaining negative through 2022. Following a sharp contraction of 9.5 percent in 2020, global trade is expected to experience a modest pickup to an average of 5.1 percent in 2021-22. For additional details, see the Global Outlook section of chapter 1.

Downside scenario

Pandemic assumptions. Insufficient pandemic management and lax compliance with social distancing measures leads to notably higher levels of new cases in many countries in 2021, requiring longer-lasting and more stringent pandemic-control measures. Relative to the baseline scenario, vaccine deployment in advanced economies and major EMDEs is slowed by supply bottlenecks and the reluctance of a higher proportion of the population to receive vaccinations.[d] As in other scenarios, rollout in other EMDEs and LICs begins up to four quarters after rollout in advanced economies and major EMDEs owing to logistical issues. Caseloads decline only gradually through 2022, mostly due to sustained social distancing.

Macroeconomic channels. Activity remains depressed, as households fear contact-intensive services, including recreation and tourism, and grapple with stringent social distancing measures. Firms—facing pandemic-control policies, a bleak outlook for consumer demand, and elevated uncertainty—curtail investment and hiring plans.

---

[b] The Oxford Global Economic Model—a large-scale global semi-structural projection model—is used to conduct the simulations described here (Oxford Economics 2020). The model includes 81 individual countries (35 advanced economies and 46 EMDEs), most of which are available at a quarterly frequency, with behavioral equations governing domestic economic activity, monetary and fiscal policy, global trade, and commodity prices.

[c] In all scenarios, the effectiveness of COVID-19 vaccines is assumed to be 85 percent—slightly lower than recently reported effectiveness—to accommodate for the rollout of several vaccines of varying effectiveness (Fitch 2020; Moderna 2020; Pfizer 2020). The vaccine rollout in advanced economies and large EMDEs is assumed to proceed at a slow pace initially and accelerate quickly as logistical and supply impediments are overcome. In the baseline scenario, the share of the population amenable to inoculation is assumed to be about two-thirds based on global survey evidence (Lazarus et al. 2020).

---

[d] Only about half of the population in advanced economies and major EMDEs is assumed to be amenable to vaccination, a level broadly consistent with the lower bound from global survey evidence (Lazarus et al. 2020).

BOX 1.4 Global growth scenarios *(continued)*

FIGURE B1.4.1 Global growth scenarios

The recovery will depend heavily on controlling the spread of the pandemic—in part a function of vaccine outcomes. In the baseline scenario, a decline in cases, a vaccine rollout that gathers pace in early 2021, and the eventual easing of pandemic-control measures underpin a modest rebound. In the downside scenario, persistently higher caseloads, more stringent involuntary social distancing, and slow vaccine development markedly weaken the recovery. In the severe downside scenario, widespread financial stress and mounting firm bankruptcies trigger financial crises, causing a second year of global recession. In the upside scenario, effective pandemic management, coupled with prompt widespread vaccination, allows activity to recover faster.

A. Global growth

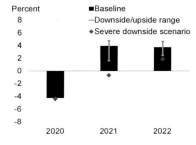

B. Growth in advanced economies

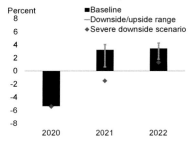

C. Growth in EMDEs

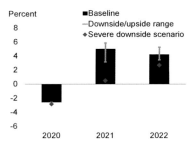

D. Trade growth

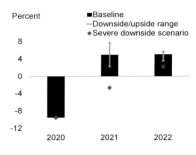

E. Average 2021-22 growth in EMDE regions

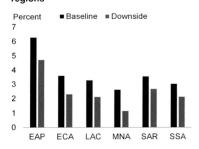

F. Primary balance sustainability gap in EMDEs, 2022

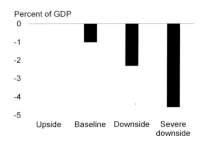

Sources: Oxford Economics; World Bank.
Note: Aggregate growth rates calculated using GDP weights at 2010 prices and market exchange rates.
F. A negative gap indicates a primary balance that would set government debt on a rising path. Gaps calculated as in Kose, Kurlat et al. 2020.

Financial conditions tighten markedly through 2021, as financial market sentiment continuously deteriorates in tandem with a string of unexpected vaccine delays and insufficient control of the pandemic, and as corporate and bank balance sheets deteriorate over prolonged demand weakness and forbearance requirements. While accommodative monetary policy keeps financial crises at bay, fiscal sustainability concerns limit the size of additional fiscal stimulus, leading to insufficient income support to the unemployed and struggling small- and medium-sized firms.

Growth outcome. The downside scenario features a much weaker and more protracted recovery, with global growth

limited to 1.6 percent in 2021 and 2.5 percent in 2022.[e] In the downside scenario, the recovery in advanced economies is stunted, with growth averaging less than 2 percent over 2021-22. Similarly, projected output growth in EMDEs would be markedly reduced from an average of nearly 5 percent in the baseline scenario to about 3.3

---

[e] Slower vaccine distribution leads to higher COVID-19 caseloads relative to the baseline, requiring additional voluntary and involuntary social distancing. On its own, the downside vaccine assumption is estimated to reduce global growth by 0.1 percentage point in 2021 and 0.8 percentage point in 2022. The remainder of the downward revision relative to the baseline scenario reflects increased involuntary social distancing brought on by persistently higher caseloads and tighter financial conditions.

BOX 1.4 Global growth scenarios *(continued)*

FIGURE B1.4.2 Scenario assumptions

Vaccination is assumed to begin slowly at first and then ramp up quickly as impediments are overcome. Vaccination helps reduce new cases. Social distancing and pandemic-control policies are eased as caseloads decline. Financial conditions are assumed to remain mostly benign in all scenarios other than the severe downside scenario, which envisions a sharp tightening of financial conditions. Oil prices are assumed to reflect variations in global demand across scenarios.

A. Assumed share of effectively vaccinated population: advanced economies and major EMDEs

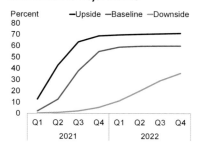

B. Impact of vaccine assumptions on number of COVID-19 cases in major economies

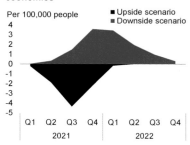

C. Impact of alternative pandemic assumptions on social distancing

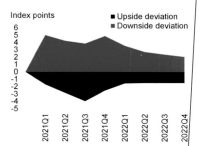

D. VIX assumptions relative to baseline for 2021

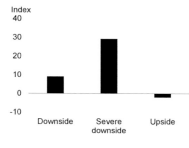

E. Corporate borrowing spread assumptions relative to baseline for 2021

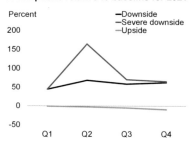

F. Oil price assumptions

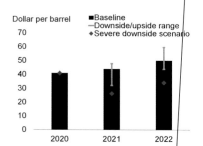

Sources: Oxford Economics; World Bank.
A. Solid lines are vaccine distribution assumptions for advanced economies and major EMDEs (China, India, and Russia).
B. Blue (red) areas show the difference of new daily confirmed COVID-19 cases per 100,000 individuals between the upside (downside) scenario and the baseline pandemic scenario.
C. Blue (red) areas show the difference of an index of involuntary social distancing between the upside (downside) scenario and the baseline pandemic scenario.
D. Chart shows the combined exogenous and endogenous deviation of the VIX, the Chicago Board Options Exchange's Volatility Index, from the baseline scenario in 2021.
E. Chart shows simple average of corporate borrowing spreads in the G7 (Canada, France, Germany, Italy, Japan, the United Kingdom, and the United States) and EM7 (China, India, Brazil, Mexico, Russia, Indonesia and Turkey). Corporate borrowing spread is defined as the difference between the 5-year corporate BBB bond yield and the 10-year sovereign bond yield.
F. Oil price is the simple average of Brent, Dubai, and West Texas Intermediate prices.

percent over 2021-22. By 2022, global and EMDE output would still be 3.5 and 2.5 percent, respectively, below output in the baseline scenario. Weaker growth would worsen debt sustainability across EMDEs. Even in 2022, after two years of recovery, the gap between the debt-stabilizing and the actual primary balance for EMDEs would still be about twice as large in the downside scenario as in the baseline scenario, setting government debt on a steeper rising path. Global trade growth would recover somewhat faster than global output growth, in line with

elasticities seen during past global recessions, but would remain around its modest 2010s average.

The materialization of the downside scenario would hit commodity- and tourism-dependent EMDEs particularly hard (chapter 2). Among EMDE regions, growth would be lowest in LAC, MNA and SSA, reflecting a heavy reliance on exports of oil and industrial commodities, the prices of which would be reduced by weak global demand. Moreover, a worsening of the pandemic across all regions

BOX 1.4 Global growth scenarios *(continued)*

would lead to extended travel restrictions with dire consequences for tourism-dependent economies.

Severe downside scenario

Pandemic assumptions. As in the downside scenario, the pandemic in the severe version is much more difficult to manage than in the baseline scenario, and the vaccine rollout is delayed. Longer-lasting and more stringent pandemic-control measures are needed through 2021 and beyond to achieve a sustained reduction in caseloads.

Macroeconomic channels. The severe downside scenario differs from the downside scenario's assumptions in the authorities' inability to stave off widespread financial market stress. The prolonged period of depressed consumption and investment caused by persistent social distancing erodes corporate balance sheets to an extent that triggers widespread corporate defaults and concerns about bank balance sheets. Banks, in turn, sharply curtail their lending activities at a time when sovereigns are hard-pressed to expand emergency lending programs, with fiscal space constrained by the realization of loan guarantees in advanced economies and capital flight in EMDEs. Several countries experience financial crises, which reverberate through the global economy in the form of sharply tighter financial conditions, diminished domestic and foreign demand, and plummeting commodity prices. An extended period of debt-deleveraging and subdued growth follows the initial crisis, compounding the pandemic's toll on the supply side of the economy.

Growth outcome. In this scenario, widespread financial crises, combined with a prolonged pandemic and delayed vaccination, would plunge the global economy into a second year of recession in 2021, before growth returns to a subdued rate of nearly 2 percent in 2022.[f] Advanced economies and EMDEs excluding China would experience a renewed contraction in 2021. As with global output, global trade growth would contract for a second consecutive year, followed by a subdued bounceback in 2022.

Severe output losses and rising borrowing cost would cause the gap between the debt stabilizing and the actual primary

balance to balloon to almost five times that in the baseline scenario in 2022. Hence, even once the recovery starts in 2022, it would take a front-loaded fiscal consolidation of nearly 5 percent of GDP, on average in EMDEs, to stabilize debt at its long-term median.

Upside scenario

Pandemic assumptions. Following the recent upsurge in global cases, effective public education campaigns and concerted multilateral coordination efforts would ensure a high degree of compliance with pandemic-control policies around the world, allowing many economies to begin rolling back the stringency of pandemic-control measures starting in the first half of 2021. Immunization campaigns proceed promptly in advanced economies and major EMDEs at the start of 2021. Widespread vaccine deployment is achieved by mid-2021 in advanced economies and major EMDEs, and up to four quarters later in other EMDEs and LICs.

Macroeconomic channels. Activity rebounds sharply as social distancing eases and households increase their demand for services amid substantial gains in employment and wages. Simultaneously, economic uncertainty dissipates, encouraging firms to invest heavily in new equipment and technologies. Positive developments in vaccine rollout—alongside the widespread release of affordable breakthrough therapeutics—trigger a sustained surge in equity markets and more benign global financial conditions. While extraordinary monetary policy accommodation begins to wane as employment improves, fiscal policy helps support workers throughout a lengthy sectoral reallocation process. Moreover, the shared global experience of combatting COVID-19 is assumed to strengthen multilateralism, with a renewed push for global trade agreements and a rules-based international trading system contributing to stronger global trade growth.

Growth outcome. Overall, in this scenario, global growth would strengthen notably, to nearly 5 percent in 2021, with advanced economies and EMDEs growing 4.1 percent and 5.8 percent, respectively.[g] Still, world growth in 2022 would be not much stronger than the baseline,

---

[f] The degree of financial stress induced by the pandemic is assumed to be comparable to that during the global financial crisis, with the VIX volatility index averaging 53 points over 2021Q2 and 2021Q3, compared to an average of 52 in 2008Q4 and 2009Q1. Credit spreads increase by 420 basis points on average over 2021Q2 and 2021Q3, compared to an average increase of 426 basis points in 2008Q4 and 2009Q1.

[g] Faster vaccine deployment meaningfully reduces the projected number of COVID-19 cases relative to the baseline, allowing for a faster easing of social distancing. On its own, the upside vaccine assumption is estimated to increase global growth by 0.4 percentage point in both 2021 and 2022. The remainder of the upside revision relative to the baseline scenario reflects reduced involuntary social distancing brought on by a faster resolution of the pandemic, and improved financial conditions.

BOX 1.4 Global growth scenarios (continued)

with the upside to growth limited by scarring from the exceptionally severe downturn in 2020. By 2022, global and EMDE output would be only 1.7 and 1.8 percent, respectively, above the baseline scenario. Such a robust recovery might be enough to stabilize EMDE debt at its long-term median. Global trade growth would experience a strong recovery, averaging nearly 7 percent over 2021 and 2022.

rising costs for businesses, fragmentation in global economic links, and lower productivity (Antràs 2020). This could stem from the simmering trade disputes involving major economies, as well as the diminished role of global bodies in recent negotiations. In addition, many countries have signed bilateral supply agreements with vaccine manufacturers; if not properly coordinated, this could lead to an undersupply of vaccines in other countries, which would be unable to control further COVID-19 outbreaks. Similarly, some border and trade restrictions imposed to slow the spread of the pandemic could be maintained even after the health crisis dissipates.

A further erosion in global cooperation risks reducing the world's ability to deal with increasingly urgent trans-national problems, including future health crises as well as climate change and global poverty. This would be particularly damaging for countries following export-led development strategies, which become less viable when global trade is impaired.

Region-specific downside risks

Many regions remain vulnerable to civil unrest, particularly where inequality is elevated, governance is poor, and economic growth is weak—all of which could be exacerbated as a result of the pandemic. Social unrest remains at a high level in parts of LAC, ECA, and MENA, and falling per capita incomes could trigger rising discontent in SSA and elsewhere. Similarly, geopolitical risks remain an important risk, to varying degrees, across EMDE regions. Both civil and international military conflicts are associated with severe disruptions to growth.

A period of persistently low commodity prices could worsen the prospects of commodity-exporting economies and regions such as MENA. This could lead to fiscal tightening, slow their recovery from the global pandemic, and increase the risk of some countries falling back into recession should additional negative shocks occur.

Disruptions from natural disasters and weather-related events are a persistent source of severe downside risk for a host of economies, especially in LICs and island economies in East Asia and Pacific (EAP) and LAC. Many categories of extreme events are becoming more frequent as a result of climate change (Smith et al. 2020). Droughts and wildfires are making some areas uninhabitable, and potentially permanently changing ecosystems (Staal et al. 2020). Although global food stocks are elevated, food insecurity remains a concern, particularly in low-income countries, as a result of declining household incomes as well as localized price spikes in some regions.

Upside risks

Although downside risks predominate, stronger-than-expected outcomes cannot be ruled out, especially if the vaccine rollout proceeds faster than currently anticipated. As discussed in box 1.4, the pace of vaccine deployment could surpass financial market expectations, triggering a sharp rise in confidence and ushering a strong rise in domestic demand. Consumption and investment would strengthen steadily as employment recovers and pandemic-induced uncertainties dissipate, and the hardest-hit services sectors such as restaurants and tourism would experience a sharp uptick from pent-up demand.

It is also possible that the shared global experience of combatting COVID-19 ushers in a renewed move toward multilateralism. Greater support for a stable, open, and rules-based international trading system could drive a reduction in tariffs, an uptick in trade, stronger foreign investment in EMDEs and, ultimately, more robust global growth.

Over the longer-term, some of the changes in practices that took place during the pandemic may help to drive future productivity growth. New business models introduced during the pandemic may prove more efficient and durable, as may have been the case during the Great Depression (Babina, Bernstein, and Mezzanotti 2020). Widespread teleworking may allow more workers to benefit from the productivity benefits of cities without increasing congestion (Duranton and Puga 2020). A near-term surge in aggregate demand, combined with a more durable increase in productivity and investment, could mitigate the long-term damage of the pandemic.

Policy challenges

Challenges in advanced economies

In the immediate term, strengthened infection control policies in advanced economies, including effective surveillance and universal masking, have the potential to significantly alter the pandemic's course and bolster the recovery. As the crisis abates, policy makers will need to keep policy support in place to sustain the recovery, despite the sharp rise in debt levels, gradually shifting from income support toward growth-enhancing policies. With limited scope for further central bank support, policy makers will also need to consider a greater role for fiscal policy in bolstering activity. In the long run, structural reforms are needed to reverse economic scarring from the pandemic and stimulate productivity growth, including by facilitating sectoral reallocation, harnessing digital technologies, and tackling rising inequality.

Monetary and financial policies

The COVID-19 pandemic will likely contribute to the trend decline in real interest rates (Jordà, Singh, and Taylor 2020). Nominal short rates will likely remain near zero for years, leading to an extended period of markedly negative real interest rates as central banks shift from crisis management to supporting the recovery (figure 1.18.A; Henneberg and Mann 2020).

Given the growing reliance on unconventional policy tools, some major central banks have considered alternative policy regimes. For instance, the U.S. Federal Reserve has adopted average inflation targeting, under which inflation

FIGURE 1.18 Monetary and financial policies in advanced economies

Policy rates in major advanced economies are expected to remain near zero for several years as central banks support a protracted recovery. Market-based measures of inflation expectations have bounced back from their second-quarter lows, partly aided by shifts in policy regimes.

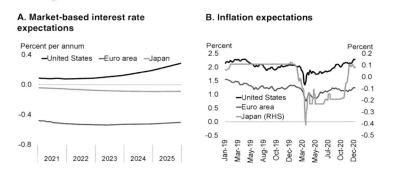

Sources: Bloomberg; World Bank.
A. Figure shows the expectations for policy rates for the euro area, Japan, and the United States obtained from Overnight Index Swaps (OIS) as of December 16, 2020.
B. Figure shows seven-year inflation swap rates for the euro area, Japan, and the United States. The last observation is December 16, 2020. The idiosyncratic increase from September 21 to September 22 (inclusive) was removed.

will be allowed to rise above target to compensate for the undershooting during downturns (Powell 2020). The anticipation of the new approach has contributed to a modest rise in market-based inflation expectations (figure 1.18.B).

Due to the severe adverse impact of COVID-19 on aggregate demand, inflation risks are squarely to the downside in the near term. That said, a sizable part of the pandemic's macroeconomic impact was in the form of a supply shock (Brinca, Duarte, and Faria e Castro 2020). If policy efforts are unable to reverse supply-side damage, inflation may resume at a faster than expected pace in the medium-term, prompting unexpected policy tightening.

Financial authorities have generally responded to COVID-19 by using the flexibility of regulatory standards, supporting affected borrowers, promoting balance sheet transparency, and maintaining operational and business continuity of banks. These measures have helped to maintain the flow of credit and mitigated financial sector stress (Nier and Olafsson 2020; IMF and World Bank 2020). Once the pandemic is effectively contained, these measures would need to be gradually tightened or reversed to guard against a

FIGURE 1.19 Fiscal policy in advanced economies

Authorities are set to withdraw fiscal support more rapidly than was the case following the global financial crisis, which could derail an already-fragile recovery. Sustained support to unemployed and vulnerable households will be needed to prevent a sharp decline in incomes. As policy makers shift their focus from crisis management to supporting the recovery, reversing the long-standing decline in infrastructure investment could be prioritized. Credible fiscal plans can help ease fiscal sustainability fears from the projected surge in sovereign debt over the outlook.

A. Fiscal impulse in advanced economies

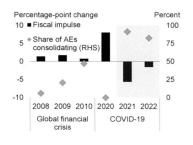

B. Disposable income: Forecast revisions in major advanced economies

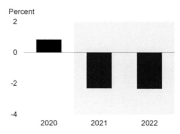

C. Government spending on infrastructure

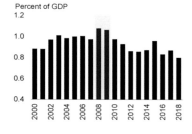

D. Gross government debt in major advanced economies

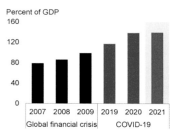

Sources: International Monetary Fund; OECD Infrastructure Investment (database); Oxford Economics; World Bank.

A.B.D. Shaded areas indicate forecasts.

A. AEs = advanced economies. Fiscal impulse is defined as the change in the cyclically-adjusted primary balance (CAPB) from the previous year. A decline in the CAPB (a negative fiscal impulse) indicates fiscal consolidation, while an increase in the CAPB (positive fiscal impulse) indicates fiscal support. Sample includes 36 economies.

B. Figure shows the percent difference in levels of real personal disposable income (PDI) between January 2021 World Bank baseline projections versus January 2020 Oxford Economics projections across major advanced economies (the euro area, Japan, and the United States). PDI is measured in constant local currency. Projections assume announced fiscal measures as of the end of October 2020. Aggregate is calculated using real U.S. dollar GDP weights at 2010 prices and market exchange rates.

C. Figure shows average of infrastructure investment as a share of GDP for 31 advanced economies. Infrastructure investment covers spending on new transport construction and improvements to existing networks. Shaded area indicates the global financial crisis spanning from 2008 until 2009.

D. Figure shows debt as a percent of GDP across major advanced economies (the euro area, Japan, and the United States). Aggregates calculated using nominal 2019 U.S. dollar GDP weights.

buildup in leverage in an environment of degraded balance sheets and low-for-long interest rates (IMF 2020f).

Fiscal policy

With monetary policy increasingly constrained, fiscal policy has taken on a critical role in

macroeconomic stabilization during the crisis, delivering unprecedented stimulus in 2020 in the form of cash transfers and income support to households and firms. Fiscal support is projected to be withdrawn more rapidly than was the case following the global financial crisis in more than 90 percent of advanced economies (figure 1.19.A). With most economies still far from potential, some further fiscal support may be needed to buttress disposable incomes and avoid derailing the fragile recovery (figure 1.19.B; Casado et al. 2020; IMF 2020c; Stone 2020).

Fiscal multipliers are high when unemployment rates are rising (Auerbach and Gorodnichenko 2015; Berge, De Ridder, and Pfajfar 2020). Policy makers could consider enhancing automatic stabilizers—for instance, by permanently adopting short-time work programs—to quicken the delivery and maximize the effectiveness of fiscal support. As fiscal authorities gradually refocus their attention on boosting a lasting recovery, spending can be reprioritized to areas with high long-term fiscal multipliers, including investments in infrastructure and public education (De Ridder, Hannon and Pfajfar 2020; Ramey 2020). For instance, one priority could be reversing the trend decline in infrastructure spending as a share of GDP experienced by more than two-thirds of advanced economies, with an emphasis on green infrastructure projects and other investments that can boost resilience to climate risks (figure 1.19.C; OECD 2020b; Vivid Economics 2020). Whereas debt dynamics remain manageable in the near term despite large increases in debt levels, credible fiscal plans can help strengthen expectations of long-run fiscal sustainability (figure 1.19.D).

Structural policies

The pandemic has had a disproportionate impact on the poor and the vulnerable, with job and income losses concentrated among low-income workers and the young. Policies can help ensure an inclusive recovery that targets lower-income and lower-skill households, including job-creating public works projects and regulatory reforms that facilitate hiring (McKinsey 2020). Moreover, increased spending on health care and pandemic preparedness—focusing on prevention and expanding support for vulnerable populations—

can play a critical role in guarding against future health crises and boost productivity (figure 1.20.A; Dyakova et al. 2017).

Policies to maintain labor attachment, including short-time work programs, were essential to alleviate the adverse effects of COVID-19 on the labor force. To avoid impinging on labor reallocation, such measures can become more targeted as the recovery progresses, including by having firms contribute to the cost of such policies and introducing time limits to mitigate the risk of supporting unviable jobs (OECD 2020c).

The rise of telework may be changing the productivity advantage of cities. Governments may have a role in increasing digital connectivity, while safeguarding the productivity-enhancing effects of dense urban areas, including an efficient sharing of local infrastructure and the promotion of new technologies and business practices (Duranton and Puga 2020).

Finally, economic damage from the pandemic is expected to reduce potential output in advanced economies (figure 1.20.B). New policies, including tax reform, expanded support for entrepreneurs, and the provision of worker training opportunities will be needed to boost productivity and take full advantage of accelerated digitalization and automation, while cushioning the process of labor reallocation (Astebro, Braguinsky, and Ding 2020).

Challenges in emerging market and developing economies

EMDEs' near-term priority is effective pandemic management, including facilitating widespread vaccine dissemination, which will be a key factor underpinning the recovery. The deterioration in bank asset quality is highlighting the challenge of preserving financial stability while still facilitating credit availability. To ensure fiscal sustainability, EMDE policy makers will need to balance nurturing the recovery against prematurely unwinding fiscal support. This trade-off underscores the need to improve domestic revenue mobilization and prioritize expenditures toward measures that yield large growth dividends. In some cases, the deterioration of public balance sheets may call for

FIGURE 1.20 Structural policies in advanced economies

Increased spending on health care—preventive care in particular—may help mitigate future health crises. The pandemic is expected to leave deep scars on potential output in advanced economies.

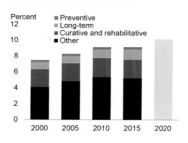

A. Government spending on health care in advanced economies

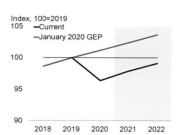

B. G7 potential output

Sources: Lorenzoni et al. (2019); OECD.stat (database); World Bank (2018b); World Bank.
A. Bars show average healthcare spending as a percentage of GDP. Grey area indicates projection for 2020 as based on baseline GDP growth projections and estimates for the growth of health care spending per capita from Lorezoni et al. (2019). Sample includes 30 advanced economies.
B. Potential output is constructed using the multivariate filter model of World Bank (2018b). Group of Seven (G7) economies include Canada, France, Germany, Italy, Japan, the United Kingdom, and the United States. Weighted average calculated using 2019 GDP at 2010 prices and market exchange rates. Last observation is 2020Q3. Shaded area indicates forecasts.

additional debt relief, particularly in LICs. In the longer run, it will be critical to mitigate the scarring of potential output caused by the pandemic, including through policies to safeguard health and education, prioritize investments in digital technologies and green infrastructure, improve governance, and enhance debt transparency.

Policy challenges in China

The COVID-19 crisis is likely to leave lasting impacts on China's economy (World Bank 2020h). Private and public debt levels, which were already elevated before the crisis, have risen further, particularly at the subnational level. This has reversed some of the deleveraging achieved since 2016 and has rendered China's economy more vulnerable to future shocks. As policy makers resume their focus on deleveraging the economy, monetary and financial policies will need to remain flexible, avoid premature and abrupt tightening, and carefully manage financial risks.

The pandemic has also exposed interlinked economic, social, and environmental fragilities (World Bank 2020i). More inclusive growth, and

FIGURE 1.21 Monetary and financial policy in EMDEs

Aggregate inflation in emerging market and developing economies (EMDEs) is low, and is expected to remain below central bank targets as a result of weak economic activity. Central bank policy rates generally remain at highly accommodative levels. Asset purchase programs have helped stabilize financial markets, but their continued use could begin to undermine financial stability in the absence of clearly defined objectives that are consistent with central bank mandates. Although EMDE banking sector capitalization remains high, on average, it is at risk of being eroded by higher nonperforming loans.

A. EMDE inflation during the pandemic and global financial crisis

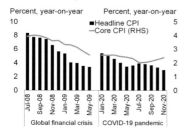

B. Expected EMDE inflation deviation from target

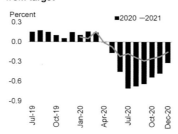

C. EMDE policy interest rates

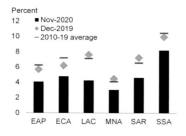

D. EMDE announced or completed asset purchases

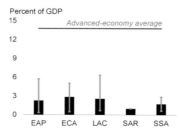

E. Impact of EMDE asset purchases: EMDE 10-year bond yields

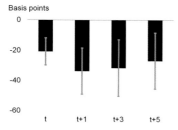

F. Proportion of firms in arrears or expecting to be within 6 months

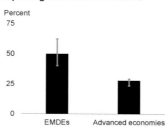

Sources: Apedo-Amah et al. (2020); Consensus Economics; Haver Analytics; National sources; World Bank.
Note: EMDEs = emerging market and developing economies; EAP = East Asia and Pacific, ECA = Europe and Central Asia, LAC = Latin America and the Caribbean, MNA = Middle East and North Africa, SAR = South Asia, SSA = Sub-Saharan Africa.
A. Aggregates calculated using 2019 real U.S. dollar GDP weights. "Headline" and "Core" samples include 15 and 11 EMDEs, respectively. Last observation is November 2020.
B. Median of monthly Consensus forecasts deviations from central bank targets. Sample includes 38 EMDEs. Last observation is December 2020.
C. Figure shows regional averages of policy interest rates. Sample includes 67 EMDEs.
D. Announced or completed purchases (where no announcement exists) relative to 2019 nominal GDP as of November 2020. Bar shows average in each region. Orange whiskers show regional range. Red line shows average of advanced-economy programs launched in 2020.
E. Panel regression results based on daily financial asset prices in 26 EMDEs. A total of 25 asset purchase announcements in 14 EMDEs are studied. Horizontal axes indicate days after the announcements of quantitative easing (t = 0). Orange lines indicate 90 percent confidence intervals.
F. Unweighted averages. Figure shows proportion of firms responding yes to "is it expected that this establishment will fall in arrears in any of its outstanding liabilities in the next six months?" as in Apedo-Amah et al. (2020). Survey of 100,000+ firms in 51 countries during April-August 2020.

a shift from public investment to consumption as its main driver, would help China's recovery be more sustainable. Structural policies should focus on encouraging investment in human capital, reducing regulatory burdens, addressing market distortions, and improving access to social services. In addition, the government could work to close the gaps in disease surveillance and control, reduce public health risks, and strengthen international collaboration.

EMDE monetary and financial policies

As a result of weak demand and subdued energy prices, EMDE inflation has fallen below central bank targets, on average, since May (figures 1.21.A and 1.21.B). Nevertheless, the fall in inflation in EMDEs has been less broad based than in advanced economies, reflecting the effects of sharp currency depreciations as well as rising domestic food prices in some countries (Ebrahimy, Igan, and Martinez Peria 2020). Whereas underlying inflationary pressures in most EMDEs are likely to remain subdued amid persistently soft demand, negative output gaps following the collapse in activity may not be as sizable as currently envisioned due to the pandemic's damage to potential growth. This could eventually fuel a pickup in inflation.

Central bank policy rates have mostly remained stable at very accommodative levels (figure 1.21.C). The prospect of generally contained inflationary pressures, along with recent changes to the monetary policy framework of the U.S. Federal Reserve that is likely to keep U.S. policy rates low for an extended period, may enable a number of EMDE central banks to maintain their accommodative policy stances during the recovery (Arteta et al. 2015; Kose, Nagle et al. 2020). Lower borrowing costs could also help lessen the financing burden on EMDEs with high debt loads and associated financial risks. These benefits may, however, be elusive for those EMDEs facing lingering vulnerabilities, such as large external imbalances or dwindling reserve buffers.

Several EMDE central banks have also continued their use of asset purchase programs, which appear to have helped stabilize financial markets (figures

1.21.D and 1.21.E; Arslan, Drehmann, and Hofmann 2020; Hartley and Rebucci 2020). The medium- to long-term effect of these programs on EMDE output and inflation is untested, and prolonged use of these unconventional tools may create new risks (chapter 4). If asset purchase programs continue to expand without clearly articulated goals that are consistent with policy mandates, hard-won central bank independence and credibility may be at risk of being eroded. Furthermore, if central bank asset purchases are perceived to fund unsustainable budget deficits, they could trigger capital flight and raise risk premia, as well as result in large currency depreciations and persistently higher inflation (Drakopoulos et al. 2020; Ha, Stocker, and Yilmazkuday 2020).

Although banking sector capital adequacy ratios remain above regulatory minimums, on average, a large proportion of firms are reporting to be in, or expect to fall into, loan arrears, as the collapse in activity continues to weigh on household and corporate income (figure 1.21.F). Policy makers face the challenge of balancing the need to extend the easing of macro- and micro-prudential policies to support activity through credit availability—such as the relaxation of minimum liquidity and capital requirements, and the slackening of borrower loan-to-value ratios to encourage lending—against upholding regulatory standards to prevent the buildup of greater systemic risks in the financial sector.

Measures to support lending to firms suffering from temporary liquidity constraints, such as regulatory forbearance and payment moratoria, need to be reassessed periodically to ensure they remain appropriate and do not impede asset quality transparency or harm bank capitalization. Inefficient insolvency regimes, and measures to increase flexibility over nonperforming loan classifications or reduce asset risk weighs below globally recognized standards, may heighten uncertainty around bank capitalization and asset quality, harming credit provision. Enhanced supervisory assessment of loan quality and regular stress testing can limit risks to bank solvency from rising loan arrears, while strong resolution and recovery regimes can limit contagion risks following bank failures.

EMDE fiscal policy

Fiscal support packages have been large in many EMDEs, with discretionary measures, such as increased expenditures or foregone revenues, constituting a substantial share of the support. The amount of support, however, has varied by region, reflecting the availability and use of policy space (figure 1.22.A). In general, EMDEs provided less fiscal support than advanced economies, in part reflecting revenue constraints in industrial-commodity exporters due to the decline in commodity prices and in LICs due to low revenue mobilization (figure 1.22.B). Fiscal support measures have been financed through debt issuance; the drawdown of buffers such as sovereign wealth and development funds; reallocation of existing spending; and external support, with 44 EMDEs benefiting from the G20 Debt Service Suspension Initiative. The fiscal response, combined with output contractions, is expected to trigger a nearly 10 percentage point rise in government debt in the median EMDE by 2022, to a record high of about 62 percent of GDP, with particularly sharp increases in South Asia (SAR) and MENA (box 1.1). Overall, the rise in debt is broad-based, with more than 80 percent of EMDEs projected to have higher debt-to-GDP ratios in 2022 relative to 2019.

Given the size of the COVID-19 shock and the lack of fiscal space, some EMDEs may need to rely on new or continued external support and debt relief to enable them to assist vulnerable households and viable firms (Truman 2020). The existing framework for debt relief is unlikely to fill the sizable financing gaps of many EMDEs, which may warrant more permanent solutions (OECD 2020a; Stubbs et al. 2020). Additionally, many EMDEs will not be able to maintain the level of expenditures needed to support the recovery, which could force some countries into premature fiscal tightening (figure 1.22.C). Particularly vulnerable countries include those where debt was already on a rising trajectory or where a large share of fiscal revenues is absorbed by debt-servicing costs (figure 1.22.D; UNCTAD 2020). The situation is worse in LICs, where nearly half were either in debt stress, or at high risk of it, prior to the pandemic (Mühleisen, Klyuev, and Sanya 2020).

FIGURE 1.22 Fiscal policy in emerging market and developing economies

Many emerging market and developing economies (EMDEs) have provided substantial fiscal packages, albeit with wide regional variation. Fiscal support, combined with output contractions, has sharply raised EMDE debt levels and service costs, which could eventually weigh on growth by forcing many countries into premature fiscal tightening. Sizable fiscal losses due to spending inefficiency further reduce policy space and growth dividends. Fiscal support for energy measures has mostly targeted fossil fuels rather than green technologies.

A. Composition of fiscal support packages, by EMDE region

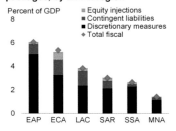

B. Fiscal impulse in EMDEs

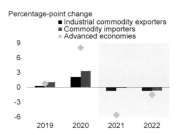

C. Share of EMDEs pursuing fiscal consolidation

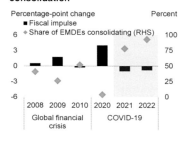

D. External debt service, by EMDE group

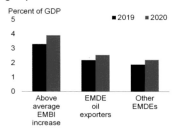

E. Public infrastructure spending losses due to inefficiency

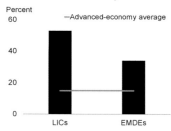

F. Amount of support committed toward energy initiatives in 2020

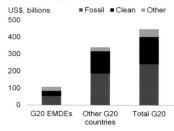

Sources: Energy Policy Tracker; International Monetary Fund; International Monetary Fund (2020h); World Bank.
Note: EMDEs = emerging market and developing economies; LICs = Low-income countries; EAP = East Asia and Pacific, ECA = Europe and Central Asia, LAC = Latin America and the Caribbean, MNA = Middle East and North Africa, SAR = South Asia, SSA = Sub-Saharan Africa. Aggregates calculated using 2019 U.S. dollar GDP at 2010 prices and market exchange rates.
A. Announced fiscal support packages as a share of 2019 nominal GDP, using data from the October 2020 IMF *Fiscal Monitor*. Aggregates calculated using unweighted averages. "Discretionary measures" includes revenue and expenditure measures; "Equity injections" includes equity injections, loans, and asset purchases; and "Contingent liabilities" includes loan guarantees and other quasi-fiscal measures. Sample includes 121 EMDEs.
B.C. Fiscal impulse is defined as the change in the cyclically-adjusted primary balance (CAPB) from the previous year. A decline in the CAPB (a negative fiscal impulse) indicates fiscal consolidation, while an increase in the CAPB (positive fiscal impulse) indicates fiscal expansion. Sample includes up to 27 EMDEs and 34 advanced economies due to data availability. Shaded areas indicate forecasts.
D. Figure shows the unweighted average of debt service on external debt in percentage of current GDP. "Other EMDEs" indicates EMDEs not included in other categories. Sample includes 87 EMDEs.
E. Data are the percentage deviation from full efficiency that are generated from planning, allocation, and implementation, as calculated in IMF (2020h). Sample includes 60 EMDEs.
F. Figure shows G20 commitments to types of energy policies as a percentage of total commitments since the pandemic began. Data as of December 16, 2020.

The expected deterioration in fiscal positions has made achieving fiscal sustainability more challenging. Providing a clear exit strategy for unwinding substantial support—alongside strengthening fiscal frameworks and debt transparency and efficiency—would help bolster credibility and keep borrowing costs contained. It would also put governments in a better position to address fiscal risks such as the realization of contingent liabilities, particularly those that arise from state-owned enterprises.

The trade-off between strengthening fiscal positions and continuing to provide support can be made more palatable through improvements on the part of both revenues and expenditures. On the revenue side, ensuring that the tax structure and statutory rates are efficient could help mobilize domestic revenues and soften the drag from fiscal consolidation. On the expenditure side, improving public investment efficiency, as well as the quality of public procurement, can ensure that expenditures yield high growth dividends and offset the impact of consolidation (Bosio, Grujicic, and Iavorskyi 2020). Strengthening governance, for instance, could halve the expenditure losses incurred by public infrastructure inefficiencies (figure 1.22.E; IMF 2020h). Additionally, expenditures could be prioritized toward measures that bolster inclusive and sustainable growth and also help ensure fiscal sustainability, such as investment in human capital or priority sectors, including green technology. That said, roughly half of the fiscal support directed toward energy initiatives in the G20 last year were committed to fossil fuels (figure 1.22.F).

EMDE structural policies

EMDE policy makers' top near-term priority will continue to be pandemic control and, once the immediate crisis abates, boosting preparedness for future health emergencies. Policy action will also be needed to mitigate the pandemic's distributional consequences and, critically, the damage it has caused to potential growth (figure 1.23.A; box 3.1; World Bank 2020n). Some of the most pressing policy goals include safeguarding health and education, prioritizing investments in digital and green infrastructure, improving governance, and enhancing debt transparency.

Improving the preparedness of health systems

As EMDEs continue to tackle the challenge of controlling the pandemic, several lessons can be drawn from the experience of countries that have achieved more durable containment of COVID-19. Perhaps most importantly, these underscore the need for pandemic-control policies to reduce the spread of the virus with limited economic disruptions, such as universal masking and effective surveillance systems with high volumes of testing and large-scale contact tracing. Additionally, sustained and transparent communication efforts are required to build trust, help guard against pandemic-control fatigue, encourage proper social-distancing practices, and maintain widespread facial masking (figure 1.23.B). In particular, governments can leverage digital communication technologies to track the effects of COVID-19 in real time. As effective vaccines continue to be produced, EMDEs will need to shift focus to supporting vaccine procurement and dissemination.

The pandemic has highlighted the large gaps in healthcare systems across many EMDEs. In the longer run, increased investment in the domestic provision of health-care-related goods and services will be needed to enhance the preparedness of domestic health care systems. In addition, increased spending on epidemic preparedness measures is paramount to minimizing the human and economic costs of future health crises. Authorities need to leverage the power of mobile data to monitor and contain epidemics and assess resource and equipment needs in real time (World Bank 2020o).

Fostering food security and education

Policy efforts are required to minimize the long-term scarring of human capital. Alleviating food insecurity is a top priority, as sharp income losses have induced poor households to cut back on food consumption (World Bank 2020h). Indeed, the number of people facing food crises is estimated to have doubled from 130 million to about 270 million by end-2020 (CARE 2020; WFP 2020a). Ensuring the effective delivery of food assistance for those in need, in part by supporting local markets via cash transfers, could help avoid

FIGURE 1.23 Structural policies in emerging market and developing economies

The lasting damage from the pandemic may contribute to a further decline in potential growth for emerging market and developing economies. Authorities can promote universal masking as a low-cost and relatively growth-friendly approach to help contain the pandemic. The recovery can be enhanced by expanding access to digital technologies and addressing infrastructure gaps, partly through green investments. In the longer run, reforms to improve governance, reduce corruption, and enhance debt transparency are needed to support potential growth.

A. EMDE potential growth

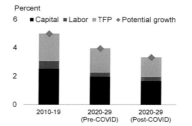

B. Prevalence of mask use

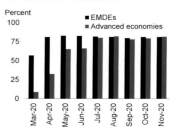

C. Access to digital technologies

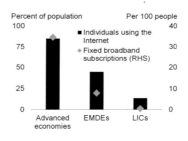

D. Average annual gap between projected infrastructure spending and needs, 2016-30

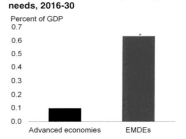

E. Cumulative response of long-term growth forecasts after institutional-reform advances and setbacks

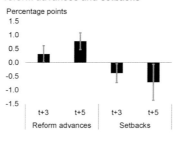

F. Debt transparency across EMDE regions

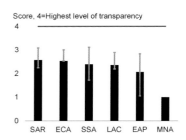

Sources: Consensus Economics; Haver Analytics; International Crisis Risk Group (database); Kilic Celik, Kose, and Ohnsorge (2020); McKinsey (2016); Rivetti (2020); World Bank; YouGov.com.
Note: EMDEs = emerging market and developing economies; LICs = low-income countries; TFP = total factor productivity; EAP = East Asia and Pacific, ECA = Europe and Central Asia, LAC = Latin America and the Caribbean, MNA = Middle East and North Africa, SAR = South Asia, SSA = Sub-Saharan Africa.
A. Real GDP-weighted average for 52 EMDEs. Potential growth based on a production function approach described in Chapter 3.
B. Bars show median values for the share of respondents that wear masks in public. Sample includes 10 EMDEs and 16 advanced economies. Last observation is November 2020.
C. Figure shows the average share of the population using the Internet and fixed broadband subscriptions per 100 people in 2017. Sample includes 36 advanced economies, 155 EMDEs, and 29 LICs.
D. Sample includes eight advanced economies and nine EMDEs.
E. Coefficient estimates of a local projection estimation of 10-year-ahead growth forecasts on reform advances and setbacks in 57 countries. Reform advances (setbacks) are defined as years in which the average of indicators by the International Crisis Risk Group increase (decrease), and are sustained for at least three years. Vertical orange lines show the 90-percent confidence interval.
F. Figure shows average score from the World Bank's Debt Reporting Heat Map. Red line is highest level of transparency. Orange lines represent the interquartile range.

chronic malnutrition, which can permanently impair maternal and child health and learning abilities (Martins et al. 2011; WFP 2020b). The international community can play a key role in supporting efforts to alleviate food insecurity. For instance, the International Development Association (IDA) is committing $5.3 billion for food security (IDA 2020). Moreover, equitable access to health care—especially for vulnerable households with reduced income—needs to be prioritized.

Safeguarding access to education is critical in promoting better long-run growth outcomes (chapter 3; Sala-i-Martin, Doppelhofer, and Miller 2004). Increased investment in infrastructure related to education can improve the quantity and quality of human capital (Francisco and Tanaka 2020; Barrett et al. 2019). Digital approaches to remote learning developed during the pandemic can also be leveraged to gradually broaden access to affordable education across EMDEs over the long term (Li and Lalani 2020).

Boosting public investment in digital and green infrastructure

In the short term, authorities can spur the accelerated adoption and development of fintech platforms that enhance the delivery of secure cash payments to a broader group of vulnerable households, which can also help alleviate the sharp rise in inequality (Davidovic et al. 2020; Gévaudan and Lederman 2020). Once the pandemic is contained, funding an expansion of broadband and mobile internet access would enable a larger share of the population to access digital services (figure 1.23.C). In addition to its productivity-enhancing effects, wider internet access has been found to increase female labor force participation (Viollaz and Winkler 2020). At the same time, policies that promote a secure online environment and deepen access to data, combined with an easing of regulatory barriers to market entry, can help grow a vibrant domestic information and communications technology sector (World Bank 2020o).

Addressing gaps between current spending on infrastructure and the level needed to meet Sustainable Development Goals can contribute to

a sustained rise in per capita incomes (figure 1.23.D; chapter 3; Canning and Pedroni 2008). Prioritizing investment in green infrastructure projects with high economic returns, and fostering the widespread adoption of environmentally-sustainable technologies, can also support higher growth levels in the long-run while contributing to climate change mitigation (OECD 2020b; Strand and Toman 2010). Building green objectives into recovery packages will increase EMDE's resilience to future shocks as well as reduce risks. Green stimulus packages, including efforts to improve energy efficiency such as retrofitting buildings, can have large fiscal multipliers as they are both labor intensive and productivity enhancing (Agrawala, Dussaux, and Monti 2020; IEA 2020).

Nonetheless, the social and economic consequences of green policies need to be carefully managed—particularly job losses in traditional energy industries. Governments can work with the private sector, leveraging public-private partnerships, to increase public investment. This type of government spending has large multiplier effects in countries where the stock of public capital is low (Izquierdo et al. 2019). Environmental protection policies and regulatory reform to improve energy efficiency are also vital to improving long-run climate, health, and growth outcomes (IMF 2020g).

Improving governance

Improving governance is also urgently needed to overcome development obstacles exacerbated by the pandemic and foster an environment conducive to higher long-run growth. Structural reforms that raise the quality of economic governance can facilitate the process of sectoral reallocation and structural transformation accelerated by the pandemic, while increasing productivity and investment (figure 1.23.E; box 3.2). Such policies include trade liberalization and regulatory reform to increase global value chain participation, tax reform, and enhanced contract enforcement (Chari, Henry, and Reyes 2020). Social safety nets will also need to be strengthened to cushion the temporary adverse impacts on employment of productivity-enhancing reforms and accelerated investments in automation and digitalization.

Reducing corruption is paramount in light of the expansion of government activity induced by the pandemic (World Bank 2020p). Among other factors weighing on institutional quality, corruption weighs on the effectiveness of resource allocation (Avellan, Galindo, and Leon-Diaz 2020). Addressing corruption can play a crucial role in bolstering the recovery. Fostering a more predictable investment climate can help countries attract FDI, seize new trade opportunities brought on by ongoing global value chain reconfiguration, and address balance of payments difficulties (World Bank 2020q). Reducing corruption can also help increase the quality of government expenditures, the effectiveness of social benefit systems, and, by boosting government revenues, the amount of fiscal space (Peisakhin and Pinto 2010).

Enhancing debt transparency, in part by adopting sound debt management practices, can support a durable recovery by fostering public trust and macroeconomic stability (Bulow et al. 2020; Malpass 2020). A firm commitment to enhancing debt transparency can help countries assess and manage the sharp accumulation in external debt brought on by the pandemic. Furthermore, it can also facilitate the establishment of sustainable debt covenants for public and private stakeholders, thereby increasing the fiscal space to fund growth-enhancing policies (World Bank 2020r). There remains considerable scope to increase debt transparency across EMDEs (figure 1.23.F).

Global coordination and cooperation

The COVID-19 pandemic is a truly global crisis that necessitates a coordinated global response (World Bank 2020s). Only once the pandemic is effectively managed in all countries will individual countries be safe from resurgence, allowing global growth outcomes to improve materially (Ghebreyesus 2020). Nevertheless, the resources to contain the pandemic and cushion its severe health, social and economic consequences are unequally distributed across countries. Although many EMDEs deployed unprecedented fiscal stimulus compared to past crises, their policy

response was constrained by limited fiscal space and was insufficient to address the pressing needs of their vulnerable populations (Gates and Gates 2020; Reinhart and Reinhart 2020).

Given the pandemic's lingering effects across fiscally constrained EMDEs, there is a pressing need for the global community to collaborate in alleviating debt burdens, particularly for the poorest countries (Shetty 2020). For example, the Brady Plan of 1989-94 achieved external debt reductions of about one-third for the 18 participating debtor countries (Cline 1995; Rieffel 2003). These large reductions helped launch recoveries in the 1990s (Kose, Nagle et al. 2020; Reinhart and Trebesch 2016).[1]

The G20's recently announced common approach to providing debt relief for the poorest countries is a step to facilitate coordination among both Paris Club and non-Paris Club bilateral lenders (G20 2020). However, besides enhancing transparency, increased participation of private creditors and their equal treatment with official bilateral creditors will be critical to achieving an equitable and durable outcome (Bulow et al. 2020; World Bank 2020t).

On the health front, coordinated global efforts across governments, the private sector, and multilateral institutions in developing, producing, and disseminating COVID-19 vaccines are critically important to ensure timely and equitable access across countries and a sustained reduction in global infection rates (Weintraub, Yadav, and Berkley 2020). In particular, countries with high vaccine development and production capacity can actively participate in coordinated international approaches to vaccine dissemination, seeking to promote the affordable and equitable distribution of vaccines amongst their lower-income peers (Ghebreyesus 2020).

In the longer term, safeguarding multilateral institutions, including their role in settling dis-

---

[1] Another historical example is the London Debt Agreement of 1953, under which 20 sovereign states collaborated to reduce West Germany's external debt by about 50 percent, contributing to West Germany's postwar economic revival (Guinnane 2015; Kaiser 2013).

putes and upholding a rules-based international trading system, is essential to sustained growth (Goldin 2020; IMF 2020g). These institutions, working hand in hand with governments, can play a crucial role in developing equitable and sustainable solutions to challenges of defeating the pandemic, reducing poverty, eliminating data sovereignty barriers, and tackling climate change.

TABLE 1.2 Emerging market and developing economies[1]

Commodity exporters[2]		Commodity importers[3]	
Afghanistan	Kyrgyz Republic	Albania	Romania
Algeria*	Lao PDR	Antigua and Barbuda	Samoa
Angola*	Liberia	Bahamas, The	Serbia
Argentina	Madagascar	Bangladesh	Sri Lanka
Armenia	Malawi	Barbados	St. Kitts and Nevis
Azerbaijan*	Mali	Belarus	St. Lucia
Bahrain*	Mauritania	Bhutan	St. Vincent and the Grenadines
Belize	Mongolia	Bosnia and Herzegovina	Thailand
Benin	Morocco	Bulgaria	Tonga
Bolivia*	Mozambique	Cambodia	Tunisia
Botswana	Myanmar*	China	Turkey
Brazil	Namibia	Croatia	Tuvalu
Burkina Faso	Nicaragua	Djibouti	Vanuatu
Burundi	Niger	Dominica	Vietnam
Cabo Verde	Nigeria*	Dominican Republic	
Cameroon*	Oman*	Egypt, Arab Rep.	
Central African Republic	Papua New Guinea	El Salvador	
Chad*	Paraguay	Eritrea	
Chile	Peru	Eswatini	
Colombia*	Qatar*	Georgia	
Comoros	Russian Federation*	Grenada	
Congo, Dem. Rep.	Rwanda	Haiti	
Congo, Rep.*	São Tomé and Príncipe	Hungary	
Costa Rica	Saudi Arabia*	India	
Côte d'Ivoire	Senegal	Jamaica	
Ecuador*	Seychelles	Jordan	
Equatorial Guinea*	Sierra Leone	Kiribati	
Ethiopia	Solomon Islands	Lebanon	
Fiji	South Africa	Lesotho	
Gabon*	South Sudan*	Malaysia	
Gambia, The	Sudan	Maldives	
Ghana*	Suriname	Marshall Islands	
Guatemala	Tajikistan	Mauritius	
Guinea	Tanzania	Mexico	
Guinea-Bissau	Timor-Leste*	Micronesia, Fed. Sts.	
Guyana	Togo	Moldova	
Honduras	Uganda	Montenegro	
Indonesia*	Ukraine	Nepal	
Iran, Islamic Rep.*	United Arab Emirates*	North Macedonia	
Iraq*	Uruguay	Pakistan	
Kazakhstan*	Uzbekistan	Palau	
Kenya	West Bank and Gaza	Panama	
Kosovo	Zambia	Philippines	
Kuwait*	Zimbabwe	Poland	

* Energy exporters.

1. Emerging market and developing economies (EMDEs) include all those that are not classified as advanced economies and for which a forecast is published for this report. Dependent territories are excluded. Advanced economies include Australia; Austria; Belgium; Canada; Cyprus; the Czech Republic; Denmark; Estonia; Finland; France; Germany; Greece; Hong Kong SAR, China; Iceland; Ireland; Israel; Italy; Japan; the Republic of Korea; Latvia; Lithuania; Luxembourg; Malta; the Netherlands; New Zealand; Norway; Portugal; Singapore; the Slovak Republic; Slovenia; Spain; Sweden; Switzerland; the United Kingdom; and the United States.

2. An economy is defined as commodity exporter when, on average in 2017-19, either (i) total commodities exports accounted for 30 percent or more of total exports or (ii) exports of any single commodity accounted for 20 percent or more of total exports. Economies for which these thresholds were met as a result of re-exports were excluded. When data were not available, judgment was used. This taxonomy results in the classification of some well-diversified economies as importers, even if they are exporters of certain commodities (for example, Mexico).

3. Commodity importers are all EMDEs that are not classified as commodity exporters.

ANNEX 1.1 Methodology

The global growth scenarios are developed using a combination of models and assumptions. The baseline and downside scenarios are constructed from individual country estimates consistent with the scenario assumptions on the path of the pandemic, the extent of social distancing, and financial conditions. These bottom-up scenarios rely on a combination of large-scale macro-econometric models, time series models, and economist judgement.

The upside and severe downside scenarios are model-based as deviations from the baseline and downside scenarios, respectively, and generated in a sequential process. First, epidemiological projections are established using a Susceptible-Infected-Recovered (SIR) model estimated with daily new confirmed cases data up to November 2020 (Kermack and McKendrick 1927; Zhou and Ji 2020). The SIR model is augmented to incorporate a vaccine following the approach of Feng, Towers and Yang (2011), and estimated for major advanced economies and largest EMDEs. Projections for daily infection rates are produced conditional on alternative assumptions for the evolution of the pandemic and the rollout of vaccines (Figures 1.3.2).[1]

The projected attenuation of the pandemic, influenced in part by vaccine outcomes, is assumed to set the stage for a gradual easing of voluntary social distancing and the removal of government-imposed pandemic-control measures, boosting activity. Following Coibion (2020) and IMF (2020), the impact of infection and lockdown measures on consumption is estimated based on pooled panel regression as follows:

$$FE_{i,t} = \beta_1 \, stringency_{i,t} + \beta_2 \, covid19_{i,t} + u_{i,t} \qquad (1)$$

where a country $i = 1, . . .21$, at a time $t = 2020Q1-Q3$. $FE_{i,t}$ is the forecast revision of real consumption using the difference between pre-pandemic forecast and the latest forecast by

Oxford Economics; $stringency_{i,t}$ is *Oxford* COVID-19 government response *stringency index*; and $covid19_{i,t}$ is COVID-19 cases per capita estimated by Imperial College London and is assumed to proxy voluntary social distancing measures. [2]

Using parameters from equation (1) and the SIR model's epidemiological projections, future consumption shocks are extrapolated to consider the impact of both voluntary and involuntary social distancing on private consumption. Consumption shocks are projected forward for the G7 (Canada, France, Germany, Italy, Japan, the United Kingdom, and the United States) and EM7 excluding China (India, Brazil, Mexico, Russia, Indonesia, and Turkey).

Projected consumption shocks—representing the mobility and confidence effects associated with COVID-19 cases and government-imposed pandemic-control measures—are then mapped into the Oxford Global Economic Model (Oxford Economics 2019). The model permits the quantification of the domestic and global economic implications of these shocks for the outlook.[3] Thus, increased (reduced) stringency of pandemic-control measures and voluntary social distancing trigger an increase (decrease) in consumption expenditures, employment, business investment, and foreign demand for exports. Moreover, a decrease in business investment lowers the level of potential output by reducing the capital stock.

In addition, the scenarios differ in their assump-tions about financial conditions.[4] Exogenous shocks to financial conditions, proxied by

---

[1] The vaccine rollout is assumed to follow a sigmoid curve: a slow initial rollout gives way to large-scale vaccination efforts and a subsequent tapering as the population amenable to vaccination rapidly declines.

[2] The estimated number of new daily cases from the Imperial College of London model is accessed via the Our World in Data (OWID) COVID-19 database. The shocks are broadly consistent with the recent behavioral SIR model literature (Bethune and Korinek 2020; Eichenbaum et al. 2020). The stringency index projection is based on projected COVID-19 cases per capita.

[3] In the model simulations, monetary policy is assumed to respond endogenously to developments in activity and inflation, cushioning the epidemiological shock's economic consequences. Fiscal policy is assumed to be exogenous beyond existing automatic stabilizer mechanisms except for the United States, where fiscal transfers are increased in the downside scenario.

[4] Higher risk premia raise corporate borrowing rates, exacerbating the rise in the cost of capital. Sovereign spreads rise among the most vulnerable EMDEs caused by capital outflows to safe havens as investor risk aversion increases.

unexpected movements in the CBOE Volatility Index (VIX), capture volatile financial market expectations surrounding the pandemic's project-ed evolution. In the severe downside scenario, a large spike in volatility, coupled with a sharp and unexpected reduction in credit supply, are used to simulate the economic consequences of wide-spread financial crisis.[5] In all scenarios, shocks to financial conditions notably affect real activity domestically, and those that occur in major financial centers such as the United States are assumed to spill over to other countries via the model's financial channels.

References

Agrawala, S., D. Dussaux, and N. Monti. 2020. "What Policies for Greening the Crisis Response and Economic Recovery? Lessons Learned from Past Green Stimulus Measures and Implications for the Covid-19 Crisis." OECD Environment Working Paper 164, OECD, Paris.

Altavilla, C., F. Barbiero, M. Boucinha, and L. Burlon. 2020. "The Great Lockdown: Pandemic Response Policies and Bank Lending Conditions." Working Paper Series 2465, European Central Bank, Frankfurt.

Antràs, P. 2020. "De-Globalisation? Global Value Chains in the Post-COVID-19 Age." NBER Working Paper 28115, National Bureau of Economic Research, Cambridge, MA.

Apedo-Amah, M. C., B. Avdiu, X. Cirera, M. Cruz, E. Davies, A. Grover, L. Iacovone, et al. 2020. "Unmasking the Impact of COVID-19 on Businesses: Firm Level Evidence from Across the World." Policy Research Working Paper 9434, World Bank, Washington, DC.

Arslan, Y., M. Drehmann, and B. Hofmann. 2020. "Central Bank Bond Purchases in Emerging Market Economies." BIS Bulletin No. 20, Bank for International Settlements, Basel, Switzerland.

Arteta, C., M. A. Kose, F. Ohnsorge, and M. Stocker. 2015. "The Coming U.S. Interest Rate Tightening Cycle: Smooth Sailing or Stormy Waters?" Policy Research Note 15/02, World Bank, Washington, DC.

---

[5] The VIX index rises to an average of 53 over 2021Q2 and 2021Q3 and credit spreads increase by 424 basis points on average over the same period. Exchange rates in EMDEs depreciate, reflecting the flight to safe havens.

Arthi, V., and J. Parman. 2020. "Disease, Downturns, and Wellbeing: Economic History and the Long-Run Impacts of Covid-19." NBER Working Paper 27805, National Bureau of Economic Research, Cambridge, MA.

Asonuma, T., M. Chamon, A. Erce, and A. Sasahara. 2020. "Costs of Sovereign Defaults: Restructuring Strategies and the Credit-Investment Channel." https://ssrn.com/abstract=3557035.

Astebro, T., S. Braguinsky, and Y. Ding. 2020. "Declining Business Dynamism among Our Best Opportunities: The Role of the Burden of Knowledge." NBER Working Paper 27787, National Bureau of Economic Research, Cambridge, MA.

Auerbach, A., and Y. Gorodnichenko. 2015. "How Powerful Are Fiscal Multipliers in Recessions?" NBER Reporter 2015 Number 2: Research Summary. National Bureau of Economic Research Cambridge, MA.

Avellan, L., J. A. Galindo, and J. Leon-Diaz. 2020. "The Role of Institutional Quality on the Effects of Fiscal Stimulus." IDB Working Paper Series 01113, Inter-American Development Bank, Washington, DC.

Azcona, G., A. Bhatt, S. E. Davies, S. Harman, J. Smith, and C. Wenham. 2020. "Spotlight on Gender, COVID-19 and the SDGs: Will the Pandemic Derail Hard-won Progress on Gender Equality?" United Nations Entity for Gender Equality and the Empowerment of Women, Geneva.

Azevedo, J. P., A. Hasan, D. Goldemberg, S. A. Iqbal, and K. Geven. 2020. "Simulating the Potential Impacts of Covid-19 School Closures on Schooling and Learning Outcomes: A Set of Global Estimates." Policy Research Working Paper 9284, World Bank, Washington, DC.

Babina, T., A. Bernstein, and F. Mezzanotti. 2020. "Crisis Innovation." NBER Working Paper 27851, National Bureau of Economic Research, Cambridge, MA.

Banerjee, R. N., and B. Hofmann. 2020. "Corporate Zombies: Anatomy and Life Cycle." BIS Working Paper 882, Bank for International Settlements, Basel.

Banerjee, R. N., E. Kharroubi, and U. Lewrick. 2020. "Bankruptcies, Unemployment and Reallocation from Covid-19." *BIS Bulletin*, No. 31, Bank for International Settlements, Basel.

Banerjee, R. N., G. Cornelli, and E. Zakrajšek. 2020. "The outlook for business bankruptcies." *BIS Bulletin*, No. 30, Bank for International Settlements, Basel.

Kose, M. A., P. Nagle, F. Ohnsorge, and N. Sugawara. 2020. *Global Waves of Debt: Causes and Consequences.* Washington, DC: World Bank.

Kose, M. A., and F. Ohnsorge, eds. 2019. *A Decade after the Global Recession.* Washington, DC: World Bank.

Kose, M. A., F. Ohnsorge, and N. Sugawara. 2020. "Benefits and Costs of Debt: The Dose Makes the Poison." Policy Research Working Paper 9166, World Bank, Washington, DC.

Kose, M. A., N. Sugawara, M. E. Terrones. 2020. "Global Recessions." Policy Research Working Paper 9172, World Bank, Washington, DC.

Kozlowski, J., L. Veldkamp, and V. Venkateswaran. 2020. "Scarring Body and Mind: The Long-Term Belief-Scarring Effects of COVID-19." NBER Working Paper 27439, National Bureau of Economic Research, Cambridge, MA.

Kubota, M., and A. Zeufack. 2020. "Assessing the Returns on Investment in Data Openness and Transparency." Policy Research Working Paper 9139, World Bank, Washington, DC.

Laeven, L., and F. Valencia. 2020. "Systemic Banking Crises Database II." *IMF Economic Review* 68 (2): 307-361.

Lakner, C., D. G. Mahler, M. Negre Rossignoli, and E. B. Prydz. 2020. "How Much Does Reducing Inequality Matter for Global Poverty?" Global Poverty Monitoring Technical Note 13, World Bank, Washington, DC.

Lakner, C., N. Yonzan, D. G. Mahler, R. A. Aguilar, and H. Wu. 2021. "Updated Estimates of the Impact of COVID-19 on Global Poverty: Looking Back at 2020 and the Outlook for 2021." *Data Blog*, January 5, 2021. https://blogs.worldbank.org/opendata.

Lazarus, J. V., S. C. Ratzan, A. Palayew, L. O. Gostin, H. J. Larson, K. Rabin, S. Kimball, and A. El-Mohandes. 2020. "A Global Survey of Potential Acceptance of a COVID-19 Vaccine." October 20. *Nature Medicine.* https://doi.org/10.1038/s41591-020-1124-9.

Li, C., and F. Lalani. 2020. "The COVID-19 Pandemic has Changed Education Forever. This is How." WEforum.org, April 29. https://www.weforum.org/agenda/2020/04/coronavirus-education-global-covid19-online-digital-learning/.

Lorenzoni, L., A. Marino, D. Morgan, and Ch. James. 2019. "Health Spending Projections to 2030: New Results Based on a Revised OECD Methodology." Organisation for Economic Co-operation and Development, Paris.

Loughran, T., and B. McDonald. 2011. "When Is a Liability Not a Liability? Textual Analysis, Dictionaries, and 10-Ks." *The Journal of Finance* 66 (1): 35-65.

Malpass, D. 2020. "Debt and Investment Transparency for Fetter Outcomes." *Voices* (blog), June 19, 2020, World Bank, Washington, DC.

Martins, V. J. B., T. M. M. Toledo Florêncio, L. P. Grillo, Maria do Carmo P. Franco, P. A. Martins, A. P. G. Clemente, C. D. L. Santos, M. de Fatima A. Vieira, and A. L. Sawaya. 2011. "Long-Lasting Effects of Undernutrition." *International Journal of Environmental Research and Public Health* 8 (6): 1817-46.

Mattoo, A., N. Rocha, and M. Ruta. 2020. *Handbook of Deep Trade Agreements.* Washington, DC: World Bank.

Mbaye, S., M. M. Moreno-Badia, and K. Chae. 2018. "Bailing Out the People? When Private Debt Becomes Public." IMF Working Paper 2018/141, International Monetary Fund, Washington, DC.

McKinsey. 2016. "Bridging Global Infrastructure Gaps." June. McKinsey Global Institute. https://www.mckinsey.com/business-functions/operations/our-insights/bridging-global-infrastructure-gaps.

McKinsey. 2020. "Saving our livelihoods from COVID-19: Toward an economic recovery." McKinsey & Company, April 19. https://www.mckinsey.com/industries/public-and-social-sector/our-insights/saving-our-livelihoods-from-covid-19-toward-an-economic-recovery#.

Mühleisen, M., V. Klyuev, and S. Sanya. 2020. "Courage under Fire: Policy Responses in Emerging Market and Developing Economies to the COVID-19 Pandemic." *IMF Blog*, June 3, 2020. https://blogs.imf.org/2020/06/03/courage-under-fire-policy-responses-in-emerging-market-and-developing-economies-to-the-covid-19-pandemic/.

Nier, E., and T. T. Olafsson. 2020. "Main Operational Aspects for Macroprudential Policy Relaxation." Special Series on COVID-19. September. International Monetary Fund, Washington, DC.

OECD (Organisation for Economic Co-operation and Development). 2020a. *Policy Responses to Coronavirus (Covid-19) Tourism Policy Responses to the coronavirus (Covid-19).* Paris: OECD.

OECD (Organisation for Economic Co-operation and Development). 2020b. "Building Back Better: A Sustainable, Resilient Recovery After COVID-19." OECD Policy Responses to Coronavirus (COVID-19). OECD, Paris.

OECD (Organisation for Economic Co-operation and Development). 2020c. "Job Retention Schemes During the COVID-19 Lockdown and Beyond." OECD Policy Responses to Coronavirus (COVID-19). OECD, Paris.

OECD (database). "Quarterly National Accounts: GDP-expenditure Approach." Organisation for Economic Co-operation and Development. Accessed on December 16, 2020. https://stats.oecd.org.

OECD Infrastructure Investment (database). Organisation for Economic Co-operation and Development. Accessed on December 16, 2020. https://doi.org/10.1787/b06ce3ad-en.

OECD.stat (database). Organisation for Economic Co-operation and Development. Global Health Expenditure Database. Accessed on December 2, 2020. https://stats.oecd.org.

Okonjo-Iweala, N., B. S. Coulibaly, T. Thiam, D. Kaberuka, V. Songwe, S. Masiyiwa, L. Mushikiwabo, and C. Duarte. 2020. "Africa Needs Debt Relief to Fight COVID-19." Project Syndicate Op-ed. https://www.project-syndicate.org/commentary/africa-needs-debt-relief-to-fight-covid19-by-ngozi-okonjo-iweala-and-brahima-coulibaly-2020-04.

Our World in Data (database). "Coronavirus Pandemic (COVID-19)." Accessed December 16, 2020. https://ourworldindata.org/coronavirus.

Our World in Data (database). "How Epidemiological Models of COVID-19 Help Us Estimate the True Number of Infections." Accessed December 16, 2020. https://ourworldindata.org/covid-models.

Oxford Economics. 2019. "The Oxford Global Economic Model." July. Oxford Economics, Oxford, U.K.

Peisakhin, L., and P. Pinto. 2010. "Is Transparency an Effective Anti-Corruption Strategy? Evidence from a Field Experiment in India." *Regulation and Governance* 4 (3): 261-280.

Pfizer. 2020. "Pfizer and BioNTech Announce Vaccine Candidate Against COVID-19 Achieved Success in First Interim Analysis from Phase 3 Study." November 9. https://www.pfizer.com/news/press-release/press-release-detail/pfizer-and-biontech-announce-vaccine-candidate-against.

Powell, J. H. 2020. "New Economic Challenges and the Fed's Monetary Policy Review." Board of Governors of the Federal Reserve System, August 27. https://www.federalreserve.gov/newsevents/speech/powell20200827a.htm.

Quayyum, S. N., and R. K. Kpodar. 2020. "Supporting Migrants and Remittances as COVID-19 Rages On." *IMF Blog*, September 11, 2020. https://blogs.imf.org/2020/09/11/supporting-migrants-and-remittances-as-covid-19-rages-on/.

Ramey, V. A. 2020. "The Macroeconomic Consequences of Infrastructure Investment." NBER Working Paper 27625, National Bureau of Economic Research, Cambridge, MA.

Reinhart, C., and V. Reinhart. 2020. "The Pandemic Depression: The Global Economy Will Never Be the Same." *Foreign Affairs*, September/October. https://www.foreignaffairs.com/articles/united-states/2020-08-06/coronavirus-depression-global-economy.

Reinhart, C., V. Reinhart, and K. Rogoff. 2015. "Dealing with Debt." *Journal of International Economics* 96 (S1): S43-S55.

Reinhart, C., and M. Sbrancia. 2015. "The Liquidation of Government Debt." *Economic Policy* 30 (82): 291-333.

Reinhart, C., and C. Trebesch. 2016. "Sovereign Debt Relief and its Aftermath." *Journal of the European Economic Association* 14 (1): 215-251.

Rieffel, L. 2003. *Restructuring Sovereign Debt: The Case for Ad Hoc Machinery*. Washington, DC: Brookings Institution Press.

Rivetti, D. 2020. "Visualizing debt transparency." *Data Blog*, World Bank, July 13 2020. https://blogs.worldbank.org/opendata/visualizing-debt-transparency.

Sala-i-Martin, X., G. Doppelhofer, and R. Miller. 2004. "Determinants of Long-Term Growth: A Bayesian Averaging of Classical Estimates (BACE) Approach." *American Economic Review* 94 (4): 813-835.

Schünemann, H. J., E. A. Akl, R. Chou, D. K. Chu, M. Loeb, T. Lotfi, R. A. Mustafa, et al. 2020. "Use of Facemasks During the COVID-19 Pandemic." *The Lancet Respiratory Medicine* 8 (10).

Shetty, S. 2020. "Accelerating Progress of Low-Income Countries Towards the SDGs: Balancing Realism and

Ambition in a Post-COVID-19 World." CGD Policy Paper 194, Center for Global Development, Washington, DC.

Shmis, T., A. Sava, J. E. N. Teixeira, and H. A. Patrinos. 2020. "Response Note to COVID-19 in Europe and Central Asia: Policy and Practice Recommendations." World Bank, Washington, DC.

Smith, A. J. P., M. W. Jones, J. T. Abatzoglou, J. G. Canadell, and R. A. Betts. 2020. "Climate Change Increases the Risk of Wildfires." September. *ScienceBrief Review.* https://news.sciencebrief.org/wildfires-sep2020-update/.

Staal, A., I. Fetzer, L. Wang-Erlandsson, J. H. C. Bosmans, S. C. Dekker, E. H. van Nes, J. Rockström, and O. A. Tuinenburg. 2020. "Hysteresis of Tropical Forests in the 21st Century." *Nature Communications* 11 (4978).

Stiglitz, J., and H. Rashid. 2020. "Averting Catastrophic Debt Crises in Developing Countries." CEPR Policy Insight 104, Center for Economic Policy Research, London.

Stone, C. 2020. "Fiscal Stimulus Needed to Fight Recessions: Lessons from the Great Recession." Center on Budget and Policy Priorities, April 16. https://www.cbpp.org/research/economy/fiscal-stimulus-needed-to-fight-recessions.

Strand, J., and M. Toman. 2010. "Green Stimulus, Economic Recovery, and Long-Term Sustainable Development." Policy Research Working Paper 5163, World Bank, Washington, DC.

Stubbs, T., W. Kring, C. Laskaridis, A. Kentikelenis, and K. Gallagher. 2020. "Whatever it Takes? The Global Financial Safety Net, Covid-19, and Developing Countries." *World Development* 137 (January): 105171.

Taskin, T. Forthcoming. "Demand and Supply Shocks During the COVID-19 Recession: Evidence from Earning Calls."

Truman, E. M. 2020. "Sovereign Debt Relief in the Global Pandemic: Lessons from the 1980s." PIIE Policy Brief 20-13, Peterson Institute for International Economics, Washington, DC.

UNCTAD (United Nations Conference on Trade and Development). 2020. *Global Trade Update.* June. Geneva: UNCTAD.

UNESCO (United Nations Educational, Scientific, and Cultural Organization). 2020. "COVID-19 Educational Disruption and Response." https://en.unesco.org/covid19/educationresponse.

UNESCO. "Institute for Statistics" (database). Accessed December 16, 2020. http://data.uis.unesco.org.

U.S. Bureau of Economic Analysis Quarterly (database). "National Data – National Income and Product Account, Personal Income and Outlays." Accessed on December 16, 2020. https://apps.bea.gov/iTable/index_nipa.cfm.

Viollaz, M., and H. Winkler. 2020. "Does the Internet Reduce Gender Gaps? The Case of Jordan." Policy Research Working Paper 9183, World Bank, Washington, DC.

Vivid Economics. 2020. *Greenness of Stimulus Index: An Assessment of COVID-19 Stimulus by G20 Countries and Other Major Economies in Relation to Climate Action and Biodiversity Goals.* https://www.vivideconomics.com/wp-content/uploads/2020/10/201028-GSI-report_October-release.pdf.

Weintraub, R., P. Yadav, and S. Berkley. 2020. "A Covid-19 Vaccine Will Need Equitable, Global Distribution." *Harvard Business Review*, April 2. https://hbr.org/2020/04/a-covid-19-vaccine-will-need-equitable-global-distribution.

WFP (World Food Programme). 2020a. "WFP Global Update on COVID-19: Growing Needs, Response to Date and What's to Come in 2021." November. World Food Programme, Rome.

WFP (World Food Programme). 2020b. "Food Assistance: Cash and In-kind." Accessed in October 23, 2020. https://www.wfp.org/food-assistance.

WHO (World Health Organization). 2020. "Social, Environmental Factors Seen Behind Africa's Low COVID-19 Cases." *WHO Regional Office for Africa* newsletter.

World Bank. 2017. *Global Economic Prospects: A Fragile Recovery.* June. Washington, DC: World Bank.

World Bank. 2018a. *World Development Report 2018: Learning to Realize Education's Promise.* Washington, DC: World Bank.

World Bank. 2018b. *Global Economic Prospects: Broad-based Upturn, but for How Long?* January. Washington, DC: World Bank.

World Bank. 2019. *Global Economic Prospects: Darkening Skies.* January. Washington, DC: World Bank.

World Bank. 2020a. *The African Continental Free Trade Area: Economic and Distributional Effects.* Washington, DC: World Bank.

World Bank. 2020b. *FDI Watch Quarterly Report.* December. Washington, DC: World Bank

World Bank. 2020c. *Commodity Markets Outlook: Persistence of Commodity Shocks.* October. Washington, DC: World Bank.

World Bank. 2020d. *Global Economic Prospects: Pandemic, Recession: The Global Economy in Crisis.* January. Washington, DC: World Bank.

World Bank. 2020e. "World Bank Group's Operational Response to COVID-19 (coronavirus) - Projects List." World Bank Brief. https://www.worldbank.org/en/about/what-we-do/brief/world-bank-group-operational-response-covid-19-coronavirus-projects-list.

World Bank. 2020f. "Saving Lives, Scaling-up Impact and Getting Back on Track." World Bank Group COVID-19 Crisis Response Approach Paper. World Bank, Washington, DC.

World Bank. 2020g. *Africa's Pulse: An Analysis of Issues Shaping Africa's Economic Future.* October. Washington, DC: World Bank.

World Bank. 2020h. *East Asia and Pacific Economic Update: From Containment to Recovery.* October. Washington, DC: World Bank.

World Bank. 2020i. *China Economic Update: Leaning Forward—COVID-19 and China Reform Agenda.* July. Washington, DC: World Bank.

World Bank. 2020j. "COVID-19 Crisis Trough a Migration Lens." Migration and Development Brief 33, World Bank, Washington, DC.

World Bank. 2020k. *Global Economic Prospects: Slow Growth, Policy Challenges.* January. Washington, DC: World Bank.

World Bank. 2020l. *Human Capital Project: Year 2 Progress Report.* Washington, DC: World Bank.

World Bank. 2020m. *Poverty and Shared Prosperity Report 2020: Reversing Reversals of Fortune.* Washington, DC: World Bank.

World Bank. 2020n. "Lasting Scars of the COVID-19 Pandemic." In *Global Economic Prospects,* 143-88. Washington, DC: World Bank.

World Bank. 2020o. "Saving Lives, Scaling-up Impact and Getting Back on Track." World Bank Group COVID-19 Crisis Response Approach Paper, World Bank, Washington, DC.

World Bank. 2020p. *Enhancing Government Effectiveness and Transparency: The Fight Against Corruption.* Washington, DC: World Bank.

World Bank. 2020q. *World Development Report 2020: Trading for Development in the Age of Global Value Chains.* Washington, DC: World Bank.

World Bank. 2020r. *International Debt Statistics 2021.* Washington, DC: World Bank.

World Bank. 2020s. *Protecting People and Economies: Integrated Policy Responses to COVID-19.* Washington, DC: World Bank.

World Bank. 2020t. "COVID 19: Debt Service Suspension Initiative." Brief. World Bank, Washington, DC. Updated on September 15, 2020.

World Bank and IMF (International Monetary Fund). 2018. "G-20 Note: Strengthening Public Debt Transparency: The Role of the IMF and the World Bank." World Bank, Washington, DC: International Monetary Fund, Washington, DC.

World Travel & Tourism Council (database). World Travel & Tourism Council, London, United Kingdom. Accessed December 17, 2020. https://tool.wttc.org.

Zhou, T., and Y. Ji. 2020. "Semiparametric Bayesian Inference for the Transmission Dynamics of COVID-19 with a State-space Model." Department of Public Health Sciences, University of Chicago.

Outlook

Regional growth is projected to accelerate to 7.4 percent in 2021, led by a strong rebound in China (figure 2.1.3.A). This is predicated on the rollout of effective vaccines gathering pace in early 2021 in major economies and somewhat later in other emerging market and developing economies (EMDEs). Effective vaccination will support a gradual improvement in global and regional confidence, consumption, and trade (chapter 1). However, despite the subsiding pandemic and a recovery of domestic and global demand, regional activity is expected to remain somewhat below its pre-pandemic trend by late 2021, reflecting lasting damage caused by the pandemic.

Investment and productivity are expected to remain persistently depressed amid elevated uncertainty (World Bank 2020b). Regional output is expected to remain around 3 percent below pre-pandemic projections in 2022, with these losses being broad-based (figure 2.1.3.B). Cumulatively over 2020-22, output losses are expected to total $1.7 trillion, equivalent to the combined 2019 GDP of Indonesia and Thailand (figures 2.1.3.C.D.E).

Growth in China is projected to accelerate to 7.9 percent this year—1 percentage point above the June forecast—reflecting the release of pent-up demand and a quicker-than-expected resumption of production and exports. Growth is expected to slow to 5.2 percent in 2022, well below its pre-pandemic potential rate, leaving output about 2 percent below pre-pandemic projections (figure 2.1.3.B).

In the rest of the region, the recovery is expected to be more protracted. Following last year's contraction, output in the region excluding China is expected to expand by 4.9 percent in 2021 and 5.2 percent in 2022, to a level around 7.5 percent below pre-pandemic projections, with significant cross-country variations (figure 2.1.3.B). Vietnam was able to control the pandemic at modest human and economic costs and its exports have remained resilient despite global headwinds. The country is projected to suffer an output loss of around 4 percent compared to pre-pandemic

FIGURE 2.1.2 **China: Recent developments**

Following a sharp contraction, the economy returned to growth in 2020Q2, albeit at an uneven pace. Industrial production has recovered much faster than consumption and services. Import growth has lagged a rebound in exports, contributing to widening trade and current account surpluses. Industrial profits have improved, and government revenue has been strengthening. Sizable policy support pushed total debt to new heights.

A. GDP growth

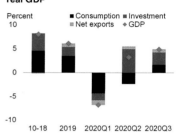

B. GDP growth and contributions to real GDP

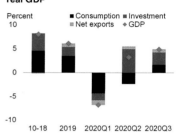

C. Goods import and export growth

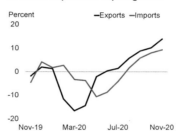

D. Current account and capital flows

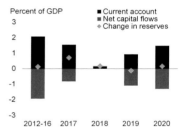

E. Industrial profits and revenue

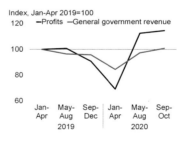

F. Fiscal support measures, government debt

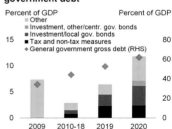

Sources: Haver Analytics; National Bureau of Statistics of China.
A. Quarter-on-quarter annualized change of real GDP in 2015 prices. Year-on-year change of total real industrial value added (2005=100) and non-seasonally adjusted nominal retail sales. Last observation is 2020Q3 for GDP and November 2020 for industrial production and retail sales.
B. Figure shows year-on-year growth and contributions to growth. Data based on official estimates published by the Chinese National Statistics agency. Last observation is November 2020.
C. Values of goods exports and imports. 3-month moving average of year-on-year change. Last observation is November 2020.
D. Net capital flows include errors and omissions. Net capital flows are estimates. 2020 is based on January-September official balance of payments statistics. Last observation is 2020Q3.
E. Figure shows seasonally adjusted profits for all industrial enterprises. Data for January and February are not published by the statistical source due to the Chinese New Year. Haver Analytics calculates figures for January and February by allocating the published February year-to-date figures to January and February using the number of working days as weights. Last observation is November 2020.
F. Figure shows estimated fiscal stimulus by categories, including investment, tax and non-tax measures, and other spending, which includes transfers to households. Augmented fiscal deficit includes net borrowing for the consolidated balance of four separate budgetary accounts: i) public finance budget balance, ii) government finance budget (including investment financed by local government bonds and land sales), iii) social security fund balance, and iv) SOE management fund balance. Government debt includes contingent debt associated with liabilities of local government finance vehicles. Data for 2020 are forecasts.

FIGURE 2.1.3 EAP: Outlook and risks

Regional growth is projected to accelerate to 7.4 percent in 2021, led by a strong rebound in China. The recovery is expected to be more protracted in the rest of the region, with activity in 2022 remaining around 7.5 percent below pre-pandemic projections. Risks are amplified by existing vulnerabilities, including high and rising public and private debt levels.

A. GDP growth

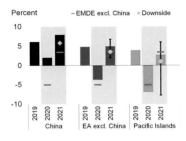

B. GDP level, deviation from January 2020 GEP forecasts

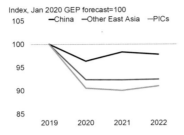

C. Cumulative output losses, two year after recession, China

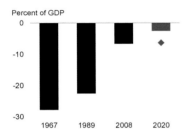

D. Cumulative output losses, two years after recession, East Asia excl. China

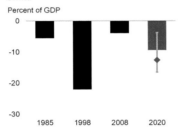

E. Cumulative output losses, two years after recession, Pacific Islands

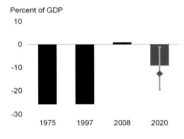

F. Public and private debt, 2020

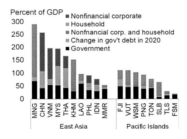

Sources: Bank for International Settlements; Haver Analytics; Institute of International Finance; World Bank.

A. Year-on-year change of real GDP in 2010 prices. "EAP excl. China" includes Cambodia, Indonesia, Lao PDR, Malaysia, Mongolia, Myanmar, Philippines, Thailand, and Vietnam. "Pacific Islands" includes Fiji, Kiribati, Marshall Islands, Micronesia, Palau, Papua New Guinea, Samoa, Solomon Islands, Timor-Leste, Tonga, Tuvalu, and Vanuatu. Aggregate growth rates are calculated using GDP weights in 2010 prices and market exchange rates. Blue lines denote forecast ranges under the baseline scenario. Data in shaded areas are forecasts.

B. "PICs" refers to Pacific Island countries. Deviation from the levels under the baseline scenario implied by January 2020 GEP forecasts.

C.D.E. Cumulative losses of GDP, two years after recession. Data are in percent of respective GDP in year t-1. Years on the horizontal axis show years of recessions. GDP losses are computed as deviations from trend GDP in constant 2010 U.S. dollars, respectively. Trend is assumed to grow at the average GDP growth rate during five years prior to each recession. For 2020, the projections released in the January 2020 *Global Economic Prospects* report are used to construct the trend. Orange lines denote ranges of estimated cumulative loses for the respective sub-groups under the baseline scenario. Red diamonds denote the losses under the downside scenario.

F. Country code definitions are available at https//wwwiban.com/country-codes. Chart shows a projected stock of government and private debt. Includes inter-company loans. Private debt stock is based on 2019 data and estimated projections for selected major economies, including China, Indonesia, Malaysia, the Philippines, and Vietnam. Public debt data for 2020 are forecasts. Last observation in 2020Q1.

---

projections by 2022. In contrast, Pacific Island countries have been largely spared by the pandemic, but have been devastated by the collapse in global tourism and travel. These economies are expected to remain around 9 percent below their pre-pandemic projected level. The cumulative output loss over 2020-22 is estimated to be around ten percent of its 2019 level (figure 2.1.3.E).

The near-term outlook remains highly uncertain. The recovery is expected to be uneven and fragile, and the materialization of a number of downside risks could derail the projected regional economic recovery (chapter 1, box 1.4). The downside scenario of a delayed vaccine rollout globally features a much weaker and more protracted recovery, with regional growth limited to 0.6 percent in 2021 and 4.7 percent on average in 2021-22 (figure 2.1.3.A). Weaker growth would worsen debt sustainability.

The pandemic's effects on demand by households, firms, and governments are likely to be long-lasting. For example, households may continue to maintain a high level of precautionary savings and avoid services that depend on face-to-face contact. The pandemic is also expected to leave lasting scars on productivity and potential growth in the region. The pandemic has weakened investment, and human capital has been eroded by disruptions in education and prolonged unemployment.

The pandemic's impact on productivity is likely to compound the deceleration in regional potential growth that was already apparent prior to the pandemic because of the policy-induced investment slowdown in China and population aging in China, Thailand, and Vietnam (World Bank 2018). The pre-pandemic baseline projected that EAP potential growth would decline by up to 2 percentage points—from around 8 percent on average in 2010-19 to below 6 percent in 2020-2029. Considering the negative impact of COVID-19 on investment, productivity, and labor participation, regional potential growth would decline more sharply to below 5 percent on average in 2020-29, with the decline mostly the result of weaker labor input and subdued investment (chapter 3, world Bank 2020a).

additional policy rate cuts, especially for countries with inflation near or above target ranges. Some countries have also used unconventional policies, such as asset purchases (Croatia, Hungary, Poland, Romania, Turkey).

Outlook

The regional economy is projected to expand by a moderate 3.3 percent in 2021, as the resurgence of COVID-19 causes persistent disruptions to activity. The regional forecast has been downgraded in 2021, reflecting downward revisions in nearly 75 percent of ECA's economies amid the rapid spread of the virus and elevated geopolitical tensions. Growth is expected to pick up in 2022, to 3.9 percent, as the economic effects of the pandemic gradually wane and the recovery in trade and investment gathers momentum (tables 2.2.1 and 2.2.2). Despite the improvement in 2022, GDP is projected to remain over 3 percent below pre-pandemic forecasts. Five or more years of per capita income gains are estimated to have been erased due to the pandemic in about one-fifth of the economies in 2020 (figure 2.2.2.A). The pandemic is also expected to further exacerbate the slowdown in productivity growth over the long run, through its damaging effects on investment and human capital accumulation (chapter 3; Dieppe 2020; World Bank 2020e).

The outlook is predicated on the distribution of effective vaccines gathering pace in early 2021 in advanced economies and major EMDEs, including Russia, then later in the year for others. It also assumes that geopolitical tensions will not re-escalate in the region. Due to considerable uncertainty surrounding the pandemic and subsequent growth forecasts, a downside scenario is considered, where the vaccine rollout is delayed by one to two quarters and financial conditions tighten substantially (figure 2.2.2.B; box 1.4).

Growth in Russia is envisioned to pick up only modestly in 2021, to 2.6 percent, as the country grapples with a renewed acceleration in COVID-19 infections. Vaccine deployment in early 2021, however, is expected to aid the recovery, with growth eventually rising to 3 percent in 2022. Growth will be further supported by a rise in

FIGURE 2.2.2 ECA: Outlook and risks

The recovery in ECA is forecast to be a modest 3.3 percent in 2021 as the region recovers from the current rapid acceleration in COVID-19 cases. Growth is then expected to rise to 3.9 percent in 2022 as the impact of the pandemic wanes and domestic demand strengthens. The pandemic is expected to erase at least five years of per capita income gains in about a fifth of the region's economies and to raise the poverty headcount. The region's recovery, however, is constrained by structural challenges, heightened financial pressures, and limited fiscal space. In addition, the recovery could be interrupted by a re-escalation of geopolitical tensions. In Central Europe, however, policies that increase the absorption of EU structural funds could boost investment.

A. Years of per capita income gains reversed in 2020

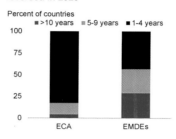

B. Growth in ECA

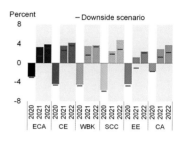

C. GDP in the Russian Federation and EMDEs

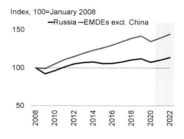

D. Policy uncertainty

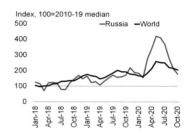

E. Average government debt levels in ECA, 2021-22

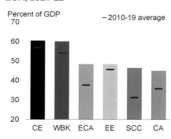

F. EU structural funds to Central Europe

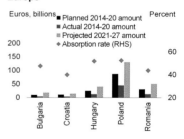

Sources: Baker, Bloom, and Davis (2015); International Monetary Fund; World Bank.
Note: CA = Central Asia; CE = Central Europe; ECA = Europe and Central Asia; EE = Eastern Europe; EMDEs = emerging market and developing economies; SCC = South Caucasus; WBK = Western Balkans. Aggregates calculated using U.S. dollar GDP per capita at 2010 prices and market exchange rates. Shaded areas indicate forecasts.
A. Figure shows the percentage of EMDEs by number of years of lost per capita income gains, measured as the difference between 2020 and the latest year of per capita income that is below 2020 value over the 2000-19 period.
B. Figure shows the downside scenario as presented in box 1.4.
D. Policy uncertainty is the Economic Policy Uncertainty Index computed by Baker, Bloom, and Davis (2015). Black horizontal line denotes 2010-19 median.
E. Aggregates are 2021-22 unweighted averages of general government gross debt. Horizontal line corresponds to 2010-19 unweighted averages. Sample includes 23 ECA countries.
F. Figure shows the total amount of EU funds that were planned to be disbursed as part of the Multiannual Financial Framework 2014-20, the total net payments that occurred, and the resulting absorption rate calculated as the ratio of net payments over planned amount. Absorption rates are calculated over 2014-20 but funds could continue to be absorbed over the next three years, thus final rates could be higher. Projected 2021-27 amount calculated using the pre-allocated amount of the Multiannual Financial Framework 2014-20, which does not include Next Generation EU funds.

industrial-commodity prices, as well as the continuation of supportive policy measures. These include sustaining the policy interest rate at a record low and more accommodative fiscal policy. As has been the case in past recoveries, the rebound will be constrained by structural rigidities (figure 2.2.2.C).

Turkey's economy avoided a contraction in 2020, with activity growing an estimated 0.5 percent amid a substantial expansion in credit. Growth is projected to rise to 4.5 percent in 2021, as a recovery in domestic demand takes hold. Despite hikes in the policy interest rate, the lira hit new lows against the U.S. dollar, which eroded balance sheets and limited the space available for additional countercyclical policy responses. The outlook has been downgraded as the sharp acceleration in new COVID-19 cases, weaker-than-expected international tourism, and tighter-than-anticipated monetary policy weigh on the recovery.

Growth in Central Europe is envisioned to firm in 2021, to 3.6 percent, supported by the recovery in trade as activity rebounds in the euro area. The outlook has been downgraded, however, amid the recent surge in COVID-19 cases. Exceptional policy accommodation is expected to continue throughout 2021, including near-zero policy interest rates (Hungary, Poland). Among the ECA subregions, fiscal support packages have been largest in Central Europe, at 9 percent of GDP, reflecting sizable discretionary measures and loan guarantees and other credit measures. The European Union (EU) structural fund package to Central Europe as part of its COVID-19 response could help support medium-term growth.

Growth in the Western Balkans is expected to rebound to 3.5 percent in 2021, assuming that consumer and business confidence are restored as COVID-19 is brought under control and that political instability eases. Tourism-dependent economies, particularly Albania and Montenegro, are projected to experience a more robust rebound in activity than the subregion's other countries. Rising fiscal liabilities in the subregion have reduced space for fiscal support, while at the same time, government budgets will be further stretched by additional spending necessary to counter the damaging economic effects of the COVID-19 outbreak. Despite these headwinds, medium-term growth and productivity in Albania and North Macedonia should be boosted by accelerating structural reforms in preparation for EU membership, assuming negotiations surrounding the accession process are not further delayed (Rovo 2020; World Bank 2020f). The subregion is also expected to benefit from the EU's recently adopted Economic and Investment Plan, which will mobilize funding to support sustainable connectivity, human capital, competitiveness and inclusive growth, and green and digital transition.

The sub-regional economy of Eastern Europe is projected to rise to a tepid 1.3 percent in 2021, reflecting continued challenges related to the pandemic, heightened political tensions in Belarus, subdued domestic demand, and ongoing structural weakness. Substantial forecast downgrades in Eastern Europe were driven by the intensification of political tensions and the associated deterioration in investor sentiment, which is expected to weigh heavily on investment.

Growth in the South Caucasus subregion is projected to rise to 2.5 percent in 2021, as the shocks related to the pandemic and conflict dissipate, and as tourism recovers alongside improving consumer and business confidence. Activity is expected to expand in Azerbaijan over the forecast horizon as oil prices stabilize and the economy benefits from investment and reconstruction spending. The peace statement between Armenia and Azerbaijan is expected to help alleviate geopolitical tensions in the region.

In Central Asia, growth is expected to recover to 3 percent in 2021, supported by a modest rise in commodity prices and foreign direct investment as the subregion deepens its integration with China's Belt and Road Initiative. Forecasts for a rebound, however, have been downgraded due to rising policy uncertainty in Central Asia, particularly in the Kyrgyz Republic, following political tensions and social unrest.

Risks

Risks to the outlook are markedly tilted to the downside, despite the development of multiple COVID-19 vaccines with high efficacy rates in trials. The near-term growth outlook for ECA is clouded by the sharp rise in uncertainty over the surge in new cases, which has contributed to social unrest in some countries, as well as the risk of geopolitical tensions re-escalating (figure 2.2.2.D). Several euro area countries have been forced to re-impose nationwide lockdowns, which may weaken external demand in ECA. Similarly, rising cases within ECA could also lead to more stringent restrictions and responses by households and firms, which would weigh on private consumption and investment. If the downturn in travel is prolonged, growth outcomes could be much weaker, particularly in tourism-dependent economies (Central Europe, Turkey, the Western Balkans). Delays in the production, procurement, or distribution of COVID-19 vaccines, lower-than-expected vaccine effectiveness, or the continuation of pandemic-related restrictions could also delay the economic recovery. The challenges of distribution and inoculation are particularly elevated in Central Asia, where health care capacity is weaker than in other parts of ECA.

In the context of capital outflows, foreign exchange reserves have been drawn down sharply in some ECA economies, constraining the capacity of central banks to buffer the impact of further negative external shocks. A sudden reassessment of investor sentiment could lead to cascading defaults and rising non-performing loans, especially given the sharp increase in government debt (figure 2.2.2.E; chapter 1). Despite exceptional liquidity support, corporate balance sheet pressures in ECA have continued to rise in the wake of COVID-19 due to lower earnings and substantial exchange-rate depreciation, putting strain on the banking sector. For banks that are undercapitalized or operate in countries with narrow fiscal space, borrower assistance has intensified stress (Demirgüç-Kunt, Pedraza, and Ruiz-Ortega 2020). The pandemic has also amplified the risk that contingent liabilities will be realized, which could further strain public finances.

The pandemic also poses medium-term risks if protracted spells of unemployment and school closures have a significant impact on human capital development through lost opportunities to acquire skills and gain knowledge (Dieppe 2020; Shmis et al. 2020; World Bank 2020e). Renewed school closures in response to a worsening of the pandemic would exacerbate these risks. Investment prospects have eroded further in response to the slowdown in capital expenditures, with the exception of Central Europe. The sizable EU structural funds package to Central Europe as part of its COVID-19 response could help mitigate the weakness in investment, but the boost could be tempered by low absorption of funds due to challenges surrounding administrative capacity and governance (figure 2.2.2.F).

The rise in geopolitical tensions in ECA also presents headwinds to growth. An unraveling of the peace statement between Armenia and Azerbaijan, further political pressures in Belarus or the Kyrgyz Republic, or renewed involvement by the region's largest economies in conflicts in Libya, the Syrian Arab Republic, or Ukraine could trigger additional sanctions and generate substantial financial market pressures. A protracted deterioration in investor sentiment—whether from uncertainty related to the pandemic, geopolitical tensions, or delays in EU accession negotiations—could have material implications for ECA and erode the outlook (World Bank 2016).

TABLE 2.2.1 Europe and Central Asia forecast summary

(Real GDP growth at market prices in percent, unless indicated otherwise)

Percentage point differences from June 2020 projections

	2018	2019	2020e	2021f	2022f	2020e	2021f
EMDE ECA, GDP[1]	**3.4**	**2.3**	**-2.9**	**3.3**	**3.9**	**1.8**	**-0.3**
GDP per capita (U.S. dollars)	2.9	1.9	-3.2	3.1	3.7	1.8	-0.3
EMDE ECA, GDP excl. Turkey	3.5	2.7	-4.0	2.9	3.5	1.0	-0.3
(Average including countries with full national accounts and balance of payments data only)[2]							
EMDE ECA, GDP[2]	3.3	2.1	-2.9	3.4	3.9	2.0	-0.3
PPP GDP	3.4	2.2	-3.0	3.3	3.8	1.8	-0.4
Private consumption	3.2	3.1	-3.6	3.6	3.0	0.1	0.7
Public consumption	3.0	3.0	3.2	-0.6	0.9	-2.0	-2.6
Fixed investment	2.8	0.4	-6.6	4.8	6.6	1.9	-1.9
Exports, GNFS[3]	5.8	2.6	-13.5	5.9	5.9	-1.7	1.9
Imports, GNFS[3]	3.3	3.6	-11.4	6.8	7.3	-0.7	2.1
Net exports, contribution to growth	1.0	-0.2	-1.3	-0.1	-0.2	-0.4	-0.1
Memo items: GDP							
Commodity exporters[4]	2.8	1.9	-3.9	2.7	3.2	1.2	-0.2
Commodity importers[5]	3.9	2.6	-2.0	3.9	4.5	2.3	-0.4
Central Europe[6]	4.9	4.3	-4.4	3.6	4.2	0.6	-0.2
Western Balkans[7]	4.0	3.5	-4.5	3.5	3.7	-1.3	-1.1
Eastern Europe[8]	3.4	2.6	-4.4	1.3	2.5	-0.8	-1.1
South Caucasus[9]	2.7	3.6	-5.7	2.5	4.8	-2.6	-0.5
Central Asia[10]	4.5	4.9	-1.7	3.0	3.8	0.0	-0.7
Russia Federation	2.5	1.3	-4.0	2.6	3.0	2.0	-0.1
Turkey	3.0	0.9	0.5	4.5	5.0	4.3	-0.5
Poland	5.4	4.5	-3.4	3.5	4.3	0.8	0.7

Source: World Bank.

Note: e = estimate; f = forecast; PPP = purchasing power parity; EMDE = emerging market and developing economy. World Bank forecasts are frequently updated based on new information and changing (global) circumstances. Consequently, projections presented here may differ from those contained in other Bank documents, even if basic assessments of countries' prospects do not differ at any given moment in time. Due to lack of reliable data of adequate quality, the World Bank is currently not publishing economic output, income, or growth data for Turkmenistan, and Turkmenistan is excluded from cross-country macroeconomic aggregates.

1. GDP and expenditure components are measured in 2010 prices and market exchange rates.

2. Aggregates presented here exclude Azerbaijan, Bosnia and Herzegovina, Kazakhstan, Kosovo, Montenegro, Serbia, Tajikistan, and Turkmenistan, for which data limitations prevent the forecasting of GDP components.

3. Exports and imports of goods and nonfactor services (GNFS).

4. Includes Armenia, Azerbaijan, Kazakhstan, the Kyrgyz Republic, Kosovo, the Russian Federation, Tajikistan, Ukraine, and Uzbekistan.

5. Includes Albania, Belarus, Bosnia and Herzegovina, Bulgaria, Croatia, Georgia, Hungary, Moldova, Montenegro, North Macedonia, Poland, Romania, Serbia, and Turkey.

6. Includes Bulgaria, Croatia, Hungary, Poland, and Romania.

7. Includes Albania, Bosnia and Herzegovina, Kosovo, Montenegro, North Macedonia, and Serbia.

8. Includes Belarus, Moldova, and Ukraine.

9. Includes Armenia, Azerbaijan, and Georgia.

10. Includes Kazakhstan, the Kyrgyz Republic, Tajikistan, and Uzbekistan.

TABLE 2.2.2 Europe and Central Asia country forecasts[1]

(Real GDP growth at market prices in percent, unless indicated otherwise)

Percentage point differences from June 2020 projections

	2018	2019	2020e	2021f	2022f	2020e	2021f
Albania	4.1	2.2	-6.7	5.1	4.4	-1.7	-3.7
Armenia	5.2	7.6	-8.0	3.1	4.5	-5.2	-1.8
Azerbaijan	1.5	2.2	-5.0	1.9	4.5	-2.4	-0.3
Belarus	3.1	1.2	-1.6	-2.7	0.9	2.4	-3.7
Bosnia and Herzegovina[2]	3.7	2.7	-4.0	2.8	3.5	-0.8	-0.6
Bulgaria	3.1	3.7	-5.1	3.3	3.7	1.1	-1.0
Croatia	2.7	2.9	-8.6	5.4	4.2	0.7	0.0
Georgia	4.9	5.1	-6.0	4.0	6.0	-1.2	0.0
Hungary	5.1	4.6	-5.9	3.8	4.3	-0.9	-0.7
Kazakhstan	4.1	4.5	-2.5	2.5	3.5	0.5	0.0
Kosovo	3.8	4.2	-8.8	3.7	4.9	-4.3	-1.5
Kyrgyz Republic	3.8	4.5	-8.0	3.8	4.5	-4.0	-1.8
Moldova	4.3	3.6	-7.2	3.8	3.7	-4.1	-0.2
Montenegro	5.1	4.1	-14.9	6.1	3.9	-9.3	1.3
North Macedonia	2.7	3.6	-5.1	3.6	3.5	-3.0	-0.3
Poland	5.4	4.5	-3.4	3.5	4.3	0.8	0.7
Romania	4.4	4.1	-5.0	3.5	4.1	0.7	-1.9
Russian Federation	2.5	1.3	-4.0	2.6	3.0	2.0	-0.1
Serbia	4.4	4.2	-2.0	3.1	3.4	0.5	-0.9
Tajikistan	7.3	7.5	2.2	3.5	5.5	4.2	-0.2
Turkey	3.0	0.9	0.5	4.5	5.0	4.3	-0.5
Ukraine	3.4	3.2	-5.5	3.0	3.1	-2.0	0.0
Uzbekistan	5.4	5.6	0.6	4.3	4.5	-0.9	-2.3

Source: World Bank.

Note: e = estimate; f = forecast. World Bank forecasts are frequently updated based on new information and changing (global) circumstances. Consequently, projections presented here may differ from those contained in other Bank documents, even if basic assessments of countries' prospects do not significantly differ at any given moment in time.

1. Data are based on GDP measured in 2010 prices and market exchange rates, unless indicated otherwise.

2. GDP growth rate at constant prices is based on production approach.

LATIN AMERICA and THE CARIBBEAN

Latin America and the Caribbean (LAC) has been severely affected by the COVID-19 pandemic, from both a health and an economic perspective. Pandemic-control measures, risk aversion among households and firms, and spillovers from a shrinking global economy resulted in an estimated 6.9 percent GDP contraction in 2020, the deepest among the six emerging market and developing economy (EMDE) regions. A modest recovery to 3.7 percent growth is projected for 2021 as restrictions are relaxed, vaccine rollouts gather pace, oil and metal prices rise, and external conditions improve. Risks to the outlook remain tilted to the downside, however. Key risks include a failure to slow the spread of the pandemic, difficulties distributing a vaccine, external financing stress amid elevated debt, a resurgence of social unrest, and disruptions related to climate change and natural disasters.

Recent developments

COVID-19 has had devastating health and economic impacts in Latin America and the Caribbean (LAC). Although the region is home to less than 10 percent of the global population, it accounts for nearly 20 percent of confirmed cases, and high positive test rates in numerous countries suggest that cases are significantly underreported. Five of the 10 emerging market and developing economies (EMDEs) with the highest COVID-19 deaths per capita are in LAC (Argentina, Brazil, Chile, Mexico, Peru; figure 2.3.1.A).

Outbreaks have spread despite the stringent mitigation measures that were in place for much of 2020 (figure 2.3.1.B). High levels of informal employment, which forced some people to leave their homes to earn income, together with limited enforcement capacity in some areas, may have contributed to noncompliance with restrictions. Outbreaks may also have been aggravated by health system shortcomings, including inequitable access to health care (OECD and World Bank 2020).

The regional economy contracted by an estimated 6.9 percent in 2020 as households and firms

exhibited risk-averse behavior and pandemic-control measures restricted activity in the formal sector. In one out of three LAC economies, GDP is estimated to have contracted by 10 percent or more in 2020, compared to one out of seven of all EMDEs.

Formal employment, hours worked, and labor income dropped sharply (figure 2.3.1.C; ILO 2020b). Women and youth, who are highly represented in the industries most disrupted by the pandemic (hotels, restaurants, and personal services), have borne a disproportionate share of job losses. Households at the lowest end of the income distribution have reported substantially higher job losses than those at the highest end (Bottan, Hoffmann, and Vera-Cossio 2020). Lower incomes have contributed to rising food insecurity (World Food Program 2020). Food insecurity has been exacerbated by higher food price inflation in some countries, and in Central American economies by damage from Hurricanes Eta and Iota (World Bank 2020g).

The region has also suffered from cross-border spillovers. The volume of goods exports dropped 8 percent year-on-year in the first three quarters of 2020. Tourism arrivals came to a halt, with Caribbean economies most exposed. Inflows of worker remittances slowed in numerous countries, but have been remarkably resilient in the

Note: This section was prepared by Dana Vorisek. Research assistance was provided by Hrisyana Doytchinova.

FIGURE 2.3.1 LAC: Recent developments

Latin America and the Caribbean (LAC) has experienced the highest number of COVID-19 infections per capita of the six emerging and developing economy (EMDE) regions, despite stringent mitigation measures. Economic activity indicators and employment plunged in the first half of 2020, and remittance inflows grew more slowly last year in many countries than in previous years. Financing conditions have eased for most economies compared to the start of the pandemic, but are still tighter than a year ago.

A. COVID-19 cases

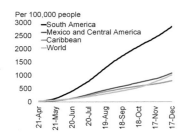

B. Stringency of COVID-19 mitigation measures

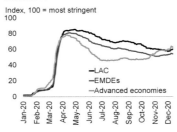

C. Employment

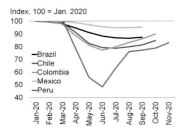

D. Remittance inflows

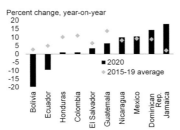

E. Bond spreads

F. Industrial production and retail sales

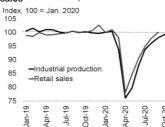

Sources: Central Bank of Bolivia; Central Bank of Colombia; Central American Monetary Council; Hale et al. (2020); Haver Analytics; Johns Hopkins University Coronavirus Resource Center; Mexican Institute of Social Security; Standard & Poor's; World Bank.

Note: EMDEs = emerging market and developing economies; LAC = Latin America and the Caribbean.

A. Lines show cumulative cases per capita. Last observation is December 17, 2020.

B. Lines show unweighted averages. The stringency index refers to the average sub-indexes of nine mitigation measures: school closures, workplace closures, cancellation of public events and public transport, restriction on gatherings, stay-home requirements and restrictions to international and domestic travel and public information campaigns. Sample includes a maximum of 32 LAC countries, 136 EMDEs, and 37 advanced economies. Last observation is December 13, 2020.

C. Data is seasonally adjusted; lines show 3-month moving averages. Last observation is November 2020 for Peru, October 2020 for Chile and Colombia, and September 2020 for Brazil and Mexico. For Peru, employment data covers only the Lima metropolitan area.

D. Percent change is calculated using the sum of January-November inflows to the Dominican Republic, El Salvador, and Guatemala; January-October inflows to Bolivia, Colombia, Honduras, Mexico, and Nicaragua; January-September inflows for Jamaica; and January-June for Ecuador.

E. Lines show medians. Investment grade economies include Chile, Colombia, Mexico, Panama, Peru, Trinidad and Tobago, and Uruguay. Below investment grade economies include Argentina, Belize, Brazil, Costa Rica, the Dominican Republic, Ecuador, El Salvador, Guatemala, and Jamaica. Last observation is December 9, 2020.

F. Lines show GDP-weighted averages of Argentina, Brazil, Chile, Colombia, and Mexico. Retail sales for Argentina are proxied by supermarket sales. Last observation is October 2020 for industrial production and September 2020 for retail sales.

Dominican Republic, Jamaica, Mexico, and Nicaragua, and in some countries inflows have been higher than expected in early 2020 (figure 2.3.1.D). The sharp downturn in energy prices strained output in oil and gas producers (Bolivia, Colombia, Ecuador). In Guyana, offshore oil field development was impeded by the impacts of the pandemic, logistics challenges, and delays in government approvals, leading to substantially weaker growth in 2020 than projected mid-year.

Financial conditions have broadly eased. Sovereign bond spreads have fallen from the peaks reached early in the pandemic yet remain elevated relative to pre-pandemic levels for below-investment-grade issuers (figure 2.3.1.E). Portfolio flows stabilized in the second half of 2020 after the region experienced outflows amounting to about 1 percent of 2019 GDP in the first half. Domestic banks, which were well capitalized at the start of the pandemic, have not shown signs of systemic stress. However, currencies remain notably weaker than a year ago, particularly for Argentina and Brazil.

Activity in the region began to improve in the third quarter of 2020 as pandemic-control measures were loosened somewhat, fiscal and monetary stimulus continued, and external demand picked up. As of September, retail sales and industrial production had nearly returned to January 2020 levels (figure 2.3.1.F). Consumer and business sentiment remain subdued.

Key components of fiscal stimulus programs have included direct payments to households, tax relief and deferrals, business lending programs, and additional health spending. Social transfers have covered a particularly large share of the population of Bolivia, Brazil, Chile, Colombia, the Dominican Republic, and Peru (World Bank 2020h). Increased public spending has been largely financed by public debt issuance, but also by official lending. The monetary policy response has been multipronged, including provision of liquidity; temporary loosening of reserve requirements for banks; policy interest rate cuts; foreign exchange market interventions; and, in Chile and Colombia, quantitative easing programs (chapter 4).

Outlook

The regional economy is projected to grow at a moderate pace of 3.7 percent in 2021 as pandemic mitigation measures are relaxed, COVID-19 vaccine rollouts gather pace, key commodity prices firm, and external conditions improve. Growth will then soften to 2.8 percent in 2022 as the boost from these factors wanes (tables 2.3.1 and 2.3.2). Relative to the size of the regional recession in 2020, the rebound will be muted, and it follows a decade of already sluggish growth (figure 2.3.2.A). In a downside growth scenario, the deployment of COVID-19 vaccines would be delayed, consumer and business confidence would remain depressed, and financial conditions would tighten markedly (box 1.4). In this scenario, growth in LAC would be a mere 1.9 percent in 2021 and 2.3 percent in 2022.

The outlook is predicated on important assumptions that are subject to a greater than usual level of uncertainty. The baseline assumes that COVID-19 vaccination gathers pace during the second half of 2021 and that oil and metal prices will be higher than forecast in June, with oil prices averaging $44 per barrel in 2021 and $50 in 2022.

In Brazil, the recovery in private consumption and investment in the second half of 2020 is expected to continue in early 2021, supported by improving confidence and benign credit conditions, pushing growth to 3 percent in 2021. The rebound is expected to be uneven across sectors; industry and agriculture are expanding more rapidly than the services sector due to a lingering risk aversion among consumers affecting travel, tourism, and restaurants, in particular. Momentum is expected to slow as the year proceeds, in part due to the withdrawal of monetary and fiscal stimulus, bringing growth down to 2.5 percent in 2022.

The growth rebound in Mexico in 2021 is based mainly on higher exports as the U.S. economy picks up and trade policy uncertainty fades after the United States-Mexico-Canada Agreement entered into force in July 2020. The forecast of 3.7

FIGURE 2.3.2 LAC: Outlook and risks

The regional economy is expected to expand by a moderate 3.7 percent in 2021 after a severe contraction in 2020 that erased a decade or more of per capita GDP gains in 40 percent of economies in the region. The impacts of the pandemic are expected to be persistent, weighing on already-slowing potential growth. The materialization of risks related to debt sustainability could hold back the post-pandemic recovery. The sudden increase in poverty in 2020, alongside long-standing concerns about inequality of opportunity and government effectiveness, could contribute to a resurgence of the social unrest the region experienced in late 2019. Disruptions and damages related to climate change and natural disasters are a persistent risk for much of the region.

A. Growth

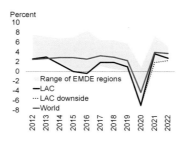

B. Years of per capita GDP gains reversed in 2020

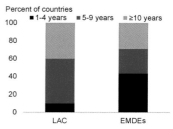

C. Potential growth

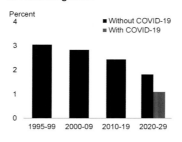

D. Government debt

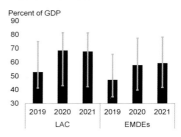

E. Poverty and government effectiveness

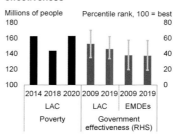

F. Exposure to natural disaster risk, 2019

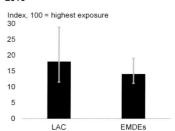

Sources: Bündnis Entwicklung Hilft and Institute for International Law of Peace and Armed Conflict; International Monetary Fund; Lakner et al. (forthcoming); Penn World Table; UN Population Prospects; World Bank (PovcalNet, Worldwide Governance Indicators).
Note: LAC = Latin America and the Caribbean; EMDEs = emerging market and developing economies.
A. Grey area shows minimum and maximum GDP growth in the six EMDE regions.
B. Sample includes 30 LAC economies and 146 EMDEs.
C. Bars show simple averages of annual GDP-weighted average of Argentina, Brazil, Chile, Colombia, Mexico, and Peru during year spans indicated.
D. Bars show medians; lines show interquartile ranges. Sample includes 24 LAC economies (excluding Argentina and República Bolivariana de Venezuela, for which 2020 or 2021 estimates are not available) and 151 EMDEs.
E. Poverty is measured as the share of the population below the poverty line of $5.50 per day in 2011 purchasing power parity terms. "Government effectiveness" measures perceptions of the quality of public services, the quality of the civil service and the degree of its independence from political pressures, the quality of policy formulation and implementation, and the credibility of government commitment to such policies. For government effectiveness, bars show medians and lines show interquartile ranges. For government effectiveness, sample includes 34 LAC economies and 155 EMDEs.

percent growth in 2021 is insufficient to reverse last year's output losses, and is being held back by factors including planned fiscal consolidation and long-standing weakness in investment. Growth is projected to slow to 2.6 percent in 2022 as external demand growth softens and the boost to economic activity from labor market improvements begins to fade.

Argentina's economy is forecast to grow by 4.9 percent this year, which would be the first positive growth rate in four years. A loosening of pandemic mitigation measures and fading uncertainty surrounding the recent debt restructuring are expected to support private consumption and investment. As consumption slows, growth is projected to soften to 1.9 percent in 2022.

In Colombia, growth is projected to reach 4.9 percent in 2021, underpinned by solid domestic demand. The energy sector is expected to benefit from rising oil prices. Growth is projected to be sustained at 4.3 percent in 2022.

Activity in Chile is projected to expand by 4.2 percent in 2021, building on momentum already evident in late 2020. Growth in Peru is poised to recover to 7.6 percent this year after suffering one of the region's deepest recessions in 2020 amid a particularly large COVID-19 outbreak and accompanying mitigation measures, which included lengthy mine closures. Growth in both countries will benefit from rising copper prices and ongoing easy monetary policy, before softening in 2022.

In Central America, growth is forecast to bounce back to 3.6 percent in 2021, underpinned by stronger remittance inflows and more robust export demand, as well as reconstruction after Hurricanes Eta and Iota in November and, in El Salvador, two other severe tropical storms last year. Growth in the Caribbean is projected to rebound to 4.5 percent in 2021, boosted by a partial recovery of tourism to pre-pandemic levels, and with it employment.

Despite a return to growth in the short term, the economic impacts of the pandemic will linger. By 2022, real GDP in LAC is projected to still be

nearly 7 percent below the level projected in January 2020. In half of LAC economies, the recession in 2020 is estimated to have set back per capita GDP to levels last seen five to nine years ago, compared to about one-quarter of all EMDEs, while two-fifths of LAC economies have experienced per capita GDP setbacks of 10 or more years (figure 2.3.2.B).

High levels of uncertainty and tighter financing conditions during the pandemic have led to delays in infrastructure spending and cuts to research and development, hindering future productivity (Dieppe 2020; World Bank 2020i). Human capital is being eroded due to large number of workers being separated from their jobs for a prolonged period and schools being closed. Potential growth in the region, already weakening due in large part to anemic productivity, will be further set back by the pandemic (figure 2.3.2.C).

Risks

Risks to the baseline outlook for LAC are weighted to the downside. Economic activity could be dragged down further by a failure to slow the spread of the pandemic, strains related to debt and external financing, a resurgence of social unrest, deeper-than-expected economic damage from the pandemic in the medium term, and disruptions related to climate change and natural disasters.

An improvement in economic conditions will depend on the extent to which the pandemic can be controlled. Renewed outbreaks; difficulties obtaining or distributing vaccines, especially in countries without domestic production capabilities; or challenges surrounding the efficacy of vaccines could force the reintroduction of mitigation measures, with grave economic consequences. External demand could be curtailed by the reimposition of control measures in major global economies, some of which experienced a resurgence of COVID-19 in late 2020.

Deterioration of investor sentiment is a significant risk to the economic outlook. Fiscal stimulus was necessary to cushion the economic blow of the pandemic, but it has largely depleted limited fiscal space. Government debt in the median LAC economy has risen sharply, from 53 percent of GDP in 2019 to 69 percent in 2020 (figure 2.3.2.D). Creditworthiness has already fallen across the region. Several sovereigns and large corporations have received credit rating downgrades since the start of the pandemic.[1] Policy makers will need to carefully prioritize spending while removing temporary measures that reduced revenues in 2020. A sudden tightening of bond yields, sharp currency depreciation, or further credit downgrades could interrupt capital inflows and make debt servicing significantly more challenging, with possible knock-on stress for domestic banking systems. However, these risks are partly mitigated by increasingly deep local-currency debt markets in some economies. Countries lacking credible medium-term plans to reduce fiscal deficits and debt levels face particular risks related to adverse shifts in market sentiment.

The large income shock caused by the pandemic is estimated to have pushed millions of people in the region into poverty, reversing the long-term downward trend in the poverty headcount (figure 2.3.2.E). Combined with entrenched inequality of opportunity and a worsening perception of government effectiveness over time, the rise in poverty could reignite the social unrest that the region experienced in 2019.

The adverse long-term impacts of the pandemic could be worse than expected. The process of reabsorbing the large number of formal workers who have become unemployed or inactive during the past year could be prolonged, extending the strain of income losses. Knowledge and skills lost during schooling disruptions could impede long-term productivity and earnings potential more than expected. Failure to pursue policies to boost low productivity, such as investments in new technologies and infrastructure, or workforce retraining and skills development programs, could dampen and prolong the economic recovery from the pandemic (Beylis et al. 2020).

Finally, unexpected disruptions related to climate change and natural disasters are a persistent source of severe downside risk for a host of LAC economies (figure 2.3.2.F). Caribbean countries are particularly vulnerable, losing an average of 3.6 percent of aggregate GDP per year during 2000-19, on average, to damages related to natural disasters, compared to 0.3 percent in all EMDEs.[2]

---

[1] Argentina and Ecuador were upgraded by Standard & Poor's since early 2020, in part due to the conclusion of debt restructuring, but bond spreads in Argentina have risen after an immediate postrestructuring fall.

[2] Calculations of GDP losses from natural disasters are calculated using EM-DAT data.

TABLE 2.3.1 Latin America and the Caribbean forecast summary

(Real GDP growth at market prices in percent, unless indicated otherwise)

Percentage point differences from June 2020 projections

	2018	2019	2020e	2021f	2022f	2020e	2021f
EMDE LAC, GDP[1]	**1.9**	**1.0**	**-6.9**	**3.7**	**2.8**	**0.3**	**0.9**
GDP per capita (U.S. dollars)	0.8	-0.1	-7.8	2.8	2.0	0.3	0.9
(Average including countries with full national accounts and balance of payments data only)[2]							
EMDE LAC, GDP[2]	1.9	1.0	-6.9	3.7	2.8	0.3	0.9
PPP GDP	1.9	0.9	-7.1	3.8	2.9	0.0	0.9
Private consumption	2.2	1.2	-7.1	4.0	3.0	1.2	1.1
Public consumption	1.7	0.0	-2.2	0.6	0.4	-4.0	0.5
Fixed investment	2.7	-0.6	-12.3	5.3	4.9	-1.2	0.6
Exports, GNFS[3]	4.3	0.7	-8.4	6.1	4.4	4.1	-0.8
Imports, GNFS[3]	5.0	-0.9	-12.2	6.9	5.0	1.0	1.0
Net exports, contribution to growth	-0.2	0.4	0.9	-0.1	-0.1	0.7	-0.2
Memo items: GDP							
South America[4]	1.6	1.1	-6.1	3.7	2.8	1.3	1.0
Central America[5]	2.7	2.5	-6.1	3.6	3.5	-2.5	0.0
Caribbean[6]	5.1	3.4	-7.7	4.5	4.0	-5.9	1.2
Brazil	1.8	1.4	-4.5	3.0	2.5	3.5	0.8
Mexico	2.2	-0.1	-9.0	3.7	2.6	-1.5	0.7
Argentina	-2.6	-2.1	-10.6	4.9	1.9	-3.3	2.8

Source: World Bank.
Note: e = estimate; f = forecast; PPP = purchasing power parity; EMDE = emerging market and developing economy. World Bank forecasts are frequently updated based on new information and changing (global) circumstances. Consequently, projections presented here may differ from those contained in other Bank documents, even if basic assessments of countries' prospects do not differ at any given moment in time. Due to lack of reliable data of adequate quality, the World Bank is currently not publishing economic output, income, or growth data for República Bolivariana de Venezuela, and the country is excluded from cross-country macroeconomic aggregates.
1. GDP and expenditure components are measured in 2010 prices and market exchange rates.
2. Aggregate includes all countries in table 2.3.2 except Dominica, Grenada, Guyana, Haiti, St. Kitts and Nevis, St. Lucia, St. Vincent and the Grenadines, and Suriname.
3. Exports and imports of goods and nonfactor services (GNFS).
4. Includes Argentina, Bolivia, Brazil, Chile, Colombia, Ecuador, Paraguay, Peru, and Uruguay.
5. Includes Costa Rica, El Salvador, Guatemala, Honduras, Nicaragua, and Panama.
6. Includes Antigua and Barbuda, The Bahamas, Barbados, Belize, Dominica, the Dominican Republic, Grenada, Guyana, Haiti, Jamaica, St. Kitts and Nevis, St. Lucia, St. Vincent and the Grenadines, and Suriname.

TABLE 2.3.2 Latin America and the Caribbean country forecasts[1]

(Real GDP growth at market prices in percent, unless indicated otherwise)

Percentage point differences from June 2020 projections

	2018	2019	2020e	2021f	2022f	2020e	2021f
Argentina	-2.6	-2.1	-10.6	4.9	1.9	-3.3	2.8
Belize	2.1	-2.0	-20.3	6.9	2.2	-6.8	0.2
Bolivia	4.2	2.2	-6.7	3.9	3.5	-0.8	1.7
Brazil	1.8	1.4	-4.5	3.0	2.5	3.5	0.8
Chile	3.9	1.1	-6.3	4.2	3.1	-2.0	1.1
Colombia	2.5	3.3	-7.5	4.9	4.3	-2.6	1.3
Costa Rica	2.7	2.1	-4.8	2.6	3.7	-1.5	-0.4
Dominica	0.5	8.6	-10.0	1.0	3.0	-6.0	-3.0
Dominican Republic	7.0	5.0	-6.7	4.8	4.5	-5.9	2.3
Ecuador	1.3	0.1	-9.5	3.5	1.3	-2.1	-0.6
El Salvador	2.4	2.4	-7.2	4.6	3.1	-1.8	0.8
Grenada	4.1	2.0	-12.0	3.0	5.0	-2.4	-3.5
Guatemala	3.2	3.8	-3.5	3.6	3.8	-0.5	-0.5
Guyana	4.4	5.4	23.2	7.8	3.6	-27.9	-0.3
Haiti[2]	1.7	-1.7	-3.8	1.4	1.5	-0.3	0.4
Honduras	3.7	2.7	-9.7	3.8	3.9	-3.9	0.1
Jamaica	1.9	0.9	-9.0	4.0	2.0	-2.8	1.3
Mexico	2.2	-0.1	-9.0	3.7	2.6	-1.5	0.7
Nicaragua	-4.0	-3.9	-6.0	-0.9	1.2	0.3	-1.6
Panama	3.7	3.0	-8.1	5.1	3.5	-6.1	0.9
Paraguay	3.2	-0.4	-1.1	3.3	4.0	1.7	-0.9
Peru	4.0	2.2	-12.0	7.6	4.5	0.0	0.6
St. Lucia	2.6	1.7	-18.0	8.1	5.2	-9.2	-0.2
St. Vincent and the Grenadines	2.2	0.4	-5.0	0.0	5.0	0.5	-4.0
Suriname	2.6	0.3	-13.1	-1.9	-1.5	-8.1	-4.9
Uruguay	1.6	0.2	-4.3	3.4	3.2	-0.6	-1.2

Source: World Bank.

Note: e = estimate; f = forecast. World Bank forecasts are frequently updated based on new information and changing (global) circumstances. Consequently, projections presented here may differ from those contained in other Bank documents, even if basic assessments of countries' prospects do not significantly differ at any given moment in time.

1. Data are based on GDP measured in 2010 prices and market exchange rates.

2. GDP is based on fiscal year, which runs from October to September. For example, 2019 refers to October 2018 to September 2019.

MIDDLE EAST and NORTH AFRICA

Output in the Middle East and North Africa (MENA) is estimated to have contracted by 5.0 percent in 2020. Significant disruptions related to COVID-19 have been compounded by the sharp fall in oil prices and oil demand. This contraction adds to already-slowing growth in the region and compounds pre-pandemic per capita income losses. Growth is expected to improve to a modest 2.1 percent in 2021, as the pandemic is brought under control and lockdown restrictions are eased, global oil demand rises, and policy support continues. The pandemic is expected to leave lasting economic scars on the region, however, and dampen potential growth. A resurgence of COVID-19, further disruptions related to geopolitical tensions and political instability, renewed downward pressure on oil prices, and additional balance of payments stress are key downside risks to the outlook.

Recent developments

The COVID-19 pandemic has caused deep output losses, on the order of 5.0 percent in 2020, in the Middle East and North Africa (MENA). Domestic cases in the region initially spiked in the Islamic Republic of Iran, followed by Gulf Cooperation Council (GCC) countries in mid-2020, but have since spread and intensified elsewhere in the region (figure 2.4.1.A).[1] Risk aversion by households and firms, along with strict lockdown measures, severely damaged activity. At their peak during 2020Q2, foot traffic around workplaces fell by about half of normal levels, and around retail spaces by even more (figure 2.4.1.B). More recently, in economies facing renewed outbreaks, mobility data is again showing weakness. In Jordan, for example, the contraction in foot traffic around work and retail spaces was about three-quarters the size of that seen at the start of the outbreak. Employment losses spiked in many economies and employment remains depressed (figure 2.4.1.C). The income shock from the pandemic is expected to increase the number of people below the $5.50 per day poverty line in the region by tens of millions by the end of this year (Lakner et al., forthcoming).

Output in MENA oil exporters is estimated to have contracted by 5.7 percent in 2020. Although domestic COVID-19 outbreaks have slowed from mid-2020 peaks in most GCC countries, the pace of new infections has reached new highs in other oil exporters (Algeria, the Islamic Republic of Iran), and has led to the reimposition of domestic mitigation measures. Oil sector output growth continues to be constrained by commitments to the OPEC+ oil production cut agreement.[2] Although the sub-region has seen a modest rebound in activity in 2020H2, with high-frequency indicators improving and equity markets stabilizing, conditions remain fragile (figure 2.4.1.D). Slowing demand is compressing inflation in most GCC economies.

Oil importers experienced a milder contraction of 2.2 percent in 2020, reflecting limited COVID-19 outbreak early in the year and lower oil prices. The pace of new infections has since risen rapidly, and fresh political uncertainty has compounded the impact of pandemic-related disruptions on

Note: This section was prepared by Franz Ulrich Ruch and Lei Sandy Ye. Research assistance was provided by Heqing Zhao and Hrisyana Doytchinova.

[1] The high number of cases in GCC countries reflects, in part, robust testing efforts in Bahrain and Qatar.

[2] OPEC+ includes 13 OPEC members and 10 other non-OPEC major oil producers.

FIGURE 2.4.1 MENA: Recent developments

Output in the Middle East and North Africa (MENA) is estimated to have contracted by 5.0 percent in 2020, as the region struggles with the dual shocks of the pandemic and the decline in oil prices. COVID-19 infection rates remain on the rise in many economies. Activity has recovered but remains subdued. Exports and industrial production contracted through much of 2020, and employment has fallen markedly in several economies. The economic policy response to COVID-19 in MENA, especially in GCC economies, has been more supportive than in other emerging market and developing economies.

A. COVID-19 cases

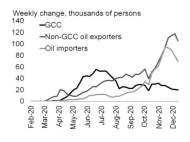

B. Workplace and retail mobility

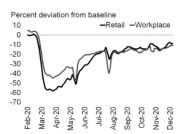

C. Employment

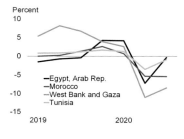

D. Composite purchasing managers indexes

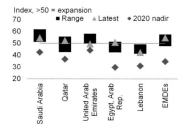

E. Export growth

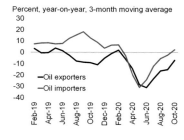

F. COVID-19 policy response

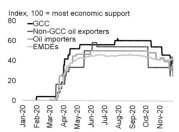

Sources: Google COVID-19 Community Mobility Reports; Hale et al. (2020); Haver Analytics; Johns Hopkins University; World Bank.
Note: EMDEs = emerging market and developing economies; GCC = Gulf Cooperation Council.
A. Lines show weekly change in confirmed COVID-19 cases. Last observation is the week of December 14, 2020.
B. Index of workplace and retail foot traffic based on mobile phone location data. In percent deviation from baseline which is the median of identical days of the week during the period between January 3 and February 6, 2020. 7-day moving average. Last observation is December 13, 2020.
C. Year-on-year change. Last observation is 2020Q3.
D. Range is the 5th and 95th percentile. Last observation is November 2020.
E. Goods exports. Sample includes five oil exporters and five oil importers with available monthly data. Last observation is October 2020.
F. Lines show unweighted averages. Index assesses economic support, including income support, fiscal measures, and debt relief, made during the COVID-19 pandemic. Based on Hale et al. (2020). Highest value is 100. Last observation is November 30, 2020.

activity. Exports and industrial production have contracted in many economies by double digits (figure 2.4.1.E). While the Arab Republic of Egypt's economy has been heavily disrupted by the pandemic, a contraction for the year was avoided thanks to previous reforms that rebuilt policy buffers, resilient consumption expenditure, and international assistance. Agricultural production continued to contract in Morocco in 2020 owing to the effects of drought. Lebanon is facing a political and economic crisis that has been compounded by COVID-19 and the Beirut port explosion (World Bank, European Union, and United Nations 2020). The country has defaulted on its sovereign debt and for the first time in its history, inflation has breached 100 percent, the effective exchange rate has collapsed, and electricity and food shortages are commonplace.

Given the magnitude of the economic damage and uncertainty generated by COVID-19, most economies in the region have announced fiscal stimulus packages that include increased spending on health and social safety nets, tax payment reductions and deferrals, and loans and guarantees to firms (figure 2.4.1.F). Increased public spending has been financed in part by increased international debt issuance (Egypt, Oman, Qatar, United Arab Emirates), although in some cases with higher yields than in early 2020. Some economies have also used resources in sovereign wealth funds to mitigate fiscal pressure (Bahrain, the Islamic Republic of Iran, Kuwait). The scope for fiscal support, however, has been limited in oil exporters by the collapse in oil prices (Saudi Arabia) and in some oil importers by high government debt (Egypt, Tunisia). In some cases, higher spending is being partially offset by policies to increase revenues (Saudi Arabia, Tunisia) and diversify economic activity (Saudi Arabia). Saudi Arabia, for example, raised value added taxes from 5 to 15 percent in July 2020 to stem a decline in revenues, which dampened consumption.

Monetary policy adjustments have also helped to cushion the economic impact of the pandemic, with the average policy rate declining by over 125 basis points, and by 400 basis points in Egypt. Central banks in the region have also implemented measures to support liquidity in the banking system (Jordan), provided credit to small and medium enterprises (Egypt), and lowered capital adequacy requirements for some financial institutions (Kuwait, United Arab Emirates).

Outlook

The regional economy is projected to recover only modestly in 2021, expanding by 2.1 percent, weaker than previously expected, and accelerate to 3.1 percent in 2022 (figure 2.4.2.A). This modest recovery reflects an expectation that the COVID-19 pandemic and low oil prices will do lasting damage in the region (figure 2.4.2.B). By 2022, regional output is expected to be almost 8 percent below the level projected in January 2020, a larger gap than in most other emerging market and developing economy regions (figure 2.4.2.C). The outlook assumes that the pandemic will be contained, oil prices stabilize, and no further escalation of geopolitical tensions. The baseline forecast further assumes that COVID-19 vaccines will be administered on a large-scale basis in the region in the second half of 2021. Oil prices are envisaged to be higher than forecast in June, averaging $44 per barrel in 2021 and $50 in 2022.

Among oil exporters, growth is expected to recover to 1.8 percent in 2021 supported by normalizing oil demand, a scheduled easing of the OPEC+ oil production cuts, policy support, and gradual phasing out of domestic pandemic-related restrictions. In Saudi Arabia, activity will be further supported by a resumption of public capital investment projects (postponed during the pandemic) and a recovery of demand after the sharp rise in value added tax. Growth in the Islamic Republic of Iran is expected to recover as domestic consumption and tourism begin to normalize, and disruptions related to COVID-19 taper. Oil production in MENA is expected to rise as global oil demand recovers. In Libya, oil production has expanded rapidly following a ceasefire agreement (IEA 2020). The continuation of planned diversification programs and a pickup in infrastructure investment are projected to sustain medium-term growth among GCC economies. While additional liquidity support by monetary authorities will help the recovery of oil

FIGURE 2.4.2 MENA: Outlook and risks

The regional economy is expected to grow by a modest 2.1 percent in 2021, supported largely by firming global oil demand and easing domestic lockdowns. The outlook, which has been downgraded from previous forecasts, is highly sensitive to a resurgence of COVID-19 infections and to volatility in oil prices. Among oil importers, additional challenges, such as sluggish progress on reforms, political risks, and susceptibility to agricultural sector shocks, may compound the adverse labor market impacts of the pandemic.

A. Growth

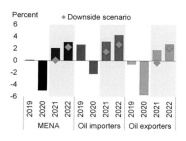

B. Output

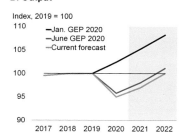

C. Output losses, by 2022

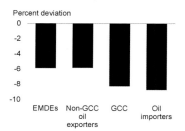

D. Pace of new COVID-19 cases

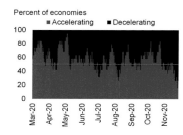

E. Global oil demand

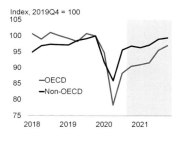

F. Political stability

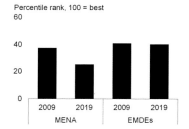

Sources: Haver Analytics; International Energy Agency; Johns Hopkins University; World Bank's Worldwide Governance Indicators; World Bank.
Note: EMDEs = emerging market and developing economies; GCC = Gulf Cooperation Council; GEP = Global Economic Prospects; MENA = Middle East and North Africa; OECD = Organisation for Economic Co-operation and Development.
A. Country groupings are GDP-weighted averages of real GDP growth.
C. Percent deviation in 2022 output between the January 2020 and January 2021 *Global Economic Prospects* forecasts.
D. Share of 18 MENA economies in which 7-day moving average new case count is accelerating or decelerating on a weekly basis. Last observation is the week of December 14, 2020.
E. Grey area denotes International Energy Agency estimates/forecasts.
F. Measures perceptions of the likelihood of political instability and/or politically-motivated violence, including terrorism.

exporters, fiscal strains will continue to limit the strength of their recovery in the medium term. By 2022, however, output in the subregion is expected to still be about 7 percent below the level projected in January 2020.

Output losses in oil importers are expected to be large, leaving them 9 percent below levels projected in January 2020 by 2022. Growth is expected to only rebound to 3.2 percent in 2021 as mobility restrictions are gradually eased and exports and domestic demand recover slowly. More generally, the recovery in the subregion is expected to be held back by tepid investment, reflecting high uncertainty related to the pandemic and political risk, subdued external demand due to weak growth prospects in the euro area, and limited fiscal space. In Egypt, growth is expected to slow to 2.7 percent in FY2020/21, amid a collapse in tourism, gas extractives and a slowdown in other key sectors such as manufacturing. Medium-term growth hinges on policy makers maintaining the momentum for reform. Morocco is expected to rebound to 4.0 percent in 2021 as agricultural output recovers from drought and domestic lockdowns ease. In Lebanon, the unfolding crises will likely result in output losses through 2022.

The outlook for growth is highly uncertain. One way to reflect this uncertainty is through scenarios (box 1.4). In a downside scenario, growth prospects are undermined by a sharper upsurge of the virus globally, the delayed rollout of vaccines, a deterioration in global financing conditions, weaker business and consumer confidence, and lower oil prices. If this was to occur, growth in MENA in 2021 would be close to zero with oil exporters experiencing a contraction for four straight years. The largest revisions to growth among oil exporters would be in Bahrain, Iraq, and Oman. In oil importers, growth would be only 1.5 percent in 2021 and 2.7 percent in 2022.

COVID-19 is expected to leave lasting scars on productivity and potential growth in the region (Dieppe 2020; Kilic Celik, Kose, and Ohnsorge 2020; World Bank 2020i). Capital accumulation is likely to be dampened, including because of uncertainty about the course of the pandemic and

its economic impacts, ongoing security concerns, lower growth expectations, and sharply reduced confidence. Productivity will also be weaker than previously expected due to the detrimental impacts of education disruptions and lengthy periods of unemployment on human capital.

Risks

Risks to the growth outlook are tilted to the downside. Key risks emanate from the trajectory of the pandemic and its social impacts, downward pressure on oil prices, domestic political uncertainty, and geopolitical tensions.

Further resurgence of COVID-19 outbreaks or delayed vaccination rollouts are significant risks. Mitigation measures have already been reimposed in parts of some countries (Algeria, Jordan, Lebanon), and may become more widespread given that about a third of economies were still seeing an accelerating pace of new infections in late 2020 (figure 2.4.2.D). More severe outbreaks in large regional economies could impose intraregional spillover effects, even if smaller economies do not experience large outbreaks (World Bank 2016). For example, oil importers (Egypt, Jordan, Lebanon, Republic of Yemen) depend heavily on remittances from the GCC. The socioeconomic consequences of the outbreak, including rising joblessness, food insecurity, and poverty, may further raise social unrest and compound losses in fragile economies.

A downturn in oil prices, excessive volatility, or an extension of the OPEC+ oil production cuts could hinder growth in oil-exporting EMDEs in the region. Oil prices have stabilized somewhat since mid-2020, but prospects remain highly uncertain and rely on both a recovery in global demand and the absence of adverse geopolitical developments (figure 2.4.2.E). Additional downward pressure on oil prices or an extension of production cuts implies that fiscal space and the scope for policy support for a recovery would further deteriorate. Oil importers could also be affected indirectly by a renewed downturn in oil prices via lower remittances and foreign direct investment (FDI) from oil-exporting MENA economies. At the same time, an unexpectedly sharp tightening of financing conditions would put further strain on already-elevated government debt burdens in some countries (Egypt, Jordan, Tunisia).

Domestic political tensions and geopolitical tensions remain a risk to growth and undermine greater trade integration (World Bank 2020j). Geopolitical tensions have eased in some respects, including the normalization of relations between Israel and some GCC countries. Tensions between the Islamic Republic of Iran and the United States continue to be elevated. Political uncertainty is high in several MENA economies (Lebanon, Tunisia, Republic of Yemen). Ceasefire agreements in Libya and Republic of Yemen present an opportunity to further improve security in the region and decrease rising food insecurity domestically. In the long term, failure to improve political stability will be detrimental to growth (figure 2.4.2.F).

There are also important risks on the policy front. Progress on the implementation of structural reforms need to be maintained, especially in some oil importers (Egypt, Jordan). It is unclear whether the pandemic will help accelerate reforms or rather hold them back as policy priorities shift. Moreover, while recent measures to ease financial conditions have helped mitigate the collapse in output, these will need to be managed and withdrawn carefully to avoid sowing the seeds of future instability. Changes in financing conditions pose additional risks to economies with large current account deficits but low FDI inflows (World Bank 2020j). In some economies (Egypt, Jordan, Tunisia) urgent balance of payment needs have already resulted in rapid financial assistance from the IMF in 2020 (IMF 2020a, 2020b, 2020c).

Finally, a worse-than-expected recovery in advanced economies could hold back the regional recovery. Given the euro area's importance as an export destination for many MENA economies, especially those in the Maghreb, worse-than-expected pandemic control in these advanced economies could set back growth in MENA.

TABLE 2.4.1 Middle East and North Africa forecast summary

(Real GDP growth at market prices in percent, unless indicated otherwise)

Percentage point differences from June 2020 projections

	2018	2019	2020e	2021f	2022f	2020e	2021f
EMDE MENA, GDP [1]	**0.5**	**0.1**	**-5.0**	**2.1**	**3.1**	**-0.8**	**-0.2**
GDP per capita (U.S. dollars)	-1.3	-1.6	-6.5	0.5	1.6	-0.7	-0.3
(Average including countries with full national accounts and balance of payments data only) [2]							
EMDE MENA, GDP [2]	0.5	-0.4	-4.8	2.0	2.8	-1.0	-0.3
PPP GDP	0.6	-0.3	-4.3	2.2	3.0	-0.8	-0.2
Private consumption	1.4	1.9	-2.5	1.6	2.5	-0.7	0.0
Public consumption	2.5	0.3	-1.6	1.0	1.7	-1.6	-0.7
Fixed investment	-0.2	-0.8	-11.7	6.1	3.6	-9.7	2.0
Exports, GNFS [3]	4.7	-6.4	-9.6	3.2	4.5	-2.7	0.1
Imports, GNFS [3]	2.0	-2.9	-8.7	2.6	4.0	-5.2	0.1
Net exports, contribution to growth	1.6	-2.2	-1.4	0.5	0.6	0.7	0.0
Memo items: GDP							
Oil exporters [4]	-0.3	-0.6	-5.7	1.8	2.8	-0.7	-0.3
GCC countries [5]	1.8	0.7	-5.7	1.6	2.7	-1.6	-0.6
Saudi Arabia	2.4	0.3	-5.4	2.0	2.2	-1.6	-0.5
Iran, Islamic Rep. [6]	-6.0	-6.8	-3.7	1.5	1.7	1.6	-0.6
Oil importers [7]	3.8	2.7	-2.2	3.2	4.3	-1.4	0.0
Egypt, Arab Rep. [6]	5.3	5.6	3.6	2.7	5.8	0.6	0.6

Source: World Bank.

Note: e = estimate; f = forecast; PPP = purchasing power parity; EMDE = emerging market and developing economy. World Bank forecasts are frequently updated based on new information and changing (global) circumstances. Consequently, projections presented here may differ from those contained in other Bank documents, even if basic assessments of countries' prospects do not differ at any given moment in time.

1. GDP and expenditure components are measured in 2010 prices and market exchange rates. Excludes Libya, the Syrian Arab Republic, and the Republic of Yemen due to data limitations.
2. Aggregate includes all economies in notes 4 and 6 except Djibouti, Iraq, Qatar, and West Bank and Gaza, for which data limitations prevent the forecasting of GDP components.
3. Exports and imports of goods and nonfactor services (GNFS).
4. Oil exporters include Algeria, Bahrain, the Islamic Republic of Iran, Iraq, Kuwait, Oman, Qatar, Saudi Arabia, and the United Arab Emirates.
5. The Gulf Cooperation Council (GCC) includes Bahrain, Kuwait, Oman, Qatar, Saudi Arabia, and the United Arab Emirates.
6. Fiscal-year based numbers. The fiscal year runs from July 1 to June 30 in the Arab Republic of Egypt, with 2020 reflecting FY2019/20. The Islamic Republic of Iran run from March 21 through March 20, with 2020 reflecting FY2020/21.
7. Oil importers include Djibouti, the Arab Republic of Egypt, Jordan, Lebanon, Morocco, Tunisia, and West Bank and Gaza.

TABLE 2.4.2 Middle East and North Africa economy forecasts[1]

(Real GDP growth at market prices in percent, unless indicated otherwise)

Percentage point differences from June 2020 projections

	2018	2019	2020e	2021f	2022f	2020e	2021f
Algeria	1.2	0.8	-6.5	3.8	2.1	-0.1	1.9
Bahrain	1.8	1.8	-5.2	2.2	2.5	-0.7	-0.1
Djibouti	8.4	7.5	-1.0	7.1	7.2	-2.3	-2.1
Egypt, Arab Rep. [2]	5.3	5.6	3.6	2.7	5.8	0.6	0.6
Iran, Islamic Rep. [2]	-6.0	-6.8	-3.7	1.5	1.7	1.6	-0.6
Iraq	-0.6	4.4	-9.5	2.0	7.3	0.2	0.1
Jordan	1.9	2.0	-3.5	1.8	2.0	0.0	-0.2
Kuwait	1.2	0.4	-7.9	0.5	3.1	-2.5	-0.6
Lebanon [3]	-1.9	-6.7	-19.2	-13.2	...	-8.3	-6.9
Morocco	3.1	2.5	-6.3	4.0	3.7	-2.3	0.6
Oman	0.9	-0.8	-9.4	0.5	7.9	-5.4	-1.5
Qatar	1.2	0.8	-2.0	3.0	3.0	1.5	-0.6
Saudi Arabia	2.4	0.3	-5.4	2.0	2.2	-1.6	-0.5
Tunisia	2.7	1.0	-9.1	5.8	2.0	-5.1	1.6
United Arab Emirates	1.2	1.7	-6.3	1.0	2.4	-1.8	-0.4
West Bank and Gaza	1.2	1.4	-7.9	2.3	2.4	-0.3	-2.8

Source: World Bank.

Note: e = estimate; f = forecast. World Bank forecasts are frequently updated based on new information and changing (global) circumstances. Consequently, projections presented here may differ from those contained in other Bank documents, even if basic assessments of economies' prospects do not significantly differ at any given moment in time.

1. Data are based on GDP measured in 2010 prices and market exchange rates. Excludes Libya, the Syrian Arab Republic, and the Republic of Yemen due to data limitations.
2. Fiscal-year based numbers. The fiscal year runs from July 1 to June 30 in the Arab Republic of Egypt, with 2020 reflecting FY2019/20. The fiscal year in the Islamic Republic of Iran runs from March 21 through March 20, with 2020 reflecting FY2020/21.
3. Forecasts for Lebanon beyond 2021 are excluded due to a high degree of uncertainty.

SOUTH ASIA

The pandemic has had a devastating impact on South Asia (SAR), leading to an estimated 6.7 percent output contraction in 2020. The region is projected to grow by 3.3 percent in 2021 and 3.8 percent in 2022, substantially weaker growth than during the decade leading up to the pandemic. COVID-19 is expected to inflict long-term damage on growth prospects by depressing investment, eroding human capital, undermining productivity, and depleting policy buffers. The outlook is highly uncertain and subject to multiple downside risks, including the possibility of more severe and longer-lasting damage from the pandemic, financial and debt distress related to an abrupt tightening of financing conditions or widespread corporate bankruptcies, adverse effects of extreme weather and climate change, weaker-than-expected recoveries in key partner economies, and a worsening of policy- and security-related uncertainty. Financial sector fragility in many economies requires active intervention by policy makers to mitigate the risk of crisis.

Recent developments

The pandemic has caused deep output losses and has contributed to a sharp rise in unemployment and poverty in South Asia (SAR). Close to a hundred million new poor—those below the $1.90 per day poverty line—will be living in the region by the end of this year (Lakner et al., forthcoming). While new cases of COVID-19 are again accelerating in some parts of the region—thereby exerting renewed pressure on economic activity—the total number of new cases and deaths remain below mid-2020 peaks (figure 2.5.1.A). The South Asia region overall has less total cases on a per capita basis than other emerging market and developing economies (EMDEs) and advanced economies. The actual extent of COVID-19 infection prevalence in SAR, however, is highly uncertain due to limited testing (Bangladesh, Pakistan).

Output in SAR contracted by an estimated 6.7 percent in 2020, reflecting the effects of severe COVID-19 outbreaks and nationwide lockdowns,

Note: This section was prepared by Franz Ulrich Ruch and Lei Sandy Ye. Research assistance was provided by Heqing Zhao and Hrisyana Doytchinova.

particularly in Bangladesh and India (figure 2.5.1.B). Economies in the region are highly dependent on activities that require extensive social interaction, which have been hit the hardest by the pandemic (hospitality, retail, transport). Following a collapse in early-2020, economic activity rebounded in 2020H2, led by industrial production, as initial stringent lockdowns have been eased. Goods exports recovered to their pre-pandemic levels as global trade firmed (figure 2.5.1.C). Tourist arrivals remains near-nil, however, reflecting continued impediments to international travel.

In India, the pandemic hit the economy at a time when growth was already decelerating. Output is projected to fall by 9.6 percent in FY2020/21, reflecting a sharp drop in household spending and private investment. The pandemic dispropor-tionately affected activity in the services sector (mainly in urban areas, such as retail), paralyzed consumption, and caused significant unemploy-ment. Recent high frequency data indicate that the services sector recovery is gaining momentum (figure 2.5.1.D). The informal sector, which accounts for four-fifths of employment, also suffered severe income losses (Elgin et al., forthcoming; World Bank 2019, 2020j).

FIGURE 2.5.1 SAR: Recent developments

The COVID-19 outbreak has resurged in many parts of the South Asia region, with ongoing restrictions on movement and activity. Exports have benefited from a rebound in China, but inbound tourism remains moribund. In India, damage to the services sector was significant, with the sector contracting for most of 2020. Fiscal policy has provided some support, but more may be needed. Monetary policy actions have brought real interest rates into negative territory.

A. COVID-19 deaths

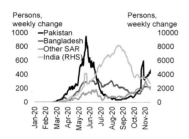

B. Lockdown stringency

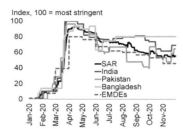

C. Activity indicators

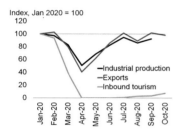

D. India: Purchasing managers indexes

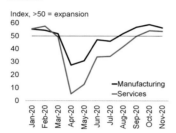

E. Primary fiscal balance

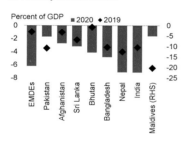

F. Real interest rates

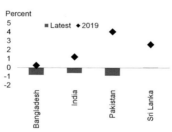

Sources: Consensus Economics; Hale et al. (2020); Haver Analytics; International Monetary Fund; World Bank; World Tourism Organization.

Note: EMDEs = emerging market and developing economies; SAR = South Asia region.

A. Unweighted averages. Last observation is December 14, 2020. "Other SAR" includes Afghanistan, Bhutan, Maldives, Nepal, and Sri Lanka.

B. Unweighted averages. The stringency index refers to the average sub-indexes of nine mitigation measures: school closures, workplace closures, cancellation of public events and public transport, restriction on gatherings, stay-home requirements and restrictions to international and domestic travel and public information campaigns. Last observation is November 30, 2020.

C. Unweighted averages. Industrial production and merchandise exports for Bangladesh, India, Sri Lanka, and Pakistan. Inbound tourism for Bhutan, India, Maldives, Nepal, and Sri Lanka. Last observation October 2020.

E. "EMDEs" refers to an unweighted average of 156 economies. Calendar year basis.

F. Real interest rates are nominal policy rates less expected inflation. Consensus Forecasts for 2020 are from December 2019; forecasts for 2021 are from December 2020. 2019 policy rates are end of year.

In the region excluding India, the economic impact of COVID-19 has been somewhat less severe but still significant. Spillovers from the global recession have amplified domestic challenges and caused a 0.7 percent output contraction in 2020, with economies that rely heavily on tourism and travel especially hard hit (Maldives, Nepal, Sri Lanka). Maldives is likely to see more than a decade of per capita income gains wiped out in 2020. In Bangladesh, which had been one of the fastest-growing EMDEs prior to the pandemic, growth decelerated to an estimated 2.0 percent in FY2019/20, as the pandemic suppressed both domestic activity and caused a double-digit contraction in exports. In Pakistan, growth is estimated to have contracted by 1.5 percent in FY2019/20, reflecting the effects of localized COVID-19 containment measures, as well as the impact of monetary and fiscal tightening prior to the outbreak (World Bank 2020j). In Sri Lanka, the pandemic-induced shock further increased an already-high risk of debt distress with its sovereign spread over a thousand basis points above pre-pandemic levels.

Shallow fiscal buffers limited the fiscal response to COVID-19 in the region with primary fiscal deficits widening less in large SAR economies than in other EMDEs (figure 2.5.1.E; chapter 1). Nevertheless, the region will register the largest average primary budget deficit in more than three decades. Rising food prices and a large decline in basic incomes prompted the authorities to implement policies to mitigate food insecurity and support the agriculture sector in most economies. Monetary policy in the region responded aggressively to preserve financial stability, focusing on ensuring adequate liquidity provision and other prudential regulatory support. Policy rate cuts of about 250 basis points on average in 2020, and 625 basis points in Pakistan, moved real interest rates into negative territory (figure 2.5.1.F).

Financial conditions have eased across much of the region, but remain tighter than before the pandemic, with sovereign spreads still above pre-pandemic levels. Capital inflows resumed in the second half of last year following significant outflows in 2020H1 but have not yet offset earlier losses in many economies. Remittance inflows remained robust in 2020 with double-digit growth in Bangladesh and Pakistan due to the increased use of formal channels to repatriate funds, government incentives, and the return of migrant workers. These inflows have contributed to the improvement of current accounts, and in some cases with international assistance, allowed several major regional economies to increase their foreign reserves (Bangladesh, India, Pakistan). India is expected to post a current account surplus in FY2020/21, mainly driven by weak domestic demand, after almost two decades of deficits. Equity markets in the region have regained all losses suffered during the first half of 2020 and foreign exchange rates are only slightly weaker than pre-pandemic valuations.

Outlook

The region is projected to grow by 3.3 percent in 2021 and 3.8 percent in 2022, substantially weaker rates than during the decade leading up to the pandemic. Weak growth prospects reflect a protracted recovery in incomes and employment, especially in the services sector; limited credit provisioning, constrained by financial sector vulnerabilities; and muted fiscal policy support (figure 2.5.2.A). Output in 2022 is projected to remain about 16 percent below pre-pandemic levels, the biggest loss among EMDE regions (figure 2.5.2.B). The baseline forecast assumes that vaccines will be distributed on a large scale in the region in the second half of 2021 and that there is no widescale and significant resurgence in infections.

In India, growth is expected to recover to 5.4 percent in 2021, as the rebound from a low base is offset by muted private investment growth given financial sector weaknesses. The pandemic will likely lower potential growth, including through eroding human capital and investment growth. In the financial sector, nonperforming loans were already at high levels before the pandemic and the economic downturn may lead to further insolvencies among financial and nonfinancial corporations. Indeed, the ratio of gross non-performing loans to assets of commercial banks in

FIGURE 2.5.2 SAR: Outlook and risks

Growth in South Asia (SAR) is projected to rebound to 3.3 percent in 2021, supported by a pickup in manufacturing and services activity, along with policy support. Output, however, is estimated to be about 16 percent below pre-pandemic trends. Risks are tilted to the downside. Despite some buildup of international reserves, heightened financial sector stress may set back the recovery and aggravate capital outflows. Climate-related events could damage agricultural activity, which in turn could weaken real incomes by boosting food prices.

A. Growth outlook

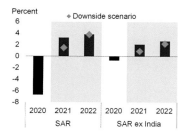

B. Output

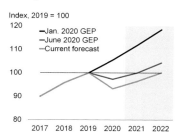

C. Pace of new COVID-19 cases

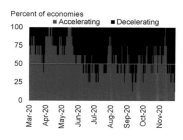

D. Cumulative portfolio capital flows since January 2020

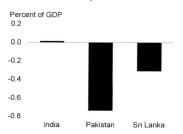

E. Share of global poor affected by high food inflation

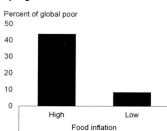

F. Sovereign spreads

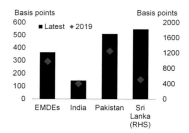

Sources: Haver Analytics; Institute of International Finance; Johns Hopkins University; World Bank.
Note: EMDEs = emerging market and developing economies; GEP = Global Economic Prospects; SAR = South Asia region.
C. Share of eight SAR economies where the 7-day moving average of new cases is accelerating or decelerating on a weekly basis. Last observation is December 15, 2020.
D. Ratio of cumulative equity and debt portfolio outflows in 2020 to 2019 GDP. Last observation is November 2020.
E. High and low food inflation is defined as economies in the top and bottom quartile of the average food inflation rate from 2000 to 2018. Poverty data for 2018 and includes data for 164 economies.
F. "2019" reflects end of year. Latest observation is the week of December 11, 2020. "EMDEs" refers to J.P. Morgan's Emerging Market Bond Index (EMBI) global diversified spread.

India could be as high as 15 percent by March 2021 (Reserve Bank of India 2020).

In Pakistan, the recovery is expected to be subdued, averaging 1.3 percent over the next two fiscal years—slightly better than expected in June 2020 but below potential growth. Growth is projected to be held back by continued fiscal consolidation pressures and services sector weakness. The outlook is predicated on main-taining reform momentum and adherence to a macroeconomic-sustainably framework. Limited prospects for a strong rebound in the services sector will aggravate poverty. This sector represents about half of Pakistan's output and are an important source of income for low-income households.

In economies that rely on external sources of growth, such as manufacturing exports (Bangladesh) and tourism (Bhutan, Maldives, Nepal, Sri Lanka), the recovery is likely to be particularly modest. Export growth is forecast to remain weak in Bangladesh, especially in the readymade garment sector. Tourism revenue is likely to remain significantly below pre-pandemic levels because of depressed demand as potential tourists remain wary of social interactions and continued restrictions on international travel. The projected drag from remittances on the region's economies (Bangladesh, Nepal, and Sri Lanka) is less certain given their recent strength. Remittances may be adversely affected by the weak recovery in Gulf Cooperation Council (GCC) countries, the resurgence of outbreaks in the United States and Europe, and difficulties facing migrants trying to return to host countries (World Bank 2020c).

The growth outlook is highly uncertain and one way to reflect this uncertainty is through scenario analysis (box 1.4). In the downside scenario, growth prospects are undermined by a sharper upsurge of the virus globally, delayed rollout of vaccines, a deterioration in global financing condi-tions, weaker business and consumer confidence, and lower oil prices. As a result, growth in SAR would be 1.8 percentage points lower than projected, at 1.5 percent in 2021 and unchanged in 2022 (figure 2.5.2.A). In the region excluding

India, the impact on growth would be slightly smaller; growth would slow to 0.9 percent in 2021 (on a calendar year basis) instead of 2.1 percent. Afghanistan, Maldives, and Pakistan are likely to see the largest downgrades.

The pandemic is expected to leave lasting scars on the region. Recent estimates suggest that potential growth will be more than 1 percentage point lower, on average, during 2020-25 compared to a no-COVID counterfactual (World Bank 2020j). These losses occur through multiple channels. The pandemic is likely to dampen capital accumulation as uncertainty, weak confidence, limited fiscal space, and financial fragilities undermine invest-ment. The pandemic will damage productivity by disrupting educational gains, making certain activities unviable, and may see labor shift to lower -productivity sectors (Dieppe 2020; World Bank 2020j). Human capital will be eroded by higher long-term unemployment, disruptions in educa-tion, and deteriorating health outcomes. These disruptions have a disproportionate impact on women, who often face a higher likelihood of job losses and a higher burden of dependent care than men, and who account for the majority of informal jobs and jobs requiring face-to-face interactions (Alon et al. 2020; Azevedo et al. 2020; ILO 2020a; Montenovo et al. 2020). Elevated fiscal and financial sector vulnerabilities increase the risk of financial crises in the region, which would further increase losses in potential growth (Dieppe 2020; Kilic Celik, Kose, and Ohnsorge 2020; World Bank 2020i).

Risks

Risks to the outlook are tilted to the downside. They include more severe and longer-lasting infection rates from the pandemic, financial and debt distress caused by an abrupt tightening of financing conditions or widespread corporate bankruptcies, adverse effects of extreme weather and climate change, weaker-than-expected recov-eries in key partner economies, and a worsening of policy- and security-related uncertainty.

Recurring COVID-19 outbreaks or delays in the procurement and distribution of vaccines is a significant risk. Hotspots of new cases are still appearing in parts of the region, which would require decisive action to avoid further spread through additional nonpharmaceutical measures (figure 2.5.2.C). The limited used of nonpharmaceutical interventions, especially the lack of testing in some economies, may undermine the ability to control further outbreaks.

Although financial sectors in the region have benefited from the easing of global financing conditions, additional stress on domestic banks could be triggered by the economic consequences of a sharp and sustained resurgence of infections within the region or globally. This could further increase corporate bankruptcies and weaken already-vulnerable balance sheets of the banking and nonbanking financial sectors in several regional economies (Bangladesh, Bhutan, India, Sri Lanka). Although capital inflows have stabilized after falling sharply in the first half of 2020, they remain subdued and renewed outflows would pose refinancing pressures in economies dependent on foreign capital (for example, Afghanistan and Sri Lanka; figure 2.5.2.D). External vulnerabilities have been some-what mitigated by the uptake of the Debt Service Suspension Initiative in Afghanistan, Maldives, Nepal, and Pakistan (G20 2020). Further policy intervention, however, is needed to minimize the risk of crisis, including greater debt transparency (box 1.1; Kose et al. 2020).

Extreme weather events, including flooding and cyclones, and impacts of climate change remain an important risk to regional growth. In addition to loss of lives and severe infrastructure damage, these events have been accompanied by higher food prices. For example, Cyclone Amphan and the flooding that occurred in Bangladesh in 2020 lifted food price inflation to an almost three-year high. Surges in food prices tend to depress incomes and consumption, and increase food insecurity, with the most severe impact felt by the poor. Economies with high food inflation rates tend to have a larger share of the global poor and higher rates of poverty (figure 2.5.2.E).

Weaker-than-expected growth elsewhere in the world may undermine the recovery in SAR. Growth outcomes in China, the European Union, and the United States, for instance, have a direct impact on growth in many economies in the region by lowering export demand and remittances, and limiting access to external financing (World Bank 2016). For example, Bangladesh's garment exports are heavily reliant on markets in the United States and Europe. Some economies in the region are also heavily dependent on remittance flows from GCC countries, which may be affected by potential renewed decline in oil prices, perhaps because of the economic impacts of the pandemic or to a sudden shift in OPEC policy.

Some economies also face considerable policy and security-related uncertainties. The policy space needed to implement long-term growth strategies has been eroded by the impact of the pandemic, and further increases the risk of financial and sovereign debt crises. The risk of debt distress is elevated in several economies, especially Maldives, Pakistan, and Sri Lanka, with decisive action required to maintain macroeconomic stability (figure 2.5.2.F). Security-related uncertainties could weigh on activity in Afghanistan, India, Nepal, and Pakistan.

TABLE 2.5.1 South Asia forecast summary

(Real GDP growth at market prices in percent, unless indicated otherwise)

Percentage point differences from June 2020 projections

	2018	2019	2020e	2021f	2022f	2020e	2021f
EMDE South Asia, GDP [1,2]	**6.5**	**4.4**	**-6.7**	**3.3**	**3.8**	**-4.0**	**0.5**
GDP per capita (U.S. dollars)	5.2	3.2	-7.8	2.1	2.7	-4.0	0.4
(Average including countries with full national accounts and balance of payments data only)[3]							
EMDE South Asia, GDP [3]	6.5	4.4	-6.7	3.3	3.8	-4.0	0.5
PPP GDP	6.5	4.4	-6.8	3.2	3.8	-4.0	0.4
Private consumption	7.1	5.2	-8.9	2.6	4.4	-6.3	-0.7
Public consumption	8.4	10.7	3.5	6.3	3.2	-4.9	0.0
Fixed investment	10.8	-0.4	-14.6	4.9	5.6	-6.4	3.7
Exports, GNFS [4]	10.5	1.1	-7.6	4.1	7.3	4.9	0.0
Imports, GNFS [4]	13.1	-5.1	-16.2	5.4	9.4	-2.6	2.8
Net exports, contribution to growth	-1.4	1.7	2.7	-0.4	-0.8	1.6	-0.5
Memo items: GDP [2]	**2017/18**	**2018/19**	**2019/20e**	**2020/21f**	**2021/22f**	**2019/20e**	**2020/21f**
South Asia excluding India	6.0	5.1	2.4	-0.7	2.1	0.3	0.0
India	7.0	6.1	4.2	-9.6	5.4	0.0	-6.4
Pakistan (factor cost)	5.5	1.9	-1.5	0.5	2.0	1.1	0.7
Bangladesh	7.9	8.2	2.0	1.6	3.4	0.4	0.6

Source: World Bank.
Note: e = estimate; f = forecast; PPP = purchasing power parity; EMDE = emerging market and developing economy. World Bank forecasts are frequently updated based on new information and changing (global) circumstances. Consequently, projections presented here may differ from those contained in other Bank documents, even if basic assessments of countries' prospects do not differ at any given moment in time.
1. GDP and expenditure components are measured in 2010 prices and market exchange rates.
2. National income and product account data refer to fiscal years (FY) while aggregates are presented in calendar year (CY) terms. (For example, aggregate under 2020/21 refers to CY 2020). The fiscal year runs from July 1 through June 30 in Bangladesh, Bhutan, and Pakistan; from July 16 through July 15 in Nepal; and April 1 through March 31 in India.
3. Subregion aggregate excludes Afghanistan, Bhutan, and Maldives, for which data limitations prevent the forecasting of GDP components.
4. Exports and imports of goods and nonfactor services (GNFS).

TABLE 2.5.2 South Asia country forecasts

(Real GDP growth at market prices in percent, unless indicated otherwise)

Percentage point differences from June 2020 projections

	2018	2019	2020e	2021f	2022f	2020e	2021f
Calendar year basis [1]							
Afghanistan	1.2	3.9	-5.5	2.5	3.3	0.0	1.5
Maldives	8.1	7.0	-21.5	9.5	11.5	-8.5	1.0
Sri Lanka	3.3	2.3	-6.7	3.3	2.0	-3.5	3.3
Fiscal year basis [1]	**2017/18**	**2018/19**	**2019/20e**	**2020/21f**	**2021/22f**	**2019/20e**	**2020/21f**
Bangladesh	7.9	8.2	2.0	1.6	3.4	0.4	0.6
Bhutan	3.8	4.3	0.7	-0.7	2.3	-0.8	-2.5
India	7.0	6.1	4.2	-9.6	5.4	0.0	-6.4
Nepal	6.7	7.0	0.2	0.6	2.5	-1.6	-1.5
Pakistan (factor cost)	5.5	1.9	-1.5	0.5	2.0	1.1	0.7

Source: World Bank.
Note: e = estimate; f = forecast. World Bank forecasts are frequently updated based on new information and changing (global) circumstances. Consequently, projections presented here may differ from those contained in other Bank documents, even if basic assessments of countries' prospects do not significantly differ at any given moment in time.
1. Historical data is reported on a market price basis. National income and product account data refer to fiscal years (FY) with the exception of Afghanistan, Maldives, and Sri Lanka, which report in calendar year. The fiscal year runs from July 1 through June 30 in Bangladesh, Bhutan, and Pakistan; from July 16 through July 15 in Nepal; and April 1 through March 31 in India.

SUB-SAHARAN AFRICA

Sub-Saharan Africa has been hard hit by the COVID-19 pandemic, with activity in the region shrinking by an estimated 3.7 percent last year. Growth is forecast to resume at a moderate average pace of 3 percent in 2021-22—essentially zero in per capita terms and well below previous projections—as persistent outbreaks in several countries continue to inhibit the recovery. COVID-19 is likely to weigh on growth in Sub-Saharan Africa for a long period, as the rollout of vaccines in the region is expected to lag that of advanced economies and major EMDEs, further dampening growth. As a result, living standards are likely to be set back a decade and tens of millions of people in the region could be pushed into extreme poverty cumulatively in 2020-21. Risks to the regional outlook are tilted to the downside, and include weaker-than-expected recoveries in key trading partner economies, logistical hurdles that further impede vaccine distribution, and scarring of labor productivity that weakens potential growth and income over the longer term.

Recent developments

Output in Sub-Saharan Africa contracted by an estimated 3.7 percent—a per capita income decline of 6.1 percent and the deepest contraction on record—as the COVID-19 pandemic and associated lockdown measures disrupted activity through multiple channels. The hardest hit countries were those with large domestic outbreaks, those heavily dependent on travel and tourism—which virtually slowed to a near-complete halt—as well as commodity exporters, particularly of oil. Although a few countries have managed to slow some large outbreaks (Ethiopia, Kenya, South Africa), outbreaks persisted in the second half of 2020 in several countries with little sign of abating (figure 2.6.1.A). Various mitigation measures have remained in place as a result, weighing further on activity.

The pandemic has exacted a large human toll in Sub-Saharan Africa. That being said, the spread of the virus across the region has not been as rapid as initially feared, despite weak health systems and large informal sectors in many Sub-Saharan African countries (Nguimkeu and Okou 2020). By mid-October, the number of confirmed cases per million people in the region was one-quarter the EMDE average. Experience from past epidemics in the region may have encouraged authorities to preemptively impose lockdowns and social-distancing measures before large domestic outbreaks occurred, helping to slow the spread of the virus. Limited transport networks likely helped further inhibit its spread. Moreover, the region also benefits from a younger population, which seems less vulnerable to COVID-19 than the elderly (Nguimkeu and Tadadjeu 2020). However, the true size and the impact of the pandemic may be understated as weak health sector capacity likely constrains widespread testing and accurate monitoring of pandemic-related deaths (figure 2.6.1.B; World Bank 2020l).

In Nigeria and South Africa—the two largest economies in the region—output fell sharply last year. The economy of Nigeria is estimated to have shrunk 4.1 percent in 2020—0.9 percentage point more than previously projected—as the effects of the COVID-19 pandemic and associated measures were worse than expected and affected activity in all sectors. Agriculture growth slowed amid difficulties in transporting inputs and products to markets, while falling oil sector activity reflected

Note: This section was prepared by Cedric Okou and Rudi Steinbach. Research assistance was provided by Maria Hazel Macadangdang.

FIGURE 2.6.1. SSA: Recent developments

COVID-19 has continued to spread throughout the region; however, the pace has been less rapid than initially feared. In countries where health care infrastructure is weaker, the true intensity of outbreaks could be understated amid reduced testing capacity. These outbreaks have led to a near-complete halt of international tourist arrivals. Exchange rates have depreciated relative to pre-pandemic levels, contributing to higher and above-target inflation in several economies. The pace of monetary policy easing slowed in the second half of last year.

A. COVID-19 total infections in SSA

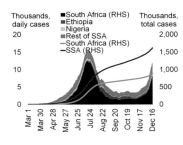

B. Confirmed COVID-19 cases and health care spending

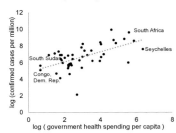

C. International tourist arrivals for selected SSA countries

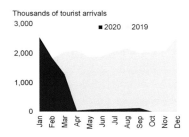

D. Exchange rates

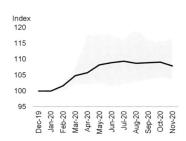

E. Inflation

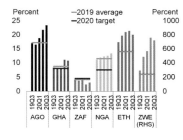

F. Policy interest rate changes

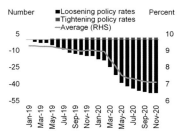

Sources: Haver Analytics; John Hopkins University; Seychelles National Bureau of Statistics; World Bank; Zimbabwe National Statistics.
Note: SSA = Sub-Saharan Africa.
A. Last observation is December 17, 2020.
B. Sample includes 47 countries. Cases per capita as of December 17, 2020. Government health spending per capita reflects 2017 data.
C. Aggregate international tourism arrivals for selected SSA countries including Kenya, Mauritius, Seychelles, and South Africa.
D. Change in USD exchange rates since December 2019. Monthly averages. Last observation is November 2020. Index (100 = December 2019). Values above 100 indicate depreciation.
E. AGO = Angola; ETH = Ethiopia; GHA = Ghana; NGA = Nigeria; ZAF = South Africa; ZWE = Zimbabwe. Latest observation is 2020Q3. Purple lines show 2020 inflation targets for Ghana, Nigeria, and South Africa.
F. Sample includes 14 Sub-Saharan countries. Last observation is November 2020.

the effects of weaker international prices and OPEC quotas.

With economic activity in South Africa already on a weak footing before the pandemic hit, output is expected to have fallen 7.8 percent last year. The country suffered the most severe COVID-19 outbreak in Sub-Saharan Africa, which prompted strict lockdown measures and brought the economy to a standstill. However, sizable and decisive monetary and fiscal policy support—which included measures to strengthen health sectors, emergency food distribution, tax relief, and loan guarantees—likely prevented an even deeper downturn.

The deep contraction in activity in the region extended beyond its large economies. Oil exporters grappled with sharply lower prices (Angola, Republic of Congo, Equatorial Guinea, South Sudan), while those with large travel and tourism sectors suffered from near-complete shutdowns of tourism-related activity (Cabo Verde, Ethiopia, Mauritius, Seychelles; figure 2.6.1.C). Contractions in agricultural commodity exporters were typically less steep, with some even avoiding outright recessions (Benin, Côte d'Ivoire, Malawi, Uganda). This partly reflects the agricultural sector's somewhat reduced exposure to the pandemic, as agricultural commodity prices declined far less than most industrial commodities, as well as relatively smaller services sectors in many of these economies. In Sudan, however, pandemic-related disruptions to activity were exacerbated by falling real incomes due to surging inflation and multiple natural disasters, including devastating floods (FAO 2020).

Exchange rates across the region remained about 5 percent weaker than levels prior to the pandemic, on average, following sharp depreciations in the first half of 2020 (figure 2.6.1.D). Inflation trends were uneven last year, as persistently soft demand helped contain inflationary pressures in some countries (Kenya, South Africa), whereas inflation remained elevated, or even accelerated, in response to weaker currencies and food price pressures in others (Angola, Ethiopia, Ghana, Nigeria, Senegal; figure 2.6.1.E). Rising food prices weighed on households incomes and consumption. This has prompted governments to implement policy measures to improve food provision, support the agriculture sector, and provide cash transfers to the poor. The pace of monetary policy easing across the region slowed in the second half of last year, particularly in countries experiencing inflationary pressures (figure 2.6.1.F). Following unprecedented capital outflows in the first half of 2020, the recovery inflows were anemic. In total, foreign direct investment flows collapsed by an estimated 30 to 40 percent last year, while remittance inflows—a vital source of household income and foreign currency receipts—are estimated to have plummeted by 9 percent in the region (OECD 2020; UNCTAD 2020; World Bank 2020c).

There was a step-change in government indebtedness in 2020, as economic activity and government revenues sharply fell while pandemic-related spending rose appreciably. Government debt in the region jumped on average 8 percentage points to 70 percent of GDP (IMF 2020d). In cash-strapped economies, governments faced severe difficulties to pay their sovereign debts. As a result, Angola and Zambia have sought to restructure their public debts. Two of Angola's largest creditors have agreed, outside of the G20 Debt Service Suspension Initiative, to defer the principal payments on Angola's debt for three years, whereas unsuccessful debt reprofiling discussions contributed to Zambia's sovereign debt default.

Outlook

Growth in Sub-Saharan Africa is expected to rebound only moderately to 2.7 percent in 2021—0.4 percentage point weaker than previously projected—before firming to 3.3 percent in 2022 (figure 2.6.2.A). While the rebound in private consumption and investment is forecast to be slower than previously envisioned, export growth is expected to accelerate in line with the rebound in economic activity among major trading partners. Despite the envisioned recovery, the level of regional GDP in 2022 is forecast to remain below the level projected in January 2020. The sluggish recovery reflects persistent outbreaks in several economies that have inhibited the resumption of economic activity, particularly in services sectors such as tourism. Although

FIGURE 2.6.2 **SSA: Outlook and risks**

After contracting steeply last year, growth in the region is forecast to resume at only a modest pace in 2021-22, with particularly sluggish recoveries in private consumption and investment. The pandemic is expected to leave lasting scars on already slowing potential growth. Falling per capita incomes mean that living standards have been set back by a decade or more in a quarter of SSA economies. The region will likely face additional hurdles in the distribution of pandemic vaccines—vaccine coverage among children in SSA countries is already lower than in other EMDEs—which could further dampen the recovery. Persistently wide budget deficits and growing interest burdens could raise debt sustainability concerns in some economies.

A. GDP growth

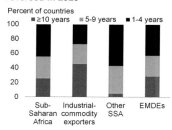

B. Potential growth

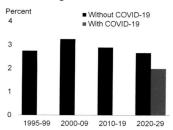

C. Years of per capita GDP gains reversed in 2020

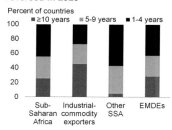

D. Evolution of per capita GDP in SSA

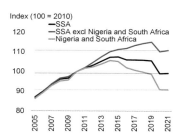

E. Vaccine coverage among children

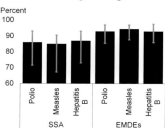

F. Fiscal balance

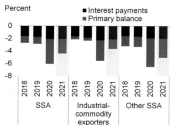

Sources: International Monetary Fund; Kilic Celik, Kose, and Ohnsorge (2020); World Bank; World Health Organization.
Note: SSA = Sub-Saharan Africa. EMDEs = emerging market and developing economies.
A. "Industrial-commodity exporters" represents oil and metal exporting countries. Aggregate growth rates calculated using GDP weights at 2010 prices and market exchange rates. "Industrial-commodity exporters" excludes Nigeria and South Africa. Diamonds correspond to the downside scenario.
B. Bars show simple averages of annual GDP-weighted average of 17 SSA economies during year spans indicated. Aggregates of production function-based potential output growth estimates calculated using real 2010 US dollar GDP at 2010 prices and market exchange rates.
C. Aggregates calculated using US dollar GDP per capita at 2010 prices and market exchange rates. Figure shows the share of countries by number of years of lost per capita income gains, measured as the difference between 2020 and the latest year of per capita income that is below 2020 value over the 2000-19 period. Sample includes 47 SSA economies, 22 "industrial-commodity exporters," and 146 EMDEs.
D. Chart reflects the evolution of real per capita GDP using 2010 USD exchange rates and weights. "SSA" sample includes 47 countries.
E. Chart shows the share of 1-year-old children covered by specific vaccines in 2019. Bars reflect medians; whiskers reflect inter-quartile ranges. "EMDEs" excludes SSA economies.
F. Simple averages of sub-groups.

COVID-19 vaccine rollouts are expected to gather pace in early 2021 among advanced economies and major EMDEs—bolstering business and consumer confidence—logistical impediments are expected to delay vaccine distribution in the region. The pandemic is set to further scar potential output growth—which was already losing steam owing to a contraction in total factor productivity—and leave a damaging legacy in the region (figure 2.6.2.B; Dieppe 2020; World Bank 2020b).

The pandemic caused an estimated 6.1 percent fall in per capita income last year and is expected to lead to a further 0.2 percent decline in 2021, before firming somewhat in 2022. The resultant decline in per capita income is expected to set average living standards back by a decade or more in a quarter of Sub-Saharan African economies, with even more severe setbacks in Nigeria and South Africa—home to one-quarter of the region's population (figures 2.6.2.C and 2.6.2.D). In all, this reversal is projected to push tens of millions more people in the region into extreme poverty cumulatively in 2020 and 2021 (World Bank 2020m).

Growth in Nigeria is forecast to resume at 1.1 percent in 2021—markedly weaker than previous projections—and edge up to 1.8 percent in 2022, as the economy faces severe challenges. Activity is expected to be dampened by low oil prices, falling public investment due to weak government revenues, constrained private investment due to firm failures, and subdued foreign investor confidence. Moreover, private consumption prospects will be weighed down by lost incomes and higher precautionary saving among nonpoor households, as well as lower remittances and the depletion of savings among poor and unemployed households amid inadequate social safety nets (World Bank 2020n).

In South Africa, growth is expected to rebound to 3.3 percent in 2021—0.7 percentage point below previous forecasts—before softening to a near-potential pace of 1.7 percent in 2022. Weaker growth momentum into 2021 partly reflects the lingering impact of the pandemic, as some mitigation measures are envisioned to remain in place. Preexisting structural constraints, such as persistent power-supply disruptions, are expected to become binding again as economic activity firms. Debt sustainability concerns may require fiscal consolidation, which, if prematurely implemented, is likely to further soften the recovery.

Elsewhere in the region, the rebound is forecast to be somewhat more pronounced, with growth resuming at an average of 4.1 percent in 2021-22, as the headwinds related to the pandemic gradually fade and external demand recovers. The recovery is expected to be slightly stronger—though still well below historical averages—among agricultural commodity exporters, averaging 4.5 percent in 2021-22. Higher international prices for agricultural export commodities are expected to support activity. These growth rates also partly reflect a resumption of investment, including foreign direct investment, as uncertainty gradually wanes, progress toward the full implementation of the African Continental Free Trade Area agreement, and continued implementation of reforms to improve business environments (Côte d'Ivoire, Togo). The pandemic has, however, resulted in delays to some large growth-enhancing infrastructure projects, such as hydrocarbon production in Senegal, which is now expected to come on stream only in 2023.

The projected rebound is expected to be more sluggish among industrial commodity exporters. Excluding Nigeria and South Africa, growth in these economies is forecast to average 2.8 percent in 2021-22, following 3.4 percent contraction last year. Although metals prices recovered somewhat in the second half of 2020, oil prices remain well below 2019 levels, weighing on the pace of recovery in oil-exporting economies (Angola, Chad, Republic of Congo, Equatorial Guinea, Gabon, Ghana). In Ghana—the region's fourth-largest economy—the expected resilience in agriculture will not be sufficient to offset the pandemic's lingering adverse impact on oil and other sectors. As a result, the growth forecast for 2021-22 has been downgraded to 1.9 percent.

Current account deficits widened in the median economy last year, as collapsing exports—including tourism receipts—exceeded the falls in imports induced by contracting domestic activity (Angola, Gabon, Mauritius, Rwanda). Deficits are expected to narrow somewhat in 2021 as improving external demand, as well as firming commodity prices, underpin a recovery in export earnings. Financing these deficits may, however, continue to be challenging, as capital inflows—including both portfolio and foreign direct investment flows—are likely to recover slowly from last year's troughs.

Risks

Risks to the outlook are tilted to the downside. Despite upward revisions to the projected pace of recovery in China, growth in major economies and key trading partners of the region could still disappoint, as has recently been the case for the euro area and the United States. A weaker-than-anticipated recovery in Sub-Saharan Africa could be the result of lingering adverse effects of the pandemic, or the delayed distribution of effective vaccines, especially if combined with a marked uptick in new domestic cases. Moreover, new waves of infections would slow growth in non-regional trading partners, which would dampen the projected growth pickup in Sub-Saharan Africa through lower export demand—particularly for tourism—and reduced investment.

Although there has been substantial progress in COVID-19 vaccine development, widescale vaccine distribution in Sub-Saharan Africa is likely to face many hurdles. These include poor transport infrastructure and distribution systems, weak health system capacity to implement large-scale vaccination programs, and outdated or insufficient cold storage systems to preserve vaccines (Akwataghibe et al. 2019; Bangura et al. 2020; Songane 2018). Childhood vaccination coverage in the region is already lower than in other EMDEs, partly reflecting some of these obstacles (figure 2.6.2.E). Moreover, with only a limited number of ongoing COVID-19 vaccine trials on the continent, there could be uncertainty about the effectiveness of vaccines for local populations. High production costs can also limit the ability of many fiscally strained economies to purchase the needed quantities to implement national vaccination programs. These constraints

could delay the region's recovery, absent international assistance.

Government debt in the region has increased sharply to an estimated 70 percent of GDP, on average, in 2020—up 8 percentage points from 2019—and is expected to rise further this year, elevating concerns about debt sustainability in some economies. This reflects expectations of persistently wide budget deficits as fiscal revenues remain below pre-pandemic levels, while health and pandemic-related spending needs continue to be elevated (figure 2.6.2.F). Moreover, greater interest payment burdens in most economies due to the pickup in indebtedness are bound to further weigh on budget deficits and could undermine required development spending. In all, 29 Sub-Saharan African countries—of the 44 Debt Service Suspension Initiative (DSSI) country partici-pants—are benefiting from debt relief assistance from official bilateral creditors. Relief amounts to $4.6 billion in debt service suspension—almost half of the total potential DSSI savings. Although the DSSI is providing some breathing room for financially strained economies, some countries such as Angola and Zambia are still struggling to pay their sovereign debts. Angola has secured a debt reprofiling with two of its largest creditors outside DSSI, with a three-year deferral of principal payments. Meanwhile, Zambia—the second-largest copper producing country in Sub-Saharan Africa—defaulted on its sovereign debt. This underscores the need for external assistance—predicated on debt transparency, including through coordinated international debt relief from both private and public creditors (UNECA 2020; World Bank 2020l). A high debt burden is likely to limit the ability of many Sub-Saharan countries to fund post-COVID reforms. The pandemic could, however, create a momentum to implement major reforms such as removing inefficient fuel subsidies, liberalizing the telecommunication sector, and promoting competition in the energy sector (Ethiopia, Nigeria, South Africa).

Banks may still face sharp increases in non-performing loans as companies struggle to service their debt due to falling revenues. The risk is substantial if the unprecedented fiscal and monetary support undertaken by several countries is prematurely withdrawn. To meet debt service obligations, high external public debt levels can compel governments to curb labor productivity-enhancing investments (Nabi and Drine 2009; World Bank 2020o). In countries with international capital market access, this may trigger increases in investor risk premia and borrowing costs that can heighten the probability of debt overhangs and debt distress (Kalemli-Özcan, Laeven, and Moreno 2018; Poirson, Pattillo, and Ricci 2004). In countries with large foreign-currency-denominated debt burdens, flight to safety and the accompanying domestic currency deprecations pose an additional risk.

The pandemic may also have worse-than-expected longer-term effects on regional growth. These could arise from the effects of higher debt loads on investment, the impact of lockdowns on schooling and human capital development, and weaker health outcomes. Many countries in the region have less developed health care systems, limited capacity for remote work and virtual education, and constrained fiscal space. Bolstered investments in broadband infrastructure could help these countries leverage digital technologies. Promising areas include health service provision, social protection delivery, remote work, online learning, and improved labor productivity. Without external financial support to help overcome these difficulties, a number of countries in the region are at risk of suffering prolonged losses of labor productivity, weaker income growth, and higher poverty.

There were already over 150 million food insecure people in 2019 in Sub-Saharan Africa—one-fifth more than the remaining five EMDE regions combined (WFP 2020). A combination of the COVID containment restrictions and adverse weather events (floods, droughts, locust infestations) have contributed to localized food price spikes in the region (Angola, Ethiopia, Ghana, Nigeria, Senegal). Food price surges are bound to worsen inequality and raise food insecurity among the poor. Political instability and violence are expected to make food insecurity worse in some countries, by threatening the lives and livelihoods of conflict-stricken populations.

Rising insecurity, conflicts, insurgencies, and the associated displacement of populations may further weigh on economic activity in several economies—particularly in the Sahel. Increased political tensions also threaten the safety of populations, as many countries are entering presidential election cycles.

TABLE 2.6.1 Sub-Saharan Africa forecast summary

(Real GDP growth at market prices in percent, unless indicated otherwise)

Percentage point differences from June 2020 projections

	2018	2019	2020e	2021f	2022f	2020e	2021f
EMDE SSA, GDP[1]	**2.6**	**2.4**	**-3.7**	**2.7**	**3.3**	**-0.9**	**-0.4**
GDP per capita (US dollars)	-0.1	-0.3	-6.1	0.1	0.7	-0.8	-0.4
(Average including countries with full national accounts and balance of payments data only)[2]							
EMDE SSA, GDP[2,3]	2.5	2.3	-3.8	2.7	3.3	-1.0	-0.4
PPP GDP	2.8	2.5	-3.5	2.8	3.5	-1.1	-0.4
Private consumption	3.3	1.2	-4.1	1.8	2.6	-2.4	-0.9
Public consumption	5.1	3.3	3.8	1.1	2.0	0.2	-0.8
Fixed investment	7.5	3.0	-6.8	3.0	5.6	-1.8	-1.1
Exports, GNFS[4]	2.6	4.5	-8.6	6.9	5.7	2.1	2.7
Imports, GNFS[4]	5.5	3.0	-8.5	2.8	3.4	-1.3	-0.7
Net exports, contribution to growth	-0.8	0.5	-0.1	1.2	0.8	1.0	1.0
Memo items: GDP							
SSA excluding Nigeria, South Africa, and Angola	4.4	3.9	-1.4	3.5	4.8	-1.1	-0.6
Oil exporters[5]	1.5	2.1	-3.5	1.1	2.2	-0.6	-0.8
CFA countries[6]	3.7	4.1	-1.4	3.1	4.8	-1.3	-1.0
CEMAC	0.3	1.5	-3.8	1.4	2.7	-1.1	0.2
WAEMU	6.4	6.0	0.3	4.2	6.2	-1.6	-2.1
SSA3	1.0	1.0	-5.7	2.0	1.9	-0.7	-0.3
Nigeria	1.9	2.2	-4.1	1.1	1.8	-0.9	-0.6
South Africa	0.8	0.2	-7.8	3.3	1.7	-0.7	0.4
Angola	-2.0	-0.9	-4.0	0.9	3.5	0.0	-2.2

Source: World Bank.

Note: e = estimate; f = forecast; PPP = purchasing power parity; EMDE = emerging market and developing economies. World Bank forecasts are frequently updated based on new information and changing (global) circumstances. Consequently, projections presented here may differ from those contained in other Bank documents, even if basic assessments of countries' prospects do not differ at any given moment in time.

1. GDP and expenditure components are measured in 2010 prices and market exchange rates.

2. Subregion aggregate excludes the Central African Republic, Eritrea, Guinea, São Tomé and Príncipe, Somalia, and South Sudan, for which data limitations prevent the forecasting of GDP components.

3. Subregion growth rates may differ from the most recent edition of Africa's Pulse (https://www.worldbank.org/en/region/afr/publication/africas-pulse) due to data revisions and the inclusion of the Central African Republic and São Tomé and Príncipe in the subregion aggregate of that publication.

4. Exports and imports of goods and nonfactor services (GNFS).

5. Includes Angola, Cameroon, Chad, the Republic of Congo, Equatorial Guinea, Gabon, Ghana, Nigeria, South Sudan.

6. The Financial Community of Africa (CFA) franc zone consists of 14 countries in Sub-Saharan Africa, each affiliated with one of two monetary unions. Cameroon, the Central African Republic, Chad, the Republic of Congo, Equatorial Guinea, and Gabon comprise the Central African Economic and Monetary Union (CEMAC), whereas Benin, Burkina Faso, Côte d'Ivoire, Guinea-Bissau, Mali, Niger, Senegal, and Togo comprise the West African Economic and Monetary Union (WAEMU).

TABLE 2.6.2 Sub-Saharan Africa country forecasts[1]

(Real GDP growth at market prices in percent, unless indicated otherwise)

Percentage point differences from June 2020 projections

	2018	2019	2020e	2021f	2022f	2020e	2021f
Angola	-2.0	-0.9	-4.0	0.9	3.5	0.0	-2.2
Benin	6.7	6.9	2.0	5.0	6.5	-1.2	-1.0
Botswana	4.5	3.0	-9.1	5.7	4.0	0.0	1.5
Burkina Faso	6.8	5.7	-2.0	2.4	4.7	-4.0	-3.4
Burundi	1.6	1.8	0.3	2.0	2.5	-0.7	-0.3
Central African Republic	3.7	3.1	0.0	3.2	4.1	-0.8	-0.3
Cabo Verde	4.5	5.7	-11.0	5.5	6.0	-5.5	0.5
Cameroon	4.1	3.7	-2.5	3.0	3.4	-2.3	-0.4
Chad	2.4	3.2	-0.8	2.4	3.3	-0.6	-2.3
Comoros	3.4	1.9	-1.4	2.4	3.6	0.0	-0.8
Congo, Dem. Rep.	5.8	4.4	-1.7	2.1	3.0	0.5	-1.4
Congo, Rep.	-6.2	-3.5	-8.9	-2.0	1.3	-2.7	-0.9
Côte d'Ivoire	6.8	6.9	1.8	5.5	5.8	-0.9	-3.2
Equatorial Guinea	-6.4	-5.6	-9.0	-2.8	-1.2	-0.6	-1.2
Eritrea	13.0	3.7	-0.6	3.5	5.5	0.1	-2.2
Eswatini	2.4	1.3	-3.5	1.5	0.9	-0.7	-1.2
Ethiopia[2]	8.4	9.0	6.1	0.0	8.7	2.9	-3.6
Gabon	0.8	3.9	-2.4	1.9	3.8	0.8	4.5
Gambia, The	6.5	6.0	-1.8	3.1	5.3	-4.3	-3.4
Ghana	6.3	6.5	1.1	1.4	2.4	-0.4	-2.0
Guinea	6.2	5.6	5.2	5.5	5.2	3.1	-2.4
Guinea-Bissau	3.8	4.6	-2.4	3.0	4.0	-0.8	-0.1
Kenya	6.3	5.4	-1.0	6.9	5.7	-2.5	1.7
Lesotho	1.5	1.4	-5.3	3.1	3.8	-0.2	-2.4
Liberia	1.2	-2.3	-2.9	3.2	3.9	-0.3	-0.8
Madagascar	4.6	4.8	-4.2	2.0	5.8	-3.0	-2.0
Malawi	3.2	4.4	1.3	3.3	4.9	-0.7	-0.2
Mali	4.7	5.0	-2.0	2.5	5.2	-2.9	-1.5
Mauritania	2.1	5.9	-0.6	3.7	4.8	1.4	-0.5
Mauritius	3.8	3.0	-12.9	5.3	6.8	-6.1	-1.1
Mozambique	3.4	2.2	-0.8	2.8	4.4	-2.1	-0.8
Namibia	0.7	-1.1	-7.9	2.2	2.0	-3.1	-0.8
Niger	7.0	5.8	1.0	5.1	11.8	0.0	-3.0
Nigeria	1.9	2.2	-4.1	1.1	1.8	-0.9	-0.6
Rwanda	8.6	9.4	-0.2	5.7	6.8	-2.2	-1.2
São Tomé and Príncipe	2.9	1.3	-6.5	3.0	5.5	3.0	-3.1
Senegal	6.4	5.3	-0.7	3.5	5.6	-2.0	-0.5
Seychelles	4.1	2.0	-15.9	3.1	3.8	-4.8	-3.2
Sierra Leone	3.4	5.5	-2.3	4.1	4.6	0.0	0.1
South Africa	0.8	0.2	-7.8	3.3	1.7	-0.7	0.4
Sudan	-2.3	-2.5	-8.4	2.5	3.1	-4.4	2.0
South Sudan[2]	-3.5	-0.3	9.3	-3.4	0.0	13.6	20.2
Tanzania	5.4	5.8	2.5	5.5	6.0	0.0	0.0
Togo	4.9	5.3	0.0	3.0	4.5	-1.0	1.0
Uganda[2]	6.2	6.8	2.9	2.8	5.9	-0.4	0.9
Zambia	3.5	1.4	-4.5	1.9	3.4	-3.7	0.5
Zimbabwe	4.8	-8.1	-10.0	2.9	3.1	0.0	0.0

Source: World Bank.
Note: e = estimate; f = forecast. World Bank forecasts are frequently updated based on new information and changing (global) circumstances. Consequently, projections presented here may differ from those contained in other Bank documents, even if basic assessments of countries' prospects do not significantly differ at any given moment in time.
1. Data are based on GDP measured in 2010 prices and market exchange rates.
2. Fiscal-year based numbers.
3. For Togo, growth figures in 2018 and 2019 are based on pre-2020 rebasing GDP estimates.

References

Akwataghibe, N. N., E. A. Ogunsola, J. E. W. Broerse, O. A. Popoola, A. I. Agbo, and M. A. Dieleman. 2019. "Exploring Factors Influencing Immunization Utilization in Nigeria—A Mixed Methods Study." *Frontiers in Public Health* 7: 392.

Alon, T. M., M. Doepke, J. Olmstead-Rumsey, and M. Tertilt. 2020. "The Impact of COVID-19 on Gender Equality." NBER Working Paper 26947, National Bureau of Economic Research, Cambridge, MA.

Azevedo, J. P., A. Hasan, D. Goldemberg, S. A. Iqbal, and K. Geven. 2020. "Simulating the Potential Impacts of COVID-19 School Closures on Schooling and Learning Outcomes: A Set of Global Estimates." Policy Research Working Paper 9284, World Bank, Washington, DC.

Baker, S. R., N., Bloom, and S. J., Davis. 2016. "Measuring Economic Policy Uncertainty." *Quarterly Journal of Economics* 131 (4): 1593-1636.

Bangura, J. B., S. Xiao, D. Qiu, F. Ouyang, and L. Chen. 2020. "Barriers to Childhood Immunization in Sub-Saharan Africa: A systematic Review." *BMC Public Health* 20 (1): 1-15.

Beylis, G., R. Fattal Jaef, M. Morris, A. R. Sebastian, and R. Sinha. 2020. *Going Viral: COVID-19 and the Accelerated Transformation of Jobs in Latin America and the Caribbean.* Washington, DC: World Bank.

Bottan, N., B. Hoffmann, and D. A. Vera-Cossio. 2020. "The Unequal Impact of the Coronavirus Pandemic: Evidence from Seventeen Developing Countries." Working Paper IDB-WP-1150, Inter-American Development Bank, Washington, DC.

Dieppe, A., ed. 2020. *Global Productivity: Trends, Drivers, and Policies.* Washington, DC: World Bank.

Demirgüç-Kunt, A., M. M., Lokshin, and I., Torre. 2020. "The Sooner, the Better: The Early Economic Impact of Non-Pharmaceutical Interventions During the COVID-19 Pandemic." Policy Research Working Paper 9257, World Bank, Washington, DC.

Demirgüç-Kunt, A., A., Pedraza, and C., Ruiz-Ortega. 2020. "Banking Sector Performance During the COVID-19 Crisis." Policy Research Working Paper 9363, World Bank, Washington, DC.

Elgin, C., A. Kose, F. Ohnsorge, and S. Yu. Forthcoming. "Measuring the Informal Economy and its Business Cycles." Mimeo, World Bank, Washington, DC.

FAO (Food and Agricultural Organization). 2020. *The Sudan: 2020 Flood Response Overview.* Geneva: Food and Agricultural Organization of the United Nations.

G20 (Group of Twenty). 2020. *Communiqué: G20 Finance Ministers and Central Bank Governors Meeting.* April 15, 2020.

Hale, T., N. Angrist, E. Cameron-Blake, L. Hallas, B. Kira, S. Majumdar, A. Petherick et al. 2020. Oxford COVID-19 Government Response Tracker, Blavatnik School of Government. https://www.bsg.ox.ac.uk/ research/research-projects/coronavirus-government-resp onse-tracker.

IEA (International Energy Agency). 2020. *Oil Market Report.* November. Paris: International Energy Agency.

ILO (International Labour Organization). 2020a. *ILO Monitor: COVID-19 and the World of Work.* Sixth edition. Geneva: International Labour Office.

ILO (International Labour Organization). 2020b. "Labour Overview in Times of COVID-19: Impact on the Labour Market and Income in Latin America and the Caribbean." Technical Note, Second Edition. International Labour Organization, Geneva.

IMF (International Monetary Fund). 2020a. "Arab Republic of Egypt: Request for Purchase Under the Rapid Financing Instrument—Press Release; Staff Report; And Statement by The Executive Director for The Arab Republic of Egypt." September. International Monetary Fund, Washington, DC.

IMF (International Monetary Fund). 2020b. "Jordan: Request for Purchase Under the Rapid Financing Instrument—Press Release; Staff Report; And Statement by The Executive Director, Alternative Executive Director, and Advisor for Jordan." May. International Monetary Fund, Washington, DC.

IMF (International Monetary Fund). 2020c. "Tunisia: Request for Purchase Under the Rapid Financing Instrument-Press Release; Staff Report; and Statement by the Executive Director for Tunisia." April. International Monetary Fund, Washington, DC.

IMF (International Monetary Fund). 2020d. *Fiscal Monitor: Policies for the Recovery.* October. Washington, DC: International Monetary Fund.

Kalemli-Özcan, S., L. Laeven, and D. Moreno. 2018. "Debt Overhang, Rollover Risk, and Corporate Investment: Evidence from the European Crisis." NBER Working Paper 24555, National Bureau of Economic Research, Cambridge, MA.

Kilic Celik, S., M. A. Kose, and F. Ohnsorge. 2020. "Subdued Potential Growth: Sources and Remedies." In *Growth in a Time of Change: Global and Country Perspectives on a New Agenda*, edited by H.-W. Kim and Z. Qureshi. Washington, DC: Brookings Institution.

Kose, M. A., P. Nagle, F. Ohnsorge, and N. Sugawara. 2020. *Global Waves of Debt: Causes and Consequences*. Washington, DC: World Bank.

Lakner, C., N. Yonzan, D. Gerszon Mahler, R. A. Castaneda Aguilar, and H. Wu. Forthcoming. "Updated Estimates of the Impact of COVID-19 on Global Poverty: Looking Back at 2020 and the Outlook for 2021." *Data Blog*, January 2021. https://blogs.worldbank.org/opendata.

Montenovo, L., X. Jiang, F. L. Rojas, I. M. Schmutte, K. I. Simon, B. A. Weinberg, and C. Wing. 2020. "Determinants of Disparities in Covid-19 Job Losses." NBER Working Paper 27132, National Bureau of Economic Research, Cambridge, MA.

Nabi, M. S., and I. Drine. 2009. "External Debt, Informal Economy and Growth." *Economics Bulletin* 29 (3): 1695–1707.

Nguimkeu, P., and C. Okou. 2020. "A Tale of Africa Today: Balancing the Lives and Livelihoods of Informal Workers During the COVID-19 Pandemic." Africa Knowledge in Time Policy Brief 1-3, World Bank, Washington, DC.

Nguimkeu, P., and S. Tadadjeu. 2020. "Why is the Number of COVID-19 Cases Lower than Expected in Sub-Saharan Africa?" *World Development*. https://doi.org/10.1016/j.worlddev.2020.105251.

OECD (Organisation for Economic Co-operation and Development). 2020. *Covid-19 in Africa: Regional Socio-economic Implications and Policy Priorities*. Paris: OECD.

OECD (Organisation for Economic Co-operation and Development) and World Bank. 2020. *Health at a Glance: Latin America and the Caribbean 2020*. Paris: OECD.

Poirson, H., C. Pattillo, and L. Ricci. 2004. "What Are the Channels Through Which External Debt Affects Growth?" IMF Working Paper 04/15, International Monetary Fund, Washington, DC.

Quayyum, S. N., and R. K. Kpodar. 2020. "Supporting Migrants and Remittances as COVID-19 Rages On." *IMFblog*, September 11, 2020. https://blogs.imf.org/2020/09/11/supporting-migrants-and-remittances-as-covid-19-rages-on/.

Reserve Bank of India. 2020. *Financial Stability Report*. July. Mumbai: Reserve Bank of India.

Rovo, N. 2020. "Structural Reforms to Set the Growth Ambition." Policy Research Working Paper 9175, World Bank, Washington, DC.

Shmis, T., A., Sava, J. E. N., Teixeira, and H. A., Patrinos. 2020. "Response Note to COVID-19 in Europe and Central Asia: Policy and Practice Recommendations." World Bank, Washington, DC.

Songane, M. 2018. "Challenges for Nationwide Vaccine Delivery in African Countries." *International Journal of Health Economics and Management* 18 (S1): 197–219.

UNCTAD (United Nations Conference on Trade and Development) 2020. *World Investment Report 2020: International Production Beyond the Pandemic*. Geneva: UNCTAD.

UNECA (United Nations Economic Commission for Africa) 2020. *Building forward together*. Addis Ababa, Ethiopia: UNECA.

WFP (World Food Programme). 2020. "WFP Global Update on COVID-19: Growing Needs, Response to Date and What's to Come in 2021." World Food Programme, Rome.

World Bank. 2016. *Global Economic Prospects: Spillovers amid Weak Growth*. January. Washington, DC: World Bank.

World Bank. 2018. "Building Solid Foundations: How to Promote Potential Growth." In *Global Economic Prospects: Broad-based Upturn, But for How Long?*, 157–217. Washington, DC: World Bank.

World Bank. 2019. *Global Economic Prospects: Darkening Skies*. January. Washington, DC: World Bank.

World Bank. 2020a. *East Asia and Pacific Economic Update: From Containment to Recovery*. September. Washington, DC: World Bank.

World Bank. 2020b. "Lasting Scars of the COVID-19 Pandemic." In *Global Economic Prospects*, 143–88. June. Washington, DC: World Bank.

World Bank. 2020c. "COVID-19 Crisis Trough a Migration Lens." Migration and Development Brief 33, World Bank, Washington, DC.

World Bank. 2020d. *Europe and Central Asia Economic Update: COVID-19 and Human Capital.* October. Washington, DC: World Bank.

World Bank. 2020e. "Pandemic, Recession: The Global Economy in Crisis." In *Global Economic Prospects.* June. Washington, DC: World Bank

World Bank. 2020f. *Global Economic Prospects: Slow Growth, Policy Challenges.* January. Washington DC: World Bank.

World Bank. 2020g. *Commodity Markets Outlook: Persistence of Commodity Shocks.* October. World Bank, Washington, DC.

World Bank. 2020h. *The Cost of Staying Healthy— Semiannual Report of the Latin America and the Caribbean Region.* Washington, DC: World Bank.

World Bank. 2020i. *Global Economic Prospects.* June. Washington, DC: World Bank.

World Bank. 2020j. *MENA Economic Update: Trading Together.* October. Washington, DC: World Bank.

World Bank. 2020k. *South Asia Economic Focus: Beaten or Broken? Informality and COVID-19.* Fall. Washington, DC: World Bank.

World Bank. 2020l. *Africa's Pulse: Charting the Road to Recovery.* October. Washington, DC: World Bank.

World Bank. 2020m. *Poverty and Shared Prosperity Report 2020: Reversing Reversals of Fortune.* Washington, DC: World Bank.

World Bank. 2020n. *Nigeria in Times of COVID-19: Laying Foundations for a Strong Recovery—Nigeria Development Update.* June. Washington, DC: World Bank.

World Bank. 2020o. *Global Economic Prospects: Slow Growth, Policy Challenges.* January. Washington, DC: World Bank.

World Bank, European Union, and United Nations. 2020. "Beirut Rapid Damage and Needs Assessment." World Bank, Washington, DC.

CHAPTER 3

GLOBAL ECONOMY

Heading into a Decade of Disappointments?

The COVID-19 pandemic has caused major disruptions in the global economy. Economic activity has been hit by reduced personal interaction, owing both to official restrictions and private decisions; uncertainty about the post-pandemic economic landscape and policies has discouraged investment; disruptions to education have slowed human capital accumulation; and concerns about the viability of global value chains and the course of the pandemic have weighed on international trade and tourism. As with previous economic crises, the pandemic is expected to leave long-lasting adverse effects on global economic activity and per capita incomes. It is likely to steepen the slowdown in the growth of global potential output—the level of output the global economy can sustain at full employment and capacity utilization—that had earlier been projected for the decade just begun. If history is any guide, unless there are substantial and effective reforms, the global economy is heading for a decade of disappointing growth outcomes. Especially given weak fiscal positions and elevated debt, institutional reforms to spur growth are particularly important. A comprehensive policy effort is needed to rekindle robust, sustainable, and equitable growth. A package of reforms to increase investment in human and physical capital and raise female labor force participation could help avert the expected impact of the pandemic on potential growth in emerging market and developing economies (EMDEs) over the next decade. In the past, the growth dividends from reform efforts were recognized and anticipated by investors in upgrades to their long-term growth expectations.

Introduction

The global economy headed into the COVID-19 pandemic on the heels of a decade of slowing productivity growth and weak investment. By 2018, labor productivity growth in advanced economies and emerging market and developing economies (EMDEs) had slowed to 0.8 and 3.5 percent, respectively, from 1.0 and 4.1 percent during the first decade of the 2000s (Dieppe 2020). In 2019, investment growth was below its 2000-09 average in two-thirds of the world's economies and in three-quarters of EMDEs (World Bank 2019a).

As these fundamental drivers of long-term growth weakened, growth in global potential output—the output that can be sustained at full employment and capacity utilization—had fallen to 2.2 percent in 2019, well below its annual average of 3.3 percent in the first decade of the 2000s. This decline in potential growth was broad-based, affecting three-quarters of countries, including two-thirds of EMDEs (World Bank 2018a; Kilic Celik, Kose, and Ohnsorge 2020).

In recognition of this weakening, forecasters repeatedly downgraded their long-term growth

expectations over the past decade. By 2019, ten-year-ahead forecasts for global growth had fallen to 2.4 percent, down from 3.3 percent in 2010. Over 2010-19, long-term growth forecasts were downgraded for almost all countries. For EMDEs, ten-year-ahead growth forecasts fell to 3.9 percent in 2019, down from 6.1 percent in 2010.

Since durable per capita income gains and poverty reduction can be achieved only with sustained improvements in potential growth, poverty reduction has slowed over the past decade. In the decade that ended in 2017, the prevalence of global extreme poverty declined by 9 percentage points of the global population, down from 11 percentage points in the preceding decade.

The new decade that began in 2020 was ushered in with the most severe global recession since the Second World War, triggered by the COVID-19 pandemic (World Bank 2020a). In less than a year, by December 2020, COVID-19 had cost the lives of more than 1.5 million people around the world and was gathering momentum once again in many advanced economies and some EMDEs (chapters 1 and 2). Like earlier severe economic disruptions, the pandemic will likely leave lasting economic and financial scars. Productivity-enhancing investment has plunged, education has been disrupted, and the pandemic has cast doubt on many countries' growth strategies, including global value chain participation, reliance on production and export of commodities, and

_____

Note: This chapter was prepared by Sinem Kilic Celik, M. Ayhan Kose, Franziska Ohnsorge, and Naotaka Sugawara, with contributions from Sergiy Kasyanenko, Yoki Okawa, and Dana Vorisek. Research assistance was provided by Ipek Ceylan Oymak and Kaltrina Temaj.

specialization in hospitality and tourism (Dieppe 2020). The pandemic is also poised to increase inequality because it risks causing large human capital losses particularly among people who are already disadvantaged, making it harder for countries to return to inclusive growth even after the shock recedes (World Bank 2020b).

Against this backdrop, this chapter examines the following questions.

- What has been the impact of the pandemic on long-term growth prospects?

- What are the implications for growth expectations over the next decade?

- What policy options are available to boost growth prospects in the post-pandemic world?

Contributions. This chapter contributes to the literature in several dimensions.

- *Impact of the pandemic on long-term growth prospects.* This chapter breaks new ground by examining the impact of the pandemic on long-term global growth prospects. Earlier studies, such as World Bank (2020a) and Dieppe (2020), estimated the impact of past economic disruptions on growth in the subsequent few years. This chapter focuses on growth prospects over the next decade.

- *Two measures of long-term growth prospects.* This chapter uses two measures of long-term growth prospects: model-based estimates of potential growth and survey-based long-term growth forecasts. The model-based potential growth estimates are intended to capture major long-term drivers of growth: investment, quantity and quality of labor supply, and total factor productivity (TFP). The survey-based long-term growth forecasts are intended to capture the expectations underlying the decisions of investors and households about investment and consumption.[1]

- *Weaker-than-expected growth after adverse events.* This chapter builds on a literature on evidence for a tendency towards initial over-optimism and subsequent disappointments by documenting how growth tends to be lower after adverse events and identifying the country features and circumstances that are most robustly associated with such growth outcomes. Previous studies have pointed to below-trend output and new IMF programs as correlates of disappointments (Ho and Mauro 2016). This chapter expands the range of correlates and compares them with current conditions. The patterns in disappointments serve as cautionary guidance to policy makers in countries that share these features and circumstances.

- *Possible over-optimism after the pandemic.* Previous research has established that growth forecasts over the past two to three decades have had a significant optimistic bias.[2] Sizeable short-term forecast errors and a failure to predict business cycle turning points a year in advance have been documented in large cross-country datasets.[3] Over-optimism—that is, disappointing growth outcomes compared to forecasts—has been documented for forecasts at the three-year horizon (Frankel 2011), five-year horizon (Pritchett and Summers 2014), and five- to ten-year horizon, with greater over-optimism as the forecast horizon expanded (Ho and Mauro 2016).[4] This study is the first to

---

[1] Consumers facing weaker income growth prospects will tend to rein in their consumption (Bayer et al. 2019; Mody, Ohnsorge, and Sandri 2012); investors with weaker prospects for sales and earnings growth will delay investments (Cummins, Hassett, and Oliner 2006;

Gennaioli, Ma, and Shleifer 2016). Therefore, weak long-term growth forecasts may create a self-fulfilling equilibrium (Chen and Shimomura 1998).

[2] The accuracy of short-term growth forecasts has been tested, for example, for China (Sun, Wang, and Zhang 2018), the euro area (Bowles et al. 2007), and Mexico (Capistrán and López-Moctezuma 2014).

[3] Some of these studies use *World Economic Outlook* forecasts (Ager, Kappler, and Osterloh 2009; Batchelor 2007; Loungani 2001; Timmermann 2007) whereas others consider Consensus Economics forecasts (Juhn and Loungani 2002).

[4] Forecasts several decades ahead have also proven overly optimistic. Forecasts in Onishi (1988) of 3.3 to 3.8 percent global growth over 1986-2000 also turned out to be higher than those that eventually materialized (3.0 percent). The optimism of growth forecasts partly reflects an initial underappreciation of structural headwinds in the economy, for example, demographics and weak investment. It could also be an outcome of the failure to predict negative shocks that trigger crises or turning points of business cycles.

examine the likely implications of such over-optimism for the current recovery from the pandemic.

- *Reforms in the post-pandemic world.* This chapter examines the link between growth-boosting reforms and long-term growth prospects. Econometric exercises examine the responses of investment and total factor productivity as well as long-term growth expectations to institutional reform advances and setbacks. A large literature on the link between specific reforms and growth is reviewed and its lessons are applied to the current growth outlook.

Main findings. The study reports the following findings (figure 3.1).

- *Damage from the pandemic to long-term growth prospects.* Even before the pandemic, trends in fundamental drivers of growth suggested that annual average potential output growth would slow by 0.4 percentage point globally and 1.0 percentage point in EMDEs over the 2020s. As a result the pandemic, the slowdown in potential growth over the 2020s may be 0.3 and 0.6 percentage point per year steeper for the global economy and EMDEs, respectively, than anticipated before the pandemic—unless effective policy action is taken or major technological advances materialize.

- *Prospect of a decade of growth disappointments.* Past recessions were typically followed by several years of disappointing growth outcomes and downgrades of long-term growth expectations. After the 2008 global financial crisis, long-term (ten-year-ahead) global growth forecasts were repeatedly downgraded, to 2.4 percent in 2019, 0.9 percentage point below their 2008 forecast (Kose, Ohnsorge, and Sugawara, forthcoming). Five years after country-specific recessions, long-term growth expectations were typically 1.5 percentage points lower than in countries without recessions. Long-term expectations were also weaker several years after financial crises. This experience suggests that the recent pandemic-related

FIGURE 3.1 Long-term growth prospects

The global economy headed into the COVID-19 pandemic after a decade of forecast disappointments and slowing potential output growth. The pandemic is expected to steepen the slowdown previously projected over the 2020s. However, ambitious policy reforms to support investment, improve education, and raise labor force participation could reverse much of the adverse impact of the pandemic on potential growth prospects over the next decade. Institutional reforms could strengthen investment and output growth prospects, as they have done in the past.

A. Global potential output growth

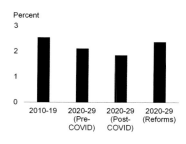

B. Ten-year-ahead growth forecasts for global output and per capita income

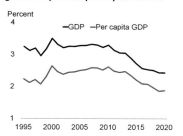

C. Ten-year-ahead output growth forecasts

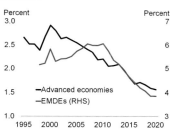

D. Global output levels

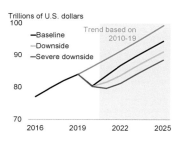

E. Cumulative change in EMDE investment two to four years after reform episodes

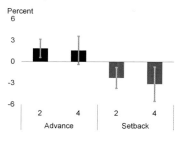

F. Cumulative response of long-term growth forecasts after institutional reform advances

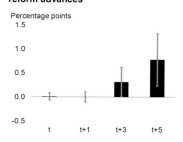

Sources: Consensus Economics; Haver Analytics; International Country Risk Guide (database); Kilic Celik, Kose, and Ohnsorge (2020); World Bank; World Population Prospects 2019 (database).
Note: EMDEs = emerging market and developing economies.
A. GDP-weighted average (at 2010 prices and exchange rates) for 82 economies. Potential growth estimates based on a production function approach as described in Kilic Celik, Kose, and Ohnsorge (2020). "Pre-COVID," "Post-COVID," and "Reforms" defined as in figures 3.2, 3.4, and 3.12.
B.C. Aggregate GDP growth calculated using GDP at 2010 prices and market exchange rates as weights. Per capita GDP growth is the difference between GDP growth and population growth. Results from the latest Consensus Economics surveys in each year are presented. Sample includes 84 countries (33 advanced economies and 51 EMDEs). The horizontal axis shows the years when Consensus Economics forecasts are surveyed.
D. Data are in U.S. dollars at 2010 prices and market exchange rates. Shaded area indicates forecasts. Trend and baseline output is defined in figures B3.1.1 and 3.7. The downside and severe downside scenarios are described in boxes 1.4 and 3.1.
E. Coefficients estimates of a local projection estimation for 71 EMDEs during 1998-2018 of cumulative investment growth on reform advances and setbacks at forecast horizons of two and four years. Reforms are defined in box 3.3. Vertical lines show 90 percent confidence intervals.
F. Cumulative impulse responses of ten-year-ahead growth forecasts on reform advances started in year t, based on local projection estimations for 57 countries during 1990-2020. Reforms are defined in annex 3.1. Vertical orange lines show the 90 percent confidence intervals.

recession may well be followed by several years of disappointing growth outcomes.

- *Reforms to boost growth prospects.* To avoid a repeat of the historical pattern of initial over-optimism followed by subsequent disappointments, a comprehensive policy effort is needed to promote a recovery that strengthened the foundations for growth. Such an effort would include reforms to improve governance and business climates; increase competition and level the playing field for firms; encourage productivity-enhancing investment in human and physical capital; foster economic flexibility; and diversify economies where activity is concentrated in a few sectors. If every country repeated its best ten-year improvement in investment and schooling and managed to close the gap between male and female labor force participation rates by as much as the most successful quartile of reformers, the adverse impact of the pandemic on EMDE potential growth could be reversed. A particular priority at the current juncture, when fiscal positions have been extremely stretched by the policy responses to the pandemic, are institutional reforms that have been associated with increased investment and stronger growth. In the past, investors have recognized the growth potential of such reform efforts, raising their long-term growth expectations by 0.8 percentage point, on average, five years after the reforms.

Data. This study use two measures of long-term growth prospects. The first is potential output growth derived from a production function approach.[5] Annual data and projections are available for 82 economies (including 30 advanced economies and 52 EMDEs, of which 12 are low-

income countries) for 1995-2029 (time series for 2020-29 are projections). These countries accounted for 95 percent of global GDP over the past five years.[6] The second measure consists of ten-year-ahead output growth forecasts compiled by *Consensus Economics*. These are available on a semi-annual or quarterly basis for up to 86 economies (33 advanced economies and up to 53 EMDEs) as well as the euro area over 1990-2020. These countries accounted for 92 percent of global GDP over the past five years. Long-term output growth forecasts are complemented by long-term investment and private consumption growth forecasts which are available for a smaller set of up to 46 economies (24 advanced economies and up to 22 EMDEs) and the euro area.

Pre-pandemic decade of economic weakness

The pre-pandemic decade was marked by weakening momentum in all major drivers of potential growth and a series of growth disappointments. These were broad-based across countries and components of growth.

Structural weaknesses in growth

Weakening drivers of growth. The pre-pandemic decade was marked by structural weaknesses that weighed on growth. Global working-age population growth slowed from 2010, chiefly because of a slowdown in EMDEs (World Bank 2018a). The pace of sectoral reallocation slowed such that labor productivity gains from this source waned (Dieppe and Matsuoka 2020). Other major productivity growth drivers slowed as gains in life expectancy as well as school achievement and enrollment levelled off and global value chains—a major driver of productivity-enhancing investment and technology transfer—appeared to mature (Dieppe 2020). Governance reform efforts slowed as well. Global investment growth weakened to 2.5

---

[5] For details of this methodology, see as in Kilic Celik, Kose, and Ohnsorge (2020) and World Bank (2018a). Potential labor supply is derived from the labor force participation predicted by a panel regression of labor force participation in five age groups for each gender on education and health indicators, as well as cohort effects. Potential total factor productivity (TFP) growth is derived from the predicted value of a panel regression of trend TFP growth on education and health indicators, investment, and research· and development spending. Potential capital is assumed to match actual capital.

[6] The latest available vintage in a year is used as the annual data series. Data on consensus forecasts are available since 1989, but long-term forecasts start in 1990. A full panel of data is available for 45 economies, including 18 EMDEs, for 1998-2020. The number of economies increased from 57 economies in the April 2019 vintage of consensus forecasts.

percent in 2019 from 3.3 percent, on average, in 2000-09 as crises disrupted bank finance in major advanced economies and FDI and other capital flows into EMDEs slowed. China implemented a policy-guided slowdown towards more sustainable growth, and policy uncertainty weighed on investment in EMDEs.

Broad-based slowdown in potential growth. Global potential output growth declined to 2.5 percent in 2010-19, well below its average of 3.3 percent a year in the preceding decade (figure 3.2). Almost one-half of this decline can be attributed to slower TFP growth, just over one-quarter to weaker capital accumulation, and the remainder to slower labor supply growth. The slowdown in global potential growth mainly reflected weaker potential growth in many EMDEs and in all EMDE regions except South Asia (SAR).

- *In advanced economies,* potential growth remained anemic at 1.4 percent a year, on average, over the 2010s as a substantial decline in capital accumulation and TFP growth (of about 0.3 percentage point a year each) relative to the preceding decade was compounded by slowing growth in the labor supply amid population aging.

- *In EMDEs,* potential growth slowed to 5.0 percent a year during the 2010s (and further to 4.4 percent a year in the second half of the 2010s), from 5.6 percent a year in the preceding decade. Four-fifths of this decline is accounted for by slower TFP growth, with the remainder the result of a slowdown in labor supply growth.

- *Investment-driven slowdowns: EAP, LAC, MNA, SSA.* The steepest regional decline in potential growth occurred in East Asia and Pacific (EAP): it weakened to 5.9 percent a year in 2018-19 from its 2010s average of 7.6 percent a year. This mostly reflected slowing capital accumulation, as China implemented a policy-guided rebalancing from investment to consumption. As in EAP, in Latin America and the Caribbean (LAC), the Middle East and North Africa (MNA), and Sub-Saharan Africa (SSA), at least half of the decline in

FIGURE 3.2 Evolution of growth prospects over the pre-pandemic decade

The global economy headed into the COVID-19 pandemic on the heels of a decade of slowing productivity growth, weak investment, and declining potential output growth.

A. Working-age population

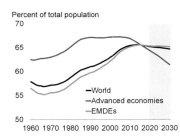

B. Contribution to labor productivity growth

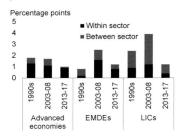

C. Investment growth

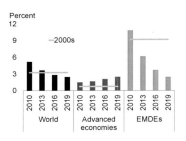

D. Global potential growth prospects

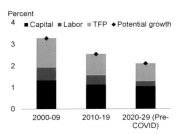

E. EMDE potential growth prospects

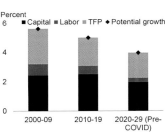

F. Potential growth in EMDE regions

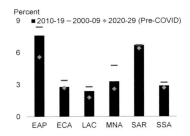

Sources: Dieppe and Matsuoka (2020); Haver Analytics; Kilic Celik, Kose, and Ohnsorge (2020); World Bank; World Population Prospects 2019 (database).

Note: EMDEs = emerging market and developing economies, LICs = low-income countries, EAP = East Asia and Pacific, ECA = Europe and Central Asia, LAC = Latin America and the Caribbean, MNA = Middle East and North Africa, SAR = South Asia, SSA = Sub-Saharan Africa. TFP = total factor productivity.

A. Population-weighted averages. Working-age population is defined as population aged 15-64 years. Shaded area indicates forecasts.

B. Based on samples of 94 countries during 1995-99 and 103 countries during 2003-17. Median of countries' annual average productivity growth. Within-sector contribution is the contribution of real value-added weighted sectoral productivity growth. Between-sector contribution is the contribution of changes in sectoral employment shares. Medians of country-specific contributions.

C. Investment refers to gross fixed capital formation. Aggregate growth calculated using investment at 2010 prices and market exchange rates as weights. Sample includes 97 countries, consisting of 34 advanced economies and 63 EMDEs.

D.-F. GDP-weighted average (at 2010 prices and exchange rates) for 82 countries, including 52 EMDEs. Potential growth estimates and projections are based on a production function approach as described in Kilic Celik, Kose, and Ohnsorge (2020). Pre-COVID projections for the 2020s assume that investment grows at its historical average rate, working-age population and life expectancy evolve as envisaged by the UN *Population Projections,* and secondary and tertiary school enrollment and completion rates improve at their historical average rate.

potential growth in 2018-19 was due to slowing capital accumulation.

- *TFP and labor supply driven slowdown: ECA.* Europe and Central Asia (ECA) was the only EMDE region where investment growth picked up in the 2010s, but this was offset by shrinking labor supply and slowing TFP growth, leaving potential growth roughly unchanged.

- *Productivity-driven acceleration: SAR.* In SAR, a modest softening in labor supply growth was more than offset by increases in TFP growth and accelerating capital accumulation, causing the rate of potential growth to rise in 2018-19 above the decade average.

Lower potential growth prospects before COVID-19. Based on pre-pandemic trends and population forecasts, global and EMDE potential growth would already have been expected to slow further in the coming decade. Global and EMDE potential growth over 2020-29 would have been 0.4 and 1.0 percentage point a year, respectively, lower than in the 2010s, falling to averages of 2.1 and 4.0 percent a year, respectively, during the 2020s.[7] In this pre-pandemic scenario, almost half of the decline would have resulted from slowing labor supply growth amid population aging and more than one-third from weakening TFP growth.[8] At this pace, there would have been limited progress towards narrowing the large per capita income gaps between advanced economies and EMDEs, where per capita incomes current amount to one-fifth of those in advanced economies on average (Dieppe 2020).

Downgraded expectations

Repeated global growth downgrades. The pandemic followed a decade of successive down-grades in long-term growth expectations (as measured by *Consensus Economics* forecasts) after a turning point marked by the global financial crisis

of 2008 (figure 3.3). In the decade preceding the global financial crisis (1998-2007), long-term global growth expectations had improved slightly (from 3.0 percent to 3.3 percent a year) and had been upgraded for about one-half of countries (Kose, Ohnsorge, and Sugawara, forthcoming). In the decade following the global financial crisis, however, long-term global growth expectations declined steadily, from 3.3 percent a year in 2010 to 2.4 percent a year in 2019.

Broad-based downgrades across countries, drivers. Downgrades in expectations for long-term growth between 2010 and 2019 applied to almost all countries. The decline in long-term output growth expectations over the past decade was accompanied by weakening prospects for global investment and consumption growth as well as per capita income growth. Long-term expectations of global per capita income growth declined from 2.6 percent in 2010 to 1.9 percent in 2019. Expectations for EMDE per capita income growth ten years ahead fell from 5.3 percent in 2010 to 3.2 percent in 2019, narrowing the gap between EMDE and advanced-economy per capita income growth—and hence the pace of income convergence—by 1.7 percentage points. The downgrade to long-term expectations for per capita income growth was broad-based, applying to 95 percent of EMDEs and advanced economies. Over 2010-19, long-term expectations of global investment growth declined from 4.3 percent to 2.6 percent. During the same period, long-term forecasts of global consumption growth declined by 0.4 percentage point, to 2.1 percent in 2019.[9]

Economic impact of the pandemic

The pandemic has disrupted key drivers of long-term economic growth. Unless this disruption is offset by technological and policy breakthroughs, the pandemic is likely to weaken growth prospects for the decade just begun.

---

[7] This scenario assumes that investment grows at its historical average rate, working-age population evolves as envisaged by the UN *Population Projections,* and secondary and tertiary school enrollment and completion rates improve at their historical average rates (Kilic Celik, Kose, and Ohnsorge 2020).

[8] The specific assumptions underlying this scenario are detailed in Kilic Celik, Kose, and Ohnsorge (2020).

---

[9] Long-term per capita income growth expectations were downgraded from 2.6 percent in 2010 to 1.9 percent in 2019, below their 1998 level. Forecast downgrades to per capita growth largely reflected downgrades to aggregate output growth.

Channels. The pandemic may set back long-term growth prospects through multiple channels. The deep economic contractions across many countries and heightened uncertainties about the post-pandemic global economic landscape may discourage investment. A prolonged period of depressed capital spending would be particularly damaging to long-term growth prospects in EMDEs, coming on the heels of several years of weak investment (World Bank 2017a, 2019a). Higher unemployment is likely to erode human capital, while disruptions to education and training can obstruct human capital accumulation (World Bank 2020a). Supply chains and working arrangements in many industries may go through costly reconfigurations as companies attempt to accommodate physical distancing of employees and customers and diversify the sourcing of inputs and the destination of outputs. The latter is a process that may have already begun as a result of rising trade tensions over the past few years. There may also be long-lasting shifts in consumer behavior, including in the composition of spending. Households may also opt for increased precautionary saving in view of heightened uncertainty about health care costs and employment and income prospects (Jordà, Singh, and Taylor 2020; Mody, Ohnsorge, and Sandri 2012). Both consumer spending and business investment may suffer from sustained declines in confidence.

Already large output losses. The pandemic-induced global recession has already turned the 2010s into a lost decade for many EMDEs (box 3.1). In about 30 percent of EMDEs, per capita income losses in 2020 have reversed 10 years or more of gains; in more than half of EMDEs, at least half a decade of income gains has been reversed (figure 3.4). In LAC and MNA, income gains of at least half a decade have been reversed in more than 80 percent of countries. The number of people living in poverty, globally, is estimated to rise by more than a hundred million by 2021 compared to pre-pandemic trends, reversing several years of poverty reduction (World Bank 2020b; Lakner et al., forthcoming).

Increase in inequality. As a result of the pandemic, 60 percent of households in nearly 100

FIGURE 3.3 Evolution of growth expectations over the pre-pandemic decade

In recognition of structural growth weaknesses, forecasters have repeatedly downgraded their long-term growth forecasts over the past decade.

A. Ten-year-ahead global output and per capita income growth forecasts

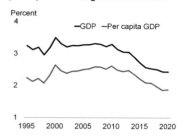

B. Three-, five-, and ten-year-ahead global growth forecasts

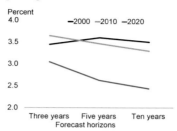

C. Ten-year-ahead global investment and consumption growth forecasts

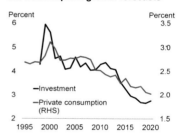

D. Ten-year-ahead output growth forecasts

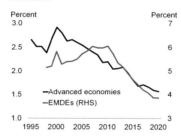

Sources: Consensus Economics; World Bank; World Population Prospects 2019 (database).
Note: EMDEs = emerging market and developing economies. Aggregate growth calculated using weights based on GDP (panels A, B, D), or investment and private consumption (panel C) at 2010 prices and market exchange rates. Per capita GDP growth is computed as the difference between GDP growth and population growth. Results from the latest Consensus Economics surveys in each year are presented. Sample for GDP growth includes 84 economies, consisting of 33 advanced economies and 51 EMDEs. Sample for investment and private consumption includes 44 countries.
A.C.D. The horizontal axis shows the years when Consensus Economics forecasts were compiled.

countries reported income losses in April-July 2020 and those with lower education levels were at greater risk of losing jobs; yet, only 20 percent of households reported receiving public social assistance (Sanchez-Paramo and Narayan 2020). COVID-19 is expected to increase global inequality, both within and between countries (Furceri et al. 2020). Within countries, the pandemic has hit particularly hard lower-paid workers—the informally employed, women, immigrants, and the low-skilled.[10]

After past epidemics, unemployment increases were larger and more persistent among lower-

---

[10] See IMF (2020a) for a literature review.

BOX 3.1 Global economy: A lost decade ahead?

Past global recessions were associated with highly persistent output losses. The pandemic-induced global recession has already reversed a decade or more of per capita income gains in roughly 30 percent of emerging market and developing economies (EMDEs). By 2025, global output is still expected to be 5 percent below the pre-pandemic trend—a cumulative output loss that is equivalent to 36 percent of the world's 2019 output. Policy makers need to undertake comprehensive and credible reform programs to set the stage for stronger long-term growth.

Introduction

After experiencing its worst recession in 2020 since World War II, the global economy is expected to recover in 2021 (figure B3.1.1). However, the pandemic-induced global recession has already turned the 2010s into a lost decade for many emerging market and developing economies (EMDEs; Kose and Sugawara, forthcoming). In about 30 percent of EMDEs, per capita income losses in 2020 reversed ten years or more of gains; in more than half of these economies, at least half a decade of income gains has been reversed. In Latin America and the Caribbean and in the Middle East and North Africa, income gains of at least half a decade were reversed in 80 percent of countries. As a result, the number of people living in poverty, globally, is estimated to rise by more than a hundred million by 2021 compared to pre-pandemic trends, reversing several years of poverty reduction (World Bank 2020b; Lakner et al., forthcoming).

Against this backdrop, this box examines the following questions.

- What were the consequences of past recessions for output?

- How much larger could output losses be in a downside scenario?

- How large have output losses been after previous global recessions?

Consequences of recessions: Large output losses

Past country-specific recessions were associated with persistent output losses. A wide range of factors led to these losses: depressed capacity utilization discouraged investment and led to a legacy of obsolete capacity; elevated uncertainty and expectations of weak growth depressed investment; weak investment delayed the adoption of capital-embodied productivity-enhancing

technologies; and protracted unemployment caused losses of human capital and reduced job-search activity.

Five years after the average country-specific recession, potential output was still about 6 percent below baseline in EMDEs (World Bank 2020a). Recessions in EMDEs that were accompanied by financial crises were associated with even larger potential output losses in EMDEs, of 8 percent relative to baseline after five years. The pandemic is likely to exacerbate the trend slowdown in growth of potential output and productivity that had been underway for a decade, particularly by increasing uncertainty about growth prospects, disrupting human capital accumulation, and raising concerns about the viability of global value chains (Dieppe 2020; Kilic Celik, Kose, and Ohnsorge 2020).

Looming danger: Even larger income losses

Output losses in the baseline scenario. Even after the recovery gets underway, there is expected to be a protracted period of below-trend global output, with substantial per capita income losses. In the baseline scenario, global output in 2025 would be about 5 percent below the pre-pandemic trend and there would be a cumulative output loss during 2020-25 equivalent to 36 percent of 2019 global GDP.

Output losses in risk scenario. A more protracted pandemic than expected could lead to even larger income losses (box 1.4). In a downside scenario of persistently higher caseloads and delayed vaccination, global output in 2025 would be about 8 percent below earlier expectations and there would be a cumulative loss equivalent to 54 percent of 2019 global output. Delays in vaccine deployment could disappoint financial markets and trigger a repricing of risks. Amid record-high debt, higher borrowing costs could tip many firms into bankruptcy, weakening bank balance sheets, possibly to an extent that could trigger a financial crisis. In such a severe downside scenario, global output could contract by another 0.7 percent in 2021. Cumulative output losses over 2020-25 could amount to 68 percent of 2019 output globally and 78 percent of 2019 output for EMDEs, with wide variation across EMDE regions. Small-state IDA countries

---

Note: This box was prepared by Naotaka Sugawara.

BOX 3.1 Global economy: A lost decade ahead? *(continued)*

FIGURE B3.1.1 Repercussions of the COVID-19 pandemic

The pandemic has already reversed a decade of income gains in a considerable share of countries. It is expected to cause lasting output losses over the next half-decade.

A. World Bank Group growth scenarios

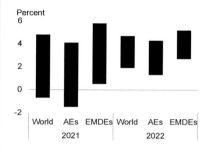

B. Share of countries, by years of per capita income gains reversed in 2020

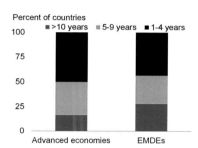

C. Share of countries, by years of per capita income gains reversed in 2020, by region

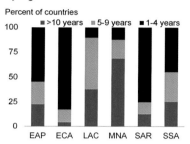

D. Global output levels

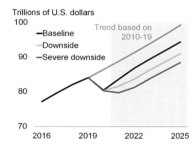

E. Global and EMDE cumulative output losses, 2020-25

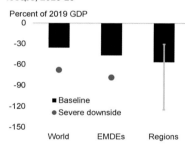

F. Cumulative output losses during 2020-25, by country characteristics

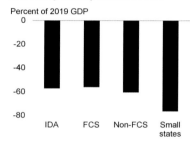

Sources: Consensus Economics; World Bank.

Note: AEs = advanced economies, EMDEs = emerging market and developing economies, EAP = East Asia and Pacific, ECA = Europe and Central Asia, LAC = Latin America and the Caribbean, MNA = Middle East and North Africa, SAR = South Asia, SSA = Sub-Saharan Africa.

A. Bars show ranges of growth scenarios for 2021 and 2022, depending on rollout of vaccines and financial stress, as discussed in box 1.4. Aggregate growth calculated using GDP at 2010 prices and market exchange rates as weights.

B.C. The share of countries with per capita income gains reversed in 2020, by the number of years indicated.

D.-F. Data are in U.S. dollars at 2010 prices and market exchange rates. Shaded area indicates forecasts. Trend is assumed to grow at the regression-estimated trend growth rate of 2010-19. For global and EMDE output, baseline output is based on the baseline estimates and forecasts in chapter 1 over 2020-22 and, for 2023-25, is assumed to grow at the rates computed with long-term consensus forecasts surveyed n October 2020. The downside and severe downside scenarios are described in the main text of the chapter and box 1.4. For regions and IDA aggregates, baseline output is assumed to grow at the baseline estimates and forecasts in chapter 1 over 2020-22 and, for 2023-25, is assumed to grow at the same rates as in the trend. Samples for IDA include 70 IDA-eligible countries, including 31 FCS, 39 non-FCS, and 23 small states.

E.F. Bars show cumulative output losses over 2020-25, based on baseline growth forecasts, and, for regions, an average of six EMDE regions is presented. Red circles are based on growth forecasts under the severe downside scenario. A vertical yellow line for regions shows the minimum-maximum range among the six regions. Cumulative losses are computed as deviations from trend in U.S. dollars, expressed as a share of GDP in 2019.

F. "FCS" refers to economies in fragile and conflict-affected situations. "IDA" refers to countries that are eligible to borrow from the International Development Association, the part of the World Bank Group that helps the world's poorest countries.

generally face larger losses than other IDA countries or EMDEs.

An outcome to avoid: Another lost decade

Large output losses. Like its predecessors, the pandemic-induced global recession will likely lead to highly protracted output losses. In the past, the losses from global recessions were associated with a wide range of factors: depressed capacity utilization; discouraged investment because of uncertainty and weak growth expectations; slower productivity-enhancing technology adoption; and loss of human capital due to persistent unemployment. The pandemic is expected to exacerbate the trend slowdown in potential growth and productivity growth in EMDEs that had already been underway for a decade.

BOX 3.1 Global economy: A lost decade ahead? *(continued)*

FIGURE B3.1.2 Increasing fiscal risks

Fiscal support and economic contractions have raised debt to record-high levels. Unless accompanied by credible commitments to return to sustainable fiscal positions, high debt and deficits can erode the effectiveness of fiscal policy.

A. Fiscal support measures	B. Fiscal balance	C. Fiscal multipliers and debt in EMDEs
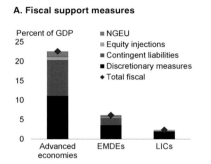	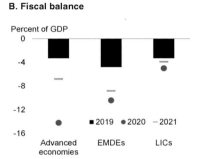	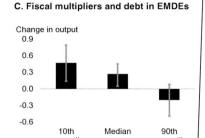

Sources: Huidrom et al. (2020); International Monetary Fund; Kose et al. (2020a); World Bank.

Note: EMDEs = emerging market and developing economies, LICs = low-income countries.

A. Fiscal stimulus measures are derived from the October 2020 IMF Fiscal Monitor database and include measures planned or under consideration. Aggregates are the GDP-weighted average of the total fiscal package and its components. "Discretionary measures" includes revenue and expenditure measures; "Contingent liabilities" includes loan guarantee and other quasi-fiscal measures; and "Equity injections" includes equity injections, loans, and asset purchases. "NGEU" refers to Next Generation EU funds. Sample includes 35 advanced economies, 139 EMDEs, and 23 LICs.

B. Aggregates computed with current GDP in U.S. dollars as weights.

C. Bars are the median conditional fiscal multipliers after two years. Fiscal multipliers are the cumulative change in output relative to cumulative change in government consumption to a 1-unit government consumption shock. Orange lines are the 16-84 percent confidence bands.

Intensifying fiscal risks. Record high debt levels may also weigh on output growth and investment in many EMDEs (box 1.1). In 2019, global total debt reached a historic record of 230 percent of GDP and global government debt rose to 83 percent of GDP (Kose et al. 2020a). Like advanced economies, EMDEs have implemented considerably larger fiscal stimulus programs than in 2009, equivalent to about 6 percent of GDP in 2020 (figure B3.1.2; World Bank 2020a). While appropriate to support aggregate demand and activity and to protect vulnerable groups and sectors during the downturn, such stimulus translated into record fiscal deficits. As a result, global government debt is expected to rise by 17 percentage points of GDP, to 100 percent of GDP in 2021 (IMF 2020b, 2020c). Current low interest rate reduce debt service cost. Nevertheless, unless accompanied by credible commitments to return to sustainable fiscal positions, record-high debt and deficits can erode the effectiveness of fiscal policy (World Bank 2015a, Huidrom et al. 2020). Past episodes of rapid debt accumulation often resulted in financial crises: about one-half of the more than 500 episodes of rapid debt accumulation in EMDEs since 1970 were associated with financial crises within two years of the

debt peak, at considerable economic cost (Kose et al. 2020c, World Bank 2020c).

New risks from unconventional monetary policy. Recognizing the benefits of prompt policy action—one of the lessons of the 2009 global recession—many central banks and governments have implemented unprecedented monetary policy easing measures. While this was appropriate to cushion the recession, it may erode the hard-won distance of central banks from political pressures and fiscal authorities in EMDEs where inflation expectations tend to be more poorly anchored (Ha, Kose, and Ohnsorge 2019). If this leads to an upward reassessment of inflation expectations, it could trigger capital outflows, depreciation, and inflationary pressures.

Conclusion

The immediate policy priorities remain to save lives, protect vulnerable groups, and preserve functioning markets. However, increasingly, policy makers need to turn their attention to averting and reversing long-term economic damage from the pandemic by strengthening policies and institutions for a resilient recovery.

skilled workers (Ma, Rogers, and Zhou 2020). Lower-income workers tend to be less able to work from home than higher-income workers and, hence, are more likely to be exposed to the pandemic at work and are more vulnerable to job or income losses due to lockdowns (Adams-Prassl et al. 2020; Brussevich, Dabla-Norris, and Khalid 2020). The share of lower-paid workers is higher in essential services where workers are more exposed to the pandemic (Goldin and Muggah 2020). Social benefits may fail to reach middle-income households that have suffered income losses but are outside existing poverty alleviation programs (Lustig et al. 2020; World Bank 2020b, 2020d). With regard to inequality between countries, lower-income countries tend to have large informal sectors that concentrate in activities, and operate in facilities, that require close interactions and are particularly vulnerable to pandemic-related disruptions (World Bank 2020a). `

Steeper slowdown in potential growth. In addition to causing losses in output *levels*, the pandemic has set back fundamental drivers of long-term output *growth*—investment, improvements in education and health, and increases in female labor force participation. Weakening fundamental drivers of growth will be reflected in lower potential growth prospects over the 2020s. Global potential growth would slow by another 0.3 percentage point a year compared with pre-pandemic trends, to 1.9 percent a year over 2020-29, below the 2.1 percent a year expected before the pandemic. The decline in EMDE potential growth over the 2020s would be 0.6 percentage point a year more than expected before the pandemic, with potential growth reaching 3.3 percent a year over 2020-29, far below its 5.0 percent average during 2010-19.

- *Investment.* Uncertainty has risen sharply as a result of COVID-19, contributing to a collapse in investment (box 3.2; Altig et al. 2020). If EMDE investment growth were to match current long-term consensus forecasts, it would slow to 2.7 percent a year, on average, over the 2020s. This would lower EMDE potential growth by 0.4 percentage point a year both directly, because of slower

FIGURE 3.4 Impact of the pandemic on long-term growth prospects

For almost one-third of EMDEs, the pandemic has wiped out a decade or more of per capita income gains. It has sharply raised poverty and lockdowns have disproportionately hit low-income workers. This adverse impact of the pandemic, along with a broader weakening of all major drivers of long-term growth, is expected to steepen the expected decline in potential growth over the next decade and cause lasting output losses.

A. Share of countries, by years of per capita income gains reversed in 2020

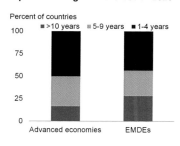

B. Global poverty relative to pre-COVID trend

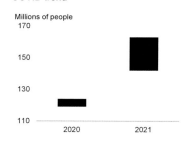

C. Average annual income of workers employed in shutdown sectors

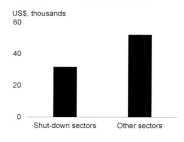

D. Global potential growth prospects

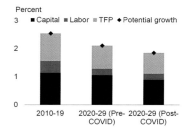

E. EMDE potential growth prospects

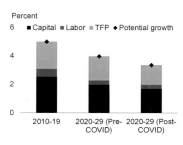

F. Potential output after recessions and financial crises

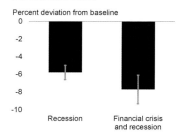

Sources: Blundell et al. (2020); Consensus Economics; Eurostat (database); Haver Analytics; Kilic Celik, Kose, and Ohnsorge (2020); U.S Bureau of Labor Statistics (database); Vavra (2020); World Bank; World Bank (2020a).
Note: EMDEs = emerging market and developing economies. TFP = total factor productivity.
A. The share of countries with per capita gains reversed in 2020, by the number of years indicated.
B. The estimated number of poor, defined with the poverty line at $1.90 per day, relative to the pre-COVID trend.
C. GDP-weighted average of annual incomes of those U.S. and euro area workers employed in shutdown sectors as defined in Blundell et al. (2020) and Vavra (2020) and in other sectors.
D.E. GDP-weighted average (at 2010 prices and exchange rates) for 82 countries, including 52 EMDEs. Potential growth estimates based on a production function approach as described in Kilic Celik, Kose, and Ohnsorge (2020). Pre-COVID prospects for the 2020s assume that investment grows at its historical average rate, working-age population and life expectancy evolve as envisaged by the UN *Population Projections*, and secondary and tertiary school enrollment and completion rates improve at their historical average rate. Post-COVID prospects assume that investment grows as expected by consensus forecasts and secondary attainment rates decline by 2.5 percentage points.
F. Bars show cumulative responses of potential output four years after respective events. Vertical orange lines show 90 percent confidence intervals. Sample includes 75 EMDEs.

growth of capital stocks, and indirectly, by dampening TFP growth, because of slower absorption of new technology embodied in new investments and a higher average age of the capital stock.[11]

- *Education.* COVID-19 has caused the "largest disruption of education systems in history" (UN 2020). As a hypothetical example to illustrate the possible impact of this disruption, the secondary school completion rate is assumed to decrease for the next half-decade and thereafter return to its trend increase, in line with evidence from the Ebola epidemic, which lowered secondary school completion rates by 2.5 percentage points in some of the affected countries.[12] Under this assumption, the secondary school completion rate would decline to 30 percent in EMDEs, on average, over the next decade. This could raise labor force participation among the young because of their earlier entry into the labor market but would reduce potential TFP growth, on balance resulting in 0.2 percentage point lower potential growth over the 2020s compared with pre-pandemic expectations.

Impact smaller than in past recessions, for now. Up to now, these effects of the pandemic on growth prospects are smaller than declines after past recessions, but further deterioration remains a risk (chapter 1). Potential output in EMDEs was, on average, 6 percent below baseline five years after past recessions, considerably more than suggested by the scenario considered here (3.1 percent; World Bank 2020a). In part, the difference reflects the unprecedented policy response to the pandemic-induced global recession of 2020. Prompt and large monetary and fiscal stimulus supported activity and, thus far at least, has averted a financial crisis. The stimulus as well as historic production cuts by OPEC, have helped

to partially reverse the initial oil price collapse. In contrast, among the past recessions in EMDEs that were considered in World Bank (2020a), many were accompanied by financial crises (23 percent of recessions) or oil price plunges (19 percent of recessions), which caused additional long-term damage.

Circumstances associated with downgraded prospects

Past recessions and financial crises were often followed by years of growth disappointments and repeated downgrades to long-term growth expectations.

Downgrades after the global financial crisis

Legacy of the last global recession. After the last global recession, in 2009, the global economy rebounded in 2010 but, in the following years, long-term growth forecasts were repeatedly downgraded, usually for the majority of countries, amid a string of growth disappointments. Growth outcomes fell short of earlier expectations in all years except in 2010. Long-term growth forecasts did not bottom out until the stimulus-fueled global upturn of 2017 (Kose, Ohnsorge, and Sugawara, forthcoming; World Bank 2018a). By 2019, expectations for long-term global growth were 0.8 percentage point lower, and expectations for long-term EMDE growth were 2.1 percentage point lower, than a decade earlier. The downgrades to output growth expectations were accompanied by repeated downgrades to expectations for investment and consumption growth (figure 3.3).

Downgrades after country-specific adverse events

Years of initial over-optimism and subsequent disappointments have not been limited to global recessions. Even after country-specific adverse events, long-term growth forecasts for the countries concerned had to be repeatedly downgraded.

Estimated of the effects of adverse events: Methodology. Two methods are used to examine the behavior of long-term (ten-year-ahead) consensus growth forecasts during and after

---

[11] Evidence of embodied technical progress in new capital investment has been found, for example, by Boileau (2002); Cummins and Violante (2002); Doraszelski and Jaumandreu (2013); Fisher (2006); Greenwood, Hercowitz, and Krusell (1997, 2000); He and Liu (2008); Hendricks (2000); and Levine and Warusawitharana (2014).

[12] Data on the impact of past epidemics on schooling is sparse. Individual country experiences may deviate materially from this illustrative example.

disruptive events. First, in a series of estimations of a local projections model as in Jordà (2005), with an adjustment as in Teulings and Zubanov (2014), the response of ten-year-ahead growth forecasts to adverse events is quantified. While the regression uses output growth forecasts as the dependent variable, the results are robust to using per capita growth forecasts. The model is estimated over a forecast horizon of up to five years using two lags of the dependent variable. The sample includes three types of "acutely adverse" events in 86 economies: 124 recessions (defined as years of per capita output contractions), 108 financial crises (defined as in Laeven and Valencia 2020), and 76 natural disasters (defined as in Dieppe 2020; annex 3.1). These are distinct events: for example, less than one-half of financial crises were associated with recessions.

Second, in a series of event studies, the behavior of long-term growth forecasts through periods of "persistently adverse" economic developments is quantified. These periods include 63 episodes when actual growth fell short of growth forecasts made in the preceding year over three or more consecutive years ("growth disappointments"); 41 episodes of negative investment growth in three or more consecutive years ("investment slowdowns"); and 49 periods of repeatedly slowing TFP growth ("productivity slowdowns"). The length of these episodes averaged four years across these episodes. Again, these periods of persistent economic pressures are distinct from recessions: Only around one-half of the episodes of growth disappointments or productivity slowdowns shared at least one year with recessions, and less than two-thirds of investment slowdowns did.

Forecast downgrades after acutely disruptive events. After an initial lag, recessions and financial crises typically ushered in periods of repeated and deepening long-term growth forecast downgrades (figure 3.5). In contrast, after natural disasters, there were no statistically significant changes to long-term growth forecasts.

- *Recessions.* After the average recession, long-term consensus forecasts were initially stable for about a year before a series of downgrades set in. These downgrades began to be

FIGURE 3.5 Long-term growth prospects after country-specific adverse events

Long-term growth forecasts for affected countries were downgraded multiple times after recessions and financial crises, but not after natural disasters.

A. Number of events

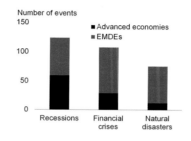

B. Cumulative response of long-term growth forecasts after recessions

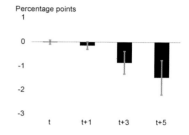

C. Cumulative response of long-term growth forecasts after financial crises

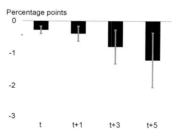

D. Cumulative response of long-term growth forecasts after natural disasters

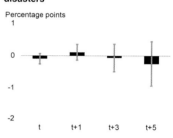

Sources: Consensus Economics; Dieppe (2020); EM-DAT (database); Laeven and Valencia (2020); World Bank.
Note: EMDEs = emerging market and developing economies.
A. The number of acutely adverse events over 1990-2020 in 86 countries where long-term Consensus Economics growth forecasts are available. The number of recessions is represented by the number of peak years identified during the sample period. For the definition of events and identification methodology, refer to annex 3.1.
B.-D. Bars are coefficient estimates for (B) a dummy on country-specific recessions, identified in a Harding-Pagan algorithm; (C) financial crises, as defined in Laeven and Valencia (2020); and (D) natural disasters, as taken from EM-DAT, in local projection estimations of ten-year-ahead growth forecasts during 1990-2020. Year t indicates the year of the business cycle peak (B), the financial crisis (C), or the natural disaster (D). Vertical orange lines show 90 percent confidence intervals. Samples include 55 countries (B), 52 countries (C), and 57 countries (D).

statistically significant from the second year following the recession and only bottomed out around five years after the recessions. Five years after the recession, the long-term growth forecast in countries with recessions was 1.5 percentage points, on average, lower than in countries without recessions.

- *Financial crises.* In contrast to recessions, financial crises were immediately followed by statistically significant forecast downgrades, with forecasts in countries with crises 0.3 percentage point lower than in those without

BOX 3.2 Impact of COVID-19 on investment: Deep, persistent, and broad based

Investment in emerging market and developing economies (EMDEs) collapsed in 2020, following a decade of persistent weakness. It is expected to expand again in 2021, but not sufficiently to reverse the decline in 2020. Based on the experience of past epidemics, investment is likely to remain weak for several years following the COVID-19 pandemic, but it is possible that renewed investment in digital technologies will spur productivity gains in some sectors. A supportive policy environment will be key to laying the groundwork for an investment rebound in EMDEs.

Introduction

The plunge in global economic activity during the COVID-19 pandemic has been accompanied by an even larger collapse in investment. The investment contraction in 2020 was deeper in advanced economies than in emerging market and developing economies (EMDEs) but the investment downturn in EMDEs was considerably sharper than during the global financial crisis.

Against this backdrop, this box addresses three questions about investment in EMDEs:

- How has the pandemic impacted investment?

- What are the prospects for it?

- What will be the long-term effects of the pandemic?

Investment before and during the pandemic

Pre-pandemic trends. As the pandemic began, the world had already experienced a decade-long slowdown in investment growth (figure B3.2.1). From a peak of 10.8 percent in 2010, investment growth in EMDEs had fallen to 2.5 percent in 2019, complicating progress toward the Sustainable Development Goals (SDGs) related to infrastructure (Vorisek and Yu 2020).[a] Periods of weakness in global commodity prices and associated adverse terms-of-trade developments, policy uncertainty, and rising corporate leverage had all curtailed investment over this period (Kose et al. 2017; World Bank 2017a, 2019a). The sluggishness of investment growth was broad-based, with more than half of EMDEs experiencing investment growth below their 2000-19 average in every year since 2012.

Deep investment collapse during the pandemic. Investment plunged particularly sharply in EMDEs excluding China as the pandemic took hold. In the full year 2020, investment in EMDEs shrank by an estimated 4.5 percent, and by a much deeper 10.6 percent if

excluding China. This contraction for EMDEs excluding China was more than 4 percentage points deeper than during the 2009 global recession, despite financial conditions being substantially easier in 2020. The contraction in 2020 was sharpest in Latin America and the Caribbean and South Asia, where GDP also declined the most. The decline in investment in 2020 was smallest in East Asia, where activity was supported by large fiscal stimulus programs in China and Vietnam and also resilient foreign direct investment (FDI) inflows to Vietnam.

Investment prospects

Subdued investment rebound, by historic standards. Even with the pandemic expected to recede in 2021, the short-term rebound in EMDE investment is projected to be much weaker in 2021, at 5.7 percent, than the rebound in 2010 (10.8 percent) following the global financial crisis. For most EMDEs, investment growth during the forecast period will remain at or below average rates during the 2010s (figure B3.2.2). These growth rates will be insufficient to reverse the investment losses during 2020. After the substantial fiscal stimulus of 2020, the transition to tighter fiscal policy in EMDEs in order to retain creditworthiness and contain debt service costs will constrain public investment projects. Private investment will be limited by uncertainty about the post-pandemic economic landscape and the viability of existing production structures. Overall investment growth in EMDEs is projected to soften to 4.3 percent in 2022. China is expected to contribute half or more of aggregate EMDE investment growth in 2021 and 2022. Without China, investment in EMDEs is projected to be still below the pre-pandemic level by 2022.

Long-term effects of the pandemic

Lasting investment losses. History suggests that the adverse effects on investment of the pandemic will linger. After epidemics in the past, losses to investment have been deeper and longer lasting than GDP losses, perhaps because of lasting effects of uncertainty and risk aversion on investment (figure B3.2.3). These same mechanisms, along with sharply lower corporate profits, can be expected

---

Note: This box was prepared by Naotaka Sugawara and Dana Vorisek.

[a] Investment is defined as gross fixed capital formation.

BOX 3.2 Impact of COVID-19 on investment: Deep, persistent, and broad based (*continued*)

FIGURE B3.2.1 Investment trends

Following a decade-long, broad-based declining trend in investment growth in EMDEs prior to the COVID-19 pandemic, investment contracted sharply in 2020. The collapse in investment was much sharper in large EMDEs (excluding China) than in large advanced economies.

A. Investment growth

B. Share of EMDEs with investment growth below 2000-19 average

C. Investment growth, by country groups

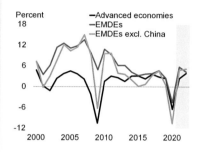
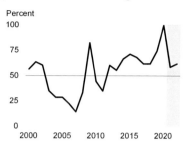
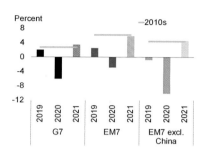

Sources: Haver Analytics; World Bank.
Note: EMDEs = emerging market and developing economies. Data for 2020 are estimates and for 2021-22 are forecasts (shaded bars and areas). Investment refers to gross fixed capital formation. Aggregate growth is calculated with investment at 2010 prices and market exchange rates as weights.
A.B. Sample includes 97 countries, consisting of 34 advanced economies and 63 EMDEs.
B. Figure shows share of EMDEs with investment growth below their own average during 2000-19.
C. "G7" includes Canada, France, Germany, Italy, Japan, the United Kingdom, and the United States. "EM7" refers to the seven largest EMDEs and includes Brazil, China, India, Indonesia, Mexico, the Russian Federation, and Turkey.

FIGURE B3.2.2 Investment prospects

The speed of recovery in investment will vary by EMDE group, but is expected to be weak overall. Excluding China, investment in EMDEs is projected to remain below pre-pandemic levels through 2022.

A. Investment growth forecasts by EMDE group

B. Contributions to EMDE investment growth

C. Investment levels

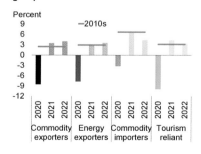
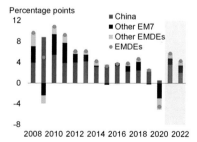
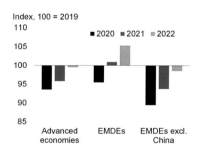

Sources: Haver Analytics; World Bank.
Note: EMDEs = emerging market and developing economies. Data for 2020 are estimates and for 2021-22 are forecasts (shaded bars or areas). Investment refers to gross fixed capital formation. Aggregate growth is calculated with investment at 2010 prices and market exchange rates as weights.
A. Sample includes 40 EMDE commodity exporters,15 EMDE energy exporters, 23 EMDE commodity importers, and 19 tourism-reliant EMDEs. Tourism-reliant EMDEs are defined as those with above-average international tourism expenditures as a share of GDP.
B. "EM7" refers to the seven largest EMDEs and includes Brazil, China, India, Indonesia, Mexico, the Russian Federation, and Turkey. "Other EMDEs" includes 56 economies.
C. Sample includes 34 advanced economies and 63 EMDEs.

BOX 3.2 Impact of COVID-19 on investment: Deep, persistent, and broad based *(continued)*

FIGURE B3.2.3 Long-term impact of the pandemic on investment

The decline in investment after pandemics tends to be deep and long lasting. The pandemic could lead to a further decline in long-term investment growth, which has already been on a downward trajectory, and will also likely hinder EMDEs' per capita income convergence with advanced economies.

A. Decline in investment and GDP levels following pandemics

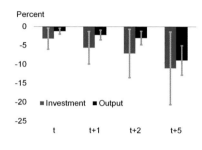

B. Long-term investment growth prospects

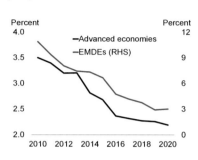

C. Difference in EMDE and advanced-economy per capita investment and GDP growth

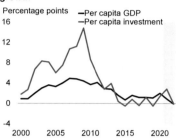

Sources: Consensus Economics; Haver Analytics; World Bank (2020a); World Bank.

Note: EMDEs = emerging market and developing economies. Investment refers to gross fixed capital formation.

A. Bars show the cumulative estimated impacts of the four most severe biological epidemics on investment and output levels relative to non-affected EMDEs. Orange lines display the range of the estimates with 90th percentile significance. The four epidemics considered are SARS (2002-03), MERS (2012), Ebola (2014-15), and Zika (2015-16). Swine flu (2009), which coincided with the 2008-09 global financial crisis, is excluded to limit possible confounding effects. Sample includes 116 economies, including 30 advanced economies and 86 EMDEs.

B. Long-term prospects refer to ten-year-ahead forecasts. The horizontal axis shows the year when long-term forecasts are surveyed. Sample includes 24 advanced economies and 20 EMDEs.

C. Data for 2020 are estimates and for 2021-22 are forecasts. Sample for per capita investment includes 97 countries, consisting of 34 advanced economies and 63 EMDEs.

to constrain investment during and after the COVID-19 pandemic (Caballero and Simsek 2020; Stiglitz 2020).

Weak investment, a source of slowing potential growth. The prospect of weak investment in EMDEs during the medium to long term, after the severe contraction in 2020, raises concerns about the effects on EMDEs' potential growth—the growth rate EMDEs can sustain at full employment and capacity. The sustained weakening of investment growth during the 2010s, together with declining total factor productivity growth, has already contributed to a slowdown in labor productivity growth in EMDEs and, as a result, limited EMDEs' convergence toward per capita income levels in advanced economies (Dieppe 2020).

Upside risk in some sectors. On the other hand, a productivity-enhancing investment surge triggered by the pandemic remains a possibility. This boost could materialize through renewed investment in digital technologies in sectors such as manufacturing, finance, and education, or through the onshoring of production of some essential products (Dieppe 2020). The pandemic also creates opportunities to shift infrastructure investment toward more resilient and environmentally sustainable options, in turn raising productivity and supporting progress toward the SDGs in the long term (Hallegatte and Hammer 2020).

Conclusion

The adverse effect of the COVID-19 pandemic on investment in EMDEs, already large, could extend for a prolonged period. Given the importance of investment in supporting productivity and per capita income gains, it is important that impediments to productive investment, including those related to financing, be reduced. For EMDEs, boosting public investment can have particularly large benefits due to high multipliers (Izquierdo et al. 2020). At the same time, improving business climates and reducing policy uncertainty is key in supporting private investment.

crises. This difference widened over time, to 1.2 percentage points after five years.

- *Natural disasters.* Natural disasters, in contrast, were not followed by significant long-term growth forecast downgrades, either initially or later. These episodes tended to be short-lived and subsequent reconstruction efforts typically triggered a growth rebound that averted long-term economic damage (Dieppe, Kilic Celik, and Okou 2020).

Forecast downgrades after persistently unfavorable growth outcomes. Given that forecasts have an element of extrapolation from recent experience, the lagged but repeated forecast downgrades after past recessions and financial crises may in part be seen as a response to persistent growth disappointments following these episodes. Since 1998, ten-year-ahead global growth forecasts have been disappointed by actual growth outcomes in every year except 2010, when the global economy rebounded from the 2009 global recession. For all countries except China, long-term and medium-term forecast errors showed over-optimism over this period; for more than half of EMDEs, long-term growth forecasts were overly optimistic by 2 percentage points a year or more, on average (figure 3.6).

- *Output growth disappointments.* In seven out of the ten years following the global recession of 2009, global output growth fell short of expectations formed in the preceding year, and, for EMDEs, this was true for eight out of the ten years. Repeated output growth disappointments were typically accompanied by significant forecast downgrades that tended to be spread evenly throughout the period. During a spell of growth disappointments, long-term growth forecasts were downgraded by a statistically significant 0.2 percentage point per year, on average. Over the average length of a spell of growth disappointments (3.8 years), this amounted to a cumulative 0.8 percentage point downgrade. Consistent with this, the repeated global growth disappointments after 2010 were accompanied by long-term global growth forecast downgrades in every year.

FIGURE 3.6 **Growth forecast errors**

Global long-term growth forecasts have been overly optimistic in every year since 1998 except 2010, when the global economy rebounded from the global financial crisis. Over-optimism in five-year-ahead and ten-year-ahead forecasts extended to all countries except China. Extended spells of economic weakness were accompanied by significant medium- and long-term growth forecast downgrades.

A. Long-term growth forecast errors

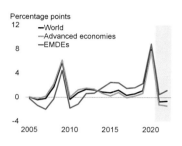

B. Medium-term growth forecast errors

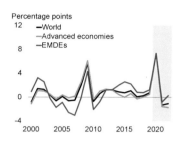

C. Share of countries with positive (overly optimistic) long-term forecast errors

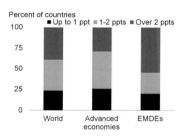

D. Share of countries with positive (overly optimistic) medium-term forecast errors

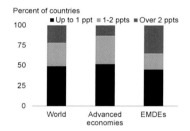

E. Average long-term growth forecast revisions during persistent events

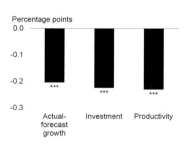

F. Average medium-term growth forecast revisions during persistent events

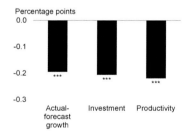

Sources: Consensus Economics; Dieppe (2020); World Bank.
Note: EMDEs = emerging market and developing economies.
A.B. Difference between ten-year-ahead (A) or five-year-ahead (B) growth forecasts and actual growth outturns. A positive number indicates an overly optimistic forecast. In shaded areas, growth forecasts in chapter 1 are used to compute the differences.
C.D. Share of countries by the size of average forecast errors computed with available data up to 2020. Positive forecast errors indicate growth forecasts made 10 years (C) or 5 years (D) ago are higher than realized growth.
E.F. Average changes in long-term (ten-year-ahead, E) and medium-term (five-year-ahead, F) growth forecasts during persistent spells of unfavorable events. *** denotes that changes during such events are statistically significantly different from zero.

- *Investment slowdowns.* Global investment growth slowed in seven out of the ten years following the global recession of 2009. Spells of multi-year investment slowdowns were accompanied by statistically significant downgrades of long-term output growth forecasts of about 0.2 percentage point a year, on average. Over the average length of a spell of consecutive investment slowdowns (3.7 years), this amounted to a cumulative 0.8 percentage point downgrade.

- *Productivity slowdowns.* In most years since the global recession of 2009, global productivity growth slowed. Spells of multi-year TFP growth slowdowns were accompanied by somewhat larger, and statistically significant, downgrades of long-term output growth forecasts of about 0.2 percentage point a year, on average. Over the average length of a spell of consecutive productivity slowdowns (3.9 years), this amounted to a cumulative 0.9 percentage point downgrade.

Hysteresis, super-hysteresis, and structural change. The successive downgrades of long-term growth forecasts documented in these exercises could stem from three sources—with differing policy implications.

- *Hysteresis.* Acute adverse events such as crises or recessions could cause hysteresis—lasting damage to output levels, in part because human capital has been depleted by long-term unemployment or capital stocks rendered outdated for lack of investment. The possibility of hysteresis implies a need for proactive macroeconomic policy stimulus to dampen the recession.

- *Super-hysteresis.* Acute adverse events could cause super-hysteresis—not only lasting damage to output levels, but also to output growth because the fundamental drivers of productivity and output growth have been dampened (Cerra, Fatas, and Saxena 2020). Like hysteresis, super-hysteresis calls for prompt macroeconomic policy stimulus, bolstered by growth-enhancing reforms.

- *Structural change.* Acute adverse events could coincide with structural change that causes long periods of slowing TFP growth, as has been hypothesized in the case of the global financial crisis more than a decade ago (Fernald et al. 2017). Such structural change calls for a focus on long-term growth-enhancing reforms.

The evidence presented here suggests that elements of all three forces have been at work. The decline in long-term forecasts of output growth, not just output levels, documented above are consistent with super-hysteresis. In addition, since there is limited overlap between recessions and persistent productivity slowdowns, the results above also suggest that structural change may have played a role in repeated forecast downgrades.

Reform options

To prevent another decade of initial growth over-optimism followed by disappointments, comprehensive reforms are needed to boost long-term growth. These include reforms to improve governance and business climates, encourage productivity-enhancing investment in human and physical capital, foster economic flexibility, and diversify economies in which activity is concentrated in few sectors.

The cost of inaction: Permanent output losses. Absent a sustained reform push to raise growth, the global economy, advanced economies, and EMDEs are likely to see permanent income and output losses relative to pre-pandemic expectations (box 3.1; figure 3.7). A major reform push may avert such an outcome and help spur a jobs-rich recovery that benefits all. Such reforms could increase, and improve the quality of, human and physical capital, and improve the efficiency of their use, for example by strengthening governance and business climates (annex 3.2). Although this section examines each of these reforms in isolation, based on the standard conceptual framework of a production function, there can be important interactions between reforms that deserve careful consideration in the design of a comprehensive reform package (annex 3.2).

Differences in country priorities. The most pressing policy priority in the short-run in most countries is likely to be rapid and widespread distribution of COVID-19 vaccines (box 1.4). However, beyond this immediate policy priority, more action is needed to promote a return to robust long-term growth. This section offers a broad menu of policy options, but priorities will differ among individual countries depending on their country characteristics. At the country level, some of the most pressing reforms are long overdue; other long-standing reform needs have been cast into a new, more urgent light by the pandemic; and yet other reforms are needed to address new challenges raised by the pandemic.

- *Where fiscal positions are stretched,* the most urgent and most cost-effective reforms need to be prioritized. Areas that need to be shielded from fiscal consolidation to ensure future growth need to be identified. In countries with long-standing challenges in raising government revenues, domestic resource mobilization could be prioritized (Kose et al. 2020b).

- *Where weak infrastructure service provision,* such as in electricity or telecommunications, as well as weak fiscal positions weigh on the recovery, reforms to foster competition or efficiency can be priorities (Rozenberg and Fay 2019).[13]

- *Where institutional weaknesses* stand in the way of limiting the economic damage from the pandemic, reforms to improve governance, strengthen government efficiency, and build trust may be priorities (Loayza et al. 2020).

- *Where economies are heavily reliant on individual sectors*—be it tourism or production or export of commodities—diversification programs can be advanced (Gill et al. 2014).

- *Where the education of today's cohort of students has been disrupted* by a lack of remote learning, digital infrastructure investment and

FIGURE 3.7 Output losses

Steep recessions during the pandemic and a subsequent potential growth slowdown are expected to cause lasting output losses.

A. Global output levels

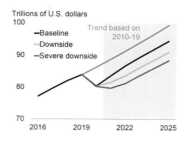

B. Cumulative global and EMDE output losses, 2020-25

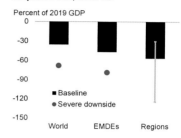

Sources: Consensus Economics, World Bank.
Note: EMDEs = emerging market and developing economies.
A. Data are in U.S. dollars at 2010 prices and market exchange rates. Shaded area indicates forecasts. Trend is assumed to grow at the regression-estimated trend growth rate of 2010-19. Baseline output is based on the baseline estimates and forecasts in chapter 1 over 2020-22 and, for 2023-25, is assumed to grow at the rates computed with long-term consensus forecasts surveyed in October 2020. The downside and severe downside scenarios are described in boxes 1.4 and 3.1.
B. Data are in U.S. dollars at 2010 prices and market exchange rates. Bars show cumulative output losses over 2020-25, based on baseline growth forecasts, and, for regions, an average of six EMDE regions is presented. Red circles are based on growth forecasts under the severe downside scenario. A vertical yellow line for regions shows the minimum-maximum range among the six regions. Cumulative losses are computed as deviations from trend in U.S. dollars, expressed as a share of GDP in 2019. For global and EMDE output, baseline output is based on the baseline estimates and forecasts in chapter 1 over 2020-22 and, for 2023-25, is assumed to grow at the rates computed with long-term consensus forecasts surveyed in October 2020. For regions, baseline output is assumed to grow at the baseline estimates and forecasts in chapter 1 over 2020-22 and, for 2023-25, is assumed to grow at the same rates as in the trend. Trend is assumed to grow at the regression-estimated trend growth rate of 2010-19. The severe downside scenarios are described in boxes 1.4 and 3.1.

redoubled efforts to improve learning outcomes, especially for the most affected groups of students, can be prioritized (Azevedo et al. 2020).[14]

- *Economies particularly at risk of damage from climate change,* especially small islands, may need to prevent climate-related damage compounding pandemic-related damage by prioritizing investment for greater climate resilience (Rozenberg and Fay 2019).

- *Fragile states* may be at particular risk because of severe institutional capacity constraints and lack of fiscal resources; they may require enhanced international support in the recovery as well as in a return to peace, in particular by addressing grievances around

---

[13] Some countries have already started on this path, such as with fuel subsidy reform (Nigeria), energy reform (South Africa), and liberalization of the telecom sector (Ethiopia).

[14] Some governments have already aimed to facilitate network expansion and reduce congestion, such as by adopting new technologies (Google's Loon network in Kenya and Mozambique) and temporary releasing additional spectrum to boost internet efficiency (Ghana, South Africa, and Zambia).

exclusion from power, opportunities, and security (World Bank 2018b).

Human capital accumulation

The pandemic has disrupted education for 90 percent of the world's children (World Bank 2020e). In quality-adjusted terms, the pandemic could lower average years of schooling by 0.6 years and raise the share of lower-secondary school children below minimum proficiency levels by one-quarter (Azevedo et al. 2020). The pandemic may roll back years of improvements in human capital—and even before the pandemic, the average newborn could only be expected to achieve 56 percent of her potential productivity as a future worker (World Bank 2020d). By 2040, about one-third of the world's workforce will be composed of individuals whose schooling was disrupted by the pandemic and, on average, human capital of the global workforce would be almost 1 Human Capital Index (HCI) point lower—equivalent to 1 percent below-potential productivity—than in the absence of the pandemic (World Bank 2020d). In addition, the global unemployment rate increased by about 2 percentage points in the first half of 2020 alone. The longer unemployment remains high, the more pronounced will be associated human capital losses. Finally, while EMDEs' younger populations may be somewhat less vulnerable to the pandemic than older populations in advanced economies, the pandemic has revealed the severe lack of capacity of EMDEs' health care systems (World Bank 2020a).

Policy measures to enhance education. The school closures caused by the pandemic have heightened educational inequalities both between countries that offer remote learning and those that cannot, and within countries between children with private tutors and remote learning, and those without (Vegas and Winthrop 2020). The learning losses associated with the shift to remote learning have led to a renewed appreciation of the value of public schooling (Reimers and Schleicher 2020). The short-term challenge is a safe re-opening of schools and keeping students, especially girls because they are at greater risk of dropout, in school while the long-term challenge is to reverse some of the pandemic-related losses in learning outcomes.

Long-term improvements start with better measurement of education outcomes to help target interventions more effectively (figure 3.8; World Bank 2019b). School meals programs and early childhood interventions can help make students better prepared for learning. To strengthen their effectiveness, teachers can be supported with coaching, motivated with incentives, and provided with appropriate technologies. Community and parent support will be critical to improve learning. Retraining programs for workers in the hardest-hit sectors can facilitate their re-employment.

Policies to improve health. The pandemic has revealed the capacity constraints of health care systems in many countries. In the short run, health systems need to be equipped to contain the pandemic. Needs include enhanced data gathering, pandemic surveillance, encouraging non-pharmaceutical interventions such as mask wearing and handwashing, and preparedness to deploy vaccines as widely and quickly as possible. COVID-19 has provided a reminder that fighting a pandemic is considerably more costly than prevention measures, such as enhanced food safety standards to prevent the spread of zoonotic diseases (Schwab 2020; van Nieuwkoop 2020).

Looking ahead, while a fully equipped health care system may exceed the resources of many countries, some lower-cost policy interventions can materially improve public health. These include child vaccination programs and services targeted at women and children during pregnancy and around child birth, as well as nutrition programs for groups at risk of malnutrition (Bhutta et al. 2013; World Bank 2015b). These need to be complemented with policies such as improving access to clean water and sanitation, and stronger safety nets that allow vulnerable populations to access health services (Galasso et al. 2017).

Infrastructure investment

The pandemic has dealt a blow to investment. In the second quarter of 2020, investment contracted by 11.0 percent, on average, in advanced economies and by 6.8 percent in EMDEs. A rebound is held back by uncertainty about the course of the pandemic and the post-pandemic economic landscape. Meanwhile, in some countries, the pandemic may have shifted investment priorities towards digital infrastructure from other forms of investment.

Policies to improve infrastructure. The fiscal stimulus packages implemented to support economies through the pandemic have provided an opportunity to help fill infrastructure gaps. Fiscally constrained governments have additional options for closing infrastructure gaps: improving the quality of infrastructure spending within existing spending envelopes, choosing a cost-effective sequencing of infrastructure investment by focusing on the projects with the highest economic returns and speeding up preparation for priority projects in the pipeline, planning immediately for new projects aligned with climate-resilient and equitable priorities, and implementing reforms that ensure more efficient use and provision of infrastructure services (Rozenberg and Fay 2019).

- *Quality.* Measures to improve the quality of infrastructure spending may include a renewed emphasis on funding maintenance and operations. For water, sanitation, and transport infrastructure, better maintenance alone could halve life-cycle cost (Rozenberg and Fay 2019).

- *Sequencing.* Infrastructure investment can be sequenced to prioritize initially lower-cost solutions to address basic needs before upgrading to costlier and more comprehensive solutions (Straub 2008). In the case of water-related infrastructure, for example, septic tanks can provide basic water and sanitation services before a fully managed sewage and sanitation system is rolled out (figure 3.9). For power infrastructure, basic access to power for small devices and lighting can be rolled out widely before rolling out access to power for large consumer appliances.

- *Efficiency.* Complementary reforms can improve the efficiency of use and provision of infrastructure services. In the power sector, for

FIGURE 3.8 Education and health outcomes

Many EMDEs have ample room to improve learning outcomes and public health.

A. PISA scores for reading

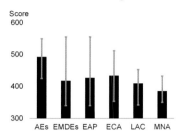

B. PISA scores for mathematics

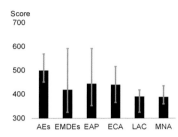

C. Share of sixth graders at pre-reading proficiency level

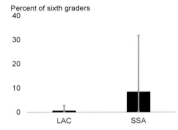

D. Share of sixth graders at pre-numeracy proficiency level

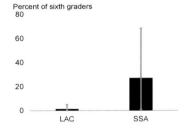

E. Prevalence of stunting

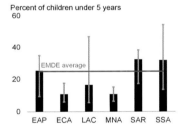

F. Mortality from poor sanitation

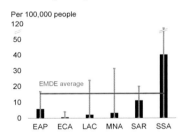

Source: World Bank.
Note: AEs = advanced economies, EMDEs = emerging market and developing economies, EAP = East Asia and Pacific, ECA = Europe and Central Asia, LAC = Latin America and the Caribbean, MNA = Middle East and North Africa, SAR = South Asia, SSA = Sub-Saharan Africa.
A.B. PISA scores in reading and mathematics for 15-year-olds in 35 advanced economies and 44 EMDEs (7 in EAP, 18 in ECA, 11 in LAC, and 8 in MNA). Bars show unweighted averages and vertical orange lines show the minimum-maximum ranges. Data are for 2018.
C.D. Percent sixth grade students in 15 EMDEs in LAC and 10 EMDEs in SSA with the lowest (pre-reading) reading proficiency level and lowest (pre-numeracy) mathematics proficiency level. Data is only available for EMDEs in LAC and SSA. Bars show unweighted averages and vertical orange lines show the minimum-maximum ranges. Data are for 2013 or 2014.
E. Percent of children aged under 5 years who are stunted, that is, whose height-for-age is more than two standard deviations below the median for the international reference population aged 0-59 months. Unweighted averages for 68 EMDEs, with vertical orange lines showing the minimum-maximum ranges. Data are for 2015-19.
F. Mortality rate attributed to unsafe water, unsafe sanitation, and lack of hygiene (per 100,000 population) in 147 EMDEs. Bars show unweighted averages and vertical orange lines show the minimum-maximum ranges. Data are for 2016.

example, smart meters can incentivize more efficient power use. In the transport sector, an integrated planning process for land use and transport can cut transport infrastructure

FIGURE 3.9 Infrastructure investment

Infrastructure investment costs can be lowered by complementary policies (such as land-use planning in the context of urban transport infrastructure) or by appropriately sequencing investment (such as providing basic infrastructure before rolling out more ambitious infrastructure). Fiscal stimulus can be reoriented towards less carbon-intensive purposes, and digital infrastructure can be expanded.

A. Average annual cost of investment in urban transport infrastructure

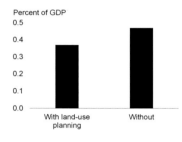

B. Annual average cost of capital, maintenance, and operation in water and sanitation

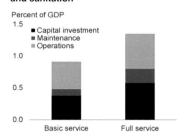

C. Amount of support committed toward energy initiatives in 2020

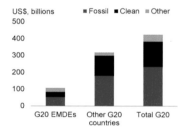

D. People making or receiving digital payments in the past year

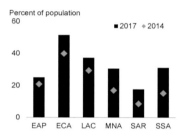

Sources: Energy Policy Tracker (database); Rozenberg and Fay (2019); World Bank.
Note: EMDEs = emerging market and developing economies, EAP = East Asia and Pacific, ECA = Europe and Central Asia, LAC = Latin America and the Caribbean, MNA = Middle East and North Africa, SAR = South Asia, SSA = Sub-Saharan Africa.
A. Estimates for low-carbon investment in urban infrastructure based on scenario for 2015-30.
B. Capital, operations, and maintenance costs are for both new and existing users. They represent the amount needed both to expand service and to continue serving existing users. "Full service" is one in which every new household served is provided with safely managed water and sanitation; "Basic service" rolls out universal access to basic services before upgrading to safely managed services. Mid-point of estimate ranges for 2015-30.
C. Figure shows the fiscal support committed toward fossil fuel-based, clean fuel-based and other energy initiatives in G20 countries. Data as of November 18, 2020.
D. Number of people having made or received digital payments in the past year, in percent of the population aged 15 years or older. Medians across countries in each region and year.

investment cost by one-quarter. This process would prioritize rail and bus transport over private road transport, incentivize rail use for passenger and freight transport, plan land use to increase density (and thus reduce mobility needs), and carefully prioritize the financing of rural roads.

Green investment. To date, fiscal stimulus in G20 countries to combat the pandemic has benefited both carbon-intensive and environmentally friendlier activities (VFDI 2020). As fiscal support

continues, a tilt towards longer-term climate and environmental goals can be considered. In addition to boosting short-term growth, investment in green infrastructure and fostering the widespread adoption of environmentally sustainable technologies can support faster growth in the long run while contributing to climate change mitigation.[15] Recovery packages that target environmental and climate-related spending will increase EMDEs' resilience to future climate-related shocks and reduce risks, and can have large fiscal multiplier effects when such spending is both labor intensive and productivity enhancing (Agrawala, Dussaux, and Monti 2020; IEA 2020). Nonetheless, the distributional effects of green policies need to be carefully managed— particularly job losses in traditional energy industries—as do the trade-offs between policies that achieve short-term goals at the expense of progress towards longer-term ones (World Bank 2013a). Beyond climate change, environmental protection policies help improve long-run health and growth outcomes (IMF 2020a).

Investment in digital infrastructure. The pandemic has pushed firms to increasingly rely on digital solutions (Apedoh-Amah et al. 2020). Education and health care systems have expanded their reliance on online learning or consultations.[16] The use of online payment

---

[15] Rozenberg and Fay (2019) show, for example, that mini-grid and off-grid electricity solutions are both environmentally sustainable technologies and cost-effective for moving toward sustainable development goals. For the short term, OECD (2020) and IMF (2020a) argue that well-designed recovery packages can promote a strong, equitable, and environmentally friendly recovery. Particularly effective policies in the short term include clean physical infrastructure, efficiency retrofits, investment in education and training, natural capital investment, and clean R&D; in lower- and middle-income countries, rural support spending can be effective (Hepburn et al. 2020). Energy efficiency, nature conservation, clean energy options, and the sustainability of transport are also priority areas for stimulus investments (Hallegatte and Hammer 2020). However, Strand and Toman (2010) caution that most "green stimulus" programs with large short-run employment and environmental effects may have less significant positive effects for long-run growth, and programs that yield larger employment effects may lead to more employment gains for largely lower-skilled workers.

[16] For experience with online teaching in Australia, see Scull et al. (2020); in Brunei and Pakistan, see Qazi et al. (2020); in China, see Sun, Tang, and Zhuo (2020); in Georgia, see Basilaia and Kvavadze (2020); in the Netherlands, see van der Spoel et al. (2020); and in Oman, see Mohammed et al. (2020). For developments in online medical care, see Hollander and Carr (2020) and Taylor, Fitzsimmons-Craft, and Graham (2020).

systems and other forms of cashless payments as well as online commerce has expanded rapidly (Barrero, Bloom, and Davis 2020; Kenney and Zysman 2020). Online food shopping has expanded, which in some cases has benefited smaller farms over agribusiness (Chang and Meyerhoefer 2020). In some countries, government assistance payments have shifted to mobile delivery (Davidovic et al. 2020; Gelb and Mukherjee 2020).

Wider availability of digital services can mitigate the impact of mobility restrictions and accelerate access to government assistance and other financial services).[17] It can facilitate job search, accelerate the discovery of new job opportunities, and increase employment (El-Mallakh 2020; Hjort and Poulsen 2019; Viollaz and Winkler 2020). It can reduce uncertainty and information asymmetries in product markets (World Bank 2019c). It can support education and learning, including where learning facilities are currently limited (Aker, Ksoll, and Lybbert 2012). Finally, it has been associated with higher firm-level productivity (Cusolita, Lederman, and Pena 2020). Expanded use of digital services requires investment in digital infrastructure but also appropriate regulation of internet and mobile operators to promote competition and ensure safety, efficiency and minimum quality standards (Agur, Martinez Peria, and Rochon 2020; Guermazi and Seligman 2020). These regulatory frameworks need to be accompanied by modern and transparent licensing frameworks and robust regulatory enforcement (Broadband Commission 2019; World Bank 2019c).

Increasing the labor supply

While job losses have been severe overall, COVID-19 has hit the services sectors, which tend to have high female employment shares, particularly hard (Alon et al. 2020). Services sectors account for 43 percent of employment in EMDEs, and women account for 61 percent of employment in services. If steep employment losses in these sectors persist, they may eventually cause female workers to exit the labor force entirely, lowering potential output. Reforms can boost employment, especially of female workers.

Policies to raise female labor force participation. Before the pandemic, several broad economic forces had helped raise female labor force participation, such as higher women's wages, changes in cultural attitudes, technological changes to have made it easier for women to work outside the home, and rapid growth in sectors that employ women intensively (Fernandez 2013; Klasen and Pieters 2015).

In addition, there have been policies aimed at raising female labor force participation, with their success depending on country circumstances (Cascio, Haider, and Nielson 2015). Early indications from advanced economies are that the pandemic has reversed some of the earlier gains in female labor force participation and exacerbated gender gaps as women with young children have disproportionately scaled back work hours and exited employment (Landivar et al. 2020). Governments can help women return to the labor market by facilitating access to high-quality childcare, lifting restrictions and disincentives to women working, and investing in education and infrastructure that increases women's longer-term attachment to the labor market. In the past, several policies have been successful in some countries. Over time, there may be a virtuous circle with rising female labor force participation shifting social norms (Duflo 2012).

- *Support for young families.* In some advanced economies, the additional within-family child care hours made necessary by the pandemic have been more equally split between fathers and mothers than pre-pandemic childcare hours (Sevilla and Smith 2020). With the right incentives, the pandemic may offer an opportunity to entrench a more equal distribution of these activities. Greater day care availability and expanded parental leave have been associated with higher female labor force participation in OECD countries and some developing economies (Dao et al. 2016; de Barros et al. 2013; Jaumotte 2004). These

---

[17] For studies documenting the impact of digital technologies on access to finance or government support, see Aker et al. (2013); Davidovic et al. (2020); Gelb and Mukherjee (2020); Ky, Rugemintwari, and Sauviat (2018); Machasio (2020); and Mbiti and Weil (2016).

policies need to be carefully crafted to encourage gender balance.[18] More flexible work arrangements to facilitate childcare by parents have generally been associated with greater female labor force participation (Dao et al. 2016). However, to the extent that these policies disproportionately encourage women to self-select into part-time work, they can lower women's labor market attachment (Blau and Kahn 2013).

- *Education.* Looking beyond the pandemic, better education for girls and women can increase their labor market attachment (Solotaroff et al. 2020). In many countries, girls' school enrollment or attainment still lags that of boys (World Bank 2013b). Even where school enrollment is comparable between boys and girls, girls tend to enroll later and drop out faster during times of economic stress, thus undermining their labor market prospects (World Bank 2012).

- *Legal and tax provisions.* The pandemic provides an opportunity to lower long-standing legal and tax barriers to female employment. The gaps between male and female labor force participation rates have been narrower in the presence of equal property, inheritance and contracting rights; joint titling rights for married couples; and equal rights to open legal proceedings, pursue a profession, or conduct economic trans-actions such as opening bank accounts (Duflo 2012; Gonzales et al. 2015). In Japan, lifting restrictions on working hours, such as on night-time work or on women's participation in professions that are considered dangerous, helped raise female labor force participation (Shambaugh, Nunn, and Portman 2017). In OECD countries, lower marginal income tax rates and the replacement of tax allowances with transferable tax credits for second-income earners have been associated with higher female labor force participation and full-time employment (Bosch and van der

Klaauw 2009; Dao et al. 2016; Jaumotte 2004).

- *Infrastructure.* The fiscal stimulus packages introduced to mitigate the economic impact of the pandemic can be geared towards infrastructure investment that can unlock female employment. In poorer countries, better infrastructure, such as access to clean water or heating materials, can free women's time for more productive employment; better infrastructure of the type that is disproportionately used by women, such as pedestrian pathways, can facilitate access to markets; better internet and mobile infrastructure can expand women's access to markets and resources and labor force participation (Das et al. 2017; Rasmussen 2016; Viollaz and Winkler 2020; World Bank 2012). Employer-provided transport can encourage female labor force participation by ensuring safety during the commute (IFC 2019).

Creating a growth-friendly environment

The pandemic may introduce lasting changes to workplaces, consumption patterns, and trade networks. It has already revealed the fragility of growth strategies concentrated on a narrow set of sectors. Economies will need to be sufficiently flexible to adjust to the demands of the post-pandemic economic landscape. This will require reforms that allow such flexibility and encourage competition and innovation.[19] Meanwhile, un-precedented macroeconomic policy stimulus may mask widespread corporate insolvency that may be revealed once stimulus is unwound. Strong macroeconomic and financial policy frameworks are needed to weather such stress.

Improving governance and business climates. There is early evidence that compliance with pandemic-control measures has been greater in countries and subnational entities with stronger

---

[18] For example, overly generous maternity leave have tended to reduce labor market attachment of women. To address this, the Nordic countries introduced "father's quotas" of parental leave that could not be transferred to mothers (Winkler 2016).

[19] The Marshall Plan offered $13 billion in financing to Europe for post-war reconstruction during 1948-51. Arguably, the conditionality for market-based reforms attached to the financing provided under the Marshall Plan was a more important catalyst for post-war growth than the financing itself (De Long and Eichengreen 1991).

trust in government (Devine et al. 2020). Improvements in governance, especially to emphasize accountability, can promote trust in government (World Bank 2017b). While progress has been made in some countries in reducing corruption, there have been setbacks in the rule of law over the past decade (box 3.3).

Governance reforms have tended to be associated with stronger growth, albeit with mixed results across countries. Governance as well as business climate reforms can raise investment and TFP growth directly by raising private returns on productivity-enhancing investment in human and physical capital. They can also promote investment and TFP growth indirectly, by removing obstacles to other drivers of long-term growth such as innovation, openness to international trade and finance, competition, and financial development. Such reforms can facilitate a re-allocation of factors of production towards more productive sectors (Dieppe and Matsuoka 2020). Major reform initiatives to improve business climates or governance have been followed by significantly higher TFP growth in the near-term and investment growth in the medium-term (figure 3.10). In contrast, reform setbacks have often been associated with TFP growth slowdowns that set in early and were not reversed over the subsequent five years.

Strengthening macroeconomic policy frameworks. The pandemic has shown once again how financial crises or deep recessions can set back years of per capita income gains. Hence, policies to moderate business and financial cycles remain one of the key components of a growth-enhancing policy agenda. To be effective, such policies need to be conducted within robust and credible frameworks.

- *Monetary policy frameworks.* Resilient monetary policy frameworks allow policy makers more room for proactive monetary policy. Exchange rate pass-through from depreciation to inflation tends to be smaller in countries with more credible, transparent, and independent central banks; inflation-targeting monetary policy regimes; and better-anchored inflation expectations (Ha, Stocker, and Yilmazkuday 2019; Kose et al. 2019).

FIGURE 3.10 Total factor productivity and investment after reform advances and setbacks

Reform advances have been associated with boosts to total factor productivity (TFP) and investment two and four years after the reform advances. Governance reform setbacks have lowered TFP.

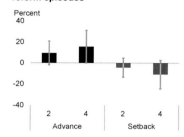

A. Cumulative change in EMDE TFP two to four years after reform episodes

B. Cumulative change in EMDE investment two to four years after reform episodes

Source: World Bank.
Note: EMDEs = emerging market and developing economies. TFP = total factor productivity. Sample includes 71 EMDEs with population exceeding 4 million people during 1998-2018; sample is smaller for TFP. Reform episodes are identified as two-standard-error changes in one of four Worldwide Governance Indicators—for 155 EMDEs and 51 advanced economies during 1996-2018. Episodes in which there were advances in one measure and simultaneous setbacks in another are excluded. A detailed methodology is available in box 3.3. TFP growth is estimated as in Dieppe (2020). Figure shows regression coefficients of cumulative TFP (A) and real investment (B) growth on dummies for reform advances and setbacks from a local projection estimation at forecast horizons of 2 and 4 years. Vertical orange lines show 90 percent confidence interval.

Establishing and maintaining resilient monetary policy frameworks is especially important against the backdrop of the recent launch of unconventional monetary policy tools—particularly asset purchases—by EMDE central banks (chapter 4).

- *Fiscal policy frameworks.* Fiscal rules can help prevent fiscal slippages, ensure that revenue windfalls during times of strong growth are prudently managed, and contain and manage risks from contingent liabilities.[20] Strong fiscal frameworks have also been associated with lower inflation and inflation volatility, suggesting that they tend to support the central bank in delivering its mandate (Ha, Kose, and Ohnsorge 2019).

---

[20] Romer and Romer (2019) show that many shifts to austerity were motivated by reasons other than lack of financial market access, including fiscal rules. Cebotari (2008) discusses in greater detail good practices for managing risks from contingent liabilities. For example, Currie and Velandia (2002) call for adding contingent liabilities to government balance sheet analysis. In another example, Ülgentürk (2017) documents the role of debt managers and the involvement of debt management offices in managing contingent liabilities.

BOX 3.3 From institutional reforms to long-term growth

Reforms to improve governance and business climates have been associated with higher total factor productivity (TFP) and investment—two key drivers of long-term output growth. Institutional reforms should be prioritized to help build the foundation for a robust and sustained economic recovery from the pandemic-induced global recession.

Introduction

The decade leading up to the pandemic-induced global recession in 2020 was marked by a steady slowdown in productivity growth and pronounced investment weakness (World Bank 2017a, 2020a). These developments were accompanied by weakening growth in potential output—the output that can be sustained at full employment and capacity utilization (World Bank 2018a). The COVID-19 pandemic has exacerbated these adverse trends. Exceptionally high uncertainty about growth prospects and policies has discouraged investment. Human capital accumulation has been set back by disruptions to education and widespread unemployment. Disruptions to global supply chains in the early stages of the pandemic may trigger a re-assessment of their viability. Lasting changes in consumer behavior, such as reduced demand for hospitality, travel, tourism, and services that involve personal interactions, may render some existing capital assets obsolete (Dieppe 2020).

A renewed boost to underlying growth is needed, a boost that could be provided by reforms to governance and business climates. Strong institutions and conducive business climates set the preconditions for vigorous growth. They encourage private sector investment and innovation by establishing secure and enforceable property rights, minimizing expropriation risk, creating a stable and confidence-inspiring policy environment, lowering the costs of doing business, and encouraging participation in the formal sector where productivity tends to be higher (World Bank 2018a, 2019d). Good governance also ensures competitive and flexible markets with limited market concentration, effective regulation, and the efficient and equitable provision of public services, including healthcare, education, and public infrastructure (Acemoglu and Johnson 2005; Dort, Méon, and Sekkat 2014; Gwartney, Holcombe, and Lawson 2006).

The potential benefits of reforms in these areas are underscored by the fact that in many emerging market and developing economies (EMDEs), weak institutions and governance remain a substantial obstacle to sustained robust growth of investment and productivity (World Bank 2018a). The lack of secure and enforceable property rights, pervasive corruption and crime, and large informal sectors are formidable constraints on the ability of private firms to invest, innovate, and close the productivity gap with high-income countries. Thus, there is considerable scope for EMDE governments to stem or reverse a slowdown in productivity and potential growth by strengthening institutions, reducing corruption, dismantling regulatory barriers to doing business and entrepreneurship, and ensuring effective regulation conducive for the efficient working of competitive markets (Kilic Celik, Kose, and Ohnsorge 2020).

Against this backdrop, this box addresses the following questions.

- Through what channels do governance and business regulations affect growth?

- How have productivity and investment growth evolved during major reform episodes?

Links between reforms and growth

Institutional quality and growth. There is now a broad consensus in the literature that market-friendly institutional reforms have been associated with stronger economic growth, albeit with wide heterogeneity across countries, and disagreements about the optimal type of institutional arrangements (Bluhm and Szirmai 2011; Nawaz 2015; Prati, Onorato, and Papageorgiou 2013). Institutional change can raise investment and productivity growth directly by raising private returns to productivity-enhancing investment in human and physical capital. Institutional reforms can also promote investment and productivity growth indirectly, by removing obstacles to other drivers of long-term growth such as innovation, openness, competition, and financial development (Acemoglu et al. 2005; Botero, Ponce, and Shleifer 2012; Glaeser et al. 2004; Glaeser, Ponzetto, and Shleifer 2007).

- *Corruption.* Over 30 percent of firms in EMDEs identify corruption and competition from the informal sector as major constraints to their growth. Several studies show that anticorruption reforms have significantly boosted long-term growth and

---

Note: This box was prepared by Sergiy Kasyanenko. Research assistance was provided by Kaltrina Temaj.

BOX 3.3 From institutional reforms to long-term growth *(continued)*

investment, albeit with substantial variation in outcomes across countries.[a]

- *Informality.* Informality is associated with considerably weaker development outcomes and well-designed reforms to reduce informality have often been associated with higher growth (World Bank 2019d). There is also a strong correlation between weak institutions—such as inefficient governance, excessive regulation, and high incidence of corruption—and informality (Guillermo et al. 2007).

- *Political stability and rule of law.* Studies show that political stability encourages stronger growth and investment, and may also improve fiscal discipline (Aisen and Veiga 2013). Security, the protection of property rights, and the removal of undue influence on courts are strongly correlated with higher growth or lower growth volatility (Acemoglu, Johnson, and Robinson 2001; Haggard and Tiede 2011; World Bank 2017b). Well-established legal systems and property rights, high-quality institutions, and mature patent laws foster deeper integration into global supply chains, which require dependable interactions between producers and suppliers across multiple stages of production and jurisdictions (Alfaro et al. 2019; WTO 2019). Global supply chains, in turn, have been associated with the absorption of productivity-enhancing technologies through foreign direct investment (Alfaro 2017).

- *Education and innovation.* By encouraging human capital accumulation and innovative activities, institutions can promote forms of economic activity that are associated with greater economic complexity and higher productivity growth (Dieppe 2020; Vu 2019). Secure intellectual property rights are critical to incentivize firms to innovate, increase research and development spending, invest in knowledge-based capital, and promote knowledge diffusion (Andrews and Criscuolo 2013; Cong 2013).

Business climates and growth. Poor business climates allow anticompetitive practices to flourish, perpetuate corruption, discourage innovation, and distort the efficient allocation of factors of production (Aghion and Schankermann 2004; Bourles et al. 2013; Buccirossi et al. 2013).

- *Reforms to improve regulatory quality.* Burdensome business regulations amplify the adverse effect of corruption on firms' labor productivity (Amin and Ulku 2019). Substantial improvement in regulatory quality is often associated with a significant increase in long-term growth as it encourages the entry of more productive firms, including multinational companies, and stimulates research and development spending (Alam, Uddin, and Yazdifar 2019; Egan 2013).

- *Reforms to increase labor market flexibility.* Labor market regulations are designed to provide social protection and improve workplace safety. If excessively distortionary or poorly enacted, they can discourage formal employment and constrain firm size.[b] Reforms to increase labor market flexibility can help improve firm-level productivity, increase labor force participation, reduce informality, and encourage a more efficient allocation of labor (Blanchard, Jaumotte, and Loungani 2013).

- *Reforms to improve business climates.* EMDEs with business-friendly regulations tend to have higher levels of economic inclusiveness, have smaller informal sectors, and grow faster (Djankov, McLiesh, and Ramalho 2006; World Bank 2014). For example, trade restrictions are associated with lower firm productivity, especially when accompanied by intrusive domestic industrial policy (Topalova and Khandelwal 2011). Weak business environments may diminish complementarities between public and foreign direct investment and domestic investment (Kose et al. 2017). Major improvements in business environments have been associated with increased output growth (Divanbeigi and Ramalho 2015; Kirkpatrick 2014).

Correlates of success of reforms. The impact of reforms often depends on the country's stage of development and the distance to the technological frontier (Dabla-Norris, Ho, and Kyobe 2016). Investments in physical and human capital are often associated with stronger long-term outcomes when the quality of institutions already exceeds certain thresholds (Hall, Sobel, and Crowley 2010; Jude and Levieuge 2017). EMDEs with stronger institutions and better regulations may achieve greater output gains from financial liberalization and trade openness (Atkin and

---

[a] See Cieślik and Goczek (2018); de Vaal and Ebben (2011); Gründler and Potrafke (2019); Hodge et al. (2011); OECD (2015); and Shleifer and Vishny (1993).

[b] See Bruhn (2011); La Porta and Shleifer (2014); Loayza, Oviedo, and Serven (2005); and Loayza and Serven (2010).

BOX 3.3 From institutional reforms to long-term growth (*continued*)

Khandelwal 2020; Slesman, Baharumshah, and Azman-Saini 2019; Williams 2019).

Political economy of reforms. The ability of governments to maintain the pace of institutional reforms is often uneven, in part because growth dividends from reforms often materialize with substantial lags and reforms may initially be politically costly, especially during elections (Alesina et al. 2020). Major growth downturns have sometimes been associated with subsequent reform accelerations; conversely, growth-enhancing reforms have also been delayed or even reversed during times of economic stress and in economies with high debt burdens (Gokmen et al. 2020; Muller, Storesletten, and Zilibotti 2019). Even during more tranquil times, meaningful reforms are often postponed due to unfavorable redistributive outcomes (Gradstein 2007).

Productivity and investment growth during major reform episodes

Methodology and data. A series of event studies and a local projection approach are used to estimate the impact of major governance and regulatory reforms on total factor productivity (TFP) and investment growth, two critical drivers of long-term output growth. Three different data sets are used to measure the quality of institutions and business climates in a large sample of EMDEs.

- *Worldwide Governance Indicators.* Major institutional reform advances (or setbacks) are defined as improvements (or deteriorations) in at least one of four *Worldwide Governance Indicators* (government effectiveness, control of corruption, rule of law, and regulatory quality) by two or more standard errors over the span of two years (as in Didier et al. 2015).

- *Doing Business indicators.* Major business climate reform advances (or setbacks) are identified in a similar manner—as those that over two years close (or widen) the gap with the best regulatory practice on at least one of ten *Doing Business* indicators by two or more standard deviations.

- *International Country Risk Guide (ICRG) indicators.* As an alternative to the *Worldwide Governance Indicators*, sustained institutional advances or setbacks are defined as an increase or decrease, respectively, in the unweighted average of four ICRG indicators—bureaucracy quality, law and order, corruption, and investment profile—provided the increase is not unwound for at least three consecutive years.

The event study examines the evolution of investment growth and total factor productivity (TFP) growth in the year immediately following the reform advance or setback. The local projection model estimates the effect of the reform event on cumulative investment growth and TFP growth over horizons of two and four years after the start of the event (annex 3.3).[c]

Progress on reforms over the past decade. Progress on institutional reforms has been mixed over the past decade (figure B3.3.1). Institutional change appears to be highly persistent: both achievements in reform advances and setbacks tend to endure (figure B3.3.2).

- *Business climate reform* advances became more common, while setbacks become less frequent (figure B3.3.1; Ruch 2020). The main reform advances were in the areas of access to credit, starting a business, and insolvency procedures, and setbacks mainly concerned paying taxes, trade, and property registration.

- *Governance reforms*, as captured in the *Worldwide Governance Indicators*, decelerated substantially in the aftermath of the global financial crisis as reform advances were offset by reform setbacks. From 1998 to 2018, less than one-fifth of all institutional reform advances in EMDEs were associated with an improvement across more than one dimension in *Worldwide Governance Indicators*, and about one in nine setbacks occurred with a simultaneous deterioration across more than one measure of institutional quality. Better control of corruption accounted for the largest proportion of the reform advances (45 percent of advances); while setbacks were most often associated with declining quality of the rule of law (37 percent of setbacks).

- *Sustained advances in the quality of institutions*, as identified by ICRG indicators, initially became less frequent after the global financial crisis when they were often offset by reform setbacks. Since the mid-2010s, however, improvements have become more frequent and setbacks rarer. Most episodes of sustained reform advances, as well as setbacks, were associated with changes in the investment profile and anticorruption measures.

Initial impact of reforms. TFP and investment growth in the year following reform episodes tended to be higher

---

[c] Sample includes up to 94 (115) EMDEs and 35 (39) advanced economies with data on TFP (investment) growth, depending on data availability for reforms.

BOX 3.3 From institutional reforms to long-term growth *(continued)*

FIGURE B3.3.1 Reform advances and setbacks

There have been a larger number of sustained improvements than setbacks in institutional quality and in business climates since the mid-2010s.

A. *Worldwide Governance Indicators*: **Number of reform advances and setbacks**

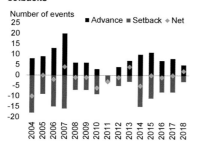

B. *Doing Business* **indicators: Number of reform advances and setbacks**

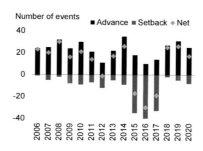

C. *International Country Risk Guide* **indicators*: Number of sustained reform advances and setbacks**

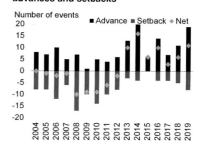

D. *Worldwide Governance Indicators:* **Sources of reform advances and setbacks in EMDEs**

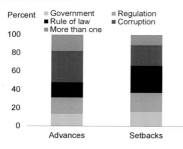

E. *Doing Business* **indicators: Sources of reform advances and setbacks in EMDEs**

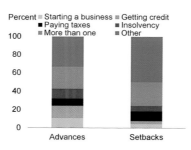

F. *International Country Risk Guide* **indicators*: Sources of sustained reform advances and setbacks in EMDEs**

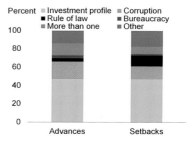

Source: World Bank.

Note: EMDEs = emerging market and developing economies. Episodes in which there were advances in one measure and simultaneous setbacks in another are excluded. A detailed methodology is available in annexes 3.1 and 3.3.

A. For *Worldwide Governance Indicators*, reform events are defined as two-standard-error changes in one of four Worldwide Governance Indicators for 155 EMDEs and 49 advanced economies during 1996-2018.

B. For *Doing Business* indicators, reform events are defined as two-standard-deviation changes in distance to frontier (the best practice across all countries) in one of ten Doing Business indicators in 67 EMDEs and 28 advanced economies during 2004-20. Sample excludes fragile and conflict states and small economies with population less than 4 million people.

C. Sustained institutional advances or setbacks are defined as an increase or decrease in the unweighted average of four *International Country Risk Guide indicators*— bureaucracy quality, law and order, corruption, and investment profile—provided the increase or the decrease is not unwound for at least three consecutive years. Sample includes 102 EMDEs and 39 advanced economies.

D. Based on 127 episodes of reform advances and 147 episodes of reform setbacks in 1998-2018 identified in 110 EMDEs with a median of 2 episodes per economy.

E. Based on 260 episodes of reform advances and 120 episodes of reform setbacks in 2006-20 identified in 67 EMDEs with a median of 6 episodes per economy.

F. Based on 106 episodes of sustained reform advances and 85 episodes of sustained reform setbacks during 2004-19 identified in 100 EMDEs with a median of 2 episodes per economy. "Other" indicates episodes when a sustained increase or decrease in the average of four indicators was not associated with any particular indicator.

than in "normal" years (without advances or setbacks), while reform setbacks were associated with lower TFP and investment growth.

- *Reform advances* reflected in *Worldwide Governance Indicators* and *ICRG* indicators, were associated with 0.8-1.2 percentage point a year higher TFP growth compared to "normal" years in EMDEs (figure

B3.3.3).[d] Reform advances that emphasized efforts to reduce corruption and strengthen the rule of law were followed by somewhat larger TFP increases. Investment growth in the year following reform

---

[d] This compares with 0.4 percent and 6.7 percent annual average global TFP growth and investment growth, respectively, during "normal" years in the median country that had neither a reform advance or setback. All comparisons refer to medians.

BOX 3.3 From institutional reforms to long-term growth *(continued)*

FIGURE B3.3.2 **Persistence of reform advances and setbacks**

Institutional change is very persistent: both achievements in reform advances and setbacks tend to endure.

A. Governance indicators around reform advances and setbacks in EMDEs	B. Business climate indicators around reform advances and setbacks in EMDEs	C. ICRG indicators around sustained reform advances and setbacks in EMDEs
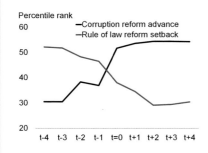	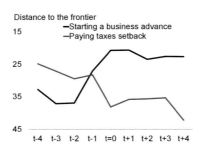	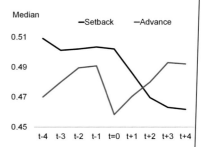

Source: World Bank.

Note: Episodes are identified in a similar way as in figure B3.3.1. A detailed methodology is available in annexes 3.1 and 3.3.

A.B. Median percentile rank (A) and distance from frontier (B). t=0 indicates the year of the reform advance or setback as identified using *Worldwide Governance Indicators* or *Doing Business Indicators*. Only the earliest episode is selected for the reform advances (setbacks) occurring in two consecutive years.

C. Average of four indicators: bureaucracy quality, law and order, corruption, and investment profile. t=0 indicates the year when a sustained reform advance or setback started as identified using *International Country Risk Guide* (ICRG) indicators.

advances was 1.5-5.0 percentage points higher in EMDEs than in "normal" years, with considerably larger increases after reform efforts to rein in corruption and strengthen the rule of law.

- *Reform setbacks,* as identified using the *Worldwide Governance Indicators* or the *ICRG* indicators, were associated with slowdons of 0.4-1.3 percentage point a year in TFP growth in EMDEs. When these reform setbacks were associated with greater corruption, EMDE TFP growth declined by an additional 0.3 percentage points. Similarly, investment growth fell by about 2 percentage points in EMDEs after reform setbacks, and by an additional 1-3 percentage points when these setbacks involved increased corruption or poorer government effectiveness.

Effects of reforms over time. The local projection estimation indicates that the effects of institutional reform advances and setbacks, identified using *Worldwide Governance Indicators* or *ICRG* indicators, have tended to accumulate over time.[c] It takes several years for TFP or

---

[c] Detailed methodology is presented in annex 3.3. A similar exercise for the *Doing Business* indicators is not possible due to data constraints.

investment growth dividends to materialize after institutional reform advances; the adverse impact of reform setbacks is more heterogeneous.

- *Reform advances.* TFP in EMDEs was about 1.9 percent above the baseline two years after reform advances reflected in *Worldwide Governance Indicators* or *ICRG* indicators. Over time, this impact became more heterogeneous and more difficult to estimate precisely. EMDE investment responded initially in a heterogeneous manner but a more well-defined effect crystallized over time. Four years after reform advances, captured by either the *Worldwide Governance Indicators* or the *ICRG* indicators, EMDE investment tended to be 16-17 percent above the baseline.

- *Reform setbacks.* EMDE TFP fell statistically significantly after reform setbacks as identified using *Worldwide Governance Indicators,* and the effect grew over subsequent years. In contrast, sustained reforms setbacks, as captured by the *ICRG* indicators, were followed by a wide range of TFP growth outcomes. Similarly, EMDE investment, evolved in too heterogeneous a manner for a well-defined estimate of the impact to be obtained but typically fell sharply below the baseline over several years.

Women, Work, and Economic Growth: Leveling the Playing Field, edited by K. Kalpana, S. Jain-Chandra, and M. Newiak, 117-126. Washington, DC: International Monetary Fund.

Datta, S. 2012. "The Impact of Improved Highways on Indian Firms." *Journal of Development Economics* 99 (1): 46-57.

Davidovic, S., S. Nunhuck, D. Prady, and H. Tourpe. 2020. "Beyond the COVID-19 Crisis: A Framework for Sustainable Government-To-Person Mobile Money Transfers." IMF Working Paper 20/198, International Monetary Fund, Washington, DC.

de Barros, R. P., P. Olinto, T. Lunde, and M. Caralho. 2013. "The Impact of Access to Free Childcare on Women's Labor Market Outcomes: Evidence from a Randomized Trial in Low-Income Neighborhoods of Rio de Janeiro." Gender Impact Evaluation Database, World Bank, Washington, DC.

de la Fuente, A. 2011. "Human Capital and Productivity." Working Paper 530, Barcelona Graduate School of Economics, Barcelona.

De Long, J. B., and B. Eichengreen. 1991. "The Marshall Plan: History's Most Successful Structural Adjustment Program," NBER Working Paper 3899, National Bureau of Economic Research, Cambridge.

de Vaal, A., and W. Ebben. 2011. "Institutions and the Relation between Corruption and Economic Growth." *Review of Development Economics* 15 (1): 108-123.

Demetriades, P., and T. Mamuneas. 2000. "Intertemporal Output and Employment Effects of Public Infrastructure Capital: Evidence from 12 OECD Economies." *Economic Journal* 110 (July): 687-712.

Devine, D., J. Gaskell, W. Jennings, and G. Stoker. 2020. "Trust and the Coronavirus Pandemic: What are the Consequences of and for Trust? An Early Review of the Literature." *Political Studies Review.* https://doi.org/10.1177/1478929920948684.

Didier, T., M. A. Kose, F. Ohnsorge, and L. S. Ye. 2015. "Slowdown in Emerging Markets: Rough Patch or Prolonged Weakness?" Policy Research Note 4, World Bank, Washington, DC.

Dieppe, A., ed. 2020. *Global Productivity: Trends, Drivers, and Policies.* Washington, DC: World Bank.

Dieppe, A., S. Kilic Celik, and C. Okou. 2020. "Implications of Major Adverse Events on Productivity." Policy Research Working Paper 9411, World Bank, Washington, DC.

Dieppe, A., and H. Matsuoka. 2020. "Sectoral Sources of Productivity Growth." In *Global Productivity: Trends, Drivers, and Policies,* edited by A. Dieppe. Washington, DC: World Bank.

Divanbeigi, R., and R. Ramalho. 2015. "Business Regulations and Growth." Policy Research Working Paper 7299, World Bank, Washington, DC.

Djankov, S., C. McLiesh, and R. Ramalho. 2006. "Regulation and Growth." *Economics Letters* 92 (3): 395-401.

Doraszelski, U., and J. Jaumandreu. 2013. "R&D and Productivity: Estimating Endogenous Productivity." *Review of Economic Studies* 80 (4): 1338-1383.

Dort, T., P. Méon, and K. Sekkat. 2014. "Does Investment Spur Growth Everywhere? Not Where Institutions Are Weak." *Kyklos* 67 (4): 482-505.

Duflo, E. 2012. "Women Empowerment and Economic Development." *Journal of Economic Literature* 50 (4): 1051-1079.

Easterly, W. 2001. "The Lost Decades: Explaining Developing Countries' Stagnation in Spite of Policy Reform 1980-1998." *Journal of Economic Growth* 6 (2): 135-157.

Easterly, W. 2005. "National Policies and Economic Growth: A Reappraisal." In *Handbook of Economic Growth,* edited by. P. Aghion and S. Durlauf, 1113-1180. Amsterdam: Elsevier.

Eckstein, Z., and O. Lifshitz. 2011. "Dynamic Female Labor Supply." *Econometrica* 79 (6):1675-1726.

Egan, P. 2013. "R&D in the Periphery? Foreign Direct Investment, Innovation, And Institutional Quality in Developing Countries." *Business and Politics* 15 (1): 1-32.

Ehrlich, I., and Y. Pei. 2020. "Human Capital as Engine of Growth—The Role of Knowledge Transfers in Promoting Balanced Growth Within and Across Countries." NBER Working Paper 26810, National Bureau of Economic Research, Cambridge.

ElFayoumi, K., A. Ndoye, S. Nadeem, and G. Auclair. 2018. "Structural Reforms and Labor Reallocation: A Cross-Country Analysis." IMF Working Paper 18/64, International Monetary Fund, Washington, DC.

El-Mallakh, N. 2020. "Internet Job Search, Employment, and Wage Growth: Evidence from the Arab Republic of Egypt." Policy Research Working Paper 9196. World Bank, Washington, DC.

Fernald, J. 1999. "Roads to Prosperity? Assessing the Link between Public Capital and Productivity." *American Economic Review* 89 (3): 619-638.

Fernald, J. G., R. E. Hall, J. H. Stock, and M. W. Watson. 2017. "The Disappointing Recovery of Output after 2009," NBER Working Paper 23543, National Bureau of Economic Research, Cambridge.

Fernández, R. 2013. "Cultural Change as Learning: The Evolution of Female Labor Force Participation Over a Century." *American Economic Review* 103 (1): 472-500.

Feyen, E., and I. Zuccardi Huertas. 2020. "Bank Lending Rates and Spreads in EMDEs Evolution, Drivers, and Policies." Policy Research Working Paper 9392, World Bank, Washington, DC.

Fisher, J. D. M. 2006. "The Dynamic Effects of Neutral and Investment Specific Technology Shocks." *Journal of Political Economy* 114 (3): 413-451.

Flabbi, L., and R. Gatti. 2018. "A Primer on Human Capital." Policy Research Working Paper 8309, World Bank, Washington, DC.

Fogli, A., and L. Veldkamp. 2011. "Nature or Nurture? Learning and the Geography of Female Labor Force Participation" *Econometrica* 79 (4): 1103-1138.

Foster, L., C. Grim, and J. Haltiwanger. 2016. "Reallocation in the Great Recession: Cleansing or Not?" *Journal of Labor Economics* 34 (S1): 293-331.

Frankel, J. 2011. "Over Optimism in Forecasts by Official Budget Agencies and its Implications." *Oxford Review of Economic Policy* 27 (4): 536-562.

Franklin, J. 2020. "Payment Holidays Squeeze Securitised Products." International Financial Law Review, London.

Fuchs, R., E. Pamuk, and W. Lutz. 2010. "Education or Wealth: Which Matters More for Reducing Child Mortality in Developing Countries?" *Vienna Yearbook of Population Research* 8: 175-199.

Furceri, D., P. Loungani, J. D. Ostry, and P. Pizzuto. 2020. "Will Covid-19 Affect Inequality? Evidence from Past Pandemics." *COVID Economics, Vetted and Real Time Papers* 12: 138-157.

Galasso, E., A. Wagstaff, S. Naudeau, and M. Shekar. 2017. "The Economic Costs of Stunting and How to Reduce Them." Policy Research Note 17/05, World Bank, Washington, DC.

Ganelli, G., and J. Tervala. 2016. "The Welfare Multiplier of Public Infrastructure Investment." IMF Working Paper 16/40, International Monetary Fund, Washington, DC.

Gelb, A., and A. Mukherjee. 2020. "Digital Technology in Social Assistance Transfers for COVID-19 Relief: Lessons from Selected Cases." CGD Policy Paper, 181, Center for Global Development, Washington, DC.

Gennaioli, N., Y. Ma, and A. Shleifer. 2016. "Expectations and Investment." *NBER Macroeconomics Annual* 30 (1): 379-431.

Gerged, A., and M. Elheddad. 2020. "How Can National Governance Affect Education Quality in Western Europe?" *International Journal of Sustainability in Higher Education* 21 (3): 413-426.

Getachew, Y. 2010. "Public Capital and Distributional Dynamics in a Two-Sector Growth Model." *Journal of Macroeconomics* 32 (2): 606-616.

Ghani, E., W. R. Kerr, and S. D. O'Connell. 2013. "Promoting Women's Economic Participation in India." Economic Premise 107, World Bank, Washington, DC.

Gill, I., I. Izvorski, W. van Eeghen, and D. de Rosa. 2014 *Diversified Development: Making the Most of Natural Resources in Eurasia.* Washington, DC: World Bank.

Glaeser, E., R. La Porta, F. Lopez-de-Silanes, and A. Shleifer. 2004. "Do Institutions Cause Growth?" *Journal of Economic Growth* 9 (3): 271-303.

Glaeser, E., G. Ponzetto, and A. Shleifer. 2007. "Why Does Democracy Need Education?" *Journal of Economic Growth* 12 (2): 77-99.

Gokmen, G., T. Nannicini, M. Onorato, and C. Papageorgiou. 2020. "Policies in Hard Times: Assessing the Impact of Financial Crises on Structural Reforms." IZA Discussion Paper 12932, Institute of Labor Economics, Bonn.

Goldin, I., and R. Muggah. 2020. "COVID-19 is Increasing Multiple Kinds of Inequality. Here's What We Can Do About It." World Economic Forum Blogs, October 9. https://www.weforum.org/agenda/2020/10/

covid-19-is-increasing-multiple-kinds-of-inequality-here-s-what-we-can-do-about-it/.

Gonzales, C., S. Jain-Chandra, K. Kochhar and M. Newiak. 2015. "Fair Play: More Equal Laws Boost Female Labor Force Participation." IMF Working Paper 15/02, International Monetary Fund, Washington, DC.

Gopalakrishnan, B. and S. Mohapatra. 2020. "Insolvency Regimes and Firms' Default Risk under Economic Uncertainty and Shocks." *Economic Modelling* 91: 180-197.

Gradstein, M. 2007. "Inequality, Democracy and the Protection of Property Rights." *Economic Journal* 117 (516): 252-269.

Grantham-McGregor S., Y. B. Cheung, S. Cueto, P. Glewwe, L. Richter, and B. Strupp. 2007. "Developmental Potential in the First 5 Years for Children in Developing Countries." *Lancet* 369 (9555): 60-70.

Greenwood, J., Z. Hercowitz, and P. Krusell. 1997. "Long-Run Implications of Investment-Specific Technological Change." *American Economic Review* 87 (3): 342-362.

Greenwood, J., Z. Hercowitz, and P. Krusell. 2000. "The Role of Investment-Specific Technological Change in the Business Cycle." *European Economic Review* 44 (1): 91-115.

Gründler, K., and N. Potrafke. 2019. "Corruption and Economic Growth: New Empirical Evidence." *European Journal of Political Economy* 60 (C): Article 101810.

Guermazi, B., and R. Seligman. 2020. "Covid-19 (Coronavirus) Response in Russia—Digital Payments." Brief, World Bank, Washington, DC.

Guillermo, P., W. Maloney, O. Arias, P. Fajnzylber, A. Mason, and J. Saavedra-Chanduvi. 2007. *Informality: Exit and Exclusion*. Washington, DC: World Bank.

Gwartney, D., R. Holcombe, and R. Lawson. 2006. "Institutions and the Impact of Investment on Growth." *Kyklos* 59 (2): 255-273.

Ha, J., M. A. Kose, and F. Ohnsorge, eds. 2019. *Inflation in Emerging and Developing Economies: Evolution, Drivers and Policies*. Washington, DC: World Bank.

Ha, J., M. Stocker, and H. Yilmazkuday.

2019. "Inflation and Exchange Rate Pass-Through." Policy Research Working Paper 8780, World Bank, Washington, DC.

Haggard, S., and L. Tiede. 2011. "The Rule of Law and Economic Growth: Where are We?" *World Development* 39 (5): 673-685.

Hall, J., R. Sobel, and G. Crowley. 2010. "Institutions, Capital, and Growth." *Southern Economic Journal* 77 (2): 385-405.

Hallegatte, S., and S. Hammer. 2020. "Thinking Ahead: For a Sustainable Recovery from COVD-19 (Coronavirus)." *Development and Changing Climate* (blog), March 30, 2020.

Hanushek, E. 2002. "Publicly Provided Education." In *Handbook of Public Economics*, edited by A. Auerbach and M. Feldstein. Amsterdam: North Holland.

Hanushek, E., and D. Kimko. 2000. "Schooling, Labor Force Quality, and the Growth of Nations." *American Economic Review* 90 (5): 1184-1208.

Hanushek, E., J. Ruhose, and L. Woessmann. 2017a. "Economic Gains from Educational Reform by US States." *Journal of Human Capital* 11 (4): 447-486.

Hanushek, E., J. Ruhose, and L. Woessmann. 2017b. "Knowledge Capital and Aggregate Income Differences: Development Accounting for U.S. States." *American Economic Journal: Macroeconomics* 9 (4): 184-224.

Hanushek, E., and L. Woessmann. 2008. "The Role of Cognitive Skills in Economic Development." *Journal of Economic Literature* 46 (3): 607-668.

Hanushek, E., and L. Woessmann. 2015a. *The Knowledge Capital of Nations: Education and the Economics of Growth*. Cambridge: MIT Press.

Hanushek, E., and L. Woessmann. 2015b. *Universal Basic Skills: What Countries Stand to Gain*. Paris: Organisation for Economic Co-operation and Development, Paris.

Hanushek, E., and L. Woessmann. 2016. "Knowledge Capital, Growth, and the East Asian Miracle." *Science* 351 (6271): 344-345.

Harding, D., and A. Pagan. 2002. "Dissecting the Cycle: A Methodological Investigation." *Journal of Monetary Economics* 49 (2): 365-381.

He, H., and Z. Liu. 2008. "Investment-Specific

Technological Change, Skill Accumulation, and Wage Inequality." *Review of Economic Dynamics* 11 (2): 314-334.

Hendricks, L. 2000. "Equipment Investment and Growth in Developing Countries." *Journal of Development Economics* 61 (2): 335-364.

Hendricks L., and T. Schoellman. 2017. "Human Capital and Development Accounting: New Evidence from Wage Gains at Migration." Working Paper 1, Opportunity and Inclusive Growth Institute, Federal Reserve Bank of Minneapolis.

Hepburn, C., B. O'Callaghan, N. Stern, J. Stiglitz, and D. Zenghelis. 2020. "Will COVID-19 Fiscal Recovery Packages Accelerate or Retard Progress on Climate Change?" Smith School Working Paper 20-02, University of Oxford, Oxford.

Hershbein, B., and L. B. Kahn. 2018. "Do Recessions Accelerate Routine-Biased Technological Change?" *American Economic Review* 108 (7): 1737-1772.

Hjort, J., and J. Poulsen. 2019. "The Arrival of Fast Internet and Employment in Africa." *American Economic Review* 109 (3): 1032-1079.

Ho, G., and P. Mauro. 2016. "Growth—Now and Forever?" *IMF Economic Review* 64 (3): 526-547.

Hodge, A., S. Shankar, D. Rao, and A. Duhs. 2011. "Exploring the Links Between Corruption and Growth." *Review of Development Economics* 15 (3): 474-490.

Hollander, J. E., and B. G. Carr. 2020. "Virtually Perfect? Telemedicine for COVID-19." *New England Journal of Medicine* 382 (18): 1679-1681.

Hu, A., and S. Liu. 2010. "Transportation, Economic Growth and Spillover Effects: The Conclusion Based on the Spatial Econometric Model." *Frontiers of Economics in China* 5 (2): 169-186.

Huffman, W. E. 2020. "Human Capital and Adoption of Innovations: Policy Implications." *Applied Economic Perspectives and Policy* 42 (1): 92-99.

Huidrom, R., M. A. Kose, J. J. Lim, and F. Ohnsorge. 2020. "Why Do Fiscal Multipliers Depend on Fiscal Positions?" *Journal of Monetary Economics* 114: 109-125.

Hulten, C. 1994. "Optimal Growth with Infrastructure Capital: Theory and Implications for Empirical Modeling." Working Paper, University of Maryland, College Park.

IEA (International Energy Agency). 2020. *Sustainable Recovery*. International Energy Agency, Paris. https://www.iea.org/reports/sustainable-recovery.

IFC (International Finance Corporation). 2019. *Tackling Childcare: A Guide for Employer-Supported Childcare*. Washington, DC: International Finance Corporation.

IMF (International Monetary Fund). 2014. *World Economic Outlook: Legacies, Clouds, Uncertainties*. Washington, DC: International Monetary Fund.

IMF (International Monetary Fund). 2015. "Making Public Investment More Efficient." Staff Report, International Monetary Fund, Washington, DC.

IMF (International Monetary Fund). 2018. *Fiscal Monitor: Managing Public Wealth*. October. Washington, DC: International Monetary Fund.

IMF (International Monetary Fund). 2020a. *World Economic Outlook: A Long and Difficult Ascent*. October. Washington, DC: International Monetary Fund.

IMF (International Monetary Fund). 2020b. *World Economic Outlook: The Great Lockdown*. April. Washington, DC: International Monetary Fund.

IMF (International Monetary Fund). 2020c. *World Economic Outlook Update: A Crisis Like No Other*. June. Washington, DC: International Monetary Fund.

Izquierdo, A., R. Lama, J. P. Medina, J. Puig, D. Riera-Crichton, C. Vegh, and G. Vuletin. 2020. "Is the Public Investment Multiplier Higher in Developing Countries? An Empirical Exploration." Working Paper 19/289, International Monetary Fund, Washington, DC.

Jaimovich, N., and H. E. Siu. 2019. "Job Polarization and Jobless Recoveries." *Review of Economics and Statistics* 102 (1): 129-147.

Jaumotte, F. 2004. "Labour Force Participation of Women: Empirical Evidence on the Role of Policy and Other Determinants in OECD Countries." *OECD Economic Studies* 2003 (2): 51-108.

Jones, B. 2014. "The Human Capital Stock: A Generalized Approach." *American Economic Review* 104 (11): 3752-3777.

Jordà, O. 2005. "Estimation and Inference of Impulse

Responses by Local Projections." *American Economic Review* 95 (1): 161-182.

Jordà, Ò., S. R. Singh, and A. M. Taylor. 2020. "Longer-Run Economic Consequences of Pandemics." NBER Working Paper 26934, National Bureau of Economic Research, Cambridge.

Jude, C., and G. Levieuge. 2017. "Growth Effect of Foreign Direct Investment in Developing Economies: The Role of Institutional Quality." *World Economy* 40 (4): 715-742.

Juhn, G., and P. Loungani. 2002. "Further Cross-Country Evidence on the Accuracy of the Private Sector's Output Forecasts." *IMF Staff Paper* 49 (1): 49-64.

Kenney, M., and J. Zysman. 2020. "COVID-19 and the Increasing Centrality and Power of Platforms in China, the U.S., and Beyond." *Management and Organization Review* 16 (4): 747-752.

Khandker, S., H. Samad, R. Ali, and D. Barnes. 2012. "Who Benefits Most from Rural Electrification? Evidence from India." Policy Research Working Paper 6095, World Bank, Washington, DC.

Kilic Celik, S., M. A. Kose, and F. Ohnsorge. 2020. "Subdued Potential Growth: Sources and Remedies." In *Growth in a Time of Change: Global and Country Perspectives on a New Agenda*, edited by H.-W. Kim and Z. Qureshi. Washington, DC: Brookings Institution.

Kirkpatrick, C. 2014. "Assessing the Impact of Regulatory Reform in Developing Countries." *Public Administration and Development* 34 (3): 162-168.

Klasen, S., and J. Pieters. 2015. "What Explains the Stagnation of Female Labor Force Participation in Urban India?" Policy Research Working Paper 7222, World Bank, Washington, DC.

Klenow, P, and A. Rodriguez-Clare. 1997. "Economic Growth: A Review Essay." *Journal of Monetary Economics* 40 (3): 597-617.

Klenow, P., and A. Rodriguez-Clare. 2005. "Externalities and Growth." In *Handbook of Economic Growth*, edited by P. Aghion and S. Durlauf, 1113-1180. Amsterdam: Elsevier.

Kose, M. A., H. Matsuoka, U. Panizza, and D. Vorisek. 2019. "Inflation Expectations: Review and Evidence." Policy Research Working Paper 8785, World Bank, Washington, DC.

Kose, M. A., P. Nagle, F. Ohnsorge, and N. Sugawara. 2020a. *Global Waves of Debt: Causes and Consequences.* Washington, DC: World Bank.

Kose, M. A., P. S. Nagle, F. Ohnsorge, and N. Sugawara. 2020b. "Can This Time Be Different? Policy Options in Times of Rising Debt." Policy Research Working Paper 9178, World Bank, Washington, DC.

Kose, M. A., and F. Ohnsorge, eds. 2019. *A Decade Since the Global Recession: Lessons and Challenges for Emerging and Developing Economies.* Washington, DC: World Bank.

Kose, M. A., F. Ohnsorge, Y. Lei, and E. Islamaj. 2017. "Weakness in Investment Growth: Causes, Implications and Policy Responses." Policy Research Working Paper 7990, World Bank, Washington, DC.

Kose, M. A., F. Ohnsorge, P. Nagle, and N. Sugawara. 2020c. "Caught by a Cresting Wave." *Finance and Development* 57(2): 41-43.

Kose, M. A., F. Ohnsorge, and N. Sugawara. Forthcoming. "Global Growth over the Next Decade: Optimistic Expectations, Disappointing Outcomes." Mimeo.

Kose, M. A., and N. Sugawara. Forthcoming. "COVID-19 Global Recession." Policy Research Working Paper, World Bank, Washington, DC.

Krueger, A., and M. Lindahl. 2001. "Education for Growth: Why and for Whom?" *Journal of Economic Literature* 39 (4): 1101-1136.

Kumar, S., and G. Rauniyar. 2011. "Is Electrification Welfare Improving? Non-experimental Evidence from Rural Bhutan." MPRA Paper 3148, University Library of Munich, Munich.

Ky, S., C. Rugemintwari, and A. Sauviat. 2018. "Does Mobile Money Affect Saving Behaviour? Evidence from a Developing Country." *Journal of African Economies* 27 (3): 285–320.

La Porta, R., and A. Shleifer. 2014. "Informality and Development." *Journal of Economic Perspectives* 28 (3): 109-126.

Laeven, L., and F. Valencia. 2020. "Systemic Banking Crises Database II." *IMF Economic Review* 68: 307-361.

Lakner, C., N. Yonzan, D. Gerszon Mahler, R. A. Castaneda Aguilar, and H. Wu. Forthcoming. "Updated Estimates of the Impact of COVID-19 on

Global Poverty: Looking Back at 2020 and the Outlook for 2021." *Voices* (blog), World Bank.

Landivar, L. C., L. Ruppanner, W. J. Scarborough, and C. Collins. 2020. "Early Signs Indicate That COVID-19 Is Exacerbating Gender Inequality in the Labor Force." *Socius* 6 (C): 1-3.

Leduc, S., and Z. Liu. 2020. "Can Pandemic-Induced Job Uncertainty Stimulate Automation?" Working Paper 2020-19, Federal Reserve Bank of San Francisco, San Francisco.

Levine, O., and M. Warusawitharana. 2014. "Finance and Productivity Growth: Firm-Level Evidence." FEDS Working Paper 2014-17, Governors of the Federal Reserve System, Washington, DC.

Loayza, N., A. Oviedo, and L. Servén. 2005. "The Impact of Regulation on Growth and Informality: Cross-Country Evidence." Policy Research Working Paper 3623, World Bank, Washington, DC.

Loayza, N., A. Sanghi, N. Shaharuddin, and L. Wuester. 2020. "Recovery from the Pandemic Crisis: Balancing Short-Term and Long-Term Concerns." Research and Policy Brief 38, World Bank, Washington, DC.

Loayza, N., and L. Servén. 2010. *Business Regulation and Economic Performance.* Washington, DC: World Bank.

Lopez-Cordova, E. 2020. "Digital Platforms and the Demand for International Tourism Services." Policy Research Working Paper 9147, World Bank, Washington, DC.

Loungani, P. 2001. "How Accurate Are Private Sector Forecasts? Cross-Country Evidence from Consensus Forecasts of Output Growth." *International Journal of Forecasting* 17 (3): 419-432.

Luo, R., Y. Shi, L. Zhang, C. Liu, S. Rozelle, B. Sharbono, A. Yue, Q. Zhao, and R. Martorell. 2012. "Nutrition and Educational Performance in Rural China's Elementary Schools: Results of a Randomized Control Trial in Shaanxi Province." *Economic Development and Cultural Change* 60 (4): 735-772.

Lustig, N., V. Pabon, F. Sanz, and S. Younger. 2020. "The Impact of COVID-19 Lockdowns and Expanded Social Assistance on Inequality, Poverty and Mobility in Argentina, Brazil, Colombia and Mexico." CGD Working Paper 556, Center for Global Development, Washington, DC.

Ma, C., J. Rogers, and S. Zhou. 2020. "Global Economic and Financial Effects of 21st Century Pandemics and Epidemics." *COVID Economics, Vetted and Real Time Papers* 5: 56-78.

Machasio, I. N. 2020. "COVID-19 and Digital Financial Inclusion in Africa: How to Leverage Digital Technologies During the Pandemic." Africa Knowledge in Time Policy Brief 1 (4), World Bank, Washington, DC.

Malmberg, H. 2016. "Human Capital and Development Accounting Revisited." Job Market Paper, IIES Stockholm University, Stockholm.

Mankiw, G., D. Romer, and D. Weil. 1992. "A Contribution to the Empirics of Growth." *Quarterly Journal of Economics* 107 (2): 407-437.

Mbiti, I., and D. N. Weil. 2016. "Mobile Banking: The Impact of M-Pesa in Kenya." In *African Successes Volume III: Modernization and Development,* edited by S. Edwards, S. Johnson, and D. N. Weil. Chicago: University of Chicago Press.

Menezes, A. 2014. "Debt Resolution and Business Exit: Insolvency Reform for Credit, Entrepreneurship, and Growth." Viewpoint, July, Trade and Competitiveness Global Practice, World Bank, Washington, DC.

Menezes, A., S. Muro. And M. Uttamchandani. 2020. "COVID-19 Outbreak: Implications on Corporate and Individual Insolvency." EFI COVID-19 Notes, World Bank, Washington, DC.

Mody, A., F. Ohnsorge, and D. Sandri. 2012. "Precautionary Savings in the Great Recession." *IMF Economic Review* 60 (1): 114-138.

Mohammed, A.O., B. A. Khidhir, A. Nazeer, and V.J. Vijayan. 2020. "Emergency Remote Teaching during Coronavirus Pandemic: The Current Trend and Future Directive at Middle East College Oman." *Innovative Infrastructure Solutions* 5(3): 1-11.

Müller, A., K. Storesletten, and F. Zilibotti. 2019. "Sovereign Debt and Structural Reforms." *American Economic Review* 109 (12): 4220-4259.

Murphy, K., A. Shleifer, and R. Vishny. 1991. "The Allocation of Talent: Implications for Growth." *Quarterly Journal of Economics* 106 (2): 503-530.

Nawaz, S. 2015. "Growth Effects of Institutions: A Disaggregated Analysis." *Economic Modelling* 45 (C): 118-126.

Norando, G. C., 2010. *Essays on Infrastructure, Female Labor Force Participation and Economic Development.* PhD (Doctor of Philosophy) thesis, University of Iowa, https://doi.org/10.17077/etd.g5h0x4jd.

OECD (Organisation for Economic Co-operation and Development). 2007. *Transport Infrastructure Investment and Economic Productivity*, Transport Research Centre, OECD, Paris.

OECD (Organisation for Economic Cooperation and Development). 2015. *Consequences of Corruption at the Sector Level and Implications for Economic Growth and Development.* Paris: OECD.

OECD (Organisation for Economic Cooperation and Development). 2020. "Building back better: A sustainable, resilient recovery after COVID-19." OECD Policy Responses to Coronavirus (COVID-19). OECD, Paris.

Onishi, A. 1988. "Projections of the OECD Economies in the Global Perspective, 1986-2000: Policy Simulations by the FUGI Global Macroeconomic Model." In *Economic Modelling in the OECD Countries*, edited by H. Motamen, 11-30. New York: Chapman and Hall.

Packard, T., U. Gentilini, M. Grosh, P. O'Keefe, R. Palacios, D. Robalino, and I. Santos. 2019. *Protecting All: Risk Sharing for a Diverse and Diversifying World of Work.* Washington, DC: World Bank.

Pereira A., and J. Andraz. 2013. "On the Economic Effects of Public Infrastructure Investment: A Survey of the International Evidence." Working Paper 108, Department of Economics, College of William and Mary, Charlottesville.

Prati, A., M. G. Onorato, and C. Papageorgiou. 2013. "Which Reforms Work and Under What Institutional Environment?" *Review of Economics and Statistics* 95 (3): 946-968.

Pritchett, L. 2000. "The Tyranny of Concepts: CUDIE (Cumulated, Depreciated, Investment Effort) Is Not Capital." *Journal of Economic Growth* 5 (4): 361-384.

Pritchett, L. 2001. "Where Has All the Education Gone?" *World Bank Economic Review* 15 (3): 367-391.

Pritchett, L. 2006. "Does Learning to Add up Add up? The Returns to Schooling in Aggregate Data." In *Handbook of the Economics of Education*, edited by E. Hanushek and F. Welch, 635-695. Amsterdam: North Holland.

Pritchett, L., and L. H. Summers. 2014. "Asiaphoria Meet Regression to the Mean." NBER Working Paper 20573, National Bureau of Economic Research, Cambridge.

Qazi, J., K. Naseer, A. Qazi, H. Al Salman, U. Naseem, S. Yang, G. Hardaker, and A. Gumaei. 2020. "Evolution to Online Education Around the Globe During a SARS-CoV-2 Coronavirus (COVID-19) Pandemic: Do Develop and Underdeveloped Cope Alike?" *Children and Youth Services Review.* https://doi.org/10.1080/02607476.2020.1802701.

Queiroz, C., and S. Gautam. 1992. "Road Infrastructure and Economic Development: Some Diagnostic Indicators." Policy Research Working Paper 921, World Bank, Washington, DC.

Rasmussen, T. 2016. "Tackling Gender Inequality in the Middle East: Gulf Cooperation Council." In *Women, Work, and Economic Growth: Leveling the Playing Field*, edited by K. Kalpana, S. Jain-Chandra, and M. Newiak, 183-185. Washington, DC: International Monetary Fund.

Reimers, F. M., and A. Schleicher. 2020. "Schooling Disrupted, Schooling Rethought: How the COVID-19 Pandemic is Changing Education." Organisation for Economic Co-operation and Development, Paris.

Reinhart, C. M., and V. R. Reinhart. 2015. "Financial Crises, Development, and Growth: A Long-term Perspective." *World Bank Economic Review* 29 (Supplement): S53–S76.

Röller, L.-H., and L. Waverman. 2001. "Telecommunications Infrastructure and Economic Development: A Simultaneous Approach." *American Economic Review* 91 (4): 909-923.

Romer, C. D., and D. H. Romer. 2019. "Fiscal Space and the Aftermath of Financial Crises: How It Matters and Why." *Brookings Paper on Economic Activity* 2019 (Spring): 239-331.

Romp, W., and J. de Haan. 2007. "Public Capital and Economic Growth: A Critical Survey." *Perspektiven der Wirtschaftspolitik* 8 (S1): 6-52.

Rozenberg, J., and M. Fay, eds. 2019. *Beyond the Gap: How Countries Can Afford the Infrastructure They Need While Protecting the Planet.* Washington, DC: World Bank.

Ruch, F. 2020. "Policy Challenges for Emerging and Developing Economies: Lessons from the Past

Decade." Policy Research Working Paper 9180, World Bank, Washington, DC.

Rud, J. 2012. "Electricity Provision and Industrial Development: Evidence from India." *Journal of Development Economics* 97 (2): 352-367.

Sala-i-Martin, X., G. Doppelhofer, and R. Miller. 2004. "Determinants of Long-Term Growth: A Bayesian Averaging of Classical Estimates (BACE) Approach." *American Economic Review* 94 (4): 813-835.

Sánchez-Páramo, C. and A. Narayan. 2020. "Impact of COVID-19 on Households: What Do Phone Surveys Tell Us?" *Voices* (blog), November 20, World Bank.

Sanchez-Robles, B. 1998. "Infrastructure Investment and Growth: Some Empirical Evidence." *Contemporary Economic Policy* 16 (1): 98-108.

Sasso, S., and J. Ritzen. 2016. "Sectoral Cognitive Skills, R&D, and Productivity: A Cross-Country Cross-Sector Analysis." IZA Discussion Paper 10457, Institute of Labor Economics, Bonn.

Schwab, J. 2020. "Fighting COVID-19 Could Cost 500 Times as Much as Pandemic Prevention Measures." WEF Covid Action Platform, August 3.

Scull, J., M. Phillips, U. Sharma, and K. Garnier. 2020. "Innovations in Teacher Education at the Time of COVID-19: An Australian Perspective." *Journal of Education for Teaching.* https://doi.org/10.1080/02607 476.2020.1802701.

Sedlacek, P. and V. Sterk. 2020. "Startups and Employment Following the COVID-19 Pandemic: A Calculator." Discussion Paper 14671, Centre for Economic Policy Research, London.

Sevilla, A., and S. Smith. 2020. "Baby Steps: The Gender Division of Childcare during the COVID-19 Pandemic." Discussion Paper 14804, Centre for Economic Policy Research, London.

Shambaugh, J., R. Nunn, and B. Portman. 2017. "Lessons from the Rise of Women's Labor Force Participation in Japan." The Hamilton Project, Brookings Institution, Washington, DC.

Shleifer, A., and R. Vishny. 1993. "Corruption." *Quarterly Journal of Economics* 108 (3): 599-617.

Sianesi, B., and J. Van Reenen. 2003. "The Returns to Education: Macroeconomics." *Journal of Economic Surveys* 17 (2): 157-200.

Slesman, L., A. Baharumshah, and W. N. W. Azman-Saini. 2019. "Political Institutions and Finance-Growth Nexus in Emerging Markets and Developing Countries: A Tale of One Threshold." *Quarterly Review of Economics and Finance* 72 (C): 80-100.

Solotaroff L. J., G. Joseph, A. T. Kuriakose, and J. Sethi. 2020. *Getting to Work: Unlocking Women's Potential in Sri Lanka's Labor Force.* Directions in Development series. March. Washington, DC: World Bank.

Steinberg, C., and M. Nakane. 2012. "Can Women Save Japan?" IMF Working Paper 12/248, International Monetary Fund, Washington, DC.

Stiglitz, J. E. 2020. "The Pandemic Economic Crisis, Precautionary Behavior, and Mobility Constraints: An Application of the Dynamic Disequilibrium Model with Randomness." NBER Working Paper 27992, National Bureau of Economic Research, Cambridge.

Strand, J., and M. Toman. 2010. "Green Stimulus, Economic Recovery, and Long-Term Sustainable Development", Policy Research Working Paper 5163, World Bank, Washington, DC.

Straub, S. 2008. "Infrastructure and Growth in Developing Countries: Recent Advances and Research Challenges." Policy Research Working Paper 4460, World Bank, Washington, DC.

Straub, S., and A. Terada-Hagiwara. 2010. "Infrastructure and Growth in Developing Asia." Economics Working Paper 231, Asian Development Bank, Manila.

Sun, L., Y. Tang, and W. Zhuo. 2020. "Coronavirus Pushes Education Online." *Nature Materials* 19 (6): 687-687.

Sun, Y., S. Wang, and X. Zhang. 2018. "How Efficient Are China's Macroeconomic Forecasts? Evidences from a New Forecasting Evaluation Approach." *Economic Modelling* 68 (C): 506-513.

Taras, H. 2005. "Nutrition and Student Performance at School." *Journal of School Health* 75 (6): 199-213.

Taylor, C. B., E. Fitzsimmons-Craft, and A. Graham. 2020. "Digital Technology Can Revolutionize Mental Health Services Delivery: The COVID-19 Crisis as a Catalyst for Change." *International Journal of Eating Disorders* 53 (7): 1155-1157.

Temple, J. 2001. "Growth Effects of Education and

Social Capital in the OECD countries." *OECD Economic Studies* 33 (C): 57-101.

Teulings, C. N., and N. Zubanov. 2014. "Is Economic Recovery a Myth? Robust Estimation of Impulse Responses." *Journal of Applied Econometrics* 29 (3): 497-514.

Timmermann, A. 2007. "An Evaluation of the *World Economic Outlook* Forecasts." *IMF Staff Papers* 54 (1): 1-33.

Topalova, P., and A. Khandelwal. 2011. "Trade Liberalization and Firm Productivity: The Case of India." *Review of Economics and Statistics* 93 (3): 995-1009.

Topel, R. 1999. "Labor Markets and Economic Growth." In *Handbook of Labor Economics*, edited by O. Ashenfelter and D. Card, 2943-2984. Amsterdam: Elsevier.

Turnovsky, S. 1996. "Fiscal Policy, Adjustment Costs, and Endogenous Growth." *Oxford Economic Papers* 48 (3): 361-381.

Ülgentürk, L. 2017. "The Role of Public Debt Managers in Contingent Liability Management." OECD Working Paper on Sovereign Borrowing and Public Debt Management 8, Organisation for Economic Co-operation and Development, Paris.

UN (United Nations). 2020. "Education during COVID-19 and Beyond." Policy Brief, August, United Nations, New York.

van der Spoel, I., O. Noroozi, E. Schuurink, and S. van Ginkel. 2020. "Teachers' Online Teaching Expectations and Experiences During the Covid-19 Pandemic in the Netherlands." *European Journal of Teacher Education* 43 (4): 623-638.

van Nieuwkoop, M. 2020. "Staying Focused on 'One Health' to Prevent the Next Pandemic." *Voices* (blog), November 11, World Bank.

Vandenbussche, J., P. Aghion, and C. Meghir. 2006. "Growth, Distance to Frontier and Composition of Human Capital." *Journal of Economic Growth* 11 (2): 97-127.

Vashakmadze, E., G. Kambou, D. Chen, B. Nandwa, Y. Okawa, and D. Vorisek. 2018. "Regional Dimensions of Recent Investment Weakness: Facts, Investment Needs and Policy Responses." *Journal of Infrastructure, Policy and Development* 2 (1): 37-66.

Vavra, J. S. 2020. "Shutdown Sectors Represent Large Share of All U.S. Employment." Key Economic Findings about COVID-19, March 27, Becker Friedman Institute for Economics, University of Chicago, accessible at https://bfi.uchicago.edu/insight/finding/shutdown-sectors-represent-large-share-of-all-us-employment/.

Vegas, E., and R. Winthrop. 2020. "*Beyond Reopening Schools: How Education can Emerge Stronger than Before COVID-19.*" Washington, DC: Brookings Institution.

Vermeersch, C., and M. Kremer. 2005. "School Meals, Educational Achievement, and School Competition: Evidence from a Randomized Evaluation." Policy Research Working Paper 3523, World Bank, Washington, DC.

VFDI (Vivideconomics and Finance for Diversity Initiative). 2020. *Greenness of Stimulus Index.* Lonson: Vivideconomics.

Viollaz, M., and H. Winkler. 2020. "Does the Internet Reduce Gender Gaps? The Case of Jordan." Policy Research Working Paper 9183, World Bank, Washington, DC.

Vorisek, D., and S. Yu. 2020. "Understanding the Cost of Achieving the Sustainable Development Goals." Policy Research Working Paper 9146, World Bank, Washington, DC.

Vu, T. 2019. "Does Institutional Quality Foster Economic Complexity?" MPRA Paper 97843, University Library of Munich, Munich.

Weil, D. 2014. "Health and Economic Growth." In *Handbook of Economic Growth*, edited by. P Aghion and S. Durlauf, 623-682. Amsterdam: Elsevier.

Wheeler, C. M., J. Baffes, A. Kabundi, G. Kindberg-Hanlon, P. S. Nagle, and F. Ohnsorge. 2020. "Adding Fuel to the Fire: Cheap Oil During the COVID-19 Pandemic." Policy Research Working Paper 9320, World Bank, Washington, DC.

Williams, K. 2019. "Do Political Institutions Improve the Diminishing Effect of Financial Deepening on Growth? Evidence from Developing Countries." *Journal of Economics and Business* 103 (May-June): 13-24.

Winkler, A. 2016. "Women's Labor Force Participation." IZA World of Labor 289. https://doi.org/10.15185/izawol.289.

Woessmann, L. 2003a. "Schooling Resources,

Educational Institutions, and Student Performance: The International Evidence." *Oxford Bulletin of Economics and Statistics* 65 (2): 117-170.

Woessmann, L. 2003b. "Specifying Human Capital." *Journal of Economic Surveys* 17 (3): 239-270.

World Bank. 2012. *World Development Report 2012: Gender Equality and Development.* Washington, DC: World Bank.

World Bank. 2013a. *Growing Green: The Economic Benefits of Climate Action.* Washington, DC: World Bank.

World Bank. 2013b. *Opening Doors Gender Equality and Development in Middle East and North Africa.* MENA Development Report. Washington, DC: World Bank.

World Bank. 2014. *Doing Business 2014. Understanding Regulations for Small and Medium-Size Enterprises.* Washington, DC: World Bank.

World Bank. 2015a. *Global Economic Prospects: Having Fiscal Space and Using It.* January. Washington, DC: World Bank.

World Bank. 2015b. *Global Monitoring Report: Development Goals in an Era of Demographic Change.* Washington, DC: World Bank.

World Bank. 2017a. *Global Economic Prospects: Weak Investment in Times of Uncertainty.* January. Washington, DC: World Bank.

World Bank. 2017b. *World Development Report 2017: Governance and the Law.* Washington, DC: World Bank.

World Bank. 2018a. *Global Economic Prospects: Broad Based Upturn, but for How Long?* January. Washington, DC: World Bank.

World Bank. 2018b. *Pathways for Peace: Inclusive Approaches to Preventing Violent Conflict.* Washington, DC: World Bank.

World Bank. 2019a. *Global Economic Prospects: Heightened Tensions, Subdued Investment.* June. Washington, DC: World Bank.

World Bank. 2019b. *Global Economic Prospects: Darkening Skies.* January. Washington, DC: World Bank.

World Bank. 2019c. *World Development Report: Learning to Realize Education's Promise.* Washington, DC: World Bank.

World Bank. 2019d. *Africa Pulse: An Analysis of Issues Shaping Africa's Economic Future.* April. World Bank, Washington, DC.

World Bank. 2020a. *Global Economic Prospects.* June. Washington, DC: World Bank.

World Bank. 2020b. *Poverty and Shared Prosperity Report: Reversals of Fortune.* Washington, DC: World Bank.

World Bank. 2020c. *Global Economic Prospects: Slow Growth, Policy Challenges.* January. Washington, DC: World Bank.

World Bank. 2020d. *The Human Capital Index, 2020 Update: Human Capital in the Time of Covid-19.* Washington, DC: World Bank.

World Bank. 2020e. *The COVID-19 Pandemic: Shocks to Education and Policy Responses.* Washington, DC: World Bank.

World Bank. 2020f. *World Development Report: Trading for Development in the Age of Global Value Chains.* Washington, DC: World Bank.

WTO (World Trade Organization). 2019. *Global Value Chain Development Report 2019. Technological Innovation, Supply Chain Trade, and Workers in a Globalized World.* Geneva: World Trade Organization.

CHAPTER 4

ASSET PUCHASES IN
EMERGING MARKETS

Unconventional Policies,
Unconventional Times

Central banks in some emerging market and developing economies (EMDEs) have employed asset purchase programs, in many cases for the first time, in response to pandemic-induced financial market pressures. These programs, along with spillovers from accommodative monetary policies in advanced economies, appear to have helped stabilize EMDE financial markets. However, the governing framework, scale, and duration of these programs have been less transparent than in advanced economies, and the effects on inflation and output in EMDEs remain uncertain. In EMDEs where asset purchases continue to expand and are perceived to finance unsustainable fiscal deficits, these programs risk eroding hard-won central bank operational independence and de-anchoring inflation expectations. Ensuring that asset purchase programs are conducted with credible commitments to central bank mandates and with transparency regarding their objectives and scale can support their effectiveness.

Introduction

The COVID-19 pandemic has tipped the global economy into its deepest recession since the Second World War. To stabilize financial markets and support activity, many central banks have employed asset purchase programs—often for the first time in the case of emerging market and developing economies (EMDEs). These have involved outright central bank purchases of longer-term financial assets, usually government bonds, and corresponding injections of reserve money into the banking system. This chapter explores how EMDE asset purchase programs have evolved, and assesses their potential benefits and costs.

The purchase of longer-term assets by central banks has both complemented and substituted for other monetary policy tools. This instrument has primarily been used in advanced economy "quantitative easing" programs with the aims of stimulating demand, boosting output, and raising inflation toward targets. Purchases of longer-term assets have usually been employed when the limits of conventional monetary policy tools have been reached—in particular, when short-term monetary policy rates have fallen near their effective lower bound. Asset purchases can directly influence specific financial market segments and asset maturities, and longer-term asset purchases can serve to lower long-term interest rates, which would be only indirectly impacted by conventional monetary policy tools (Haldane et al 2016). These programs can also be used to help

stabilize financial markets and improve market functioning during periods of high volatility and low market liquidity, an objective that did not motivate the early advanced economy asset purchase programs (Christensen and Gillan 2019).

Central banks across advanced economies and EMDEs have responded to the economic and financial market shocks induced by the COVID-19 pandemic with broad-based cuts in short-term policy rates, which in many economies are now at, or close to, their effective lower bounds. One-third of advanced economy central banks have reduced their short-term policy rates to 0 percent or lower, while around 90 percent have lowered them below 1 percent (figure 4.1). Some EMDE central banks (Chile, Costa Rica, Hungary, Paraguay, Peru, Poland, Thailand) have also cut policy rates to less than 1 percent. For additional policy easing and to contain a sharp rise in government bond yields in March 2020, many of these central banks introduced asset purchase programs (Chile, Costa Rica, Hungary, Poland, Thailand). Policy rates remain above 1 percent in 80 percent of EMDEs, but central banks in at least 13 of these EMDEs have also implemented asset purchase programs (figure 4.1).

This chapter addresses the following questions:

- How have asset purchase programs been designed in EMDEs?

- Have EMDEs benefited from these programs?

- What are the risks associated with these programs?

- What are the main policy lessons for EMDEs?

Note: This chapter was produced by Jongrim Ha and Gene Kindberg-Hanlon. Research assistance was provided by Kaltrina Temaj and Jingran Wang.

FIGURE 4.1 Policy interest rates and bond yields

In 2020, central banks in advanced economies cut policy rates close to the effective zero lower bound. Toward the end of the year, around 90 percent of advanced economy policy interest rates were below 1 percent, and one-third were at or below zero. In contrast, just 20 percent of EMDE central banks have cut policy rates below 1 percent. In addition to policy rate cuts, many advanced economies and EMDEs initiated asset purchase programs after government bond yields, including those usually considered "safe-haven" assets, spiked in March 2020.

A. Advanced economy policy rates

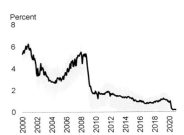

B. EMDE policy rates

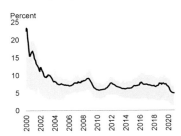

C. Distribution of policy rates: Advanced economies

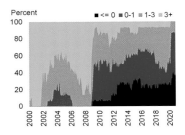

D. Distribution of policy rates: EMDEs

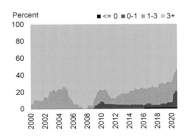

E. Peak increase in bond yields and spreads in March

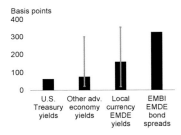

F. Advanced economy and EMDE 10-year government bond yields

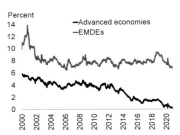

Sources: Haver Analytics; National sources; World Bank.
Note: EMDE = emerging market and developing economies; EMBI = JPMorgan Emerging Market Bond Index.
A.-D. Data for up to 16 advanced economy and 67 emerging and developing economy central banks during 2000-2020.
A.B. Solid line reflects a simple average of policy rates. Shaded region shows the inter-quartile range.
E. Maximum increase in local currency government bond yields and the JPMorgan EMBI index of EMDE foreign-currency bond spreads during March 2020 using daily data. Orange whiskers indicate the maximum and minimum increase in 10-year government bonds in 30 advanced economies and 21 EMDEs. Bars indicate the average increase.
F. Average of 10-year government bond yields for up to 30 advanced economies and 22 EMDEs.

Contributions. This chapter contributes to the literature in three ways.

First, it takes stock of the EMDE asset purchase programs that have been announced or implemented since early 2020. It discusses how the programs in EMDEs compare to those in advanced economies in their design, scale, and objectives. To shed light on the topic, the chapter also presents a review of the literature on the macroeconomic and financial effects of programs in advanced economies, including their spillovers to EMDEs.

Second, the chapter is one of the first studies to provide detailed evidence on the effects of asset purchase announcements in EMDEs on financial markets. A few earlier studies have estimated the impact of asset purchase program announcements in EMDEs on bond markets and exchange rates (Arslan, Drehmann, and Hofmann 2020; Hartley and Rebucci 2020; IMF 2020b). This chapter expands on these studies by including the effects on equity markets and by comparing the effectiveness of EMDE asset purchases to that of conventional monetary policy actions, and that of asset purchase programs in advanced economies.

Third, the chapter reviews historical experiences of central bank financing of government deficits in EMDEs. In particular, it reviews the circumstances of economies that experienced episodes of debt monetization and high inflation in the 1980s and early 1990s and draws out parallels and differences with the central bank policies and country circumstances of those EMDEs undertaking asset purchases in 2020. It assesses the circumstances—in particular elevated levels of debt, large fiscal deficits, and weak growth prospects—which may increase the risk that some EMDEs begin to resemble these historic episodes.

Findings. Several findings emerge from this chapter.

- *Diverse design of asset purchase programs in EMDEs.* As of mid-December 2020, 18 EMDEs had announced or implemented asset purchase programs. Asset purchases have been mainly focused on local currency-denominated government bonds. The size of asset purchases has varied from less than 1 to 6 percent of GDP. Many EMDE central banks have not announced the scale or duration of purchases, and while most have been purchasing only in secondary markets, some have purchased bonds directly from governments.

- *Decline in government bond yields.* Announcements of asset purchase programs appear to have helped stabilize bond markets and boost equity prices without putting pressure on exchange rates. The effects on long-term bond yields and equity prices have been on average greater than the effects of the announcements of monetary policy rate cuts in response to COVID-19. In addition, the announcement effect of EMDE asset purchases on government bond yields (but not equity prices) seems to have been larger than the announcement effects of advanced economy asset purchases. The broader macroeconomic consequences, however, remain to be seen.

- *Risks to central bank credibility and perceptions of debt-monetization.* Recent asset purchase programs in some EMDEs were initiated to support financial stability and orderly market functioning following the spike in bond yields in March 2020. In contrast, during historical episodes of EMDE debt monetization, central banks bought government bonds to finance government deficits by issuing reserve money. Previous episodes of debt monetization differed from the recent experience in being preceded by long periods of high inflation, less credible fiscal and monetary policy frameworks, external debt defaults, and stubbornly high fiscal deficits. For now, macroeconomic conditions in EMDEs are more benign than in these historical episodes. However, the earlier episodes provide a reminder of the risks to central bank credibility if asset purchase programs are used for prolonged monetary financing of fiscal deficits.

- *Effectiveness.* Based on the experience during the pandemic and, in advanced economies,

before it, asset purchase programs have helped reduce bond yields and boosted equity prices during periods of market illiquidity in EMDEs. The recent experience of asset purchase programs, however, may overstate its future effectiveness for three reasons. First, it was set against the backdrop of uniquely accommodative macro-economic policies in advanced economies. Second, it was an unanticipated departure from earlier policy guidance of EMDE central banks that had focused on buttressing their independence. Third, fragile liquidity conditions in EMDE financial markets are conducive to volatile movements in asset prices, possibly leading to unintended consequences of future asset purchases.

- *Policy implications and design of asset purchase programs.* Embedding asset purchase programs in a transparent monetary policy framework that is consistent with inflation and financial stability objectives will reduce the risk that asset purchases are perceived as monetary financing that might de-anchor inflation expectations. Current projections of large fiscal deficits and elevated public debt levels amplify the need for medium-term strategies that avoid this risk and ensure that the benefits of EMDE asset purchase programs outweigh their costs. The need for enhanced frameworks and medium-term fiscal strategies may increase in the absence of the uniquely accommodative global monetary conditions established in response to COVID-19.

The remainder of this chapter is organized into five sections. First, a brief history of asset purchase programs in advanced economies is provided, and their estimated effects on asset prices and macroeconomic outcomes are discussed. In the second section, details of the asset purchase programs in EMDEs are presented and compared to those in advanced economies. The third presents evidence on the effects of EMDE asset purchases on financial markets. The fourth section discusses potential risks of EMDE asset purchase programs. The final section concludes with policy implications. A box examines historical episodes of deficit monetization in EMDEs and considers similarities and differences with EMDEs implementing asset purchases in response to the COVID-19 pandemic.

Background: Asset purchase programs in advanced economies

Quantitative easing has increasingly become part of the monetary policy tool kit of central banks in advanced economies in recent years, when short-term policy interest rates have approached their effective lower bounds at around zero. The use of asset purchase programs by advanced economies appears to have also helped stabilize financial markets in EMDEs during the early stages of the COVID-19 pandemic.

History of asset purchase programs. In 2001, the first major asset purchase program was initiated by the Bank of Japan as short-term interest rates reached zero, consumer price inflation remained weak, and GDP growth was persistently anemic. During the 2007-09 global financial crisis, the U.S. Federal Reserve and the Bank of England cut short-term interest rates close to zero and engaged in large scale QE programs, purchasing domestic sovereign bonds and government-backed mortgage securities. They were joined by the European Central Bank (ECB) in 2015, although the ECB had earlier introduced the Securities Markets Program to ensure liquidity in government bond markets. Ahead of the COVID-19 pandemic, both the ECB and the Bank of Japan were engaged in the continued purchase of sovereign bonds and some private-sector securities.

Monetary policy response to COVID-19. In March 2020, global financial market volatility rose dramatically. Government bond yields, which had fallen in February due to expectations of a sharp decline in economic activity, began to rise in advanced economies as investors sought to increase cash holdings and market intermediaries struggled to absorb large sales volumes (figure 4.1; FSB 2020). Advanced economy asset purchases were initiated or expanded both to improve the functioning of government bond markets and to

stimulate output and inflation by lowering long-term interest rates (figure 4.2).[1] In some cases, asset purchases have since been extended to a broader set of assets—including riskier private sector assets—than in previous programs (Federal Reserve, Bank of England, and ECB).[2] Asset purchase programs in 2020 were also accompanied by substantial liquidity provision through other mechanisms, such as new credit facilities for commercial banks or lending via repurchase agreements. In many cases, these facilities enabled central banks to finance the purchase of government debt, leading to increases in their indirect exposure to the government (Feyen and Huertas 2019). As a result of these measures, the expansion of central bank balance sheets in 2020 exceeded the initial expansion during the global financial crisis.

The effects of asset purchases in advanced economies. A large literature has found that advanced economy asset purchase programs appear to have helped lift output and inflation, lower bond yields, and support asset prices (annex 4.1). Asset purchase programs that have aimed to improve market functioning, such as the ECB's Securities Market Programme, have been found to reduce risk and liquidity premia and improve market conditions (BIS 2019). Over 80 percent of studies assessing the impact of QE in advanced economies have found statistically significant positive impacts on output and inflation (Fabo et al. 2020; annex table A4.1.2).

Spillovers from advanced economy asset purchases to EMDEs. U.S. monetary policy easing has generally in the past been transmitted to EMDEs through domestic currency appreciation, lower bond yields, higher equity prices, and increased capital inflows.[3] Since March 2020,

---

[1] The New York Federal Reserve statement stated that purchases would be implemented to ensure "Smooth function of the market for Treasury securities." https://www.newyorkfed.org/markets/opolicy/operating_policy_200323.

[2] In some cases, private sector assets, such as covered bonds (ECB), and corporate bonds, equity ETFs, and real estate investment trusts (Bank of Japan) have been purchased in earlier episodes of QE.

[3] See, for instance, Bhattarai, Chatterjee, and Park (2018), Feyen et al. (2015), Rogers, Scotti, and Wright (2018), and Tillman (2016). Using novel empirical strategies, these studies provide evidence on the significant transmission of U.S. monetary policy shocks into financial markets in other open economies.

benign global financial conditions, partly driven by the launch of major asset purchase programs in advanced economies, are likely to have reduced the extent of capital outflows from EMDEs and depreciations of their currencies. More generally, advanced economy financial conditions, which have been affected by their domestic asset purchase programs, have been shown to have substantial spillovers to EMDE financial conditions during the COVID-19 pandemic (Ahmed et al. 2020).

Risks associated with asset purchase programs. By lowering longer-term interest rates, asset purchases can both reduce returns to lenders and increase those to borrowers. By raising the prices not only of bonds but also of risky assets such as equities and housing, asset purchases can increase the wealth of those who hold such assets (Colciago, Samarina, and de Haan 2019). Some studies—of the euro area, Japan, the United Kingdom, and the United States—have found that asset purchase programs have increased wealth or income inequality. [4]

However, other studies have found that the benefits to employment and incomes for lower-income workers have outweighed such regressive redistribution effects so that, overall, asset purchase programs have either had insignificant overall distributional effects or have lowered wealth or income inequality (Inui, Sudo, and Yamada 2017; Lenza and Slacalek 2018). In addition to distributional effects, low interest rates driven by asset purchase programs or other accommodative policies could lead to misallocation of capital and market concentration, and reduce technological dynamism, thus lowering productivity growth (Gopinath et al. 2017; Liu, Mian, and Sufi 2019). Finally, the portfolio channel of asset purchase programs may incentivize excessive risk-taking and lead to financial instability (Adrian and Liang 2016).

FIGURE 4.2 Scale of unconventional monetary policies

Announced and implemented asset purchases by EMDE central banks have been smaller than those in advanced economies. In both advanced economies and EMDEs, asset purchases have frequently been accompanied by increased lending to banks, such that the overall increase in central banks' balance sheet has been larger than asset purchases. In advanced economies, the response to COVID-19 has exceeded the initial response to the global financial crisis in terms of the total expansion of central bank assets.

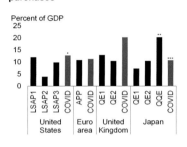

A. Advanced economy asset purchases

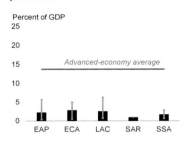

B. EMDE announced or completed purchases

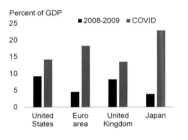

C. Advanced economy central bank balance sheet expansions

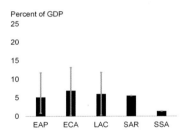

D. EMDE central bank balance sheet expansion since January 2020

Sources: Haver Analytics; National sources; World Bank.
Note: EMDE = emerging market and developing economies; EAP = East Asia and Pacific, ECA = Europe and Central Asia, LAC = Latin America and the Caribbean, SAR = South Asia, SSA = Sub-Saharan Africa. All asset purchase and balance sheet figures are estimates based on published data.
A. Announced purchases of sovereign and private sector bonds in percent of nominal GDP. In the U.S., the large-scale asset purchase (LSAP) programs began in 2008 (LSAP1), 2010 (LSAP2), and 2012 (LSAP3). The European Central Bank's 2015 Asset Purchase Program (APP) is given as the original announced program size. U.K. programs include QE1, launched in 2009, QE2, launched in 2010 and expanded in 2011, and the COVID program launched in March 2020. The Bank of Japan's first QE program during 2001-06 is given as "QE1," while the second QE program launched in 2010 is given as QE2. The "Quantitative and Qualitative" program launched in 2013 is given as QQE.
* The "COVID" package launched in March 2020 is not specified in scale, so purchases are only shown from the start of the program to November 2020.
** QQE program reflects initially announced purchases in March 2013. Subsequent expansions of the program increased liquidity by 72 percent of GDP between March 2013 and January 2020.
*** Bank of Japan COVID support package is not limited. Purchases to November are provided.
B. Announced or completed purchases (where no announcement exists) relative to 2019 nominal GDP as of November 2020. Bar shows average in each region. Orange whiskers show regional range. Red line shows average of advanced economy programs launched in 2020.
C. Increase in central bank balance sheets during August 2008-December 2009 and from January to November 2020.
D. Change in central bank balance sheets in percent of nominal GDP since January 2020 in those economies undertaking asset purchases. Monthly data to October 2020. Bar shows average in each region. Orange whiskers show regional range.

---

[4] See Bunn, Pugh, and Yeates (2018); Juan-Francisco, Gomez-Fernandez, and Ochando (2018); Mumtaz and Theophilopoulou (2017); and Taghizadeh-Hesary, Yoshino, and Shimizu (2020).

Asset purchase programs in EMDEs

In 2020, 18 EMDEs announced or implemented asset purchase programs. These tended to be smaller than programs in advanced economies. In many cases, EMDE programs have been less transparent than those in advanced economies in their objectives, duration, and scale.

EMDEs using asset purchase programs. Faced with rising government financing costs, deteriorating financing conditions, and large capital outflows in March 2020, several EMDE central banks joined central banks in advanced economies in launching asset purchase programs (World Bank 2020). Most of these EMDEs purchased government or private bonds for the purpose of meeting macroeconomic or financial stability objectives for the first time.[5] As of mid December 2020, the EMDE central banks that had announced or implemented asset purchase programs were Bolivia, Chile, Colombia, Costa Rica, Croatia, Ghana, Guatemala, Hungary, India, Indonesia, Malaysia, Philippines, Poland, Romania, Rwanda, South Africa, Thailand, and Turkey.[6] Other large EMDEs have taken legal steps to initiate purchase programs, such as lifting constitutional bans on outright monetary financing. For example, the central bank of Brazil has been granted emergency powers to purchase government bonds.

Features of asset purchase programs in EMDEs. The asset purchase programs announced by EMDE central banks vary widely in the intended scale of purchases, asset types, and duration. The full details of many programs, however, have not been specified (table 4.1).

- *Scale of purchases.* The size of announced or completed purchases has remained modest so far, ranging from 1 to 6 percent of annual GDP (figure 4.2). However, purchases may continue to be expanded in many of these economies.

- *Types of assets.* EMDE asset purchases have largely focused on local currency-denominated government debt. Several programs also have involved the purchase of bank bonds or mortgage bonds. Only a few EMDE central banks have announced the maturities of the bonds they have planned to purchase.

- *The duration of purchase programs.* The duration of asset purchase programs has generally been unspecified in EMDEs. Some central banks appear to have conducted one-off purchases at various times between March and May. Purchases have continued in many economies that have not announced details of the final program size or duration, even as government bond yields fell below their pre-COVID levels in April (figure 4.3).

- *Primary and secondary market purchases.* Most EMDE central banks have purchased, or plan to purchase, government and private bonds exclusively in secondary markets, although some have also purchased government debt directly from the government. In some cases, these latter purchases have been specifically acknowledged as being for the purpose of financing the 2020 fiscal deficit.

Comparison with asset purchase programs in advanced economies. Unlike many advanced economy central banks' recent and past asset purchase programs, many central banks in EMDEs have not announced the parameters of their asset purchase programs, including the size and duration of planned purchases.[7] They have also focused on purchasing government debt and bank bonds, whereas asset purchase programs in advanced economies have broadened their asset purchases to include riskier non-bank private sector assets.

---

[5] Pre-2020 examples of asset purchases by EMDE central banks to meet macroeconomic or financial stability objectives are rare. One exception is the case of Hungary: in December 2017, its central bank (MNB) announced the introduction of a mortgage bond purchase program to support the mortgage bond market.

[6] Programs based on long-term repurchase agreements such as in Mexico or Serbia are not included here, although these in practice may be similar in their effects to asset purchase programs. See, for details, Bank of Spain 2020; BIS 2020; Hartley and Rebucci 2020; IMF 2020a; and Yale 2020.

---

[7] Among advanced economy programs in response to COVID-19, key exceptions are the open-ended QE announcement by the Federal Reserve (March 23, 2020) and by the Bank of Japan (April 27, 2020).

EMDE central banks' asset purchases (or planned purchases) have been smaller than those in advanced economies, with most EMDE programs equivalent to less than 2 percent of annual GDP. Advanced economy asset purchase announcements or completed purchases in response to COVID-19 have averaged 14 percent of GDP. In some EMDEs, central bank balance sheets have expanded by more than asset purchases on account of increased liquidity provision to banks. At the same time, domestic banks have in turn increased their holdings of government debt in some economies (Hungary, Indonesia, Poland, Romania, South Africa; IMF 2020b).[8] In other cases, balance sheets have expanded by less than bond purchases as central banks have sought to sterilize the effect of purchases on bank reserves, for example by selling foreign-currency assets.

Finally, unlike most advanced economy central banks, most EMDE central banks launched their asset purchase programs before their policy interest rates had reached their effective lower bound, in order to reduce risk and term premia in longer-term interest rates. Policy rates averaged 3.6 percent as of end-November 2020 in EMDEs that had announced asset purchase programs, and 70 percent of these economies had monetary policy rates above 1 percent.

Benefits of EMDE asset purchase programs

Announcements of asset purchase programs by EMDE central banks in 2020 were predominantly aimed at helping to stabilize domestic financial markets. They appear to have reduced bond yields by more than announcements of policy rate cuts or advanced economy asset purchase announcements. They also appear to have boosted equity markets more than announcements of policy rate cuts, but to a lesser extent than asset purchase program announcements in advanced economies.

---

[8] In 15 EMDEs that implemented asset purchase programs, central banks' balance sheets expanded in 2020 by around 6 percentage points of GDP on average, which is around three times average annual balance sheet expansion over 2010-19.

FIGURE 4.3 **EMDE asset purchases and bond yields**

Following an increase in March 2020, EMDE government bond yields fell below their levels at the start of the year. EMDE asset purchase programs have generally continued to expand even as yields have fallen, although the pace of asset purchases has slowed since May.

A. EMDE long-term bond yields

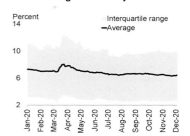

B. EMDE asset purchases

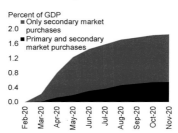

Sources: Haver Analytics; National sources; World Bank.
Note: EMDE = emerging market and developing economies.
A. Ten-year bond yields in 21 EMDEs. Shaded region shows the inter-quartile range of bond yields.
B. Cumulative asset purchases of 14 EMDEs where monthly purchase data are available, in percent of total GDP. EMDEs purchasing in both primary and secondary markets include Indonesia and the Philippines. EMDEs purchasing only in secondary markets include Bolivia, Chile, Colombia, Croatia, Hungary, Indonesia, Malaysia, Poland, Romania, South Africa, Thailand, and Turkey. In economies where November data are unavailable, purchases to October or September are used. All asset purchase figures are estimates based on published data.

Channels for the transmission of announcements of asset purchases to financial markets and the economy

Objectives of asset purchases in EMDEs: stabilizing financial markets. EMDE asset purchase programs have generally been used to provide liquidity and reduce volatility in domestic financial markets, particularly the markets for government bonds. For instance, central banks in Poland and South Africa have explicitly cited "providing liquidity" as one of the objectives of their programs.[9]

Analytical considerations: Effects on financial markets. Asset purchase programs would be expected to lower long-term interest rates through several channels, including by reducing liquidity and term premia, and by signaling that an accommodative stance of monetary policy may

---

[9] During the 2007-09 global financial crisis, different types of policies, such as in reduction in reserve requirements, were used by EMDEs to ease liquidity conditions, and they were partially effective (Ishi, Stone, and Yehoue 2009; Yehoue 2009). Similarly, to reduce market volatility during the 2013 "taper tantrum" episode, EMDEs deployed a range of policy tools, which included capital flow management measures and foreign exchange interventions (Sahay et al. 2014). Local currency-denominated bond purchases, however, were generally not used on these occasions.

persist for longer than might have been expected on the basis of policy history.[10] Empirical evidence, mainly from advanced economies, suggests that the effects of conventional monetary policy tend to be weaker during economic downturns or crises than during expansions or normal periods (Angrist, Jordà, and Kuersteiner 2018; Barnicon and Matthews 2015; Kurov 2012).[11] Asset purchases may help overcome this by lowering the longer end of the yield curve. To the extent that an announcement of asset purchases lowers returns on government bonds and improves perceptions of the economic outlook, the prices of riskier assets such as equities are also likely to benefit. Finally, by lowering longer-term interest rates, asset purchase programs may be expected to lead to depreciation of the domestic currency.

Empirical literature: Effects on financial markets. Recent studies of the impact of asset purchase announcements on EMDE financial markets conclude that they have generally helped stabilize rising long-term bond yields (Arslan, Drehmann, and Hofmann 2020; Hartley and Rebucci 2020; IMF 2020b; World Bank 2020). At least one study concluded that the impact of asset purchase programs on EMDE financial markets may even have been greater than in advanced economies, possibly because these programs generally came as a surprise and because EMDE bond markets tend to be less deep than those in advanced economies, and hence affected more by large transactions (Hartley and Rebucci 2020).

Estimating the short-term effects of asset purchases in EMDEs

Methodology. The reactions of daily financial asset prices—long-term (10-year) government bond yields, exchange rates vis-a-vis the U.S. dollar, and equity price indices—around the announcements of EMDE asset purchase programs were examined using a panel regression framework. The regression controls for time fixed effects—hence removing common global shocks—and cross-section fixed effects—hence removing country-specific factors—as well as policy rate changes and lags of the dependent variables (annex 4.2). The sample includes 26 EMDEs, 14 of which announced at least once the launch or expansion of asset purchase programs. This provides 25 announcement events since March 2020 (table 4.1).[12] The reactions of asset prices following EMDE asset purchase announcements are compared to their reactions in response to advanced economy asset purchase announcements, and to announcements of conventional policy rate cuts.[13] The response of asset prices is assessed in the narrow window of five to seven days around the announcement to ensure that the results are not contaminated by other news. In addition, an event study framework provides a robustness check for the regression analysis, as well as a more detailed analysis of country-specific results (annex 4.3).

Estimated effects of EMDE asset purchases

- *Bond markets.* The estimated initial reaction of local currency-denominated long-term bond yields suggests that the announcements of asset purchase programs in EMDEs in 2020 helped lower yields that had been rising amid heightened risk and liquidity strains. The asset purchase announcements were associated, on average, with a peak 34 basis point decline in long-term bond yields within two days (figure 4.4).[14] These effects are larger than might have been expected from the experience with pre-pandemic advanced economy programs. For example, the Bank of England and Federal Reserve's first major programs are estimated to

---

[10] On the theoretical transmission channels of asset purchase programs, and monetary policies more generally, into bond markets, see Eggertsson and Woodford (2003), Gertler and Karadi (2015), Joyce et al. (2012), and Krishnamurthy and Vissing-Jorgensen (2011).

[11] This may reflect an asymmetric response of term premia to the state of the economy, such that borrowing costs for households or firms rise, even though policy rates go down (Hanson and Stein 2015), or weaker bank credit mechanisms during crises. Alternatively, it may be that perceptions about the future path of policy rates reflect uncertainty about future policy stances and the economic outlook (Tilmann 2020; Van Nieuwerburgh and Veldkamp 2006).

---

[12] Among the EMDEs that announced asset purchase programs, four (Bolivia, Costa Rica, Guatemala, and Rwanda) were not included in the study because the announcement date is not clear or daily financial data are not available.

[13] All comparisons are relative to responses in EMDEs without asset purchase program announcements.

[14] These are based on the estimation of the baseline model. The effects based on the alternative model were similar.

have reduced domestic long-term bond yields by 15-25 basis points for programs roughly equivalent to 4 percent of GDP, twice the scale of the average asset purchase program implemented in EMDEs so far (figure 4.2; table A4.1.1; Christensen and Rudebusche 2012; Joyce et al. 2011; Williams 2014).[15]

- *Equity markets.* The asset purchase announcements in EMDEs were associated with a 1.9 percent increase in benchmark equity indices within two days of the announcements. Within five working days, equity prices increased by 3.9 percent.

- *Currency markets.* EMDE asset purchase announcements were not followed by statistically significant EMDE exchange rate movements in either direction. That said, in view of the broad-based downward pressures on EMDE currencies in March-April 2020, the multiple asset purchase announcements in advanced economies as well as EMDEs over this period may have helped stabilize currency markets and dampen further capital outflows and currency depreciations among EMDEs.[16]

Comparison with announcements of policy rate cuts

Effects of monetary policy rate cuts in EMDEs. Along with the implementation of asset purchase programs, EMDEs have responded to the COVID-19-induced recession with monetary policy rate cuts. The 14 EMDE central banks considered here implemented 34 policy rate cuts between March and July 2020, with rates lowered by 50 basis points on average. Announcements of such policy rate cuts appear to have had modest effects on long-term EMDE bond yields. Following the announcements of the policy rate

FIGURE 4.4 Effects of EMDE asset purchase announcements

The announcement of asset purchase programs in EMDEs helped stabilize domestic financial markets. Following the asset purchase announcements in EMDEs, local bond yields declined by up to 34 basis points and equity prices increased by 4 percent. The impacts on exchange rates were not statistically significant.

A. Impact of EMDE asset purchases: EMDE 10-year bond yields

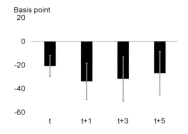

B. Impact of EMDE asset purchases: EMDE equity prices and exchange rates

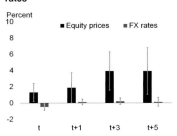

Sources: Haver Analytics; National sources; World Bank.
Note: EMDE = emerging market and developing economies. Panel regression results based on daily financial asset prices in 26 EMDEs. Twenty-five asset purchase announcements in 14 EMDEs are studied (annex 4.2). Horizontal axes indicate days after the announcements of asset purchase (t = 0). Standard errors are clustered by countries. Blue and red bars indicate point estimates and orange whiskers indicate 90 percent confidence intervals.
B. FX rates indicate foreign exchange rates of EMDE currencies vis-à-vis the U.S. dollar. An increase in the exchange rate denotes a depreciation of EMDE currencies.

cuts, long-term bond yields declined by 13 basis points, within two business days, and the impacts quickly dissipated (figure 4.5).[17] The results suggest that policy rate cuts were largely perceived to be temporary or anticipated. Other factors limiting the effect on bond yields may have included an offsetting increase in uncertainty about the path of future policy rates following the cut. From April 2020 onwards, when financial conditions had eased, the pass-through strengthened; long-term bond yields declined by up to 40 basis points per 1 percentage point policy rate cut.

Comparison with announcements of advanced economy asset purchase programs

Announcement effects in advanced economies. Announcements of asset purchase programs by the Federal Reserve and the ECB were followed by

---

[15] The effects summarize the various estimates in the literature and are scaled to be comparable (Williams 2014).

[16] For instance, when sovereign credit default swap (CDS) spreads were instead employed as the dependent variable in the regression, it was estimated that announcements of EMDE asset purchases were followed by a narrowing of the spread by around 10 basis points within two business days, although the impacts were found to quickly dissipate. These results were robust to models that controlled for various types of global factors, including US asset prices and the CBOE volatility index. This validates the baseline model with time and cross-section fixed effects.

---

[17] The estimated impacts of domestic policy rate cuts on long term yields are similar to estimates of 10-30 basis points per 1 percentage point policy rate cut by IMF (2020b).

FIGURE 4.5 Effects of policy rate cuts and asset purchase announcements in EMDEs

Announcements of central bank interest rate cuts in EMDEs were followed by declines in bond yields that were smaller than those after asset purchase announcements. Equity prices and exchange rates did not respond significantly to policy rate cuts in EMDEs.

A. Impact of EMDE policy rate cuts: EMDE 10-year bond yields

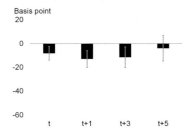

B. Impact of EMDE policy rate cuts: EMDE equity prices and currencies

C. Impact of policy rate cuts and asset purchase programs: EMDE 10-year bond yields

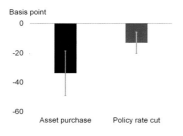

D. Impact of policy rate cuts and asset purchase programs: EMDE equity prices and currencies

Sources: Haver Analytics; National sources; World Bank.
Note: EMDE = emerging market and developing economies. Panel regressions results based on daily financial asset prices in 26 EMDEs. 34 policy rate cuts and 25 asset purchase announcements in 14 EMDEs between March and July 2020 are studied (annex 4.2). FX rates indicate foreign exchange rates of EMDE currencies vis-à-vis the U.S. dollar. An increase in the exchange rate denotes a depreciation of EMDE currencies. Blue and red bars indicate point estimates and orange whiskers indicate 90 percent confidence intervals.
A.B. Horizontal axes indicate days after the announcements of policy rate cuts (t = 0).
C.D. Maximum cumulative impact of EMDE asset purchase programs and EMDE policy rate cuts.

declines in bond yields that were generally smaller than both the declines in bond yields in EMDEs after announcements of domestic EMDE asset purchases and the declines in bond yields in advanced economies after previous advanced economy programs.[18] U.S. bond yields fell by 16-21 basis points within a day of each of the Federal Reserve's announcements on March 15 and 23 and April 9, 2020.[19] In response to the

---

[18] This result is consistent with Hartley and Rebucci (2020) and may partly reflect less deep EMDE financial markets than in advanced economies.

[19] Yields fluctuated from the second trading days after the announcements, reflecting the rising volatility in global financial markets in mid-March 2020. That said, from March 26, U.S. bond

announcement of asset purchases by the ECB on March 19, French and German long-term bond yields fell by 26 and 12 basis points, respectively, over the following three days, although there was wide heterogeneity across other euro-area economies.

Spillover effects on EMDEs of advanced economy asset purchase programs. Although the response of asset prices in advanced economies in 2020 was more muted than following their previous asset purchase programs, there were sizable spillovers to EMDE asset prices from the announcements by the Federal Reserve and the ECB.[20] Within a week of the asset purchase announcements by the Federal Reserve and the ECB, EMDE bond yields declined by up to 22 basis points, and equity prices rose by up to 5.7 percent. EMDE currencies appreciated against the U.S. dollar by around 1 percent a few business days after the announcements (figure 4.6).[21]

Risks associated with asset purchase programs in EMDEs

The experience of recent EMDE asset purchase programs during COVID-induced market volatility may overstate their future effectiveness if their use is prolonged or expanded. First, these programs were a surprise departure from the previous policy direction of EMDE central banks that had focused on reinforcing their credibility and independence. Concerns about central bank independence may grow if there is a large, persistent deterioration in fiscal positions in EMDEs, leading to rising inflation expectations and bond yields. Second, fragile liquidity in EMDE financial markets can lead to

---

yields declined persistently, partly reflecting the signaling effects of the second announcement of open-ended asset purchases.

[20] These results are consistent with the literature on evidence of significant international spillovers of advanced economy QE to EMDE financial markets (Bhattarai, Chatterjee, and Park 2018; Chen et al. 2016; Rogers, Scotti, and Wright 2018).

[21] The effects of domestic policy rate cuts and spillovers from advanced economy asset purchase program announcements were estimated based on data for the 14 EMDEs that have announced asset purchase programs. A larger group of 26 EMDEs, including 12 EMDEs that have announced no asset purchase programs, was also examined. The results were similar.

unpredictable changes in asset prices. Third, recent asset purchase programs in EMDEs were set against the backdrop of uniquely accommodative and synchronized macroeconomic policies in advanced economies.

Fragile institutional frameworks. The asset purchase program announcements in EMDEs took financial markets by surprise, after decades of central bank policy focused on establishing independence from fiscal and political institutions and building credibility. Unless asset purchase programs are viewed as consistent with central bank mandates centered on price stability, they may imperil the operational independence, transparency, and credibility of central banks that have struggled in the past to distance themselves from political pressures (Ha, Kose, and Ohnsorge 2019). Inflation remains higher in EMDEs than in advanced economies, and inflation expectations continue to be less well anchored (Ha, Stocker, and Yilmazkuday 2020; Kose et al. 2019). If asset purchases are perceived to be a signal of lasting and unsustainable debt monetization, inflation expectations may jump in EMDEs, particularly in those where they are poorly anchored (Blanchard and Pisani-Ferry 2020; Woodford 2004).

Rapidly deteriorating fiscal positions. Asset purchase programs may amplify capital flight and currency depreciations that are triggered by government solvency concerns (annex 4.4; Hofmann, Shim, and Shin 2020). Governments have appropriately responded to the disruptions caused by the COVID-19 pandemic with unprecedented fiscal stimulus. Current projections are for fiscal deficits in those EMDEs engaged in asset purchases to rise to nearly 10 percent of GDP, on average, in 2020, and to average close to 5 percent of GDP over the following five years (box 4.1). This is close to the average deficit in the cases of the 1980s and 1990s when EMDE governments turned to monetization (annex 4.4). Today's prospective fiscal deficits over the medium term amplify the risk that confidence in monetary and fiscal policies might at some point decline. EMDEs with greater foreign participation in financial markets, particularly where liabilities to foreign investors are denominated in foreign currency, may be at a higher risk of disruptions

FIGURE 4.6 Spillovers from advanced economy asset purchases to EMDEs

Asset purchase programs launched in 2020 by the U.S. Federal Reserve and the European Central Bank had substantial spillovers to EMDE financial markets. Following advanced economy asset purchase announcements, EMDE bond yields declined by over 20 basis points; equity prices rose by up to 5.7 percent; and EMDE currencies appreciated against the U.S. dollar by around 1 percent.

A. Impact of advanced economy asset purchases: EMDE 10-year bond yields

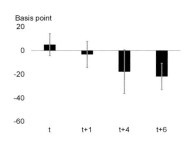

B. Impact of advanced economy asset purchases: EMDE equity prices and currencies

C. Impact of advanced economy and EMDE asset purchases: EMDE 10-year bond yields

D. Impact of advanced economy and EMDE asset purchases: EMDE equity prices and currencies

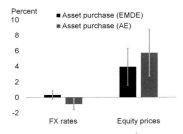

Sources: Haver Analytics; National sources; World Bank.
Note: AE = advanced economies; EMDE = emerging market and developing economy.
Panel regressions results based on daily financial asset prices in 26 EMDEs around asset purchase announcement by the U.S. Federal Reserve, the European Central Bank, and 14 EMDEs (annex 4.2). FX rates indicate exchange rates of EMDE currencies against the U.S. dollar. An increase in the exchange rate denotes a depreciation of EMDE currencies. Blue and red bars indicate point estimates and orange whiskers indicate 90 percent confidence intervals.
A.B. Horizontal axes indicate days after the announcements of asset purchase (t = 0).
C.D. Maximum cumulative impact of advanced economy and EMDE asset purchase announcements.

from changes in global sentiment centered on solvency concerns, which can trigger fire sales of bonds that put pressure on EMDE bond yields and exchange rates (Carstens and Shin 2019).

Less developed capital markets. The issuance of local currency-denominated government debt in EMDEs has doubled since 2011. Nevertheless, EMDE government bond markets are less deep than those of advanced economies. Bid-ask spreads are often substantially wider in EMDEs than in advanced economies, and have less

BOX 4.1 Remembering history: Monetary financing of fiscal deficits in EMDEs

In the past, monetary financing of fiscal deficits has been associated with severe macroeconomic instability, particularly during the 1980s and 1990s. While current EMDE policies and institutional characteristics differ materially from these earlier episodes, adverse consequences may emerge unless their lessons are heeded.

Introduction

Recent asset purchase programs in EMDEs have been largely designed to support market liquidity and improve financial conditions. In some cases, however, purchases have been used explicitly to finance fiscal deficits. These purchases may raise concerns that, over time, asset purchase programs will transition into a prolonged period of monetary financing of fiscal deficits—a practice associated with severe macroeconomic instability in the 1980s and 1990s. Historically, EMDEs where central banks have undertaken policies with some similarities to asset purchase programs, such as large-scale liquidity injections and money creation to finance government deficits, have in some cases experienced persistently high inflation and weak economic growth (Jacome et al. 2011, 2018). In this box, the characteristics of five such episodes in the 1980s and 1990s are explored: they occurred in Argentina, Brazil, Bolivia, Peru, and Turkey (annex 4.4). This box examines two questions regarding these historic episodes:

- What were the drivers and costs of monetary financing of fiscal deficits?

- How do EMDEs implementing asset purchase programs today differ from these case studies?

Drivers and consequences of monetary deficit financing

Debt monetization episodes in EMDEs. In the 1980s, several EMDEs maintained persistently large fiscal deficits that were financed to a large degree through central bank currency issuance and accompanied by exceptionally high inflation (IMF 2001). Debt monetization tended to increase in these episodes after external defaults shut down access to foreign currency borrowing (Argentina, Brazil, Bolivia, and Peru) or foreign capital inflows reversed as external imbalances grew (Turkey). Beginning in the 1980s, these episodes, especially in Latin America, resulted in prolonged output contractions or stagnation, and macroeconomic instability.

Mounting vulnerabilities. In these episodes, debt monetization was accompanied by large and sustained fiscal deficits, banking sector losses, high external debt, persistent current account deficits, and capital outflows (Kaminsky and Reinhart 1999; Reinhart and Savastano 2003). Monetization of government deficits was accompanied by prolonged periods of high inflation (in excess of 80 percent per year, on average, in the decade ahead of crises) and a de-anchoring of inflation expectations, paving the way for further instability.

Self-reinforcing spiral of deficit monetization, inflation, and deficits. External defaults in the early 1980s (Latin American economies) or rising external borrowing risk premia in the early 1990s (Turkey) required fiscal deficits to be funded by domestic sources. Many governments turned increasingly to monetization following failed attempts at fiscal consolidation (Dornbusch and de Pablo 1990; FDIC 1997; Sachs and Morales 1988). Monetary accommodation of large fiscal deficits, and the associated inflation, led to a self-reinforcing spiral of rising inflation, which eroded the real tax base and raised borrowing costs further, and was in turn met with further expansion of central bank reserve money to meet rising government financing needs. [a]

Lost decade. The financing of fiscal deficits through monetization contributed to a prolonged period of macroeconomic instability in many EMDEs and may have delayed efforts to restructure debt and reduce fiscal deficits. There were a series of external defaults and restructurings over 12-17 years in the Latin American episodes. [b] In the 1980s, output growth was on average 3-6 percentage points a year lower than in the 1970s in the affected Latin American economies (annex 4.4).

Note: This box was prepared by Gene Kindberg-Hanlon with research assistance from Kaltrina Temaj.

---

[a] There is debate over whether some hyperinflations, such as those in Brazil and Argentina in the late 1980s, were preceded by a monetization of debt, or whether rapid expansion of reserve money was an overly accomodative response to devaluations and rapidly rising country risk premia which in turn led to rapid increases in money demand (Kiguel and Liviatan 1995).

[b] In Turkey, capital inflows were largely private and there was no sovereign default, but foreign currency capital flight from the banking sector required intervention from the central bank that resulted in the loss of half of its foreign currency reserves (Celasun 1998).

TABLE 4.1 Main asset purchase announcements in EMDEs in 2020 *(continued)*

Country	Month/Day	Primary or secondary market	Bond type	Main announcements
Poland	3/17	Secondary	Government	Approved the central bank to buy an unspecified amount of government bonds on the secondary market.
	4/8		Government	Broadened the scope of purchases by announcing the central bank would not only buy government bonds but also other bonds with state guarantees (including those issued by the Polish Development Fund and Bank Gospodarastwa Krajowego).
Romania	3/20	Secondary	Government	Announced plans to provide liquidity to banks via repo transactions and purchase local leu-denominated debt on the secondary market to promote market liquidity.
South Africa	3/25	Secondary	Government	Started an unspecified amount of government bond asset purchases.
Thailand	3/20	Secondary	Government	Bought 45 billion baht of bonds and stand ready to continue to buy them to ensure sufficient liquidity.
	4/7		Corporate	Approved a law to allow the BOT to set up a 400-billion baht fund to buy good-quality corporate bonds.
Turkey	3/31, 4/17	Secondary	Government	Commenced the purchase of several billion TRY of Turkish government bonds. Limits of outright purchases were revised to boost liquidity in the government bond market.
Programs excluded from panel and event studies:				
Bolivia	N/A	Secondary	Government	Initially purchased government bonds from pension funds to boost banking system liquidity.
Costa Rica	4/15	Secondary	Government	Authorized the central bank to purchase government bonds on the secondary market up to CRC 250,000 million.
Guatemala	N/A	Primary, Secondary	Government	Congress authorized the central bank to purchase up to 11,000 million GTQ to support fiscal financing requirements in response to COVID-19.
Rwanda	3/18	Primary, Secondary	Government	Offered a 6-month window to purchase government bonds at "prevailing market rate" and reduced the waiting period for the central bank to purchase bonds in the primary market following failed auctions from 15 to 30 days.

Sources: Central bank websites; Arslan, Drehmann, and Hofmann (2020); Hartley and Rebucci (2020); IMF (2020b).
Note: Those economies listed as purchasing in the "secondary" market are not undertaking any primary purchases. In those economies where purchases are to be conducted in the primary and secondary market, all have indicated that one of the purposes of their asset purchase program is to fund fiscal deficits.
a.   See Reserve Bank of India (2020a, 2020b) for details of the announcements.
b.   See Bank Indonesia (2020a, 2020b) and MoFRoI (2020) for details of the announcements.

ANNEX 4.1 Literature on the effects of advanced economy QE programs

TABLE A4.1.1 Literature on the effects of QE programs on bond yields

Literature	Country and program	Findings	Yield impact over 1-7 days (fall)
McLaren, Banerjee, and Latto (2014)	U.K. QE1 and QE2	Gilt yields declined by around 93 basis points with local supply effects (quantity of available bonds) accounting for around half of the fall.	93bps
Gagnon et al. (2011)	U.S. LSAP1	The overall size of the reduction in the ten-year term premium in the range of 30 to 100 basis points, with most estimates in the lower and middle thirds of this range.	30-100bps
Krishnamurthy and Vissing-Jorgensen (2011)	U.S. LSAP 1	QE1 appears to have generated a large impact of QE1 on the yields on these bonds, with effects as high as 160 bps for 10-year agency and Treasury bonds.	160bps
Williams (2014)	Literature review of U.S. and U.K. programs	The central tendency of the estimates indicates that $600 billion of Federal Reserve's asset purchases lowers the yield on ten-year Treasury notes by around 15 to 25 basis points.	15-25bps for $600bn of QE, equivalent to LSAP 2 in the United States
Joyce et al. (2011)	U.K. QE1	QE1 in the U.K. may have depressed medium- to long-term government bond yields by about 100 basis points, with the largest part of the impact coming through a portfolio balance effect.	100bps
Christensen and Rudebusche (2012)	U.K. QE1 and U.S. LSAP1	Find that declines in U.S. Treasury yields mainly reflected lower policy expectations, while declines in U.K. yields appeared to reflect reduced term premiums. The existing literature on the response of fixed-income markets to the Federal Reserve's first LSAP program and the Bank of England's QE program suggests a negative effect of between 50 and 100 basis points on 10-year yields.	50-100bps

TABLE A4.1.2 Literature on the effects of QE programs on output and inflation

Literature	Country, program and methodology	Inflation impact	Output and employment impact
Weale and Wieladek (2016)	U.S. and U.K. 2008-2014 Structural VAR model	Asset purchases worth 1 percent of nominal GDP, leads to a rise in inflation of 0.58 percent in the United States and 0.32 percent in the U.K.	Asset purchases worth 1 percent of nominal GDP lead to a rise of output of about 0.62 percent in the U.S. and 0.25 percent in the U.K.
Gambacorta, Hofmann, and Peersman (2014)	Panel analysis of Canada, the euro area, Japan, Norway, Sweden, Switzerland, the United Kingdom, and the United States. 2008-2011	Six months after a 3 percent increase in the central banks' assets, the effect on consumer price inflation reach peak effects of 0.01-0.04 percent.	Six months after a 3 percent increase in the central banks' assets, output effects reach a peak of around 0.04-0.10 percent.
Wu and Xia (2016)	U.S. 2009-13	-	Unemployment rate was one percentage point lower than a counterfactual without LSAP1 and LSAP2.
Baumeister, C. and L. Benati (2013)	Effect of QE through term premia compressions in the U.K. and U.S. Estimated using a structural VAR.	Model simulations suggest that in the absence of policy interventions, the U.S. economy would have been in deflation until 2009:Q3 with annualized inflation rates as low as −1 percent. In the United Kingdom, without quantitative easing, annualized inflation would have fallen to −4 percent.	U.S. real GDP would have been 0.9 percent lower in the absence of QE and unemployment would have been 0.75 percentage points higher, reaching a level of about 10.6 percent in 2009:Q4. In the U.K., output growth would have reached a trough of −12 percent at an annual rate in the first quarter of 2009 based on the median of our counterfactual estimates.
Kapetanios et al. (2012)	U.K. QE1. Time-varying parameter structural VAR.	QE1 in the U.K. had a peak effect on annual CPI inflation of about 1.25 percentage points.	QE1 in the U.K. had a peak effect on output of about 1.5 percent.
Balatti et al. (2017)	U.S. 1982-2014 and U.K. 1971-2015 VAR model	Insignificant impact on output and inflation.	

ANNEX 4.2 Methodology: Estimation of the impact of asset purchases

This annex describes the panel regression model that is employed to assess the reaction of asset prices following asset purchase announcements in EMDEs.

Model specification. Panel regressions are estimated based on local projections in Jordà (2005).

$$\Delta X_{i,t+h} = \Psi_h(L) Y_{i,t-1} + \beta_h APP_{i,t} + Z_{i,t} + \varepsilon_{i,t+h},$$
$$h = 0, 1, 2, \ldots \text{ (Baseline model)}$$

where X_t is a dependent variable and Y_t is a vector of explanatory variables that include lags of the dependent variables and policy interest rates at time t. $Z_{i,t}$ represents other control variables including country and time fixed effects. $\Psi_h(L)$ is a polynomial in the lag operator, and APP_t is the dummy variable for the announcement of asset purchase in country i at time t. The coefficient β_h gives the response of X at time $t+h$ to the shock

(announcement) at time t. Thus, the impulse response functions are constructed as a sequence of the β_hs estimated in a series of single regressions for each horizon.

Along with the baseline model, an alternative model is considered where, instead of time fixed effects, dummy variables for conventional monetary policy announcements in EMDEs and for asset purchase announcements in advanced economies are explicitly included. Thus, in this model, the estimated asset purchase announcement effects are estimated controlling for such effects.

$$\Delta X_{i,t+h} = \Psi_h(L) Y_{i,t-1} + \beta_h^{APP} APP_{i,t} + \beta_h^{APPadv} APPadv_t$$
$$+ \beta_h^{IR} IR_{i,t}, h = 0, 1, 2, \ldots \text{ (Alternative model)}$$

where IR_t is a dummy for announcements on policy rate cuts in EMDEs and $APPadv_t$ is a dummy for asset purchase announcements in advanced economies. Other notation remains unchanged. Standard errors are clustered by country. The point estimates of coefficients along with their 90 percent confidence intervals are reported.

Data. The sample includes 26 EMDEs, 14 of which have announced the launch or expansion of asset purchase programs on 25 occasions in total between March and July 2020.[23] For dependent variables of the panel regressions, three types of asset prices are considered—local currency long-term (10-year) bond yields, equity price indices and FX rates of local currencies vis-à-vis the U.S. dollar, all at daily frequency. Three models are estimated separately for each financial asset. In addition, the announcements of 34 policy rate cuts in 14 EMDEs between March and July 2020, and the asset purchase announcements by the Federal Reserve, which were occurred on March 23 and April 9, and by the ECB on March 19, were explored as well.

Robustness checks. Time fixed effects or a dummy variable for advanced economy asset purchase announcements is included in the models to control for the impacts of global financial market developments on EMDE asset prices. Several global variables are additionally tested in both types of model to control for external influences. The variables include the Chicago Board Options Exchange Volatility Index (VIX), the EMBIG spread, US 10-year bond yields, US stock price index, US dollar index, and the principal components of 10-year bond yields or equity prices among 30 advanced economies.[24] The impact of asset purchase announcements in EMDEs was not materially affected; the differences in the reactions of EMDE long-term bond yields were at most 5 basis points across models, and do not alter any of the findings in the main text.[25]

ANNEX 4.3 Event study of asset purchase announcements

As a robustness check of the panel regressions, event studies were performed. These complement the regression analysis by analyzing country-specific announcement effects of asset purchase programs.[26] The sample includes 25 asset purchase announcements in 14 EMDEs between March and July 2020. The response of asset prices is assessed in the narrow window of five days around the announcement to ensure that the results are not contaminated by other news.

EMDE asset purchase announcement effects on financial markets. Event study results are consistent with the regression results (figure A4.3.1). Following the asset purchase program announcements, participating EMDEs experienced on average:

- declines in domestic 10-year bond yields of around 37 basis points within two days and 42 basis points within five days—compared to a negligible decline in the EMDE group that had not implemented asset purchase programs;

- a 2.4 (3.8) percent increase in benchmark equity indices within two (five) days of the announcements, compared to less than 1 percent in the EMDE group that had not implemented asset purchase programs;

- a 0.3 percent currency depreciation against the U.S. dollar within two days but with large variations across countries, and with no significant difference from the depreciations of currencies in EMDEs that had not implemented asset purchase programs;

- a decline in sovereign CDS spreads (5-year) of around 11 (5) basis points within two (five) days, but with large variations across

---

[23] Among the 18 EMDEs that announced asset purchase programs, four EMDEs (Bolivia, Costa Rica, Guatemala, and Rwanda) were not included in the study because the announcement date is not clear or daily financial data are not available. The other economies that have not announced asset purchase programs include some large EMDEs, such as Brazil, Mexico, and Russian Federation.

[24] See, for example, Ahmed et al. (2020) for the impact of global financial market developments on financial conditions in EMDEs during the COVID-19 global recession.

[25] Finally, there were some cases when the announcement dates of asset purchase in EMDEs coincided with those of domestic policy rate cuts or asset purchases in advanced economies. Dropping these cases from the sample resulted in little change to the announcement effects of EMDE asset purchases.

---

[26] While the panel regressions control for potential confounding factors based on given assumptions, the event studies simply observe the asset price movements around the asset purchase announcements.

FIGURE A4.3.1 Event study: Asset purchase announcements in EMDEs

The announcements at the launch of asset purchase programs in EMDEs were associated with declines in long-term bond yields and a boost to equity prices. These effects were consistent across most EMDEs although they varied in magnitude. On average, exchange rates did not react to asset purchase announcements.

A. Evolution of 10-year bond yields around asset purchase announcements

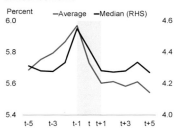

B. Evolution of exchange rates around asset purchase announcements

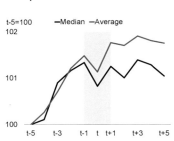

C. Evolution of equity prices around asset purchase announcements

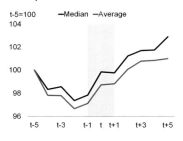

D. Impact of asset purchases on asset prices

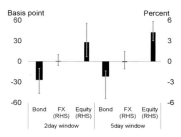

Sources: Haver; National sources; World Bank.
Note: Event studies are based on 25 asset purchase announcements in 14 EMDEs since March 2020.
A.-C. Horizontal axes indicate business days before and after the announcements of asset purchase (shaded area, t = 0).
D. Median and interquartile range of changes in bond yields or rate of returns in FX rates per U.S. dollar and sovereign equity index within 2- or 5-day window after the announcements. An increase in the exchange rate denotes an appreciation of the U.S. dollar.

countries—compared to a negligible decline in the EMDE group that had not implemented asset purchase programs;

• more effective stabilization of domestic financial markets, relative to EMDEs not announcing asset purchase programs.

Cross-country heterogeneity and differences. The effects on long-term bond yields were more pronounced in some EMDEs (Colombia, Ghana, South Africa, Turkey) than in others (India, Indonesia, Malaysia; figure A4.3.2). The effects were more sizeable on equity prices in Colombia, the Philippines, Romania, and Thailand than in other EMDEs. The asset purchase announcements

were followed by currency depreciations in Poland, Romania, and Turkey, whereas currencies appreciated in Hungary, Malaysia, and South Africa.

Heterogeneity may indicate an important role for the scale and scope of asset purchase programs as well as initial conditions. In countries that announced above-average purchase ceilings, the effects on bond yields were 30 basis points larger on average. In Colombia, Hungary, and Thailand—where asset purchase programs targeted bank and non-financial corporate bonds, as well as government bonds—the announcement effects on equity prices were more pronounced. With respect to country-specific features, some EMDEs with higher rates of inflation or larger sovereign credit spreads (Ghana, South Africa, Turkey) had larger announcement effects on bond yields, possibly reflecting the greater rise in the yields before the launch of asset purchase programs. A larger share of foreign ownership in local debt or in stock markets (Hungary, Poland, Romania, South Africa, Thailand) was associated with greater sensitivity of asset prices to asset purchase announcements.[27]

Comparison with the effects of policy rate cuts and advanced economy asset purchase programs

The reaction of asset prices following EMDE asset purchase announcements are compared with the responses to advanced economy asset purchase announcements, and to conventional monetary policy.

Effects of monetary policy rate cuts in EMDEs. Announcements of policy rate cuts had modest effects on long-term bond yields: following the announcement of policy rate cuts, long-term bond yields declined by 9 basis points, on average, within two business days (14 basis points within a week) (figure A4.3.3).

Effects of asset purchase programs in advanced economies. Announcements of asset purchase

---

[27] For instance, Arslan et al. (2020) argue that larger foreign investor participation in the local currency bond market can increase the effect of the confidence-restoring signaling effect of the asset purchase announcements.

programs by the Federal Reserve and the ECB in 2020 were followed by declines in bond yields that were generally smaller than the domestic responses to EMDE asset purchase programs and previous advanced economy programs. U.S. 10-year bond yields fell by 21 and basis points, respectively, within a day after the Federal Reserve's announcements on March 15 and 23. Following the third announcement, on April 9, US bond yields declined by a further 16 basis points within five days. In response to the announcement of asset purchases by the ECB on March 19, German bond yields fell by 12 basis points over three days while bond yields in France declined by 11 basis points within a day and 26 basis points within three days.

Spillover effects of advanced economy asset purchases to EMDEs. Although the response of asset prices in advanced economies to asset purchases in 2020 was muted relative to responses to earlier programs, there were sizable and relatively persistent spillovers to EMDE asset prices from the announcements by the Federal Reserve and the ECB. The spillovers to EMDE equity prices and exchange rates were actually larger than the impacts of EMDEs' own asset purchase programs on these variables. U.S. announcements had stronger spillover effects on non-EU EMDEs than ECB announcements.

- *U.S. Federal Reserve announcements.* The announcement by the Federal Reserve on March 23 was followed by declines in EMDE bond yields of 44 basis points on average, i.e., virtually the same as for announcements by the countries' own central banks. Within a week of the announcement, EMDE equity prices had risen by 6 percent, and EMDE currencies had appreciated vis-à-vis the US dollar by 1.4 percent. Following the announcement on April 9, EMDE bond yields declined by 27 basis points, equity prices rose by 1.8 percent, and currencies appreciated by 0.5 percent on average.

- *ECB announcements.* In the week following the announcement by the ECB on March 19, government bond yields in EMDEs declined by 7 basis points while equity prices rose by 3.9 percent. In the three EMDEs in the

FIGURE A4.3.2 Event study: Cross-country heterogeneity

The effects of asset purchase announcements were quantitatively different across EMDEs. The heterogeneity may indicate an important role for initial conditions as well as for how the measures were designed. The estimated announcement effects on bond and stock markets were more pronounced in EMDEs with greater program size and where both government and private bonds than others.

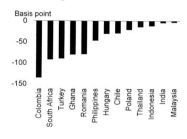

A. Declines in long-term bond yields after asset purchase announcements

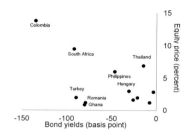

B. Asset purchase announcement effects on bond and stock markets

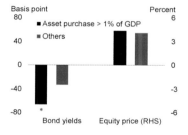

C. Impact of asset purchase announcements on bond yields and equity prices, by size of asset purchase programs

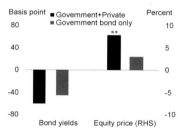

D. Impact of asset purchases on government bond yields and equity prices, by asset types

Sources: Haver; National sources; World Bank.
Note: Country- or group-specific announcement effects of asset purchase programs in EMDEs on 10-year bond yields (A.-D.) and equity prices (B.-D.). Announcement effects are measured by 2-day cumulative changes in bond yields or equity prices. In EMDEs with multiple asset purchase announcements, asset price changes are averaged across announcements.
C.D. ** and * indicate that the mean of asset purchase programs' impact is different across country groups at the significance level of 5 percent and 10 percent, respectively.

European Union (Hungary, Poland, and Romania), however, the effects of the ECB announcement were more pronounced, reflecting the large cross-border financial linkages. Sovereign bond yields in the three EU EMDEs declined on average by 50 basis points and equity prices increased by 5.6 percent within the week.

Comparison with regression results. The results based on the event studies confirm that the financial market effects of EMDE asset purchase announcements were sizeable. That said, the observed asset price movements were overall larger than the estimates based on the regressions

FIGURE A4.3.3 Event study: Policy rate cuts and individual asset purchase effects

Following announcements of policy rate cuts, long-term bond yields in EMDEs declined by around 10 basis points on average, which were smaller than the effects of asset purchase announcements. The effects on equity prices and FX rates were not statistically significant. Asset purchase programs launched by the US Federal Reserve and the European Central Bank were associated with declines in long-term bond yields, boosts to equity prices, and appreciations of currencies in EMDEs. The strength of the effects was comparable to those of domestic asset purchase announcements in EMDEs.

A. Average Policy rate cuts in EMDEs

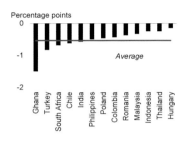

B. Impact of monetary policy rate cuts on asset prices in EMDEs

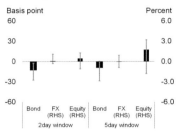

C. Impact of asset purchases on government bond yields

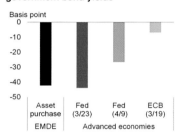

D. Impact of asset purchases on equity prices and FX rates

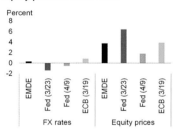

Sources: Haver; National sources; World Bank.

Note: EMDE = emerging market and developing economies. Event studies are based on asset price movements in 14 EMDEs, following 34 policy rate cuts EMDEs between March and July 2020 (A.B.), and asset purchase announcements by the U.S. Federal Reserve and the European Central Bank (C.D.). See annex 4.3 for more details.

A. Average policy rate cuts during the sample period.

B. Median and interquartile range of changes in bond yields or rate of returns in FX.

B.D. FX or FX rates indicate foreign exchange rates of EMDE currencies vis-à-vis U.S. dollar. An increase in the exchange rate denotes a depreciation of EMDE currencies.

C.D. Average announcement effects of asset purchases in EMDEs and in advanced economies on 10-year bond yields (C) and equity prices and FX rates (D) in EMDEs. Announcement effects are measured by 5-day cumulative changes in asset prices. FX rates indicate foreign exchange rates of EMDE currencies vis-à-vis U.S. dollar (or euro in the case of event studies on asset purchase announcements by the ECB).

presented in the main text. The larger effects revealed by the event studies reflect the fact that other events were also affecting EMDE asset prices that were not controlled for in the event study, but which were controlled for in the regressions. For example, asset purchase announcements by advanced economies seem to have played a critical role. Despite the large scale of policy rate cuts in EMDEs, their impact was weaker than that of their asset purchase announcements.

ANNEX 4.4 Historical case studies of EMDE debt monetization

This annex presents examples of debt monetization episodes in EMDEs in the 1980s and 1990s that were associated with extreme macroeconomic instability, such as high inflation, debt distress, and currency crises. In many of these cases, debt monetization increased following external default or the withdrawal of foreign financing and was accompanied by persistent and large fiscal deficits and high inflation for many years. Five case studies in the 1980s and 1990s are considered (figure A4.4.1). In the Latin American experiences, output losses were substantial. In Turkey, where debt monetization occurred over a shorter horizon and to a lesser degree, output losses were smaller and shorter-lived.

Argentina (1989)

The roots of the Argentinian crisis of 1989 were in the Latin American debt crisis of 1982, when Argentina and several other economies defaulted on foreign loan payments. After the country became locked out of international financial markets, expansion of the monetary base and financial repression were needed to finance large fiscal deficits (Buera and Nicolini 2019). Argentina had already experienced persistently high inflation in the 1970s and early 1980s, accompanied by rapid monetary expansion, leading to weakly anchored inflation expectations. Efforts to tighten monetary policy to control inflation involved higher interest rates, which increased debt-service costs, which were met, in turn, with monetary financing from the central bank. Persistently high inflation, interest rates, and failed fiscal consolidations led output to stagnate during 1980-88. Lost confidence in the ability of the government and central bank to meet debt-service requirements generated sharp capital outflows in 1987-88. Progressively higher interest rate risk premia drove government deficits higher, and continued monetary financing of deficits led to rapidly rising inflation beginning in 1988, accelerating further in 1989, when inflation reached over 3000 percent and output contracted by 7 percent (Beckerman 1992).

Bolivia (1985)

Bolivia received large inflows of foreign credit in the late 1970s. As global interest rates rose and capital flows subsided, a forced devaluation in 1979 exacerbated the external debt burden. In contrast to other Latin American economies facing external financing difficulties, Bolivia continued to meet debt service requirements on much, but not all, of its external debt. Stabilization efforts designed to reign in the public deficit through spending cuts or tax increases failed for political reasons throughout the early 1980s (Sachs 1987). Almost all of the large remaining financing needs of the government were met through additional money creation by the central bank (Kehoe, Machicado, and Peres- Cajias 2019). Tax revenues collapsed alongside rising inflation, falling from 9 percent of GNP in the early 1980s to 1 percent in 1985 (Sachs 1987). Revenues were further hurt by a continuous contraction in output during 1980- 85, averaging 1.8 percent a year. Annual inflation exceeded 1000 percent in 1984 and reached nearly 12,000 percent in 1985.

Brazil (1990)

Like Bolivia and Argentina, Brazil was largely cut off from external financing sources after the Mexican default of 1982, following the rise in global interest rates driven by the "Volcker disinflation" that began in 1979. High interest rates initially pushed the public sector deficit to between 6 and 8 percent of GDP during 1980-82 before a stabilization plan reduced it to 3 percent of GDP in 1983. However, the deficit remained high at 4 percent of GDP on average from 1984-8 (Pereira and Nakano 1991). Inflation routinely exceeded 100 percent annually in the early 1980s, and various attempts to control inflation using price controls and by increasing interest rates failed ("the Cruzado Plan," "Bresser Plan," and "Summer" plans). Many of these plans attempted to reduce the persistent fiscal deficit but it remained large (Ayres et al. 2018). Increasing risk premia led to rising interest rates which the central bank indirectly financed the government deficit to a large degree through repurchase agreements of government debt. As the monetary base expanded, inflation expectations became further de-anchored and inflation rose to 1,400 percent in 1989,

FIGURE A4.4.1 Characteristics of debt-monetization episodes in EMDEs

In the EMDEs considered in the case studies, inflation and debt monetization peaked after a prolonged period of accelerating inflation and large fiscal deficits, even after repeated consolidation attempts. In many of these cases (as well as in other EMDEs at the time), external debt burdens were high notwithstanding repeated defaults—sudden stops in foreign lending due to defaults or a reversal of capital inflows increased incentives to finance fiscal deficits through central bank money creation.

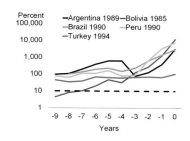

A. Inflation

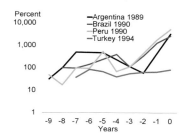

B. Growth of the monetary base

C. Government deficits

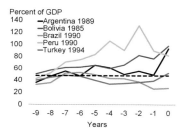

D. External debt-to-GDP ratio

Sources: Haver; IMF Historical Debt Statistics; Kigual and Liviatan (1995); Pereira and Nakano (1991); Rodriguez (1991); World Bank (World Development Indicators).
Note: Period "0" refers to the year in which the country experienced peak inflation and monetary base expansion, provided in the legend of each chart. Dotted black line reflects average for EMDEs not included in the case studies during 1979-1994 and which did not experience hyperinflation or external default. Comparison economies are not available for monetary base due to data limitations.
A. Argentina uses GDP deflator due to data constraints.
B. Percent growth in base, or "high powered" money issued by the central bank. Data unavailable for Bolivia over the required timeframe. Data interpolated through years in which there was a currency redenomination in Argentina.
C. Fiscal deficit uses IMF Historical Debt Database, supplemented by data from Kigual and Liviatan (1995), Pereira and Nakano (1991), and Rodriguez (1991).
D. External debt, percent of nominal gross national income.

increasing further to 2,700 percent in 1990. The poor macroeconomic environment led output to stagnate for three years during 1988-90.

Peru (1990)

In the mid-1980s, Peru embarked on a new set of policies designed to boost economic growth following many years of slow expansion and high inflation. As in Argentina and Brazil, Peru had defaulted or fallen into arrears with foreign creditors in the early 1980s, requiring increasing domestic financing to fund growing government deficits throughout the decade. Inflation was high but controlled, even as deficit financing was increasingly sourced through monetary expansion, through a system of price controls and subsidized government production (Pastor and Wise 1992). However, eventually, fiscal expansion and currency devaluations led to rising price pressures. The link between inflation and the budget deficit reinforced the economy's fiscal weakness, necessitating further debt monetization during the late 1980s; tax revenues fell from 13 percent of GDP in 1985 to just 4 percent in 1989 due to lags in tax collection during periods of rapidly rising inflation and a low degree of tax revenue indexation (Dornbusch, Sturzenegger, and Wolf 1990). Inflation reached over 7,000 percent in 1990, after growing deficits required increasing rates of debt monetization, and output contracted by an average of 9 percent each year during 1988-90 (Martinelli and Vega 2018).

Turkey (1994)

A successful period of export growth and capital account liberalization was halted by a period of strong currency appreciation and rapidly rising labor costs after 1988 (Celasun 1998). Public sector borrowing requirements increased rapidly in this period, peaking in 1993. Initially, financing requirements were partly covered through capital inflows, with the central bank limited to financing 15 percent of the government deficit. However, to stem rising interest costs, the government turned increasingly to monetary financing in 1993, when legal limits were raised. Auctions of domestic debt instruments were canceled to reduce interest rates and replaced with credit from central bank facilities (Ozatay 2000). Inflation reached over 100 percent in 1994 alongside a large currency devaluation, which also coincided with a significant output contraction caused by the crisis. The degree and duration of debt monetization was smaller in the 1994 crisis in Turkey than in the Latin American experiences, and the government was able to continue to service its debts. Although the impact on output was less severe, output contracted by 5 percent in 1994, after an average growth rate of 5 percent in the preceding decade.

References

Abiad, A., J. Bluedorn, J. Guajardo, and P. Topalova. 2012. "The Rising Resilience of Emerging Market and Developing Economies" IMF Working Paper 12/300, International Monetary Fund, Washington, DC.

Adrian, T., and N. Liang. 2016. "Monetary Policy, Financial Conditions, and Financial Stability." *International Journal of Central Banking* 14 (1): 73-131.

Ahmed, S., J. Hoek, S. Kamin, B. Smith, and E. Yoldas. 2020. "The Impact of COVID-19 on Emerging Market Economies' Financial Conditions." FEDS Notes, Board of Governors of the Federal Reserve System, Washington, DC.

Angrist, J. D., O. Jordà, and G. Kuersteiner. 2018. "Semiparametric Estimates of Monetary Policy Effects: String Theory Revisited." *Journal of Business & Economic Statistics* 36 (3): 371-87.

Arslan, Y., M. Drehmann, and B. Hofmann. 2020. "Central Bank Bond Purchases in Emerging Market Economies." BIS Bulletin 20, Bank for International Settlements, Basel, Switzerland.

Ayres, J., M. Garcia, D. Guillen, and P. Kehoe. 2018. "The Monetary and Fiscal History of Brazil, 1960-2016." Staff Report 575, Federal Reserve Bank of Minneapolis.

Bank of Spain. 2020. "Report on the Latin American Economy: Second Half of 2020." Economic Bulletin, Bank of Spain, Madrid.

Barnichon, R., and C. Matthews. 2015. "Measuring the Non-linear Effects of Monetary Policy." Meeting Papers, 2015-49, Society for Economic Dynamics.

Baumeister, C., and L. Benati. 2013. "Unconventional Monetary Policy and the Great Recession: Estimating the Macroeconomic Effects of a Spread Compression at the Zero Lower Bound." *International Journal of Central Banking* 9 (2): 165-212.

BIS (Bank for International Settlements). 2019. "Unconventional Monetary Policy Tools: A Corss-Country Analysis." Committee on the Global Financial System, Basel, Switzerland.

BIS (Bank for International Settlements). 2020. *Quarterly Review.* June. Basel, Switzerland: BIS.

Bank Indonesia. 2020a. "Bank Indonesia Policy Mix Economic Stimulus: Mitigating COVID-19 Impact." Press release, Bank Indonesia, Jakarta.

Bank Indonesia. 2020b. "Bank Indonesia Strengthening Measures to Maintain Monetary and Financial Stability." Press release, Bank Indonesia, Jakarta.

Bank Indonesia. 2020c. *Monetary Policy Review.* March. Jakarta: Bank Indonesia.

Beckerman, P. 1992. "Public Sector 'Debt-Distress' in Argentina, 1988-89." Policy Research Working Paper 902, World Bank, Washington, DC.

Benigno, G., J. Hartley, A. Garcia-Herrero, A. Rebucci, and E. Ribakova. 2020. "Credible Emerging Market Central Banks could Embrace Quantitative Easing to Fight COVID-19." IEMS Working Paper 2020-75, Hong Kong University of Science and Technology.

Bhattarai, S., A. Chatterjee, and W. Park. 2018. "Effects of US Quantitative Easing on Emerging Market Economies." ADBI Working Paper 803, Asian Development Bank Institute, Tokyo.

Blanchard, O., and J. Pisani-Ferry. 2020. "Monetisation: Do Not Panic." VoxEU.org, https://voxeu.org/article/monetisation-do-not-panic.

Bresser, L. C. B., and Y. Nakano. 1991. "Hyperinflation and Stabilization in Brazil: The First Collor Plan." In *Economic Problems of the 1990s,* edited by P. Davidson and J.Kregel. London: Edward Elgar.

Buera, F., and J. Nicolini. 2019. "The Monetary and Fiscal History of Argentina, 1960-2017." Staff Report 580, Federal Reserve Bank of Minneapolis.

Bunn, P.. A. Pugh, and C. Yeates. 2018. "The Distributional Impact of Monetary Policy Easing in the U.K. Between 2008 and 2014." Staff Working Paper 720, Bank of England, London.

Carstens, A. 2020. "Monetary Policy in a Global Environment." Speech at the Progress Foundation 50th Economic Conference on "Sound Money—A Noble Goal Under Constant Fire." October 8, 2020, Zurich.

Carstens, A., and H. S. Shin. 2019, "Emerging Markets Aren't Out of the Woods Yet. How They Can Manage the Risks." *Foreign Affairs,* March 15, 2020.

Celasun, O. 1998. "The 1994 Currency Crisis in Turkey." Policy Research Working Paper 1913, World Bank, Washington, DC.

Chen, Q., A. Filardo, D. He, and F. Zhu. 2016. "Financial Crisis, U.S. Unconventional Monetary Policy and International Spillovers." *Journal of International Money and Finance* 67 (C): 62-81.

Christensen, J., and J. Gillan. 2019. "Does Quantitative Easing Affect Market Liquidity." Working Paper 2013-26, Federal Reserve Bank of San Francisco.

Christensen, J., and G. Rudebusch. 2012. "The Response of Interest Rates to U.S. and U.K. Quantitative Easing." Working Paper 2012-06, Federal Reserve Bank of San Francisco.

Colciago, A., A. Samarina, and J. de Haan. 2019. "Central Bank Policies and Income and Wealth Inequality: A Survey." *Journal of Economic Surveys* 33 (4): 1199-1231.

Dornbusch, R., and J. C. de Pablo, 1990. "The Process of High Inflation." In *Developing Country Debt and Economic Performance, Volume 2: Country Studies—Argentina, Bolivia, Brazil, Mexico,* 77-91. Cambridge, MA: National Bureau of Economic Research.

Dornbush, R., F. Sturzenegger, and H. Wolf. 1990. "Extreme Inflation: Dynamics and Stabilization." *Brookings Papers on Economic Activity* 2: 1-81

Eggertsson, G., and M. Woodford. 2003. "The Zero Bound on Interest Rates and Optimal Monetary Policy." *Brookings Papers on Economic Activity* 1: 139-233.

Fabo, B., Jancokova, M., Kempf, E. and L. Pastor. 2020. "Fifty Shades of QE: Conflicts of Interest in Economic Research." NBER Working Paper 27849, National Bureau of Economic Research, Cambridge, MA.

FDIC (Federal Deposit Insurance Corporation). 1997. "History of the Eighties: Lessons for the Future. Vol. 1, An Examination of the Banking Crises of the 1980s and Early 1990s." Federal Deposit Insurance Corporation, Washington, DC.

Feyen, E. H. B., S. Ghosh, K. Kibuuka, and S. Farazi. 2015. "Global Liquidity and External Bond Issuance in Emerging Markets and Developing Economies." Policy Research Working Paper 7363, World Bank, Washington, DC.

Feyen, E., and I. Huertas. 2019. "The Sovereign-Bank Nexus in EMDEs: What is it, is it Rising, and What are the Policy Implications?" Policy Research Working Paper 8950, World Bank, Washington, DC.

Frankel, J. A., C. A. Vegh, and G. Vuletin. 2013. "On Graduation from Fiscal Procyclicality." *Journal of Development Economics* 100 (1): 32–47.

FSB (Financial Stability Board). 2020. "Holistic Review of the March Market Turmoil." Financial Stability Board, Basel, Switzerland.

Gagnon, J., M. Raskin, J. Remache, and B. Sack. 2011. "The Financial Market Effects of the Federal Reserve's Large-Scale Asset Purchases." *International Journal of Central Banking* 7 (1): 3-43.

Gambacorta, L., B. Hofmann, and G. Peersman. 2014. "The Effectiveness of Unconventional Monetary Policy at the Zero Lower Bound: A Cross-Country Analysis." *Journal of Money, Credit, and Banking* 46 (4): 615-642.

Gertler, M. L., and P. Karadi. 2015. "Monetary Policy Surprises, Credit Costs and Economic Activity." *American Economic Journal: Macroeconomics* 7 (1): 44-76.

Gopinath, G., S. Kalemli-Özcan, L. Karabarbounis, and C. Villegas-Sanchez. 2017. "Capital Allocation and Productivity in South Europe." *Quarterly Journal of Economics* 132 (44): 1915-1967.

Ha. J., M. A. Kose, and F. Ohnsorge, eds. 2019. *Inflation in Emerging and Developing Economies: Evolution, Drivers, and Policies.* World Bank, Washington, DC.

Ha, J., M. Stocker, and H. Yilmazkuday. 2020. "Inflation and Exchange Rate Pass-Through." *Journal of International Money and Finance* 105.

Haldane, A., M. Roberts-Sklar, T. Weiladek, and C. Young. 2016. "QE: The Story so Far." Staff Working Paper 624, Bank of England, London.

Hanson, S. G., and J. c. Stein. 2015. "Monetary Policy and Long-Term Real Rates." *Journal of Financial Economics* 115 (3): 429-448.

Hartley, J., and A. Rebucci. 2020. "An Event Study of COVID-19 Central Bank Quantitative Easing in Advanced and Emerging Economies." http://dx.doi.org/10.2139/ssrn.3607645.

Hofmann, B, I. Shim, and H. S. Shin. 2020. "Emerging Market Economy Exchange Rates and Local Currency Bond Markets Amid the Covid-19 Pandemic." BIS Bulletin 5, Bank for International Settlements, Basel, Switzerland.

IMF (International Monetary Fund). 2001. "The Decline of Inflation in Emerging Markets: Can it be Maintained?" In *World Economic Outlook: Fiscal Policy and Macroeconomic Stability.* Washington, DC: International Monetary Fund.

IMF (International Monetary Fund). 2013. "Global Impact and Challenges of Unconventional Monetary Policies." IMF Policy Paper, International Monetary Fund, Washington, DC.

IMF (International Monetary Fund). 2020a. "International Monetary Fund COVID-19 Policy Tracker." https://www.imf.org/en/Topics/imf-and-covid19/Policy-Responses-to-COVID-19.

IMF (International Monetary Fund). 2020b. *Global Financial Stability Report: Bridge to Recovery.* October. Washington, DC: International Monetary Fund.

IMF and World Bank. 2020a. "Recent Developments on Local Currency Bond Markets in Emerging Economies." Staff Note for the G20 International Financial Architecture Working Group (IFAWG), Washington, DC.

IMF and World Bank. 2020b. "Joint Bank-Fund Note on Public Sector Debt Definitions and Reporting in Low-Income Developing Countries." International Development Association, International Monetary Fund, Washington, DC.

Inui, N., N. Sudo, and T. Yamada. 2017. "Effects of Monetary Policy Shocks on Inequality in Japan." Bank of Japan Working Paper 17-E-3, Bank of Japan, Tokyo.

Ishi, K., M. Stone, and E. Yehoue. 2009. "Unconventional Central Bank Measures for Emerging Economies." IMF Working Paper 09/226. International Monetary Fund, Washington, DC.

Jacome, L., H. Sedik, and S. Townsend. 2011. "Can Emerging Market Central Banks Bail Out Banks? A Cautionary Tale from Latin America." IMF Working Paper 11/258, International Monetary Fund, Washington, DC.

Jacome L., H. Sedik, and A. Ziegenbein. 2018. "Is Credit Easing Viable in Emerging and Developing Economies? An Empirical Approach." IMF Working Paper 18/43, International Monetary Fund, Washington, DC.

Jordà, Ò. (2005). Estimation and inference of impulse responses by local projections. *American Economic Review* 95 (1), 161-82.

Joyce, M., A. Lasaosa, I. Stevens, and M. Tong. 2011. "The Financial Market Impact of Quantitative Easing in the United Kingdom." *International Journal of Central Banking* 7 (3): 113-161.

Joyce, M., D. Miles, A. Scott, and D. Vayanos. 2012. "Quantitative Easing and Unconventional Monetary Policy—An Introduction." *The Economic Journal* 122 (November): 271-289.

Juan-Francisco, A., N. Gomez-Francisco, and C. Ochando. 2019. "Effects of Unconventional Monetary Policy on Income and Wealth Distributions: Evidence from United States and Eurozone." *Panoeconomicus* 66 (5): 535-558.

Kaminsky, G., and C. Reinhart. 1999. "The Twin Crises: The Causes of Banking and Balance-of-Payments Problems." *American Economic Review* 89 (3): 473-500.

Kapetanios, G., H. Mumtaz, I. Stevens, and T. Theodoridis. 2012. "Assessing the Economy-wide Effects of Quantitative Easing." *The Economic Journal* 122 (564): 316-347.

Kehoe, T., C. G. Machicado, and J. Peres-Cajias 2019. "The Case of Bolivia." Macro Finance Research Program Working Paper, Federal Reserve Bank of Minneapolis.

Kigual, M., and N. Liviatan 1995. "Stopping Three Big Inflations: Argentina, Brazil, and Peru." In *Reform, Recovery, and Growth: Latin America and the Middle East,* edited by R. Dornbusch, and S. Edwards. Chicago: University of Chicago Press.

Kose, M. A., H. Matsuoka, H., U. Panizza, and D. Vorisek. 2019. "Inflation Expectations: Review and Evidence." CEPR Discussion Paper 13601, Centre for Economic Policy Research, London.

Kose, M. A, P. Nagle, F. Ohnsorge, and N. Sugawara. 2020. *Global Waves of Debt: Causes and Consequences.* Washington, DC: World Bank.

Krishnamurthy, A., and A. Vissing-Jorgensen. 2011. "The Effects of Quantitative Easing on Interest Rates: Channels and Implications for Policy." Brookings Papers on Economic Activity, 2011-2, Brookings Institution, Washington, DC.

Kurov, A. 2012. "What Determines the Stock Market's Reaction to Monetary Policy Statements?" *Review of Financial Economics* 21(4): 175-87.

Lenza, M., and J. Slacalek. 2018. "How Does Monetary Policy Affect Income and Wealth Inequality? Evidence from Quantitative Easing in the Euro Area." ECB Working Paper 2190, European Central Bank, Frankfurt.

Liu, E., A. Mian, and A. Sufi. 2019. "Low Interest Rates, Market Power, and Productivity Growth." Working Paper 2019-09, Becker Friedman Institute, University of Chicago.

Martinelli, C., and M. Vega 2018. "Monetary and Fiscal History of Peru 1960-2010: Radical Policy Experiments, Inflation, and Stabilization." Working Paper 2018-007, Banco Central Reserva Del Peru, Lima, Peru.

McLaren, N., R. Banerjee, and D. Latto. 2014. "Using Changes in Auction Maturity Sectors to Help Identify the Impact of QE on Gilt Yields." *The Economic Journal* 124 (576): 453-479.

MoFRoI (Ministry of Finance: Republic of Indonesia). 2020. "This is the Burden Sharing between the Ministry of Finance and BI to Handle Covid-19 Costs." News, Ministry of Finance, Jakarta, Indonesia.

Mumtaz, H., and A. Theophilopoulou. 2017. "The Impact of Monetary Policy on Inequality in the U.K. An Empirical Analysis." *European Economic Review* 98 (September): 410-423.

Ozatay, F. 2010. The 1994 Currency Crisis in Turkey. *The Journal of Policy Reform* 3 (4): 327-352.

Pastor, M., and C. Wise. 1992. "Peruvian Economic Policy in the 1980s: From Orthodoxy to Heterodoxy and Back." *Latin American Research Review* 27 (2): 83-117.

Pereira, L. C. B., and Y. Nakano 1991. "Hyperinflation and Stabilization in Brazil: The First Collor Plan." *Economic Problems of the 1990s.* Cheltenham, U.K.: Edward Elgar Publishing.

Reinhart, C., and M. Savastano 2003. "The Realities of Modern Hyperinflation." *Finance and Development* 40 (2): 20-23.

Reserve Bank of India. 2020a. "RBI Announces OMO Purchase of Government of India Dated Securities." Press release, Reserve Bank of India, Mumbai.

Reserve Bank of India. 2020b. "RBI Announces Special Open Market Operations (OMO) of Simultaneous Purchase and Sale of Government of India Securities." Press release, Reserve Bank of India, Mumbai.

Rodriguez, C. 1991. "The Macroeconomics of the Public Sector Deficit: The Case of Argentina." Working Paper 632, World Bank, Washington, DC.

Rogers, J. H., C. Scotti, and J. H. Wright. 2018. "Unconventional Monetary Policy and International Risk Premia." *Journal of Money, Credit and Banking* 50 (8): 1827-50.

Sachs, J. 1987. "The Bolivian Hyperinflation and Stabilization." *American Economic Review* 77 (2): 279-83.

Sachs, J., and J. A. Morales. 1988. "Bolivia: 1952-1986." International Center for Economic Growth, San Francisco.

Sahay, R., V Arora, T. Arvanitis, H. Faruqee, P. N'Diaye., and T. Mancini-Griffoli. 2014. "Emerging Market Volatility: Lessons from the Taper Tantrum." IMF Staff Discussion Note 14/09, International Monetary Fund, Washington, DC.

Taghizadeh-Hesary, F. Yoshino, N. and S. Shimizu. 2020. "The Impact of Monetary and Tax Policy on Income Inequality in Japan." *The World Economy* 43 (10): 2600-2621.

Taylor, J. B. 2009. "The Need for a Clear and Credible Exit Strategy." In *The Road Ahead for the Fed*, edited by J.D. Ciorciari and J. Taylor, chapter 6. Stanford, CA: Hoover Institution Press.

Tillmann, P. 2016. "Unconventional Monetary Policy and the Spillovers to Emerging Markets." *Journal of International Money and Finance* 66 (September): 136-156.

Tillmann, P. 2020. "Monetary Policy Uncertainty and the Response of the Yield Curve to Policy Shocks." *Journal of Money, Credit and Banking* 52 (4): 803-33.

Van Nieuwerburgh, S., and L. Veldkamp. 2006. "Learning asymmetries in real business cycles." *Journal of Monetary Economics* 53 (4): 753-772.

Weale, M., and T. Wieladek. 2016. "What are the Macroeconomic Effects of Asset Purchases?" *Journal of Monetary Economics* 79 (May): 81-93.

Williams, J. 2014. "Monetary Policy at the Zero Lower Bound: Putting Theory Into Practice." Hutchins Center on Fiscal & Monetary Policy, Brookings Institution, Washington, DC.

Woodford, M. 2004. "Inflation Targeting and Optimal Monetary Policy." *Review, Federal Reserve Bank of St. Louis* 86 (Jul): 15-42.

World Bank. 2020. *Global Economic Prospects*. June. Washington, DC: World Bank.

Wu, J., and F. Xia. 2016. "Measuring the Macroeconomic Impact of Monetary Policy at the Zero Lower Bound." *Journal of Money, Credit and Banking* 48 (2-3): 253-291.

Yale University. 2020. "Yale Program on Financial Stability COVID-19 Policy Tracker." https://docs.google.com/spreadsheets/d/1s6EgMa4KGDfFzcsZJK qwiH7yqkhnCQtW7gI7eHpZuqg/edit#gid=0.

Yehoue, E. 2009. "Emerging Economy Responses to the Global Financial Crisis of 2007-09: An Empirical Analysis of the Liquidity Easing Measures." IMF Working Paper 09/265. International Monetary Fund, Washington, DC.

STATISTICAL
APPENDIX

Real GDP growth

	Annual estimates and forecasts [1] (Percent change)					Quarterly estimates [2] (Percent change, year-on-year)					
	2018	2019	2020e	2021f	2022f	19Q2	19Q3	19Q4	20Q1	20Q2	20Q3e
World	3.0	2.3	-4.3	4.0	3.8	2.2	2.3	2.3	-1.4	..	..
Advanced economies	2.2	1.6	-5.4	3.3	3.5	1.5	1.7	1.4	-1.2	-11.3	..
United States	3.0	2.2	-3.6	3.5	3.3	2.0	2.1	2.3	0.3	-9.0	-2.9
Euro area	1.9	1.3	-7.4	3.6	4.0	1.3	1.4	1.0	-3.2	-14.7	-4.3
Japan	0.6	0.3	-5.3	2.5	2.3	0.5	1.3	-1.0	-2.1	-10.3	-5.7
Emerging market and developing economies	4.3	3.6	-2.6	5.0	4.2	3.4	3.5	3.9	-1.9	..	..
East Asia and Pacific	6.3	5.8	0.9	7.4	5.2	5.9	5.8	5.7	-5.3	0.8	3.3
Cambodia	7.5	7.1	-2.0	4.0	5.2	..	..	..	..	..	..
China	6.6	6.1	2.0	7.9	5.2	6.2	6.0	6.0	-6.8	3.2	4.9
Fiji	3.8	-0.4	-19.0	2.6	8.2	..	..	..	..	..	..
Indonesia	5.2	5.0	-2.2	4.4	4.8	5.1	5.0	5.0	3.0	-5.3	-3.5
Lao PDR	6.3	4.7	-0.6	4.9	4.8	..	..	..	..	..	..
Malaysia	4.7	4.3	-5.8	6.7	4.8	4.8	4.4	3.6	0.7	-17.1	-2.7
Mongolia	7.0	5.0	-5.2	4.3	5.4	8.4	5.7	-0.7	-10.9	-8.8	-2.7
Myanmar	6.4	6.8	1.7	2.0	8.0	..	..	..	..	..	..
Papua New Guinea	-0.3	5.9	-3.8	3.5	4.2	..	..	..	..	..	..
Philippines	6.3	6.0	-8.1	5.9	6.0	5.4	6.3	6.7	-0.7	-16.9	-11.5
Solomon Islands	3.9	1.2	-4.8	3.2	3.5	..	..	..	..	..	..
Thailand	4.1	2.4	-6.5	4.0	4.7	2.4	2.6	1.5	-2.0	-12.1	-6.4
Timor-Leste	-0.8	3.4	-6.8	3.1	4.2	..	..	..	..	..	..
Vietnam	7.1	7.0	2.8	6.7	6.5	6.7	7.5	7.0	3.7	0.4	2.6
Europe and Central Asia	3.4	2.3	-2.9	3.3	3.9	1.4	2.3	3.8	2.4	-8.9	..
Albania	4.1	2.2	-6.7	5.1	4.4	2.6	4.2	-0.1	-2.3	-10.2	..
Armenia	5.2	7.6	-8.0	3.1	4.5	..	..	..	..	..	..
Azerbaijan	1.5	2.2	-5.0	1.9	4.5	..	..	..	..	..	..
Belarus	3.1	1.2	-1.6	-2.7	0.9	0.5	1.4	1.6	-0.2	-3.3	..
Bosnia and Herzegovina	3.7	2.7	-4.0	2.8	3.5	3.0	3.3	1.8	2.2	-9.3	..
Bulgaria	3.1	3.7	-5.1	3.3	3.7	4.0	3.1	3.2	1.8	-8.5	-4.2
Croatia	2.7	2.9	-8.6	5.4	4.2	2.6	2.8	2.3	0.2	-15.4	-10.0
Georgia	4.9	5.1	-6.0	4.0	6.0	4.8	5.4	4.6	2.3	-13.2	-5.6
Hungary	5.1	4.6	-5.9	3.8	4.3	4.5	4.7	4.2	2.2	-13.6	-4.6
Kazakhstan	4.1	4.5	-2.5	2.5	3.5	4.4	4.7	5.0	2.7	-6.0	..
Kosovo	3.8	4.2	-8.8	3.7	4.9	..	..	..	..	..	..
Kyrgyz Republic	3.8	4.5	-8.0	3.8	4.5	..	..	..	..	..	..
Moldova	4.3	3.6	-7.2	3.8	3.7	5.9	4.3	0.2	0.9	-14.0	-9.7
Montenegro [5]	5.1	4.1	-14.9	6.1	3.9	..	..	..	..	..	..
North Macedonia	2.7	3.6	-5.1	3.6	3.5	4.3	3.6	3.3	0.9	-14.9	-3.3
Poland	5.4	4.5	-3.4	3.5	4.3	4.7	4.4	3.9	1.9	-8.0	-1.8
Romania	4.4	4.1	-5.0	3.5	4.1	3.5	3.4	4.7	2.4	-10.3	-6.0
Russian Federation	2.5	1.3	-4.0	2.6	3.0	1.1	1.5	2.1	1.6	-8.0	-3.4
Serbia	4.4	4.2	-2.0	3.1	3.4	2.9	4.9	6.3	5.2	-6.3	-1.4
Tajikistan	7.3	7.5	2.2	3.5	5.5	..	..	..	..	..	..
Turkey	3.0	0.9	0.5	4.5	5.0	-1.7	1.0	6.4	4.5	-9.9	6.7
Ukraine	3.4	3.2	-5.5	3.0	3.1	4.7	3.9	1.5	-1.3	-11.4	-3.5
Uzbekistan	5.4	5.6	0.6	4.3	4.5	..	..	..	..	..	..

Real GDP growth *(continued)*

	Annual estimates and forecasts [1] (Percent change)					Quarterly estimates [2] (Percent change, year-on-year)					
	2018	2019	2020e	2021f	2022f	19Q2	19Q3	19Q4	20Q1	20Q2	20Q3e
Latin America and the Caribbean	1.9	1.0	-6.9	3.7	2.8	0.7	1.0	0.8	-0.9	-15.2	..
Argentina	-2.6	-2.1	-10.6	4.9	1.9	0.4	-1.8	-1.1	-5.2	-19.0	-10.2
Belize	2.1	-2.0	-20.3	6.9	2.2	..	..	..	..	..	..
Bolivia	4.2	2.2	-6.7	3.9	3.5	2.6	2.2	1.1	0.6	-21.7	..
Brazil	1.8	1.4	-4.5	3.0	2.5	1.5	1.3	1.6	-0.3	-10.9	-3.9
Chile	3.9	1.1	-6.3	4.2	3.1	1.8	3.4	-2.1	0.3	-14.5	-9.1
Colombia	2.5	3.3	-7.5	4.9	4.3	3.1	3.5	3.5	1.2	-15.9	-9.0
Costa Rica	2.7	2.1	-4.8	2.6	3.7	0.6	2.5	3.3	0.6	-8.6	..
Dominica	0.5	8.6	-10.0	1.0	3.0	..	..	..	..	..	..
Dominican Republic	7.0	5.0	-6.7	4.8	4.5	3.7	5.0	5.8	0.0	-16.9	..
Ecuador	1.3	0.1	-9.5	3.5	1.3	0.5	-0.3	-1.0	-2.3	-12.4	..
El Salvador	2.4	2.4	-7.2	4.6	3.1	1.6	2.9	2.8	1.0	-19.3	..
Grenada	4.1	2.0	-12.0	3.0	5.0	..	..	..	..	..	..
Guatemala	3.2	3.8	-3.5	3.6	3.8	3.8	4.0	3.9	0.9	-9.6	..
Guyana	4.4	5.4	23.2	7.8	3.6	..	..	..	..	..	..
Haiti [3]	1.7	-1.7	-3.8	1.4	1.5	..	..	..	..	..	..
Honduras	3.7	2.7	-9.7	3.8	3.9	1.9	3.4	2.4	-1.0	-19.1	..
Jamaica [2]	1.9	0.9	-9.0	4.0	2.0	1.4	0.6	0.0	-2.4	-18.4	..
Mexico	2.2	-0.1	-9.0	3.7	2.6	-0.9	0.0	-0.6	-1.4	-18.7	-8.6
Nicaragua	-4.0	-3.9	-6.0	-0.9	1.2	-3.1	-3.3	0.0	1.6	-7.5	-2.7
Panama	3.7	3.0	-8.1	5.1	3.5	2.9	2.7	3.3	0.4	-38.4	..
Paraguay	3.2	-0.4	-1.1	3.3	4.0	-3.3	2.6	3.5	4.4	-6.5	..
Peru	4.0	2.2	-12.0	7.6	4.5	1.3	3.2	1.9	-3.5	-29.8	-9.4
St. Lucia	2.6	1.7	-18.0	8.1	5.2	..	..	..	..	..	..
St. Vincent and the Grenadines	2.2	0.4	-5.0	0.0	5.0	..	..	..	..	..	..
Suriname	2.6	0.3	-13.1	-1.9	-1.5	..	..	..	..	..	..
Uruguay	1.6	0.2	-4.3	3.4	3.2	0.1	1.1	0.2	-1.4	-10.6	..
Middle East and North Africa	0.5	0.1	-5.0	2.1	3.1	-1.0	-0.9	1.1	-1.5	..	..
Algeria	1.2	0.8	-6.5	3.8	2.1	..	..	..	..	..	..
Bahrain	1.8	1.8	-5.2	2.2	2.5	1.8	2.7	-0.4	-1.1	-8.9	..
Djibouti	8.4	7.5	-1.0	7.1	7.2	..	..	..	..	..	..
Egypt, Arab Rep. [3]	5.3	5.6	3.6	2.7	5.8	5.7	5.6	5.6	5.0	-1.7	..
Iran, Islamic Rep. [3]	-6.0	-6.8	-3.7	1.5	1.7	-11.7	-9.1	1.8	-6.8	-2.9	4.8
Iraq	-0.6	4.4	-9.5	2.0	7.3	..	..	..	..	..	..
Jordan	1.9	2.0	-3.5	1.8	2.0	1.7	1.9	2.1	1.3	-3.6	..
Kuwait	1.2	0.4	-7.9	0.5	3.1	1.8	0.1	-1.1	-1.0	..	..
Lebanon [6]	-1.9	-6.7	-19.2	-13.2	..	..	..	..	..	..	..
Morocco	3.1	2.5	-6.3	4.0	3.7	2.4	2.4	2.3	0.1	-14.9	-8.7
Oman	0.9	-0.8	-9.4	0.5	7.9	..	..	..	..	..	..
Qatar	1.2	0.8	-2.0	3.0	3.0	0.5	0.7	0.2	0.0	-6.1	..
Saudi Arabia	2.4	0.3	-5.4	2.0	2.2	0.5	-0.5	-0.3	-1.0	-7.0	-4.6
Tunisia	2.7	1.0	-9.1	5.8	2.0	1.2	0.9	0.9	-2.0	-20.9	-5.8
United Arab Emirates	1.2	1.7	-6.3	1.0	2.4	2.0	2.3	0.8	-0.3	..	..
West Bank and Gaza	1.2	1.4	-7.9	2.3	2.4	2.3	-0.6	-1.8	-3.4	..	..

Real GDP growth *(continued)*

	Annual estimates and forecasts [1] (Percent change)					Quarterly estimates [2] (Percent change, year-on-year)					
	2018	2019	2020e	2021f	2022f	19Q2	19Q3	19Q4	20Q1	20Q2	20Q3e
South Asia	6.5	4.4	-6.7	3.3	3.8	5.1	4.4	4.0	2.9	-23.7	..
Afghanistan	1.2	3.9	-5.5	2.5	3.3	..	..	..	..	..	..
Bangladesh [3][4]	7.9	8.2	2.0	1.6	3.4	..	..	..	..	..	..
Bhutan [3][4]	3.8	4.3	0.7	-0.7	2.3	..	..	..	..	..	..
India [3][4]	6.1	4.2	-9.6	5.4	5.2	5.2	4.4	4.1	3.1	-23.9	-7.5
Maldives	8.1	7.0	-21.5	9.5	11.5	9.2	4.0	9.9	-5.0	-51.6	..
Nepal [3][4]	6.7	7.0	0.2	0.6	2.5	..	..	..	..	..	..
Pakistan [3][4]	5.5	1.9	-1.5	0.5	2.0	..	..	..	..	..	..
Sri Lanka	3.3	2.3	-6.7	3.3	2.0	1.1	2.4	2.0	-1.7	-16.3	1.5
Sub-Saharan Africa	2.6	2.4	-3.7	2.7	3.3	2.2	2.0	2.1	1.6	-10.0	..
Angola	-2.0	-0.9	-4.0	0.9	3.5	..	..	..	..	..	..
Benin	6.7	6.9	2.0	5.0	6.5	..	..	..	..	..	..
Botswana	4.5	3.0	-9.1	5.7	4.0	3.0	3.0	1.6	2.6	-24.0	..
Burkina Faso	6.8	5.7	-2.0	2.4	4.7	..	..	..	..	..	..
Burundi	1.6	1.8	0.3	2.0	2.5	..	..	..	..	..	..
Cabo Verde	4.5	5.7	-11.0	5.5	6.0	..	..	..	..	..	..
Cameroon	4.1	3.7	-2.5	3.0	3.4	..	..	..	..	..	..
Central African Republic	3.7	3.1	0.0	3.2	4.1	..	..	..	..	..	..
Chad	2.4	3.2	-0.8	2.4	3.3	..	..	..	..	..	..
Comoros	3.4	1.9	-1.4	2.4	3.6	..	..	..	..	..	..
Congo, Dem. Rep.	5.8	4.4	-1.7	2.1	3.0	..	..	..	..	..	..
Congo, Rep.	-6.2	-3.5	-8.9	-2.0	1.3	..	..	..	..	..	..
Côte d'Ivoire	6.8	6.9	1.8	5.5	5.8	..	..	..	..	..	..
Equatorial Guinea	-6.4	-5.6	-9.0	-2.8	-1.2	..	..	..	..	..	..
Eritrea	13.0	3.7	-0.6	3.5	5.5	..	..	..	..	..	..
Eswatini	2.4	1.3	-3.5	1.5	0.9	..	..	..	..	..	..
Ethiopia [3]	8.4	9.0	6.1	0.0	8.7	..	..	..	..	..	..
Gabon	0.8	3.9	-2.4	1.9	3.8	..	..	..	..	..	..
Gambia, The	6.5	6.0	-1.8	3.1	5.3	..	..	..	..	..	..
Ghana	6.3	6.5	1.1	1.4	2.4	5.7	5.6	7.9	4.9	-3.2	-1.1
Guinea	6.2	5.6	5.2	5.5	5.2	..	..	..	..	..	..
Guinea-Bissau	3.8	4.6	-2.4	3.0	4.0	..	..	..	..	..	..
Kenya	6.3	5.4	-1.0	6.9	5.7	5.3	5.2	5.5	4.9	-5.7	..
Lesotho	1.5	1.4	-5.3	3.1	3.8	2.2	1.7	1.0	1.0	-15.8	..
Liberia	1.2	-2.3	-2.9	3.2	3.9	..	..	..	..	..	..
Madagascar	4.6	4.8	-4.2	2.0	5.8	..	..	..	..	..	..
Malawi	3.2	4.4	1.3	3.3	4.9	..	..	..	..	..	..
Mali	4.7	5.0	-2.0	2.5	5.2	..	..	..	..	..	..
Mauritania	2.1	5.9	-0.6	3.7	4.8	..	..	..	..	..	..
Mauritius	3.8	3.0	-12.9	5.3	6.8	..	..	..	..	..	..
Mozambique	3.4	2.2	-0.8	2.8	4.4	2.9	1.2	1.4	1.7	-3.3	-1.1
Namibia	0.7	-1.1	-7.9	2.2	2.0	-3.6	-2.1	4.4	-1.4	-10.1	-10.5
Niger	7.0	5.8	1.0	5.1	11.8	..	..	..	..	..	..
Nigeria	1.9	2.2	-4.1	1.1	1.8	2.1	2.1	2.5	2.0	-6.0	-3.1
Rwanda	8.6	9.4	-0.2	5.7	6.8	..	..	..	..	..	..
São Tomé and Príncipe	2.9	1.3	-6.5	3.0	5.5	..	..	..	..	..	..
Senegal	6.4	5.3	-0.7	3.5	5.6	..	..	..	..	..	..
Seychelles	4.1	2.0	-15.9	3.1	3.8	..	..	..	..	..	..
Sierra Leone	3.4	5.5	-2.3	4.1	4.6	..	..	..	..	..	..

Real GDP growth *(continued)*

	Annual estimates and forecasts[1] (Percent change)					Quarterly estimates[2] (Percent change, year-on-year)					
	2018	2019	2020e	2021f	2022f	19Q2	19Q3	19Q4	20Q1	20Q2	20Q3e
Sub-Saharan Africa (continued)											
South Africa	0.8	0.2	-7.8	3.3	1.7	0.9	0.1	-0.5	0.1	-17.5	-6.0
South Sudan [3]	-3.5	-0.3	9.3	-3.4	0.0	..	..	..	..	..	..
Sudan	-2.3	-2.5	-8.3	2.5	3.1	..	..	..	..	..	..
Tanzania	5.4	5.8	2.5	5.5	6.0	7.5	8.1	6.2	5.7	..	..
Togo [7]	4.9	5.3	0.0	3.0	4.5	..	..	..	..	..	..
Uganda [3]	6.2	6.8	2.9	2.8	5.9	6.5	8.1	8.0	1.0	-6.0	..
Zambia	3.5	1.4	-4.5	1.9	3.4	2.3	1.1	0.2	-0.3	-2.1	..
Zimbabwe	4.8	-8.1	-10.0	2.9	3.1	..	..	..	..	..	..

Sources: World Bank and Haver Analytics.

Note: e = estimate; f = forecast.

1. Aggregate growth rates calculated using GDP weights at 2010 prices and market exchange rates.

2. Quarterly estimates are based on non-seasonally-adjusted real GDP, except for advanced economies, as well as Ecuador, Morocco, Poland and Tunisia. Data for Bosnia and Herzegovina are from the production approach. Quarterly data for Jamaica are gross value added.

Regional averages are calculated based on data from following countries.

East Asia and Pacific: China, Indonesia, Malaysia, Mongolia, the Philippines, Thailand, and Vietnam.

Europe and Central Asia: Albania, Belarus, Bosnia and Herzegovina, Bulgaria, Croatia, Georgia, Hungary, Kazakhstan, Moldova, North Macedonia, Poland, Romania, the Russian Federation, Serbia, Turkey, and Ukraine.

Latin America and the Caribbean: Argentina, Bolivia, Brazil, Chile, Colombia, Costa Rica, the Dominican Republic, Ecuador, El Salvador, Guatemala, Honduras, Jamaica, Mexico, Nicaragua, Panama, Paraguay, Peru, and Uruguay.

Middle East and North Africa: the Arab Republic of Egypt, Bahrain, the Islamic Republic of Iran, Jordan, Kuwait, Morocco, Qatar, Saudi Arabia, Tunisia, the United Arab Emirates, and West Bank and Gaza.

South Asia: India, Maldives and Sri Lanka.

Sub-Saharan Africa: Botswana, Ghana, Kenya, Lesotho, Mozambique, Namibia, Nigeria, South Africa, Uganda, and Zambia.

3. Annual GDP is on fiscal year basis, as per reporting practice in the country.

4. GDP data for Pakistan are based on factor cost. For Bangladesh, Bhutan, Nepal, and Pakistan, the column labeled 2019 refers to FY2018/19. For India, the column labeled 2018 refers to FY2018/19.

5. Quarterly data are preliminary.

6. Forecasts for Lebanon beyond 2021 are excluded due to a high degree of uncertainty.

7. For Togo, growth figures in 2018 and 2019 are based on pre-2020 rebasing GDP estimates.

Data and Forecast Conventions

The macroeconomic forecasts presented in this report are prepared by staff of the Prospects Group of the Equitable Growth, Finance and Institutions Vice-Presidency, in coordination with staff from the Macroeconomics, Trade, and Investment Global Practice and from regional and country offices, and with input from regional Chief Economist offices. They are the result of an iterative process that incorporates data, macroeconometric models, and judgment.

Data. Data used to prepare country forecasts come from a variety of sources. National Income Accounts (NIA), Balance of Payments (BOP), and fiscal data are from Haver Analytics; the World Development Indicators by the World Bank; the World Economic Outlook, Balance of Payments Statistics, and International Financial Statistics by the International Monetary Fund. Population data and forecasts are from the United Nations World Population Prospects. Country- and lending-group classifications are from the World Bank. The Prospects Group's internal databases include high-frequency indicators such as industrial production, consumer price indexes, emerging market bond indexes (EMBI), exchange rates, exports, imports, policy rates, and stock market indexes, based on data from Bloomberg, Haver Analytics, IMF Balance of Payments Statistics, IMF International Financial Statistics, and J. P. Morgan.

Aggregations. Aggregate growth for the world and all sub-groups of countries (such as regions and income groups) is calculated using GDP weights at 2010 prices and market exchange rates of country-specific growth rates. Income groups are defined as in the World Bank's classification of country groups.

Forecast process. The process starts with initial assumptions about advanced-economy growth and commodity price forecasts. These are used as conditioning assumptions for the first set of growth forecasts for EMDEs, which are produced using macroeconometric models, accounting frameworks to ensure national account identities and global consistency, estimates of spillovers from major economies, and high-frequency indicators. These forecasts are then evaluated to ensure consistency of treatment across similar EMDEs. This is followed by extensive discussions with World Bank country teams, who conduct continuous macroeconomic monitoring and dialogue with country authorities and finalize growth forecasts for EMDEs. The Prospects Group prepares advanced-economy and commodity price forecasts. Throughout the forecasting process, staff use macro-econometric models that allow the combination of judgement and consistency with model-based insights.

Global Economic Prospects: Selected Topics, 2015-21

Global Economic Prospects: Selected Topics, 2015-21

Growth and Business Cycles	
Cross-border spillovers	
Who catches a cold when emerging markets sneeze?	January 2016, Chapter 3
Sources of the growth slowdown in BRICS	January 2016, Box 3.1
Understanding cross-border growth spillovers	January 2016, Box 3.2
Within-region spillovers	January 2016, Box 3.3
East Asia and Pacific	January 2016, Box 2.1.1
Europe and Central Asia	January 2016, Box 2.2.1
Latin America and the Caribbean	January 2016, Box 2.3.1
Middle East and North Africa	January 2016, Box 2.4.1
South Asia	January 2016, Box 2.5.1
Sub-Saharan Africa	January 2016, Box 2.6.1
Productivity	
How do disasters affect productivity?	June 2020, Box 3.2
Fading promise: How to rekindle productivity growth	January 2020, Chapter 3
EMDE regional productivity trends and bottlenecks	January 2020, Box 3.1
Sectoral sources of productivity growth	January 2020, Box 3.2
Patterns of total factor productivity: A firm perspective	January 2020, Box 3.3
Debt, financial crises, and productivity	January 2020, Box 3.4
Labor productivity in East Asia and Pacific: Trends and drivers	January 2020, Box 2.1.1
Labor productivity in Europe and Central Asia: Trends and drivers	January 2020, Box 2.2.1
Labor productivity in Latin America and the Caribbean: Trends and drivers	January 2020, Box 2.3.1
Labor productivity in Middle East and North Africa: Trends and drivers	January 2020, Box 2.4.1
Labor productivity in South Asia: Trends and drivers	January 2020, Box 2.5.1
Labor productivity in Sub-Saharan Africa: Trends and drivers	January 2020, Box 2.6.1
Investment slowdown	
Investment: Subdued prospects, strong needs	June 2019, Special Focus 11
Weak investment in uncertain times: Causes, implications, and policy responses	January 2017, Chapter 3
Investment-less credit booms	January 2017, Box 3.1
Implications of rising uncertainty for investment in EMDEs	January 2017, Box 3.2
Investment slowdown in China	January 2017, Box 3.3
Interactions between public and private investment	January 2017, Box 3.4
East Asia and Pacific	January 2017, Box 2.1.1
Europe and Central Asia	January 2017, Box 2.2.1
Latin America and the Caribbean	January 2017, Box 2.3.1
Middle East and North Africa	January 2017, Box 2.4.1
South Asia	January 2016, Box 2.5.1
Sub-Saharan Africa	January 2016, Box 2.6.1
Forecast uncertainty	
Scenarios of possible global growth outcomes	June 2020, Box 1.3
Quantifying uncertainties in global growth forecasts	June 2016, Special Focus 2
Fiscal space	
Having space and using it: Fiscal policy challenges and developing economies	January 2015, Chapter 3
Fiscal policy in low-income countries	January 2015, Box 3.1
What affects the size of fiscal multipliers?	January 2015, Box 3.2
Chile's fiscal rule—an example of success	January 2015, Box 3.3
Narrow fiscal space and the risk of a debt crisis	January 2015, Box 3.4
Revenue mobilization in South Asia: Policy challenges and recommendations	January 2015, Box 2.3
Other topics	
Education demographics and global inequality	January 2018, Special Focus 2
Recent developments in emerging and developing country labor markets	June 2015, Box 1.3
Linkages between China and Sub-Saharan Africa	June 2015, Box 2.1
What does weak growth mean for poverty in the future?	January 2015, Box 1.1
What does a slowdown in China mean for Latin America and the Caribbean?	January 2015, Box 2.2

Global Economic Prospects: Selected Topics, 2015-21

Prospects Group:
Selected Other Publications on the Global Economy, 2015-21

Commodity Markets Outlook	↗
Persistence of commodity shocks	October 2020
Food price shocks: Channels and implications	April 2019
The implications of tariffs for commodity markets	October 2018, Box
The changing of the guard: Shifts in industrial commodity demand	October 2018
Oil exporters: Policies and challenges	April 2018
Investment weakness in commodity exporters	January 2017
OPEC in historical context: Commodity agreements and market fundamentals	October 2016
From energy prices to food prices: Moving in tandem?	July 2016
Resource development in an era of cheap commodities	April 2016
Weak growth in emerging market economies: What does it imply for commodity markets?	January 2016
Understanding El Niño: What does it mean for commodity markets?	October 2015
How important are China and India in global commodity consumption?	July 2015
Anatomy of the last four oil price crashes	April 2015
Putting the recent plunge in oil prices in perspective	January 2015

Inflation in Emerging and Developing Economies: Evolution, Drivers, and Policies	↗
Inflation: Concepts, evolution, and correlates	Chapter 1
Understanding global inflation synchronization	Chapter 2
Sources of inflation: Global and domestic drivers	Chapter 3
Inflation expectations: Review and evidence	Chapter 4
Inflation and exchange rate pass-through	Chapter 5
Inflation in low-income countries	Chapter 6
Poverty impact of food price shocks and policies	Chapter 7

A Decade After the Global Recession: Lessons and Challenges for Emerging and Developing Economies	↗
A decade after the global recession: Lessons and challenges	Chapter 1
What happens during global recessions?	Chapter 2
Macroeconomic developments	Chapter 3
Financial market developments	Chapter 4
Macroeconomic and financial sector policies	Chapter 5
Prospects, risks, and vulnerabilities	Chapter 6
Policy challenges	Chapter 7
The role of the World Bank Group	Chapter 8

Global Waves of Debt: Causes and Consequences	↗
Debt: Evolution, causes, and consequences	Chapter 1
Benefits and costs of debt: The dose makes the poison	Chapter 2
Global waves of debt: What goes up must come down?	Chapter 3
The fourth wave: Ripple or tsunami?	Chapter 4
Debt and financial crises: From euphoria to distress	Chapter 5
Policies: Turning mistakes into experience	Chapter 6

Prospects Group:
Selected Other Publications on the Global Economy, 2015-21

Global Productivity: Trends, Drivers, and Policies	↗
Global productivity trends	Chapter 1
What explains productivity growth	Chapter 2
What happens to productivity during major adverse events?	Chapter 3
Productivity convergence: Is anyone catching up?	Chapter 4
Regional dimensions of productivity: Trends, explanations, and policies	Chapter 5
Productivity: Technology, demand, and employment trade-offs	Chapter 6
Sectoral sources of productivity growth	Chapter 7

High-Frequency Monitoring	↗
Global Monthly newsletter